THE TEXAS LEAGUE

1888–1987

A Century of Baseball

Bill O'Neal

EAKIN PRESS ★ Austin, Texas

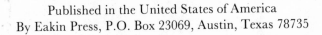
Library-of-Congress Cataloging-in-Publication Data

O'Neal, Bill, 1942–
 The Texas League.

 Bibliography: p.
 Includes index.
 1. Texas League — History. 2. Baseball — Texas — History. I. Title.
GV875.T36054   1987   796.357'09764   87-6760
ISBN 0-89015-596-8
ISBN 0-89015-609-3 (pbk.)

Dedicated to my wife

Faye
who continues to love me despite
my long affair with baseball

Contents

Foreword

My first contact with the Texas League came in 1949, when I was the catcher for the Nashville Vols in the Dixie Series against the Tulsa Oilers, champions of the Texas League. It was a typically hard-fought series, which we won, four games to three (the next year Nashville lost the Dixie Series to San Antonio, also in seven games). I played in a number of exhibition games against Texas League clubs, and later, as a major leaguer, I played alongside or against many fine athletes who had come up through the storied Texas League.

Little did I realize that one day I would serve as president of the Texas League. In 1968 I became general manager of Little Rock's Arkansas Travelers in the Texas League, and after eight years in this position I succeeded Bobby Bragan as league president. During the two decades that I have been associated with the Texas League as president or general manager, it has been my pleasure to witness our circuit shake off the doldrums that affected all of minor league baseball in the 1960s, and surge to our seventh straight million-plus attendance mark during the past season.

Today the Texas League enjoys enthusiastic fan support and a high quality of play. The traditions of the Texas League are being carried on by the club officials and players — and fans — of the 1980s. Families are coming out to the ball parks for wholesome, economical recreation. The clubs are run by bright, community-minded men, while the players are bigger and stronger and faster than ever.

The Texas League has a long and rich history. Bill O'Neal's book recaptures the exciting exploits enjoyed by fans around the league for a century. As we enter our second century, the future of the Texas League promises to be equally colorful and entertaining for fans of the future.

CARL SAWATSKI
TEXAS LEAGUE PRESIDENT

Acknowledgments

I owe my first expression of gratitude for this project to my father, W. C. O'Neal of Corsicana. He introduced me to Texas League baseball in the late 1940s, and we regularly attended games together for more than a decade. My grandfather became a Texas League fan by watching the famous Corsicana Oilers of 1902. He operated a semi-pro team for a couple of seasons, and he began taking my father to Texas League games in the 1920s. They saw Jake Atz and his Fort Worth Cats, Big Boy Kraft, Snipe Conley, Zeke Bonura, and the Texas League's first night game in Waco in 1930. During the late 1930s and the 1940s, my father traveled professionally throughout Texas, and he attended games and playoff series across the state. While working on this book I have regularly pumped my father for information. I am grateful to him for the broad fund of knowledge he shared with me — and for instilling a boyhood love of Texas League baseball that continues to linger.

When I conceived of this book I contacted Carl Sawatski, president of the Texas League. He has been enthusiastic and supportive from the beginning. Carl sent me materials from his office, provided introductions to club officials of the Texas League, generated financial support from the league to offset my research expenses, allowed me to participate in a meeting of the Texas League at mid-season of 1986, and met with me on several occasions — once while he was confined to a hospital bed. Throughout this project he responded by phone and mail to dozens of my inquiries on matters large and small, and I am deeply grateful for his cooperation and assistance.

Through the auspices of the East Texas Historical Association, I was awarded a research grant from the Ottis Lock Endowment. This grant was provided to facilitate my research of the East Texas

League and of East Texas cities which have held franchises in the Texas League. I am privileged to be a member of the Association, and I am most appreciative of the generous support of the Lock Endowment.

In Carthage I enjoy the good fortune of living in the same community with two former Texas Leaguers. Joe Vitter, a star of the 1930s and 1940s, opened his home to me on numerous occasions and permitted me to copy photographs and clippings from the scrapbooks compiled by his lovely wife, Eleanor. Jon Perlman, currently pitching for the Giants' organization, offered his enlightening reflections about four seasons spent in the contemporary Texas League. Jon loaned me photos and offered his comments on what I had written about his era. A neighbor and friend, Vivian Hanson, shared her memories of attending games in Houston during the World War I period.

At Panola Junior College in Carthage, my colleagues in M. P. Baker Library were as resourceful and cooperative as ever. Joyce Chapman, head librarian, obtained numerous sources through interlibrary loan, and staff members Mary Rose Johnson and Barbara Bell capably assisted me in chasing down one lead after another. Janna Hernandez, my secretary in 1985–86, itemized various materials and helped me with numerous other tasks.

The National Baseball Hall of Fame in Cooperstown provided a large amount of materials essential to this project, and I am especially indebted to Thomas R. Heitz, librarian, and to research associate Paul A. Cunningham. The Society for American Baseball Research also is located in Cooperstown, and I am grateful to W. Lloyd Johnson, SABR executive director, for his excellent help. I owe a debt of gratitude to Fred Graham, director of the Texas Sports Hall of Fame in Arlington, who granted me access to the superb collection of materials he has accumulated and who cordially provided every cooperation during my visit.

During the spring and summer of 1986, I traveled to the past and present cities of the Texas League, visiting libraries and ball parks and club officials. I saw a triple play in Beaumont, the Chicken in San Antonio, the opening game at Shreveport's Fair Grounds Field, a doubleheader in historic Ray Winder Field in Little Rock, and I was taken beneath the old grandstand at El Paso's Dudley Dome to view the adobe construction. I studied yellowing newspaper accounts of famous games, and I had the pleasure of talking with fans, former players, and managers in numerous locations. It was a delightful research experience, and I am indebted to the following kindred spirits for their invaluable assistance.

Lou Valentic, general manager of the Beaumont Golden Gators, was most open and helpful to me. Owner Ted Moor, Jr., and his charming wife were also extremely cooperative. I had a fascinating conversation with Al Vincent, famed Texas League manager, and I am indebted to Mrs. Dutch Lorbeer for allowing me to use a number of her excellent photographs. Staff members of the Beaumont Public Library assisted me industriously as I worked through their abundant resources.

Steve Ford, general manager of the San Antonio Dodgers, graciously took time to talk with me during a busy evening when the Chicken appeared at a Dodgers' game. Angela Ploch, a knowledgeable and devoted fan of San Antonio baseball, generously provided me with a number of needed photographs. The staff of the San Antonio Public Library helped smooth my way as I mined their collection of local baseball history.

Staff members of the El Paso Public Library helped me work the rich sources of the local sports history files. Diablos' general manager Rick Parr toured me through the Dudley Dome and offered his information and photo files to me. Naida Fordyce of the Diablos' staff provided needed materials on short notice, and club president Jim Paul also offered helpful suggestions. Marvin Nicchio, an enthusiastic Diablos' fan, shared knowledge and insight about El Paso baseball.

At the Midland Public Library, Rose Rankin conducted me through the impressive collections of the museum basement. At the Angels' offices, assistant general manager Matt Perry put aside his morning tasks to guide me through the stadium, offer information, and locate and loan me numerous photos of his team in action.

Bill Brock of the Austin History Center, Austin Public Library, greatly facilitated my explorations of the rich information and photographic collections at his institution. At the site of old Disch Field, members of the Austin Parks and Recreation Department hospitably answered my questions and toured me through the old clubhouse where their offices now are located.

At the Dallas Public Library, Travis Dudley was extremely

helpful in locating and providing copies of photographs. At the Fort Worth Public Library, Max Hill enthusiastically embraced my project and directed me to numerous discoveries among the vast collections of the Local History and Genealogy Department. Jessie Cartwright, of the photographic department of the Amon Carter Museum, provided cheerful assistance in tracking down photos.

In the impressive local history room of the Houston Public Library, staff members facilitated my search for information and photos. At Galveston's Rosenberg Library, Casey Greene of the Galveston and Texas History Center greatly aided me in locating materials. The staff at the Waco Public Library assisted in my search for information, and staff members at the Temple Public Library expedited my exploration of their fine local history collection. The Local History Department of the Corpus Christi Public Libraries located for me several illuminating items. In Longview I was aided by Pauline Cox of the Nicholson Memorial Public Library and by Ellie Bourdon Caston, director of the Gregg County Museum. Janice Robbins of Greenville expertly guided my research efforts at the W. Walworth Harrison Public Library.

Sandra Holmes, public services librarian of the Texarkana Public Library, furnished useful materials, and Dr. Bill Hughes of Texarkana College shared inside information about players he had known in his minor league days. The Local History Department of the Victoria Public Library provided excellent background information about that baseball hotbed. Daisy Harvill, director of the Aiken Regional Archives on the campus of Paris Junior College, unearthed excellent sources of information about early-day baseball in Paris, Texas.

In Sherman I was assisted by Jacqueline Barfield, assistant library director at the Sherman Public Library, and by Sheri S. McLeroy, director of the Sherman Historical Museum. Staff members of the Denison Public Library made useful suggestions in my search for materials.

At the old ball park in Wichita Falls, I encountered Felix Figuero and Alex Franco, who enthusiastically shared their knowledge of local baseball. Staff members of the Amarillo Public Library courteously helped me find needed information. In Tyler I am indebted to Richmond Dorsey, a Texas League fan since boyhood, for his encouragement and reminiscences.

xii

Jess Cummings of Corsicana, my coach in high school, provided useful information and photos. Patty Andrews, widow of former Corsicana and Dallas pitcher Jimmy Andrews, shared her memories and her scrapbook with me. Mrs. Vernon Washington graciously permitted me to visit her home in Linden, Texas, and loaned me precious photographs and scrapbooks. Mariana York, widow of the record-setting shortstop, Tony York, generously answered my questions and shared with me several excellent photos and clippings.

Elizabeth Denham, the competent assistant general manager of the Shreveport Captains, helped me on several occasions. Taylor Moore, club president, also was most cooperative, and Jon Long, general manager, offered needed information. Bill McIntyre, gentlemanly sportswriter for the *Shreveport Times*, opened his voluminous files on Shreveport baseball to a stranger. Texas League great Homer Peel visited with me by phone and at his Shreveport home.

Graydon K. Kitchens, Sr., an attorney in Minden, Louisiana, and a Texas League fan since 1926, generously proffered the use of his complete collection of Spalding and Reach Guides, and he responded promptly to my inquires. In Lake Charles, Susan Cooke, head of the Reference Department of the Calcasieu Parish Public Library, located and provided to me excellent information about Lake Charles baseball. Jeri Fahrenbach, reference librarian of the Lafayette Public Library, offered helpful suggestions. Lois Koehler, reference coordinator of the Rapids Parish Library, secured materials that I greatly needed about the Alexandria Aces.

The personable Joe Preseren, general manager of the Tulsa Drillers, gave me considerable insight into the operation of Texas League baseball today. Driller ushers Herman Brooks, Roger Thompson, and Norman McArthur regaled me with reminiscences of Tulsa baseball in past decades. Phillip Tolbert, public service librarian of Oklahoma City's Metropolitan Library System, provided guidance through his excellent collections, and staff members of the Tulsa Public Library offered similar assistance with their abundant resources. Mary B. Ruhle, reference librarian of the Ardmore Public Library, made useful suggestions regarding information sources in Ardmore.

Mike Feder, general manager of the Jackson Mets, was responsive to my inquiries in Jackson and twice in Shreveport. Con Maloney, Jackson owner, answered my questions and introduced me to veteran manager John Antonelli. A highly knowledgeable Jackson fan, John H. Callow, not only talked with me on two occasions about the Mets; he also recalled his years of watching Memphis perform in the Texas League. Bill Valentine, general manager of the Arkansas Travelers, found time to help me despite the pressures of preparing for a doubleheader. Kent Pylant, general manager of the Wichita Pilots, helpfully contributed background information on the Texas League's newest team.

A cherished friend, Frank P. Dickson, Sr., of Albuquerque, New Mexico, provided considerable information about the career of his father, the great Texas League pitcher Hickory Dickson. He also loaned me a rare original copy of the team portrait of the 1906 Cleburne Texas League champions. John Vittal, senior reference librarian of the Albuquerque Public Library, helped me track down materials from an abundant collection on local history.

Charles Baxter Miller, of Baxter's Photo Supplies in Marshall, Texas, was an unfailing source of technical expertise and advice regarding photographs. Brenda Allums, head of the Journalism Department at Panola Junior College in Carthage, was helpful on several occasions with photographic problems. William Harbour, a student and personal friend of mine, provided the dust jacket photo and developed several photos taken by my wife.

My twin daughters, Lynn and Shellie, provided invaluable aid in indexing and proofreading the manuscript. My wife Faye offered reliable tips on points of grammar, listened willingly to various portions of the manuscript, and uncomplainingly permitted me to immerse myself in the affairs of the Texas League.

1888-1899

A Lurching Start

The Texas League came into existence during the initial surge of athletic enthusiasm that swept across America in the late 1800s. During the Civil War, thousands of soldiers learned the game of baseball at hundreds of army camps, and after the war these young veterans brought the sport home to a multitude of towns and country villages. Baseball became America's first team sport, and there was enough fan interest (in those days baseball fans were called "bugs" or "kranks") for the Cincinnati Red Stockings — a team of paid professionals — to earn nearly $30,000 in gate receipts in 1869 (of course, salaries and expenses also were nearly $30,000 — the 1869 profit was $1.39!).

Two years later, nine teams formed the National Association of Professional Base-Ball Players, and in 1876 this organization was superseded by an eight-team National League. In 1882 a second "major league" was founded, the American Association, and the Union Association was organized two years later.

Three "minor leagues" — most notably the International Association — commenced play in 1877. By 1884, when three major leagues were in operation, there were eight minor leagues. Most of the junior professional franchises, like the major league clubs, were located in the industrialized, urbanized northeast. But in 1885 the Southern League was founded, and professional ball began to be

1

played in California. For years, professional ballplayers had headed west to ply their trade in the winter.

There is evidence that baseball was played in Texas as early as 1861, and a game was reported in detail in 1867. On San Jacinto Day, April 21, 1867. The Stonewalls of Houston crushed the R. E. Lees of Galveston, 35-2. Amateur nines flourished in Texas during the next few years, playing on vacant lots and cow pastures across the state. An amateur club from New Orleans, the Robert E. Lees (the name already was immortalized across the South) came to Texas in 1872 and played teams in Dallas, Waco, and Austin, traveling the dusty roads of the frontier state by stagecoach. Texas colleges began to match their nines; the famous A&M–Texas rivalry began on the diamond in 1884, a decade before students of the two state colleges clashed on a gridiron. By the 1880s some of the better baseball clubs in Texas cities were hiring skilled pitchers, catchers, and sometimes a shortstop to bolster local talent. In 1884 Samuel L. Hain, a Pennsylvanian who had moved to Houston and who had played semi-pro ball, organized a "Texas League" of clubs from Houston, Galveston, Dallas, Fort Worth, San Antonio, and Waco. These teams scheduled 15 games each, to be played between August 3 through October 16, but aside from two or three paid players per club, this operation was strictly on the amateur level.

The first appearance of an all-professional team in Texas occurred in Galveston in 1877. The Indianapolis professional club stopped over on a barnstorming tour long enough to play an amateur team, but the Texans were hopelessly overmatched. The Indianapolis pitcher, Edward "The Only" Nolan, was an experienced pro with a sharp-breaking curve. Nolan completely baffled the Texans, striking out 26 of the 27 men he faced (one Galveston "hitter" managed to tap a ground ball to short).

A decade later the first game between major leaguers occurred in Texas. In the fall of 1887, Charles Comiskey's St. Louis Browns, recently crowned champions of the American Association, and two National League clubs, the New York Giants and a team purporting to be Chicago (it was actually an aggregation of a few Chicago players and several other athletes from other National League teams) barnstormed Texas. The three major league clubs played separate schedules against local amateur and semi-pro teams, but in Houston a match was arranged between the Browns and "Chi-

cago." Fittingly, the champion Browns won Texas's first major
league game, 10-6.

During this momentous fall of 1887, "Honest John" Mc-
Closkey brought another team of professionals to Texas. The 25-
year-old McCloskey was a versatile athlete who had begun playing
professional baseball in 1882 in his home town, Louisville, Ken-
tucky. In 1884 he was one of the "Texas League's" hired catchers;
his battery mate was a gifted 15-year-old southpaw from Louisville,
"Red" Ehret. McCloskey, a born promoter, recognized the bur-
geoning baseball interest in Texas. He played for St. Joseph of the
Western League in 1887, and at the close of the season he enlisted
Ehret and other experienced Western Leaguers into a team of Joplin Independents. They first engaged in a series of 14 games with a
club formed by six-foot-five-inch "Big Mike" O'Connor, who
would become a notable Texas Leaguer. Then McCloskey's Independents, victorious in 10 of their 14 contests, headed for California
by way of Texas. McCloskey lined up games in Fort Worth and
Waco, and in Austin defeated a team of Southern League stars.
Sam French, a lumber man, and contractor Ed Byrne enthusiastically arranged a series of three games in Austin between Mc-
Closkey's team and the New York Giants. The Giants insisted on a
$1,000 guarantee, but French and Byrne stipulated that the winner
would take 85 percent. Large crowds in Austin (the magnificent
new capitol building was about to be dedicated) saw McCloskey's
upstarts defeat the Giants twice. The major leaguers left town without playing a third game.

French, Byrne, and other baseball enthusiasts joined with
McCloskey in arranging a meeting to organize a "State Base Ball
League." Representatives from Austin, Dallas, Houston, Fort
Worth, and New Orleans gathered in Austin on December 15 and
16, 1887, while Galveston, San Antonio, and Waco sent letters of
application. "Much enthusiasm was manifested by those present,"
reported the *Dallas Morning News*. Fred W. Turner of Austin was
elected president and Robert Adair of Houston vice-president (but
Turner, an insurance man, moved to Chicago before the 1888 season began, so Adair — a railroad executive who was a strong
backer of the Houston ball club — actually served as the first executive head of the Texas League). Salary limit per club was set at
$1,000, and numerous other details were discussed. A second meet-

ing was scheduled for January 18, 1888, in Houston, and work commenced in various cities to organize teams for the inaugural season. In January membership of the "Texas League of Baseball Clubs" still was not set. New Orleans had decided to enter the Southern League, and a committee was dispatched to San Antonio to enlist that major Texas city. A schedule committee was selected and an agreement was entered with A. J. Reach Company of Philadelphia to manufacture the official "Texas League ball." A league-wide admission price of twenty-five cents was set, umpires were to be paid $75 plus railroad fares, and play was scheduled to last from April 5 through mid-October of 1888.

Opening games did not take place until Sunday, April 8. Initially there were six clubs: Austin (which consisted of McCloskey and his Joplin players), Fort Worth (managed by Big Mike O'Connor, who was attracted to Texas by McCloskey), Houston, San Antonio, Galveston, and the Dallas "Hams." These teams played through April and May, with Dallas and Austin proving to be the strongest aggregations. San Antonio staggered to a 6-27 record the first two months and, with attendance understandably poor, dropped out of the league early in June. The schedule was altered to accommodate an awkward five-team complement. One team was idle for three or four days at a time while the other four played. To raise money and keep idle players in shape, games with amateur clubs were scheduled as frequently as possible, but as the summer progressed one team after another sank into financial difficulty. Fort Worth disbanded in June, and Austin was ready to fold by the end of the month.

McCloskey found backing in San Antonio and moved his players from Austin to the Alamo City, thus maintaining a four-team format. By the end of July the Southern League was disintegrating, and New Orleans transferred its team to the Texas League. The schedule committee once again went to work.

Early in September, Houston and Galveston, both with losing records, dropped out, and New Orleans realized that another road trip to Texas would be fruitless, since only San Antonio and Dallas still had teams. The last Texas League game of 1888 was played on September 2. The Dallas Hams had enjoyed a 55-27 record, but McCloskey claimed a co-championship for his Austin–San Antonio team, since his club was the only one besides Dallas to finish.

Austin 1888. Austin's first club was managed by Honest John McCloskey, center, the founder of the Texas League. Sherry Sheringhausen and Mikado Flynn were notable early-day Texas Leaguers, while Red Ehret and Buck Weaver went on to successful major league careers.
— Courtesy Austin History Center, Austin Public Library

McCloskey's won-lost mark was just 38-29, however, and Dallas had the honor of finishing atop the standings in the Texas League's inaugural year. Calling themselves the "State Fair and Exposition team," the Dallas club promptly organized a barnstorming tour of the Midwest.

Red Ehret, McCloskey's star southpaw, went to Kansas City and began an 11-year major league career, finishing out 1888 at 4-3 with the American Association's last-place club. McCloskey's right fielder, Buck Weaver, completed the year in Louisville of the American Association and eventually hit for a .285 average in 744 major league games. Harry Raymond, McCloskey's third baseman, also finished 1888 at Louisville, but before he left he helped immortalize the term "Texas Leaguer," a synonym for a blooper hit. Charles Edward "Home Run" Duffee went up to the St. Louis Browns in 1889. "Scrappy Bill" Joyce, a pugnacious infielder for Fort Worth and New Orleans, spent most of the 1890s in the National League.

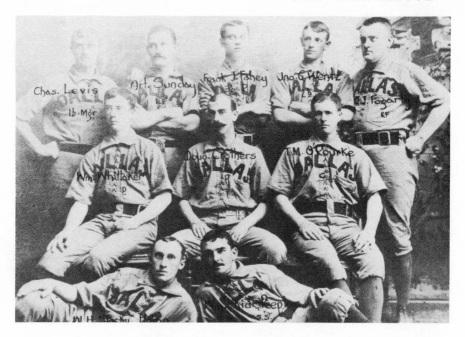

Dallas, the first Texas League champs, 1888. Note the lace-up shirts and the wide belts buckled on the side, with a big loop in the middle. On the right, reclining, is shortstop Kid Peeples, one of the most popular Texas Leaguers of the first decade. Left fielder Art Sunday, second from left, standing, was the brother of baseballer and evangelist Billy Sunday.

— Courtesy Dallas Public Library

Joyce was player-manager of New York from 1896 to 1898 — the first Texas Leaguer to manage a major league team.

Galveston had featured a battery of brothers: pitcher T. Stallings and catcher George Tweedy Stallings. George went up to Brooklyn in 1890 and later managed in the big leagues for a dozen years, leading Boston's "Miracle Braves" to a world championship in 1914. William Geiss, a Fort Worth infielder, already had spent a year with Detroit in the National League, while New Orleans shortstop "Sadie" Houck had played eight seasons with seven major league clubs before he came to Texas. Many other 1888 players were seasoned professionals, and several others would eventually make the big leagues.

Texas League kranks, therefore, witnessed a high quality of baseball in 1888. The "pitcher's point" in 1888 was a four-by-six-foot box located just 50 feet from the batter, while the "catcher's point" often was as far as 40 feet behind the hitter. Some catchers were beginning to wear bird cage masks and rudimentary chest protectors, but shin and knee guards were years away, and the catcher's mitt was a flimsy leather device. Before catchers began wearing masks there was no protection from foul tips except distance. As protective equipment evolved some catchers began to creep closer to the hitter, but in 1888 no catcher played as close as modern catchers. Their stance was more upright than today's, an advantage in throwing the ball, but the greater distance — especially to second base — gave base stealers a significant edge.

Since 1884 pitchers had been permitted to throw overhanded, but a great many hurlers still used an underhand delivery. They were 10 feet closer to the batter, however, and were allowed five balls or "wides" before a hitter walked (four balls for a walk began in 1889). Furthermore, it was customary through the 1930s for the umpire (there was only one per game) to be given just three baseballs. When a ball was fouled every effort was made to retrieve it and put it back into play. By the late innings the balls were soiled and scuffed, difficult for hitters to see, and easy for the pitchers to grip. Games usually were scheduled for 3:00 or 3:30 in the afternoon, and even though most contests were played in less than two hours (starting pitchers were expected to finish their games without help from relievers, and umpires kept players hustling so that the contest could be completed before dark), extra-inning affairs sometimes found hitters squinting through the gathering dusk at a filthy ball sailing at them from 50 feet away.

Outfielders also had trouble picking up a long fly struck late in the afternoon, and it was difficult catching any hit or thrown ball. Gloves were light, often nothing more than work gloves with the fingers cut out. In 1888 many players still operated barehanded. Ballparks were ramshackle structures built around rough, rocky diamonds. Ground balls took wicked hops, and a hard throw across the infield always sizzled a first baseman's hands. Generations of boys were taught to "catch the ball with both hands"; not until the development of enormous modern-day mitts could fielders make one-handed catches with any degree of reliability.

Old-time box scores always included "put outs" and "assists" alongside hitting information. Fielding statistics were of greater interest to kranks when hard-scrabble infields, discolored balls, and

---

YOU'VE COME A LONG WAY, BABY!

The Victorian sporting public was predominantly masculine, but early in its existence the Texas League began to court the support of women. At Galveston, for example, a Ladies' Day — free admission every Wednesday — was established in 1888, and at Beach Park a special grandstand was built "especially for the ladies from which they may view the game without being annoyed by the noisy crowd." The Austin Statesman *of June 24, 1889, proclaimed to its feminine readers:*

> *Don't fear to compromise your sex by attending the baseball game. It is affirmed on the best authority, that Mrs. Cleveland, now the first lady in the land, is enthusiastically devoted to the game. That should make it fashionable, and insure the game financial success in Texas.*

Vivian Hanson, a native of Houston and a friend of the author, happily recalls visiting with the players every Ladies' Day in seasons during the World War I era. A large representation of female fans has been present at every Texas League game the author has attended during the past four decades, and players of the 1980s can readily make the pleasant acquaintance of "Baseball Annies."

---

inadequate gloves rendered every fielding chance an uncertain adventure.

Although the club owners had lost money during the Texas League's first season, Honest John McCloskey was encouraged by the reaction the professionals had generated, and he began lining up sportsmen willing to organize clubs for 1889. Austin, Houston, Galveston, and Fort Worth again fielded teams, but Dallas accepted a franchise in the Southern League. Waco put together a club, however, and by April, Dallas had decided to play in the Texas League, making a six-team circuit.

There were many recognizable names for second-year kranks to cheer. McCloskey managed Houston and, as he had at Austin and San Antonio, played center field (during the early years of the Texas League virtually all teams employed player-managers). He brought several of his players with him to Houston: Emmett Rodgers, a star catcher and hitter; first baseman Charles Isaacson; J. C. "Sherry" Sheringhausen, a fine second sacker; and pitcher Walter Baldwin. McCloskey retained "Pop" Weikart and pitcher William Erickson from the 1888 Houston team, while acquiring outfielder Arthur Sunday and crack shortstop "Kid" Peeples from the 1888 Dallas champions.

Big Mike O'Connor was hired as manager-first baseman at Austin. Other familiar players from 1888 included "Farmer" Works, who played for three clubs in 1888, then went to Galveston (in 1889, 1890, 1895, and 1896), twice managing the Sandcrabs. Henry Fabian, a slashing hitter was back with Dallas, and would be a Texas League mainstay past the turn of the century. Outfielder "Voiceless Tim" O'Rourke was hired away from Dallas by Galveston; after a third season in the Texas League he would head for the major leagues. A lot of other roster-shuffling went on, because during the early years club rights to players virtually did not exist. Good athletes sometimes moved from team to team two or three times in a season, then would be wooed by another franchise during the off-season. Of course, the wooing was not very high-powered; for 1889, club payrolls were reduced to $800 per month. Through the early years of the twentieth century, rosters were small: eight regulars, a utility man, and perhaps three pitchers, at least one of whom could double up in the infield or outfield.

The 1889 schedule called for the six teams to play from April 8 to September 15. McCloskey's handpicked Houston "Babies" led the league all season, although Dallas, Austin, and Galveston were close behind. Actually, Dallas started poorly and in June the club was in financial difficulty. But local backers reorganized the team, and Dallas went on a tear, winning 15 straight games, although they could not catch Houston.

Doubleheaders were introduced to the Texas League in 1889. The first twin attraction was played on July 4 at Austin when McCloskey brought his Babies to town. Austinites cheered their team to a double victory over the league leaders, 13-9 and 5-2. In a July 28 doubleheader at Dallas, George R. Kittle of Austin (who had pitched for Dallas and Fort Worth in 1888) hurled both nine-inning contests. It was the Texas League's first iron-man performance, but Kittle lost both games, 3-0 and 15-3.

Despite a close pennant race, by August all of the clubs were in financial straits. Houston and Austin disbanded on August 9, and within the next five days the other teams had folded. Houston finished first, winning 54 of 98 games. Third-place Austin claimed the pennant, since Houston and second-place Dallas had not paid their league dues in full (only Austin, Galveston, and Fort Worth had submitted complete payment to the League office). After a heated

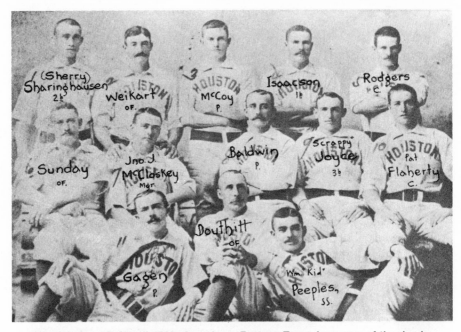

The Houston "Babies," 1889 champions. Famous Texas Leaguers of the day included Kid Peeples (bottom right), Art Sunday (second row left), player-manager
Honest John McCloskey (next to Sunday), Pat Flaherty (middle row right), Sherry
Sheringhausen (top row left), the popular Pop Weikart (next to Sheringhausen),
and Emmett Rodgers (top row right). Scrappy Bill Joyce (middle row, second from
right) became the first Texas Leaguer to manage a major league club.
— Author's Collection

newspaper squabble involving McCloskey, the club owners and the
league president, the pennant was awarded to the Houston Babies.

Unlike 1888, when spotty newspaper coverage rendered season records permanently obscure, averages were compiled for 1889.
Galveston outfielder and first baseman Farmer Works was the
league's first batting champion with a lusty .372 average. Houston
outfielder Arthur Sunday pounded out a .344 clip, while third
place went to another Galveston outfielder, Jack Huston, who hit
.326. Dallas outfielder Herman Bader simply ran wild on the basepaths. Although his club played just 91 games, Bader stole 146
bases against the remote catchers of the day. Bader's feat has never
been surpassed and has existed longer than any other league record. Waco finished last at 33-50, but boasted an outstanding
pitcher, Edgar McNabb, who somehow went 20-10 on the year. By

1893 McNabb had made it to the famous Baltimore Orioles, but before the next season opened he killed a young woman in a Pittsburgh hotel, then committed suicide.

Although the 1889 season had ended a month ahead of schedule, club owners were so enthusiastic about 1890 that they held an organizational meeting in October 1889. The 1890 season opened on March 30 with the same six clubs that had started in 1888. McCloskey again was player-manager at Houston, and Big Mike O'Connor returned to Fort Worth to hold down first base. Like many first sackers of his day, Big Mike kept one foot on his base at all times. He regarded the space between first and second as an area to be patrolled by the second baseman. Many old-style first basemen disdained to leave their bag even to pursue pop fouls. Indeed, second and third basemen long had kept a foot on "their" base, leaving only the shortstop to roam the infield. But this style of play was becoming obsolete, as third basemen and second basemen began to leave their bags to range farther and farther after ground balls and popups, and first basemen began to charge bunts and chase popups — even in foul territory. Most pitchers, however, still stayed within their box, and covering first base on a ball hit to the right side of the infield was virtually unknown. Pitchers also did little to hold baserunners close to the bag, which is one reason Herman Bader enjoyed such remarkable success on the basepaths in 1889.

Hard-hitting Pop Weikart returned for his third year at Houston in 1890. Farmer Works was Galveston's player-manager, while "Tub" Welch, an outstanding catcher, lined up behind the hitters for his third season with Dallas. Other third-year players included Kid Peeples (who brought his shortstop skills to Galveston), Sherry Sheringhausen (Fort Worth), Henry Fabian (Dallas), and Voiceless Tim O'Rourke (who played for Fort Worth and Houston, then went up to the majors at the close of the Texas League season).

The Galveston Sandcrabs, led by Farmer Works, proved to be the class of the league in 1890. McCloskey's Houston club just played .500 ball, and his catcher, Harry Elliff, died in May. Elliff, who had caught for Waco in 1889, earned the unwanted distinction of becoming the first Texas Leaguer to die during the regular season.

Before the season was two months old, the Austin franchise was in trouble. Austin disbanded on June 2, and Fort Worth folded shortly afterward. League officials tried to draw up a four-team schedule, but Waco decided to pull out and the league dissolved on June 10. No records were compiled for 1890, but Galveston, at 31-13, was far ahead of the pack.

There was general discouragement over the early dissolution of the league, and no one did anything to organize for 1891. John McCloskey put together a team of Texas Leaguers to play out of Sacramento in 1891. Viewed by a visiting Texan, McCloskey's club was dubbed the "Texas Steers." Ever the optimistic promoter, McCloskey refused to give up on the Lone Star State. He returned to Texas in April 1892 and quickly stirred up support for a resumption of league play.

Within a few weeks backing had been found for clubs in Houston, Galveston, Dallas, and Fort Worth. McCloskey again would be Houston's player-manager, and he hired catcher Tub Welch, infielder Sherry Sheringhausen, pitcher William Erickson, and other experienced pros. Charles Isaacson, one of McCloskey's 1888 originals, was engaged to manage and play first base for Galveston, and Honest John lined up the hard-hitting catcher, Emmett Rodgers, as well as several other capable players.

But Dallas and Fort Worth, scrambling to put together teams, found themselves playing with a number of local amateurs. The schedule began on Thursday, May 7, and from opening day Houston dominated the league. On May 20 Houston rapped out 24 base hits and defeated Dallas, 23-19, in the highest-scoring game of the year. Each club committed nine errors — a testimony to the difficult fielding conditions of the day. But the first triple play in Texas League history occurred on May 14 in a game between Galveston and Houston. Ollie Pickering, left fielder for the Sandcrabs, made an unexpected catch for one out, threw to second to double off a runner, and the relay to Isaacson at first recorded the third out. A week later, Pickering was hired by Houston, and he rewarded McCloskey by cracking seven consecutive singles — still the record for a single game.

By early July, McCloskey's team had raced to a 40-14 mark, while the other three teams had losing records. Fort Worth and Dallas disbanded their clubs on July 7. McCloskey and Si Packard, president of the Houston club and of the league in 1892, located sportsmen who were willing to organize teams in San Antonio and

Waco. While these new clubs were being put together, Houston and Galveston played each other almost every afternoon, with McCloskey's teams winning most of these exhibition games. One Galveston victory, however, was notable: on the evening of July 22, under makeshift illumination, the two teams played five innings. In Texas's first night game, Galveston defeated Houston, 9-8. There were other night exhibitions that season, but there would not be a night game in regulation play in the Texas League until 1930.

On July 23 play resumed between Houston, Galveston, Waco, and San Antonio. Big Mike O'Connor turned up as San Antonio's first baseman, but the team was weak overall, barely able to win one out of every three games. Waco played .500 ball. They were led by Henry Fabian, who brought his lethal bat with him from the defunct Dallas club. Ben Richards was in the Waco outfield, and played there again in 1897. Later he would be elected to several terms as mayor of Waco. The team's most remarkable player, however, was Ed Grider, a 14-year-old schoolboy who was a regular member of the pitching rotation.

These four teams started their schedule from scratch, hoping to encourage attendance with a new race. This was the first Texas League version of the split season, a device that would be regularly employed in somewhat different fashion by the circuit during the twentieth century. Houston again won more games than anyone else, but even though the race was tighter, attendance was poor for all four clubs. After the two Labor Day games, the league disbanded.

The indefatigable McCloskey went right to work, and within a week organized Dallas, Bonham, Denison, and Gainesville into a North Texas loop. The players donned new uniforms and played through September, but these games have never been counted as Texas League contests. For 1892, Houston, with a composite record of 59-26, notched their second Texas League pennant.

Four seasons and four failures. The Texas League had never completed a full schedule, and no one had made any money. There was so little interest that even Honest John McCloskey gave up — for the time being. In 1893 he managed Montgomery in the Southern League, handling two future Hall of Famers, "Iron Man" Joe McGinnity and Fred Clarke. McCloskey moved over to Savannah in 1894, then went up to Louisville in the National League.

During 1893 and 1894, there was no professional league play in Texas. But the nationwide popularity of baseball by then was phenomenal. Major league baseball of the mid-1890s was dominated by the Baltimore Orioles, a hustling, scrappy team which captured the public imagination and helped solidify baseball as the national pastime.

Sportsmen in Texas were dissatisfied with amateur quality baseball, and when Ted Sullivan, an experienced minor league organizer, began an energetic correspondence in the fall of 1894, he fanned the interest of a number of influential parties. Organizational meetings were held in Dallas in October 1894 and January 1895. By April an eight-team circuit had been formed — the first time the Texas League could promise the variety and competition of an eight-team schedule. Dallas, Fort Worth, Galveston, Houston, Austin, and San Antonio again organized clubs, while Sherman and Shreveport, Louisiana, made their first appearances in the league. Because of the addition of Shreveport, the circuit was titled the Texas–Southern League, which again was the official name in 1896, even though Shreveport was not a member that year. In 1897, 1898, and 1899 the official label was Texas Association. But by 1895 "Texas League" was so closely identified with the loop that kranks and newspaper accounts ignored conflicting official titles. Labeled the Texas League in 1888, the name has stuck for a century, even when half of the league members were located outside the Lone Star State.

When play opened on April 20, 1895, Texas League kranks witnessed a major change in the game. Pitchers, now operating atop a mound from a slab, rather than the old box, were positioned 60 feet six inches away from the hitter. Most pitchers required a few seasons to adjust the break of their curves, and the extra 10 feet gave batters a tremendous improvement. Throughout baseball in the mid-1890s, batting averages soared, and the Texas League was no exception.

The most reliable statistics to date were kept in 1895. Dallas accumulated a .310 team batting average; in 1896 San Antonio would hit .311, and in 1897 they batted at a .312 clip. The 1895 batting champ was Al McBride. An outfielder, McBride played for Waco in 1892 and managed Austin in 1895. He put himself in all but one of Austin's 95 games, and batted a galactic .444. It is the

The Fort Worth Panthers about 1890. Note the baggy pants, long sleeves, catcher's mitt, and flimsy glove. Early-day gloves were intended to provide a modicum of protection, while today's vast leather mitts are designed for entrapment.
— Courtesy Fort Worth Public Library

highest batting average ever compiled in the Texas League, and it sent McBride to the National League in 1896.

William Kemmer played 46 games for Shreveport in 1895, accumulating a lusty .405 batting average. He continued to play first base and outfield for various Texas League clubs from 1896 to 1899. Accurate statistics were not kept during the latter two seasons, but in 1896 and 1897 Kemmer hit well over .300. Veteran Texas Leaguer Pop Weikart hit .313 in 1895, .376 in 1896, and .385 in 1897. Frank Badger caught for five league clubs from 1895 through 1899, and Matt Stanley was the catcher for two teams from 1895 through 1897. Both men hit over .300 in 1895, 1896, and 1897. Irwin Isaacs, Rosie Weber, and George Keefe were popular pitchers during the 1895–1899 era, and all three men were steady .300 hitters. Charles Elsey played for Fort Worth in 1895 and San Antonio in 1896, averaging a powerful .360 for the two years. Fort Worth outfielder Ed Mackey hit .333 in 1895, and George Reilly, the Fort Worth third baseman, hit .375 in 116 games.

There were several unusually high scoring games in 1895. The season was just a week old when Shreveport edged Sherman, 21-20;

THROWN OUT AT THE PLATE ON A HOME RUN!

Nelson Leopold, Galveston club president and owner from 1920 to 1924, was fond of recalling an incident that happened when the Sandcrabs of the 1890s played a game against hated Houston at Beach Park.

"The outfield fence was right on the beach and there was a high tide on the day of the game," explained Leopold. One of the Galveston players slammed a pitch over the plank fence and began a leisurely trot around the bases. But a wave washed the ball back under the fence, and a Houston outfielder hurled the soggy horsehide toward the catcher, who tagged the startled Sandcrab slugger.

"There was the biggest hassle you ever saw about that," laughed Leopold. The beleaguered umpire finally decided that the home run would count, and Galveston went on to win the game.

---

the two teams rattled out 49 hits. Two days later Shreveport was defeated by Fort Worth, 24-20. In May, Dallas annihilated Austin, 27-3, while Shreveport walloped Houston, 26-10. Every Shreveport player got at least two hits in the game, and Shreveport stole thirteen bases.

Galveston third baseman Will Blakey owned the basepaths around the league, stealing 116 bases. The hard-running Galveston Sandcrabs stole a total of 374 bases — still the season club record. San Antonio, on its way to the cellar with a futile 21-72 mark, set less desirable team records, committing 475 errors and establishing an inept .885 fielding percentage. George Reese, Austin's shortstop, committed 100 errors during the season. The 1895 home run king was Charles Meyers, who played first base for Shreveport and Galveston. Meyers hit 15 homers, a respectable total during the dead ball era. Dallas's Jack Killacky led the league with 197 base hits, including a league-leading 44 doubles.

Despite the season-long avalanche of base hits, the Texas League exhibited several excellent pitchers in 1895. Cassie McAllister was 22-6 for Fort Worth, and he hit .351. Doubling up as an infielder and outfielder in 1896, he batted .351 and went to Cleveland at the end of the season. "Piggy" Page won 22 games for Galveston, and John McCoy and G. Mackey — who played for two clubs each in 1895 — were 21-13 and 23-14 respectively. A mysterious pitcher known only as Woodruff was perfect at 11-0 for Dallas, then disappeared permanently from baseball records. Sam McMackin was spectacular for Dallas at 28-7, while Galveston manager George Bristow went 30-16, including 16 straight victories late in the season. Al McFarland had proved himself an excellent hitter and pitcher around the league in 1890 and 1892, and for Fort Worth in 1895 he carved out a superb 34-12 record. McFarland's 34 wins are the greatest total ever compiled during a Texas League season.

Despite an exciting quality of play, however, Texas League clubs continued to suffer financially. The hard-hitting Dallas team reeled off 21 straight victories early in the season. After a month, several clubs were in such straits that reorganization was necessary, and some teams acquired new ownership. Lagging attendance spurred several owners to split the season. On June 22, Dallas was declared first-half champion, and the next day a new race began. Behind George Bristow's remarkable pitching, Galveston's Sandcrabs won 16 in a row, but Al McFarland hurled Fort Worth into the lead. On September 2, with Fort Worth atop the standings, the league halted play, just two weeks before the end of the announced schedule.

Fort Worth and Dallas added a few star players from other teams, then launched the Texas League's first playoff series. Scheduled for 15 games, the series ended because of a dispute after 13 games on September 20. Fort Worth led Dallas, 7-6, and after months of newspaper controversy (Dallas was 82-33 on the season, as opposed to Fort Worth's 77-39 record), Fort Worth was awarded the pennant at the league meeting in January 1896.

When the 1896 season began in April, the Shreveport franchise had been taken over by Denison, while the other seven clubs from 1895 again fielded teams. As had become commonplace, some teams had to reorganize under new ownership during the season. Sherman abruptly disbanded on June 10, triggering a flurry of activity. Other clubs scrambled to sign Sherman's best players, most notably Big Mike O'Connor. League president John Ward hustled up to Paris, Texas, which boasted a crack semi-pro team, and within one day organized a club to replace Sherman.

A split season was declared on July 3, but the second "half" lasted less than a month. In early August, Denison, Dallas, Paris, and Fort Worth folded, but the remaining four teams played for a few more weeks. Houston and Galveston announced a 30-game playoff, but mercifully only seven games of this marathon were staged. Although Fort Worth's Panthers had compiled a 71-29 record (.710 winning percentage), the Houston Buffaloes had lasted to season's end and were awarded the pennant on the strength of an 81-49 (.623) mark.

There were many fine performers around the league in 1896. Fleet Houston outfielder James "Rabbit" Slagle hit .367, while Houston's first baseman and manager, Charles Shaffer, hit .355 and stole 86 bases. Houston's catcher, "Dumb Henry" Cote, added 64 stolen bases. Big Mike O'Connor pounded out a league-leading .401 batting average. Houston pitcher John Roach won 29 games, while Fort Worth's Dale Gear enjoyed a sparkling 24-5 (.828) season, finishing 1896 with Cleveland. A Dallas infielder, Norman Arthur "Kid" Elberfeld, was destined for a major league career that spanned 1898-1914. Harry Steinfeldt of Fort Worth and Houston's John "Noisy" Kling (who batted .359 in 51 games) and Rabbit Slagle would spend years together on the Chicago Cubs.

Honest John McCloskey, recently discharged by Louisville, turned up in Texas toward the end of the 1896 season. The comparatively strong finish encouraged great optimism about 1897, and McCloskey began organizing a club in Dallas. The Houston and Galveston organizations remained intact, and new clubs were put together in San Antonio, Austin, Fort Worth, and Paris. New Orleans and Shreveport applied for franchises, but travel considerations prompted the decision to maintain an all-Texas loop. The eighth club for 1897 was a twin-city franchise, Sherman-Denison, although there proved to be friction between the two communities during the season. The player-manager of Sherman-Denison was an infielder known as Pierce Nuget "No Use" Chiles. No Use Chiles had played for Galveston in 1895, and he would average .301 for Philadelphia's National League entry in 1899–1900. His peculiar nickname derived from his favorite insult as a dedicated bench jockey. San Antonio's player-manager was Big Mike O'Connor, who captained his team to the early lead in league play.

The Texas League decided to begin a second half on June 28. Galveston, bolstered by league batting champ Kid Nance (who ripped opposition pitching for a .395 average in 1897), soared past everyone during the second-half schedule. Sherman-Denison was in second place, but suddenly folded on July 11. Before the day was out, however, the gifted promoter John McCloskey secured backing in Waco, and the club immediately found a new home. One of the skilled Waco amateurs enlisted to shore up the roster was a young first baseman named Ellis Hardy, who would spend a dozen years as a Texas League manager during the early twentieth century. Sunday ball was illegal in Waco, so Sabbath games with the Tigers hosting were held in Corsicana or Hillsboro, while other "home" games occasionally were staged at Cleburne and Calvert.

By early August a few teams began to drop out (Houston players quit en masse after a meager $20 gate on August 12), but some of the teams played until August 22, the scheduled end of the season. It was the first time in seven tries that at least a few clubs had made it to the conclusion of the schedule. Fort Worth outfielder J. J. "Quick" Gettman, who led the Texas League in stolen bases (55) and runs scored (122), went up to Washington, hitting .315 in 37 remaining games of the 1897 National League season. An outfielder named Hill hit .335 for Paris, and Dallas infielder Russ Hall had a fine season and went up to the National League (Hall later founded the Association of Professional Ball Players of America). Pop Weikart, manager-first baseman for Austin, hit .385. August "Cannonball" Weyhing, a veteran of 10 years in the majors, led the Texas League in games pitched (50), then spent four more seasons in the big leagues, winning a total of 267 major league games.

San Antonio won the first half (46-24), Galveston the second half (33-13), and the Sandcrabs topped the league with a 72-44 composite record for 1897. The season had been the most successful yet, with the finest caliber of ball to date. Enthusiastic promoters and prospective owners held the first meeting for 1898 in November 1897.

Only six clubs lined up for 1898: Austin, Dallas, Fort Worth, Galveston, Houston, and San Antonio. Opening games were played on April 9, but less than two weeks later the Spanish-American War erupted. Texas, with its long frontier period scarcely ended, patriotically rallied to the flag. Young men hurried to enlist, and soon Teddy Roosevelt and the colorful cavalry regiment that would earn glory as the "Rough Riders" were training in San Antonio. Baseball took a distant back seat to war fever.

On May 1 Fort Worth announced that it was quitting play. The league arbitrarily dropped Dallas — over the howls of player-manager John McCloskey — to attempt a four-team schedule in

Game action in Houston about 1890. The scoreboard was provided by the *Houston Chronicle*. Only one umpire was assigned to early games, standing behind the pitcher when men were on base. The grandstand crowd includes ladies, but only a handful of kranks are in the bleachers.

— Courtesy Houston Public Library

South Texas. But this effort lasted just from May 2 to May 13, when everyone conceded that it was futile to continue play. Dallas, at 13-7 (.650), had the best percentage, but no pennant was ever awarded for the abbreviated season of 1898.

In planning for 1899, little enthusiasm could be mustered in the northern sector of the state for resuming Texas League play. John McCloskey signed on with the Southern League as an umpire, but Big Mike O'Connor tried to place a Dallas club in the league. South Texas interests prevailed, however, and Dallas joined the Southern League. O'Connor agreed to be player-manager at Austin, while other franchises were established at Galveston, Houston, and San Antonio. This all-south Texas loop would conserve travel expenses, but with just four teams little variety of competition could be offered to the increasingly sophisticated baseball fans of Texas. Anticipating this problem, a short season — April 15 through July 15 — was planned. The customary $800 salary limit was fixed.

Two weeks after play opened, the Southern League folded

(this circuit, reorganized in 1901, became more familiarly known as the Southern Association). Many Southern League players, including a number of former Texas leaguers, gravitated to the "Texas Association," as league organizers — and practically no one else — persisted in calling it. John McCloskey returned to Texas, umpiring for the rest of the season. Houston was mired in last place, so an arrangement was reached by telegraph to transfer the Houston franchise to Mobile's club, which was leading the Southern League when it disbanded. Mobile brought most of its players to Houston, while retaining only two men from the original Buffalo roster. Pop Weikart returned to the Texas League from Mobile, as did the hard-hitting catcher, Frank Badger, and four other players who had spent two or three seasons in the Texas League.

Players on other clubs had become familiar to Texas League kranks in past years. Piggy Page, for example, had played pitcher, catcher, and infield every season since 1892, and another was picturesque Cy Mulkey, a pitcher-outfielder who was in his fifth consecutive year in the league (Cy's brother, Abe Mulkey, was a noted Texas evangelist). Austin added an outstanding pitcher from The University of Texas squad, John Douglas, who apparently was the first player signed straight out of college into the Texas League. Other new players included Ike Pendleton, Ben Shelton, George Markley, and other men who would become fixtures around the league after the turn of the century.

Galveston bolted ahead of the pack from opening day. On June 13 a split season was declared, but when Galveston again opened up a lead, fan interest lagged. On July 5 Austin announced that it was folding, and the other three teams had little choice but to disband the league, just 10 days ahead of the scheduled end of the season. Galveston was the only one of the four teams to finish 1899 with a winning record (52-26).

Since 1888 the Texas League had failed to operate only in 1891, 1893, and 1894, even though the knowledgeable Texas League historian, William B. Ruggles, stated that "it is doubtful if anyone made any money out of baseball from 1888 through 1899." Perhaps because of 12 years of steady losses, not enough Texas sportsmen could be found to back the league in 1900 or 1901. Thus 1899 clearly ended the formative period of the Texas League. Over the years Texans had become accustomed to a high quality of baseball, and certain Texas cities had become accustomed to fielding a professional team. Several Texas League players had appeared who boasted major league credentials, while a steady stream of them advanced to the big leagues. Rich Texas League traditions had been firmly established and would evolve expansively during the twentieth century.

1902–1909

A New Century

During 1901 the talk of baseball was the upstart American League. For a decade the National League had been the sole "major" circuit, but in 1901 a new loop challenged the senior league. The American League, paying higher salaries, lured numerous established stars away from the National League. Nap Lajoie of Connie Mack's Philadelphia Athletics led the majors with a .422 batting average, while the incomparable Cy Young went 31-10 for Boston.

The success of the new American League stimulated even greater popular interest in baseball across America, and gave Texas sportsmen hope that the Texas League could be revived. Joseph W. Gardner of Dallas met with fellow baseball enthusiasts in the fall of 1901, then wrote to Ted Sullivan, offering railroad fare back to Texas if Sullivan would return to the Lone Star State and resurrect the old Texas League. Sullivan worked through the winter, held an organizational meeting in Dallas in January 1902, and lined up backers in a number of North Texas cities.

By April a six-team league had been organized. Sullivan headed the Fort Worth club, and Cy Mulkey put together another twin-city franchise at Sherman-Denison. There also were teams at Fort Worth, Paris, Waco, and Corsicana, a newcomer to professional baseball. Minor leagues, caught in the middle of the turbu-

The Corsicana Oilers, spectacular 1902 champions and winners of a record 27 straight games. Standing, left to right: Bellmont Method, p; J. J. Clarke, c; Bob White, p; Big Mike O'Connor, 1B and mgr.; George Markley, 3B; Walter Morris, ss (later Texas League president). Middle row: Frank Ripley, rf; Upton Blair, president; Curley Maloney, p-cf. Bottom row: Alec Alexander, 2B-c; Lucky Wright, p; Ike Pendleton, lf.

— Courtesy *Corsicana Daily Sun*

lent conflict between the American and National leagues, met in September and October 1901 and organized a National Association, which set regulations applicable throughout baseball. Minor leagues were to be stratified as Class A, B, C, or D circuits, and the new Texas League was admitted to the National Association as a Class D loop.

J. Doak Roberts, a Corsicana businessman who would become a towering figure in the Texas League, put together a remarkable ball club for his home town. Big Mike O'Connor was his manager and first baseman, and catcher Nig Clarke was just one of three future big leaguers on the team. The Corsicana Oilers made a shambles of the 1902 race, bolting to a 58-9 start, including a record-setting 27 consecutive victories. One of these victories ranks as probably the most famous game in Texas League history.

The Sherman-Denison franchise lasted just 11 days, found a

BOX SCORE: CORSICANA VS. TEXARKANA AT ENNIS, JUNE 15, 1902

Corsicana	AB	R	H	Texarkana	AB	R	H
Maloney, cf	6	5	3	Deskin, cf	5	1	2
Alexander, 2b	8	5	8	Mulkey, 2b	4	0	1
Ripley, rf	8	6	5	Welter, 3b	4	0	1
Pendleton, lf	8	6	8	Wolfe, c	4	1	1
Markley, 3b	7	7	6	Murphey, lf	4	0	1
O'Connor, 1b	8	7	7	DeWitt, p	3	0	1
Clark, c	8	8	8	Tackaberry, 1b	4	1	1
Morris, ss	8	6	6	Gillon, rf	4	0	1
Wright, p	4	1	2	Burns, ss	4	0	0
	65	51	53		36	3	9

Stolen Bases: *Maloney, Alexander, Morris, Clark, Ripley.* **Home Runs:** *Clark (8), O'Connor (3), Alexander (3), Ripley (2), Pendleton (2), Maloney, Markley, Morris.* **Triples:** *Markley, O'Connor.* **Doubles:** *Morris, Alexander, Maloney, Pendleton, Deskin, Tackaberry, Welter.* **LOB:** *Corsicana (15), Texarkana (5).* **Errors:** *Corsicana (0), Texarkana (5).* **Double Plays By:** *Corsicana (4), Texarkana (1).* **Walks By:** *Wright (1), DeWitt (3).* **Struck Out By:** *Wright (2), DeWitt (1).* **Hit By Pitcher By:** *DeWitt (3).* **Earned Runs By:** *Corsicana (26), Texarkana (1).* **Umpires:** *Method and Cavender.* **Time:** *2:10.*

Texarkana	*010*	*000*	*020 — 3*
Corsicana	*629*	*275*	*488 — 51*

new home in Texarkana, but continued to be the weakest club in the league. Local ordinances in Corsicana prohibited Sunday baseball, so a June 15 game between the Oilers and Texarkana was moved to a small ball park in Ennis. Corsicana's explosive offense drubbed C. B. DeWitt, Texarkana's pitcher and part-owner, for 53 hits, including 16 home runs. Nig Clarke unloaded eight homers in eight times at bat, and the final score was a lopsided 51-3. A host of records were set — runs scored, hits, Clarke's eight roundtrippers, eight runs, 32 total bases, and so on — which have never been surpassed in professional baseball.

Texarkana, mired in last place, and next-to-last Paris dropped out in July. A second half was begun with four teams on July 9, but Corsicana continued to dominate, despite the loss of pitcher Bob White and infielders Walter Morris and George Markley, who left the team after clashing with management. With fan interest declining, the league halted play on August 31, a week ahead of schedule. Corsicana finished 88-23, their .793 winning percentage the highest in league history. A highlight of the season was the Texas League's first no-hitter, a 3-0 victory over Dallas hurled by Fort Worth's Bill Doyle in the first game of a July 4 doubleheader.

Club owners were elated over the successful revival of the Texas League, and Corsicana, Dallas, Fort Worth, and Paris readied teams for the 1903 season. Paris enjoyed the only winning record (32-20) in the first half, but attendance was poor despite their on-field success. When the season was split on June 25, the franchise was moved to Waco — which finished last in the second half. The second-half champion was Dallas, although Corsicana claimed that several games should be forfeited to them by Dallas, which would have given the Oilers the title. Corsicana's claims were ignored, and Dallas and Waco planned a playoff series. The entire playoff was staged in Dallas, because of greater attendance potential. Waco, with the weaker team and no home games, proved no match for Dallas, dropping the championship series to the Giants, 7-3.

In the spring of 1903 sportsmen in South Texas looked northward, observed the revived Texas League readying for a second season, and organized a circuit of their own. The South Texas League was awarded a Class C designation by the National Association, and it operated for four seasons, 1903 through 1906. Beaumont, Galveston, Houston, and San Antonio held franchises all four years. Of course, four-team leagues limit the variety of competition — and fan interest. In 1906, therefore, the South Texas League added Austin and Lake Charles, Louisiana, and operated as a six-team circuit.

In order to attract good ballplayers with marketable "names" among Texas baseball fans, the South Texas League in 1903 adopted the tactics the American League had used successfully in 1901 — the same tactics that would be used many times in the future by other upstart circuits in various sports. The South Texans offered more money for established Texas Leaguers than the North Texas clubs were paying. Beaumont not only paid high salaries, they also dispensed $10 bonuses after key victories and offered other incentives, prompting Texas sportswriters to dub Beaumont the "Millionaires." Perhaps to offset the higher salaries, the South Texas League ordered its teams to "stay away from high-priced hotels," and Beaumont's Millionaires were fined $50 for traveling regally in upper berths to San Antonio.

Most of the South Texas League stars were hired away from Texas League clubs. Fastballer Bill Sorrells was lured from Fort Worth by Houston, where he won 24 games in 1904 and led the league in strikeouts with an incredible 332. Ivy Tevis, the 1905 strikeout leader (201) who lost a no-hitter (his Galveston teammates dropped the game 0-1 to Houston) in 1906, had pitched for Paris in 1902. Eugene Burns and Eddie Taylor, who both twirled 1903 no-hitters in the South Texas League, were seduced away from Paris after the season started. San Antonio's Hickory Clark, who pitched a no-hitter (which turned into an 11-inning scoreless tie with Beaumont's Roy McFarland) in 1905, had worked for Dallas the three previous years. Baldo Luitich, a 26-game winner for Beaumont in 1904, had broken into the Texas League in 1899; Baldo pitched both ends of a doubleheader on July 9, 1904, defeating San Antonio 6-3 in the opener, but losing the second game, 7-8.

In 1903 San Antonio hired Walter Morris, Ike Pendleton, and Lucky Wright, who had starred with Corsicana's 1902 Texas League champs — and it was no coincidence that San Antonio's Bronchos won the first South Texas championship in 1903. Prince Ben Shelton, an established Texas League star, was the 1904 South Texas batting champ with a .352 average, and Ed Pleiss, who won the new loop's first hitting title with a .360 mark, had played for two Texas League clubs. The 1904 stolen base champ (47), Charles Barrett, had played for two Texas League clubs before going to San Antonio, and the 1904 doubles leader (36), Fred Schatzke, had been player-manager at Dallas for two seasons before being lured to the opposition circuit. And Dick Latham, a graceful, hard-hitting outfielder popular among baseball fans as "a beau ideal of his time," broke into the Texas League in 1898, but played three seasons for San Antonio of the South Texas circuit, leading in home runs (18) in 1904. A number of other fine players were enticed to leave the Texas League for their aggressive South Texas rivals.

Each year the South Texas League used a split season and planned a postseason playoff. In 1903 San Antonio defeated Galveston in the playoffs for the initial pennant, while Galveston triumphed over Houston in 1904. The next season Houston won both halves and took the championship without a playoff. In 1906 Austin downed Houston for the final South Texas crown.

In the meantime, the Texas League had been carrying on

Houston "Wanderers" of the 1904 South Texas League, clad in the popular double-breasted warmup jackets. Stars of the team were pitcher Ivy Tevis (top row, right) and hard-hitting Bob Edmondson (next to Tevis). Bliss Gorham (middle row, right) was league president.

— Courtesy Baxter Photo, Marshall, Texas

gamely with North Texas teams. The 1904 season was the last in which the Texas League would start as a four-team circuit. Corsicana, Dallas, and Fort Worth battled fiercely for the lead, but Paris was far off the pace and suffered accordingly at the gate. Trapper Longley, Corsicana's superb outfielder, hit .372 and sparked the Oilers to the first-half championship. But Beaumont enticed Longley and Tony Thebo, the Oilers' fleet center fielder, to jump to the South Texas League, and Corsicana dropped to second in the second half.

Fort Worth developed an excellent pitching staff and surged to the second-half lead. Charles Jackson was 26-8, including a no-hitter, for Fort Worth; Harold Christman went 21-6 to lead the league in winning percentage (.778); and Red Jarvis was the league strikeout champion (185). Dallas's Jack Huffmeister hurled an 11-inning one-hitter against Fort Worth on July 14 — but Dallas committed 16 errors and the Panthers opportunistically defeated Huffmeister,

6-5. Fort Worth dominated second-half play, and late in the season Paris disbanded. Ardmore, which boasted a top semi-pro team, played the remaining 10 games on the Paris schedule, winning three.

The league closed the season early, but a long playoff series was planned between Fort Worth and Corsicana. Corsicana aggressively recruited star players from other teams for the series, and the Oilers won 11 of 19 games over Fort Worth. Corsicana had won two pennants in their first three years in the Texas League.

For 1905 a six-team circuit took shape. Temple made its first appearance in the Texas League, Austin fielded a new team under player-manager Mike O'Connor, and Waco took the place of Paris–Ardmore. But Corsicana got off to a miserable 9-29 start, and surrendered their franchise in the face of financial ruin. The league briefly tried to run the team, then disbanded Corsicana and fifth-place Austin, which also had financial difficulties. Big Mike O'Connor moved north 110 miles, finishing 1905 as player-manager at Waco. Big Mike had played in the Texas League every season since its formation — the only man to participate in the first 13 seasons — but 1905 was his final year. His health failed suddenly, and he died in the State Hospital in Austin in 1906.

Most of the Texas League teams were brought to court in 1905 for violating the state law prohibiting Sunday amusements. Waco's team, which had been arrested en masse for a Sabbath violation, received the decisive ruling. The Texas Court of Criminal Appeals handed down the decision that the law did not apply to baseball, since the statute had been passed before the sport became a popular professional amusement. Similar cases against other Texas League teams were dropped, and the longtime problems over Sunday baseball finally ceased, except in a few communities which for a time maintained local ordinances against athletic events on the Sabbath.

This was the heart of the dead-ball era, when there were few home runs. Pitchers rather than hitters were baseball's biggest heroes, and spitballers now abounded. The old scuffed balls were "loaded" with spittle, tobacco juice, slippery elm, or other substances, and hitters found it difficult to see discolored balls. In 1905 no Texas League regular hit .300: Scott Ragsdale, catcher-first baseman for Austin and Waco, led the league with a .292 average,

while the 1906 batting champ was George Whiteman, who hit just
.281 for Cleburne. Temple took the 1905 team batting title with an
anemic .242 average (Houston led the South Texas League in 1905
with an identical .242 mark, and second-place San Antonio "hit"
just .127 as a team!). Ben Shelton and George Stovall tied for the
1905 Texas League home run championship — with five each!
There were four no-hitters in the Texas League in 1905, and five
the next season. During a July 3 doubleheader Harry Ables, Dallas's superb southpaw, shut out Fort Worth twice, 6-0 and 8-0, becoming the first Texas Leaguer to win an iron-man outing. It was
his first full season in the league — he went 17-13 with a 1.93 ERA,
and pitched six games for the St. Louis Browns at the end of the
year.

All four teams that finished the 1905 Texas League schedule
enjoyed winning records, and the race was so tight that the season
was not split. Behind the excellent pitching of Rick Adams, who
hurled seven games for Washington the last part of the season, and
another future major leaguer, Hickory Dickson, Temple made a determined run at the 1905 pennant. When the Boll Weevils finished
their home schedule they enjoyed a four-game lead over Fort
Worth. But the next day the Boll Weevils dropped a doubleheader
in Fort Worth, and the Panthers beat Temple in single games the
next two days. Fort Worth then won their final three games, and
the Panthers copped the pennant by a game and a half over the Boll
Weevils. Harold Christman enjoyed his second straight 20-win season for the Panthers, leading the league with 23 victories.

The same four teams that had finished 1905 — Fort Worth,
Temple, Waco, and Dallas — returned for the next season, while
franchises also were placed at Cleburne and Greenville. It would
prove to be the only Texas League season for the latter two cities —
an abbreviated one for Greenville, but a brilliant year for Cleburne.
League president J. Doak Roberts organized the Cleburne club,
stocking the team with proven talent from previous years. Longtime Texas League star Prince Ben Shelton would manage and play
first base. Four-year Texas Leaguer Dee Poindexter brought speed
and finesse to left field, and the picturesque, hustling Mickey Coyle
held down second. From Temple, Roberts hired the splendid pitchers Rick Adams and Hickory Dickson, as well as veteran third
baseman Roy Akin. There were two gifted rookies: big Dode Criss,

a hard-hitting pitcher who pounded out a .396 average and sometimes was placed in the outfield or at first, and an 18-year-old pitcher-outfielder from Hubbard, Tris Speaker.

It took part of a season for the magnificent Cleburne club to jell, however, and early in the year Fort Worth and Dallas fought it out for the lead. Dallas was managed by Curley Maloney, a Texas League fixture since 1889. Fort Worth was led by Alex Dupree, a brilliant pitcher who was a 20-game winner in all three of his Texas League seasons (1906, 1907, and 1908). In 1906 he was 25-7, leading the loop in victories (Rick Adams tied him). On May 28 Dupree no-hit Greenville in a 5-1 win, and on June 26 he pitched another no-hitter, defeating Waco, 1-0. Only Larry Maxie, pitching for Austin in 1961, ever matched Dupree's feat of hurling two no-hitters in a single season. While Dupree was notching his second no-hitter, that same day Eddie Rodebaugh of Dallas (who won 22 games in 1905 and enjoyed a sparkling 17-4 record in 1906) no-hit Cleburne, 3-1. The Dallas catcher in 1905, as well as in the previous year, was a young player out of Ohio Wesleyan named Branch Rickey. Rickey moved up to the St. Louis Browns at the end of 1905, and went on to become one of baseball's most progressive and influential executives.

The 1905 season was split on June 30, with Fort Worth the first-half winner. Greenville had a .500 record, but weak attendance caused the club to fold. A five-team schedule was awkward, so the league arbitrarily dropped Temple, which incensed Boll Weevil supporters. Cleburne nearly folded, too, but the club held together and surged to the second-half championship. Rick Adams notched 25 victories, but Hickory Dickson was right behind with 24. Dickson no-hit Temple on June 30, pitched a 19-inning scoreless tie against Alex Dupree on July 23, then capped a remarkable year on the next-to-last day of the season, hurling a pair of 2-0 victories over Fort Worth in a doubleheader shutout.

Cleburne, hitting on all cylinders at the end of the year, whipped second-place Fort Worth six of the last seven times the two teams played. The Panther players, apparently convinced that they would be walloped again in a playoff with Cleburne, went their own ways when the regular schedule was concluded. Cleburne won the championship by default. The next year efforts were

Cleburne's first — and only — Texas League club, the 1906 champions. Clockwise from top: Doak Roberts, owner and Texas League president; Charlie Moran, ut.; Hickory Dickson, p; Dode Criss, p-ut.; Parker Arbogast, c; rookie Tris Speaker, rf; Dee Poindexter, lf; Bobby Wright, if; Rick Adams, p; Mickey Coyle, 2B; Lucky Whiteman, cf; Roy Akin, 3B; Prince Ben Shelton, 1B and mgr. Note the double-breasted warmup jackets and the player poses, especially the upright catcher stances.
— Courtesy Frank P. Dickson, Sr., Albuquerque, New Mexico

made to organize a club, but Cleburne never reappeared in the Texas League. One season, one pennant!

Two months after the close of the 1906 season, a meeting was held in San Antonio to join the South Texas and Texas leagues. It was obvious by that time that the best cities from the two small loops could combine into a strong eight-team "All-State League." Dallas, Fort Worth, Temple, and Waco organized clubs, and were joined by Austin, Galveston, Houston, and San Antonio from the south. The new Texas League was designated Class C by the National Association, with a 140-game schedule. Each team would play every opponent 20 times — 10 at home and 10 away. It was the first balanced schedule in Texas League history that was

played out by all eight teams. Not a team folded, and 1907 was regarded in some quarters as the true beginning of the Texas League.

A number of old favorites who had defected to the South Texas
circuit now rejoined the Texas League. Piggy Page, for example,
who had broken in with Fort Worth in 1892, brought his colorful
talents back to the Texas League. At different times from 1892 to
1910 he was a 20-game winner, a catcher, infielder, manager, and
umpire. Houston pitcher Ivy Tevis, who had started with Paris in
1902, led the Texas League in 1907 with 24 victories. Austin, the
South Texas League champions in 1906, kept most of their best
players. Leadoff man Harry Short stole 78 bases in 1907 to pace the
league, while the Austin pitching staff again was sparked by southpaw Bill Bailey (the 1907 strikeout king with 234 K's), Rube Sutor
(who notched 23 victories), and William "Parson" McGill (the
1907 percentage winner — .780 on a 15-4 record).

Since the 1906 Texas League champion, Cleburne, did not
field a club in 1907, the players who did not move to a higher clas-
sification were snapped up by other Lone Star teams. Prince Ben
Shelton was player-manager at Temple, and he brought left fielder
Dee Poindexter with him, but the Boll Weevils sagged to last place.
Two of Cleburne's splendid outfielders, Tris Speaker and George
Whiteman, joined Houston, along with third sacker Roy Akin. Bob
Edmondson, who was the only player to stay with one club —
Houston — during all four seasons of the South Texas circuit,
teamed with Speaker and Whiteman to form one of the greatest
outfields in Texas League history. The hard-hitting Edmondson
was in center, flanked by Whiteman in left and Speaker in right.
Speaker was perfecting his technique of playing very shallow, snag-
ging line drives and popup "Texas Leaguers" that should have
been hits, but relying on his incredible speed to outrace deep flies.
Speaker led the league with a .314 batting average (although Sam
Stovall of San Antonio was credited with a .332 average by the
Spalding Guide), then went up to the Boston Red Sox at the end of
1907. He was in the American League for 22 seasons, had a lifetime
batting average of .344, and became a Hall of Famer.

San Antonio had a swashbuckling 1907 club led by power-hit-
ting first baseman-manager Pat Newnam and pitcher Buck Harris,
whose 23 victories included the season's only no-hitter (Harris won
22 for the Bronchos the next year). The Bronchos were chronic um-

pire baiters whose worst wrangle came during a July 23 doubleheader at Austin. The Bronchos were so enraged at the officiating
during the first game that they forfeited in the eighth inning. They
continued to skirmish with the umpire, and several players were
hauled off the field by policemen. Angrily, the Bronchos declared
that they would not play the second game, but they were reminded
that league rules would dictate a substantial fine against San Antonio. The team grudgingly agreed to play, but decided among
themselves just to go through the motions. Broncho players
swapped positions as many as three times during the game, outfielders gazed blankly as fly balls dropped at their feet, and infielders let routine grounders bounce between their legs. Austin was allowed to steal 23 bases — a league record for one game. Austin
scored 12 runs in the first inning, then romped to a 44-0 win over
the disgruntled Bronchos.

The 1907 pennant race was hard-fought, featuring tight pitching throughout the league. Houston's 24-game winner, Ivy Tevis,
Tex Covington, who fashioned a sparkling 16-6 record, and W. E.
Hester pitched a record-setting 57 consecutive innings of shutout
ball, and the Buffaloes won four straight 1-0 games. Harry Ables of
the Dallas team was 12-5 with a 1.77 ERA. Harry Guyn, the 17-17
ace of a weak Waco club, twirled 40 consecutive shutout innings to
set another league record. In early August Austin won nine straight
games, including six shutouts: five of the victories and 49 innings
were consecutive shutouts. The Austin pitching staff allowed a mis-
erly four runs and 33 hits during the nine games of this remarkable
string. On August 6, in the middle of the streak, Austin's left-
handed fastballer, Bill Bailey, went into the ninth inning with a 3-0
lead. But the leadoff batter walked and Curley Maloney doubled
him to third. Bailey, facing the third-, fourth-, and fifth-place batters, threw nine explosive pitches. One offering was fouled away,
but the other eight were waved at futilely as the meat of the order
went down swinging and Bailey preserved his shutout.

Austin went on to win the championship by one and a half
games over Dallas, and just four and a half games separated the top
four clubs. The race kept fan interest so stimulated that the season
was not split. It would be 13 years before a split schedule again was
employed, and the eight-team format was so successful that this arrangement would become permanent.

Austin's Senators won the final South Texas League pennant in 1906, and most of the players returned to win the Texas League flag in 1907. The Senators are posed beside their wooden grandstand, with female admirers in the background.
— Author's Collection

Last-place Temple, still bitter over having been forced out of the league in 1906, sold its franchise to Shreveport interests. Because of increased mileage expenses, the league required Shreveport to post a $75 guarantee to visiting clubs (the Texas teams put up a $50 guarantee). Aside from Shreveport, the league was composed of the same cities as the previous year. But the fine Austin team of the past two seasons suffered the loss of its best players (the sale of promising players was a key source of revenue for minor league owners), and the 1908 Senators plummeted to the cellar.

San Antonio filled in the power vacuum, closely pursued by Dallas. Curley Maloney, whose first Texas League season was at Dallas in 1889, batted .302 and led the circuit in hits and doubles as a player-manager for the Giants in 1908. Another figure from the 1880s, Pop Weikart, played 84 games at first base and managed Galveston. Shreveport's Tony Thebo stole 90 bases to take the theft championship, and he led the league with 63 steals the next year.

The batting champ was Houston left fielder Bob Edmondson, who hit a sizzling .391.

There were five no-hitters in 1908, and the first was the most frustrating. Fred Cook, who won more than 20 games in 1908 and again in 1909 for San Antonio, no-hit Waco on June 1. But the Bronchos could not score, and the game went into extra innings. Cook kept his no-hitter through 11 innings, his shutout through 12 — then lost his finest game, 2-0, in the 13th. Harry Ables, now pitching for San Antonio, had his usual fine year, 15-6 with a 2.04 ERA. O. C. Peters won 24 games for Dallas to lead the league in victories, and Houston's Hank Griffin went 23-9 (.719) for the highest percentage.

San Antonio won the pennant and Dallas again finished second, but Houston made by far the most humanitarian gesture of this or any other season. On their first road trip of the year, Houston players found a baby boy who had been abandoned on the train. Star third baseman Roy Akin took a special liking to the infant, but all of the Buffs rallied to the cause. The players started a fund for the baby, and during several games Buffs passed their caps to raise more money. Akin eventually adopted the foundling and raised him.

The only club to give up its franchise after the 1908 season was last-place Austin. Oklahoma City joined the league to provide the eighth team, but the Oklahomans had to guarantee visitors $100 per game (as opposed to $75 for Shreveport and $50 for the six Texas clubs). Oklahoma City fielded an excellent team, boasting the batting champ — fleet outfielder O. C. Downey, who hit .346 — and an impressive second-place finish.

The league was tough in 1909: six of the eight teams enjoyed winning records, at the expense of Galveston and last-place Waco. Houston battled its way to the pennant, signifying the start of a dynasty. The Buffs would finish on top five of the next six years. Houston's manager was old pro Hunter Hill. An infielder who had spent three seasons in the American League, Hill was obtained from the International League at the start of 1909 and made his first appearance in the Texas League since Corsicana's superb team of 1902. Hill stressed bunting, and his club led the circuit in sacrifices in 1909 and 1910. His catchers were Reindeer Bill Killefer, who went up to the majors at the end of the year and stayed

CONGRATULATIONS, CHAMPS!

San Antonio's 1908 Bronchos won the first Texas League pennant enjoyed by the Alamo City, and several wealthy fans decided to stage an appreciation banquet worthy of the occasion. The 15 Broncho players received invitations to a formal victory banquet to be held at 410 Matamoros Street — one of the largest, plushest houses in San Antonio's red light district.

San Antonio Bronchos, 1908 champs, togged out in warmup sweaters which were often unnecessary in mid-afternoon Texas heat. The great southpaw Harry Ables (325 strikeouts in 1910), stands in the middle of the top row. Owner Morris Block is seated in the middle. Outfielder Otto McIver, a 13-year Texas Leaguer, is at left in the middle row. Admirers treated the Bronchos to an evening in the red-light district.
— Courtesy Baxter Photo, Marshall, Texas

The athletes togged out in their Sunday best. George "Tex" Westerzil, the youngest Broncho, had graduated from San Antonio High School and proceeded straight to Block Stadium, hitting .301 in 58 games as a rookie third baseman. Dressing in his high school graduation suit, Westerzil solicited assurances from the older players that they would "protect" him — a dubious assurance at best.

The honored players were ushered into the Victorian establishment by a butler, and the men were escorted to the dining room by the madam and other bejeweled young women in formal gowns. Owner Morris Block was present, but the table was presided over by one of San Antonio's leading businessmen, who toasted the players to the applause of the ladies.

Following a sumptuous meal, outfielder-manager George "Cap" Leidy was presented an enormous engraved trophy. The players then were told to look under their plates, where each man found a crisp $100 bill. Further details of the evening are not known, but surely no Texas League victory celebration has ever been more appreciated by the players.

until 1921, and Brooks Gordon, a superior handler of pitchers who
had lost half a foot in a rail mishap. Pat Newnam, the Texas League
home run champ (18) in 1908, was on first, and would be with the
team in all five championship years. The outfield was excellent:
slow but hard-hitting Hub Northen in right; the graceful veteran
Trapper Longley in center; and 5'6" Joe Mowry in left. Mowry,
who spent eight years as a Buffalo, possessed a powerful, accurate
arm, he was extremely quick and a fine bunter, and he always batted leadoff.

Houston's best pitchers were southpaw Charles Rose (who
won 21 games and who, like Newnam, was with the Buffs in all five
of the championship seasons) and Harry Stewart (whose 23-8 record was the best in the league). San Antonio boasted a trio of fire-
ballers in 1909. Fred Cook had another outstanding season, leading
the league in strikeouts (264) and innings pitched (317). Harry
Ables went 19-12, working 293 innings and striking out 259. Lefthander Willie Mitchell was hired off the campus of Mississippi
A&M in 1909. He enjoyed a 13-9 rookie season, pitching a no-hitter against Shreveport on June 26, then on August 19 fanning 20
Galveston batters to set a Texas League record that would last
more than seven decades. Ables and Mitchell were moved to Cleveland at the end of the season, and Mitchell stayed in the major
leagues for 11 years.

As the decade came to a close, the Texas League found itself in
a solid position. Now more than 20 years old, the circuit had developed a tradition of aggressive, quality baseball. Texans could read
the big league box scores and follow the fortunes of numerous athletes they had seen play in the Texas League, and there was no
slowdown in the parade of players to the majors. The Texas
League, like the major circuits, now had eight teams, and had operated for an unprecedented eight seasons in a row. No longer did
clubs abruptly disband in the middle of the season, nor did the
league find it expedient to halt play for a few weeks — or months —
before the end of the regular schedule. Baseball now was firmly established as the national pastime, and in the Lone Star State —
atop a pyramid of college teams, semi-pro clubs, high school
squads, and town teams — stood the Texas League.

1910-1919

A
Baseball
Heyday

The second decade of the new century proved to be a period of dynasties in the Texas League. Houston dominated the first half of the decade, being awarded a controversial co-championship in 1910, regrouping the next year, then winning three pennants in a row. Of course, Houston had won the flag in 1909 and had retained a solid nucleus of players — the team would claim all or part of five championships during a six-year period.

Pitching was the key for Houston in 1910: only one player hit over .300 (Hub Northen, .311), although Pat Newnam batted .350 in 38 games (he played 103 games for the St. Louis Browns in 1910). Houston won with a balanced mound staff: John Eubanks, a 37-year-old ex-American Leaguer, was 10-4, while Sandy Malloy, spitballer Pep Hornsby, and Roy Mitchell won 16 apiece, and Charles Rose and curveballer Cy Watson chipped in 13 each.

But Dallas also boasted a fine pitching staff — Walter Shontz (19-9), R. Yates (13-6) and southpaw Rube Evans (15-12) — while first baseman Hank Gowdy led the league in hitting (.312) and outfielder George Jackson paced the circuit in stolen bases (55). The Dallas Giants pressured the defending champion Buffaloes all season. By now Dallas and Fort Worth were bitter rivals, as were Houston and Galveston. Texan loyalties also alienated Shreveport's Pirates and Oklahoma City's Indians. These tensions, com-

Texas League club officials, 1910. Top, left to right: W. R. Davidson, Waco owner; Jay Andrews, Oklahoma City mgr.; Joe Gardner, Dallas owner. Second row: B. C. Doherty, Galveston owner; F. H. Devers, Galveston; Harry Ehrlich, Shreveport mgr.; Doak Roberts, Houston owner. Third row: James A. Maloney, Dallas mgr.; Walter Morris, Fort Worth owner; Morris Block, San Antonio owner. Bottom row: Otto Sens, Houston owner; James Weaver, Fort Worth owner; George Leidy, San Antonio mgr.

— Author's Collection

bined with a tight pennant race, spurred more than the usual on-field rhubarbs and scuffles. "The public wants clean baseball," declared one critic, "the time has passed when the players who misbehave on the diamond will receive the sympathies of league officials, or of the public. . . ."

One important development of 1910 was the introduction of rain checks to the Texas League. Before the season opened, John J. McGraw brought his famous New York Giants to Fort Worth for an exhibition game with the Panthers. When rain halted play, Panther owner J. Walter Morris told the fans to line up at the ticket windows for refunds. But a number of fans got their money, then slipped to the back of the line for another refund. "That's when I decided to start issuing rain checks," stated Morris, and the practice quickly became common throughout the league.

The pennant race was tight through the year. San Antonio southpaw Harry Ables (who dueled Waco's Arthur Loudell 23 innings to a 1-1 tie on July 5) claimed that a Buffalo player had tried to bribe him to throw a game, and a mid-season league meeting threw out seven contests. Four of the disputed games had been Houston victories, only one of which had been protested, but an appeal to the National Association brought no response. On the final day of the season, with Houston leading Dallas by half a game, the Giants won a bitterly fought doubleheader from Fort Worth. Houston, with a postponement to make up, scheduled a tripleheader: three five-inning games with archrival Galveston. Galveston won the first, the Buffs took the second — then accepted a disputed forfeit when Galveston marched off the field during the third inning of the finale.

Although Dallas apparently had won by a full game, Houston pressed a claim to the championship. Arguments raged through the off-season, and both clubs ignored the suggestion that a seven-game playoff be arranged just prior to the opening of the 1911 season. Eventually, a co-championship was declared.

There was a change of cast for 1911, as Shreveport pulled out of the league. Austin interests purchased the franchise, and the Senators fought their way clear of a tight pennant race. Not a single Austin regular hit .300, but the Senators were led by two 20-game winners: Wiley Taylor (22-14) and Jack Ashton (21-12).

After the season, Oklahoma City sold its club to Beaumont, and the Texas League became an all-Texas aggregation for the next three seasons. During those years Houston moved back atop the circuit. Hunter Hill, the fine player-manager of 1910–11, left after a dispute with management. He was replaced by third baseman John Fillman, who stressed bunting, the hit and run, and aggressive baserunning.

Charles Rose, a slender southpaw who was destined to be one of the greatest of all Texas League hurlers (143-98 over 10 seasons), was the Buffalo mound ace. Rose pitched for all five Houston championship teams: he was 21-16 in 1909, 13-10 in 1910, 21-11 with eight shutouts in 1912, 26-7 with nine shutouts in 1912, and 24-9 in 1914 — winning 105 games for the five pennant winners.

KILL THE UMPIRE!

Wild Bill Setley was a colorful umpire who spent the 1910 season calling balls, strikes, and outs in the Texas League. It was a particularly turbulent year, wracked with more than the usual number of brawls, fist fights between managers and umpires, and fan disorders.

"I've seen them wear six-shooters to games in the Texas League," reminisced Setley 30 years later, "and when a fan pulled one out in Fort Worth and took a shot at a fly ball, I was ready to check out."

The most prominent umpire of this period was Wilson Matthews, who played in the Texas League as an infielder and outfielder in 1899 and 1902, managing Paris part of the latter season. But he was so respected and well liked that he was called upon to umpire in each season, and by 1903 he had become a full-time arbiter. He was the Texas League's finest umpire for a dozen years, until he died of tuberculosis in 1917.

By this time one man no longer was called upon to umpire Texas League games. Two-man crews became the rule, and when the Texas League began regular post-season playoff series in the 1930s it became customary to use three umpires. At the beginning of each game the head ump would face the grandstand and announce the lineups through a megaphone.

In 1981 Pamela Postema, who had four years' experience in the Gulf Coast and Florida State leagues, became the Texas League's first female umpire. She worked Texas League games for two years, and her contract was purchased by the Class AAA Pacific Coast League. Since 1986 the Texas League has used three umpires at all games.

Rose had formidable mound help. Rube Foster was 24-7 with 10 shutouts in 1912, then went to the Boston Red Sox. The 1912 pitching staff also featured Roger Edmondson (17-7, then 18-9 in 1914), while the 1913 corps boasted Andy Ware (20-14) and Dode Criss (16-4). Ware was even better in 1914 (26-8); his right hand had been maimed in a boyhood accident, but the stubs of his fingers gave a wicked spin to his pitches.

Like Rose, first sacker Pat Newnam also played for each of the five Buffalo pennant winners. He missed much of 1910 while playing in the American League, but he could not hit major league pitching and soon returned to Houston, where he took over as manager in 1914. During 16 seasons as a Texas Leaguer, Newnam stole 501 bases. The outfield mainstay in 1912, 1913, and 1914 was Red Davis, who led the league in stolen bases (65) in 1914.

But in 1914 Houston's long dominance was challenged by an-

UNASSISTED TRIPLE PLAY AT THIRD

An unassisted triple play is a rarity in baseball, but especially so when a third baseman makes the outs. Third sacker Roy Akin played Texas League ball with Galveston, Temple, Cleburne, and Houston from 1902 through 1908. Playing in the Pacific Coast League in 1911, Akin hit into an unassisted triple play, which apparently inspired him to try the trick himself. The next season Akin signed with Waco, and on May 9, 1912, the Navigators traveled to Houston for a game with the Texas League's most daring exponents of bunting and aggressive baserunning.

In the first inning Houston put John Fillman on third and Gilbert Britton on second with no outs. In similar situations Fillman, the manager, had signaled a bunt to score both baserunners, and on the pitcher's windup Fillman and Britton tore toward home. But batter Red Davis's bunt was a line drive that Akin speared. Fillman was already home and Britton had passed third when Akin tagged the base, putting both men out and producing the Texas League's first unassisted triple play.

---

other budding dynasty: the Waco Navigators. Ellis Hardy, who first appeared in the Texas League in 1897 as Waco's first baseman, had been lured from his coaching position at Texas Christian University to become the Navigator manager in 1911. By 1914 Hardy had built an imposing and remarkably stable club. Nine men played for the Navigators in each of the three consecutive title years:

Emmett "Turley" Reilly — a fine catcher with a cannon for an arm.

Eddie Donalds — a tall righthander with good control who was 30-4 in 1914, 18-12 in 1915, and 17-10 in 1916.

George Sage — a big righthander who was 13-3 in 1914, 14-9 in 1915, then slumped to 6-14 in 1916.

Cliff Hill — a southpaw control artist who picked up the slack as Donalds and Sage weakened; he was 10-5 in 1914, then 15-8 in 1915, and 23-14 in 1916.

Walter Malmquist — a flawless fielder, he was the Navigator second baseman for six years.

Harvey Grubb — he handled the hot corner superbly, but was weak at the plate.

Fred Wohleben — the tall, lumbering first baseman led the Texas League in home runs in 1913 and 1915.

Archie Tanner — one of the great Texas League shortstops, he

Houston Buffaloes, 1914 co-champs. Noted Texas Leaguers included 13-year
catcher Frank Kitchens (third from left, top), Bob Edmondson (second from right,
top), Dode Criss (top right), player-manager Pat Newnam (center of middle row),
and the superb southpaw, Charlie Rose (third from left, bottom row). For years it
was customary for fans to stick a fist through the top of their straw skimmers at the
close of the Labor Day (end of summer) doubleheader.
— Courtesy Baxter Photo, Marshall, Texas

had impressive range as a fielder, and during 14 seasons and
1,527 league games he hit .280.

Bob James — a nine-year Texas League outfielder, he hit .295 in
1914 (he spent the first part of the season with Austin), .313
in 1915 (and with eight home runs he tied Wohleben for the
lead), and .303 in 1916.

The Navigators produced the Texas League batting champ in
each title year: in 1914, his only season in the league, Robert Clemens hit .327 and also led in runs, hits, total bases, and assists by a
left fielder; in 1915 Roxy Walters batted .325, then finished the season in the American League, where he spent the next decade; and
in 1916 Clarence "Little Bit" Bittle, a 5'6" right fielder, topped the
league with a .333 average as a crack leadoff man.

Hardy's team was a formidable combination which stayed
hard on the heels of defending champion Houston throughout
1914. On the last day of the season Houston led Waco with two

The Waco Navigators, 1914 co-champs, wearing their warmup sweaters. Ten members of the Navigators played throughout the three-year pennant dynasty. Top row, left to right: Jack Ashton, Cliff Hill, George Crichlow, Ottie Ingram, Fred Baker, H. Green, William Rennard, Roy Akin. Middle row: Finley Yardley, Hatton Ogle, Walter Malmquist, Ellis Hardy, mgr., Ollie Jost, Fred Wohleben, Eddie Donalds. Bottom row: Mike Rose, Harvey Grubb, Arch Tanner, Emmett Reilly, Robert Clemens.
— Courtesy Baxter Photo, Marshall, Texas

more victories but the same number of defeats. Waco won its season-ending Labor Day doubleheader from Dallas, while the Buffaloes defeated Galveston in the first game of a double bill. In the second game, with the Buffs trailing, the umpires stopped play because of darkness in the top of the fifth — no contest. Houston claimed the pennant by a .673 to .670 percentage edge over the Navigators. But Waco protested a June game won by Houston, which in turn protested a Navigator victory. When the technicalities were examined and various games were discarded (and the umpires of the Houston-Galveston doubleheader fired), each club was awarded a 102-50 record and a co-championship.

In 1915 Waco handily outdistanced the other seven teams. One of these clubs was Shreveport, a replacement for hapless Austin, which had lost 31 consecutive games on the way to the 1914 cellar. On August 15 a ferocious storm rocked the Gulf Coast, destroying the ball parks at Houston and Galveston. The Sandcrabs

The Houston Buffaloes in the World War I era. Texas Leaguers traveled for decades by rail. Rookies were always assigned upper berths on Pullman cars. On hot summer nights Pullmans were stifling, but if windows were opened smoke and cinders flew into the car.
— Courtesy Houston Public Library

suspended operations for the final two weeks of the season, but the Buffaloes played out their schedule, utilizing fields at Austin, Corpus Christi, and Brenham for their remaining "home" games.

In 1916 Waco was fiercely challenged by the Shreveport Gassers. Late in the season, with the Navigators clinging to a slim lead, Shreveport came to Waco for a climactic three-game series. Waco took two out of three, then hung on for their third straight pennant.

By the time the 1917 season opened, the United States had entered World War I. Fans were distracted by war fever — and, increasingly, by movies, automobile driving, college football, and other popular competition for the entertainment dollar. In 1914, 42 minor leagues had opened the season, but in 1917 the Texas League was one of just 20 circuits that started the year, and by May the last-place Galveston and weak Beaumont franchises were in trouble. The clubs folded, although they were promised preference for future readmission. Their best athletes were distributed among the remaining six teams, which produced a high quality of play around the league. During the season, Sunday doubleheaders became a feature of the schedule that would be enjoyed by Texas League fans for the next several decades.

Dallas won the first of two consecutive pennants in 1917. The Submarines were led to the championship by Snipe Conley, who pitched 12 consecutive years for Dallas, 1916 through 1927. The righthander boasted a wicked spitball and fielded his position like a shortstop. Snipe enjoyed a spectacular season in 1917: he won 27 games, including 19 straight; he led the league in victories and strikeouts (171); and he swung a mean bat, posting the highest batting average (.309) on the team.

Conley and the 1917 Dallas Submarines exemplified the fact that this was a decade dominated by pitchers. Team and individual batting averages were low throughout the decade. The highest team percentages of the period were posted by Dallas in 1911 and Waco in 1915, .270 each season, while co-champion Houston won the team batting title in 1910 with an anemic .240 average. Dallas first baseman Hank Gowdy was the league batting champ in 1910 with a .312 mark, and the only hitting titlist of the decade who posted a really impressive average was Beaumont's star center fielder, Al Nixon, who hit .364 in 1919.

There were heroic pitching exploits throughout the decade. Hickory Dickson, a Texas League standout in 1905 and 1906, spent five seasons in the majors before signing with Houston in 1916. In an 18-8 year he posted a 1.06 ERA, still the league record — and, coincidentally, the first season the Texas League kept ERA records. Rube Robinson was 28-7 for Fort Worth in 1911. A fireballing southpaw who struck out 243 in 300 innings, he could enter a game with little warmup and was often called on for relief duty — he pitched in 55 games and won more games than he started. Eddie Donalds, of course, led Waco to a 1914 co-championship with a brilliant 30-4 record. Beaumont boasted a magnificent duo in 1919: 10-year Texas Leaguer "Oyster Joe" Martina enjoyed his finest season (28-13), while southpaw Bill Bailey (24-21) led the loop in strikeouts (277). Each hurler worked 378 innings, setting the all-time league record. Eugene Moore, a powerfully built Galveston lefthander, twice led the league in strikeouts (213 in 1912 when he was 19-6, and 240 in 1914 when he was 21-10), while another southpaw, the veteran Harry Ables, fanned 325 in 320 innings for San Antonio in 1910.

The three-man pitching rotation still was customary on most teams; the four-man rotation became popular during the 1920s. There were no relief specialists. Starting pitchers were expected to be ready to work relief, and the best starters were called in to work the most important late-inning situations. But starters also were expected to complete their games, including extra-inning contests. On August 7, 1915, Buddy Napier of Houston and Gus Bono of Dallas worked 15 scoreless innings before darkness halted proceedings. On June 25, 1910, Jim Durham of Oklahoma City and George Hinricksen of Galveston toiled 19 innings (Durham took the 3-2 decision), while Waco's Cliff Hill and Galveston's Jim Gudger went 20 innings on August 13, 1916 (Gudger weakened in the 20th and lost, 4-1). On May 18, 1918, with only six clubs participating in a war-shortened season, all three Texas League games were 1-0 pitchers' duels.

There were 22 no-hitters during the decade. The previous decade had featured at least 24 no-hitters, plus five in the South Texas League, but there were more strong hitting feats during the first seasons of the twentieth century than in the 1910–1919 period. On May 31, 1912, Houston's Grover Brant pitched a 12-inning no-hitter against Fort Worth, finally beating big Poll Perritt, 2-1. Brant hurled another no-hitter against Galveston in 1914, but he was only one of three pitchers to pitch two no-hitters during the decade. Hatton "Professor" Ogle, a tall righthander, pitched no-hitters for Waco in 1912 and 1914, while big Dode Criss, now playing for Houston, threw no-hitters in 1914 and 1915. Furthermore, Jimmie Zinn pitched a no-hitter for Waco in 1917 and another for Wichita Falls in 1920, the great Paul Wachtel threw no-hitters for Fort Worth in 1918 and 1924, and Jean Dale pitched a no-hitter for Dallas in 1910, then held his opponents hitless for the first 10 innings of a 1920 game.

During Andy Ware's splendid 26-8 season in 1914, the Houston righthander won 14 straight decisions. Dode Criss won 15 straight for Houston in 1913; he was only 9-4 the next year, but hit .348, and in 1915 he was 18-9 and .333 at the plate. But the longest winning streak of the decade, of course, was Snipe Conley's 19 straight in 1917. On April 15 Snipe worked 15 innings, only to lose, 2-3, to Waco. But four days later he beat Shreveport, 1-0, and he was off and running. Snipe started 17 games during the string, going the distance every time, and he also made nine relief appearances, picking up two more victories. He pitched four shutouts during his string, including a no-hitter against Fort Worth on June 24. During the Fort Worth game, Snipe struck out nine Panthers and walked one, who was cut down trying to steal. Conley faced just 27 batters and barely missed a perfect game. He went 10 innings to beat Waco, 6-5, for his 19th consecutive victory on July 8. Three days later the Navigators beat Conley, 8-3, finally snapping the streak. At the time it was thought that George Bristow, 30-16 for Galveston in 1895, had won 22 straight, but later it was found that Bristow's consecutive victory string was 16. Carl Hubbell of the New York Giants won 24 straight over the 1936 and 1937 seasons; the major league record for a single season is 19, shared by two other New York pitchers, Timothy Keefe in 1888 and Rube Marquard in 1912. Snipe Conley's 19 stands as the record for the first century of Texas League play.

Dallas made it two straight pennants in 1918, although the season was drastically curtailed by the war (just nine minor leagues started the season, and only the International League completed its schedule). The six clubs that had finished the 1917 Texas League season lined up for the next year. Although the United States had been involved in the war for a year, Washington gave out assurances that professional baseball would be allowed to continue. But on May 23 it was announced that on July 1 all men not in a necessary occupation would be called to "work or fight." Many young players did not wait to be drafted, and, as these volunteers gave up a flannel uniform for khakis (or signed up for "essential" work), numerous other players began to be drafted. "Farewell games" for departing players were held at parks around the league, while professional athletes stationed at camps in San Antonio, Waco, Austin, Houston, and Fort Worth appeared in weekend lineups.

Although the turnover on every team was continuous, Dallas pulled away from the field in June. Snipe Conley was still throwing spitballs, but the key for Dallas in 1918 was hitting. Outfielder Olen Nokes led the league in batting (.333), but scrappy third baseman Jewel Ens (.303), center fielder (and part owner and club president!) Walter "Chink" Mattick (.302), and southpaw pitcher-outfielder Walter Kinney (.301) all hit well. After July 1 operations became more difficult, and the patriotism of the Texas League increasingly was held open to question. League officials decided to halt play on July 7, with Dallas leading the pack at 52-37.

With the armistice signed on November 11, 1918, Texas League officials eagerly reorganized the circuit for 1919. Galveston and Beaumont rejoined the league, which resumed the same lineup as that which had opened the 1917 season. Postwar fans surged to the ballparks, but turbulent weather caused a flurry of rainouts, prompting the league to declare a split season for the first time since 1906.

Shreveport surged from the cellar in 1918 to the first-half championship in 1919. The Gassers were led by fiery Billy Smith, a veteran manager who had copped six pennants in the tough Southern Association. Smith put together a fine pitching staff: John Verbout topped the league in ERA (1.56) and went 11-5 (Verbout was 22-11 in 1920; in 1919 Houston's Bryan Harriss also fashioned a 1.56 ERA with a 21-14 record, then he went to the American League for a 10-year career with Philadelphia and Boston); Buddy Napier was 21-11 for the Gassers; Karl Black (whose real name was Tauschenschleger) was 15-10; and Gus Bono pitched a no-hitter for the Gassers after coming over at mid-season from Dallas.

But in the second half the Gassers sagged to fifth while Fort Worth dominated play. Panther manager Jake Atz was building a dynasty which would feature a splendid mound staff: his aces in 1919 were Joe Pate (15-4 with a 1.68 ERA), Buzzer Bill Whitaker (24-12 and 1.89), and Paul Wachtel (21-14 and 2.40).

When the two teams met for a seven-game playoff, Fort Worth held a commanding second-half margin (.651 winning percentage to Shreveport's .493), and the Panthers were consensus favorites to win. But Shreveport took the first two games at home, then went to Fort Worth and won their third straight. Fort Worth fought back gamely, winning the next two 2-1 and 2-0. Then it was back to Shreveport, where the clubs locked up at 2-2 through 10 innings before the game was called on account of darkness. Finally, the Gassers took game seven, 6-5, capturing their first Texas League flag. But the Panthers of Fort Worth, with the best overall record of the season, had just begun to flex the muscles of the most awesome dynasty the Texas League would see during its first century. The second decade of the twentieth century had been a time of two- and three-year dynasties, but Texas League fans of the 1920s would see the greatest dynasty of all.

1920–1929

The Texas League During the Golden Age of Sports

The decade of the 1920s is regarded by many as the Golden Age of Sports in America, and baseball enjoyed a heyday as the most popular professional game in the land. The ball was livelier now, and Babe Ruth led the sport into an exciting era of home run sluggers and high-scoring games. The day of tight pitchers' duels — contests which featured hit-and-run, stolen bases, and bunting to play for one run — faded rapidly under a barrage of home runs as batters swung from the heels. Fans responded eagerly to a more electric style of baseball that proved perfectly suited to the accelerated pulse rate of the Roaring Twenties.

Babe Ruth was a sensation in 1920 when he walloped an astounding 54 roundtrippers (he duplicated this total in 1928, but in 1921 he hit 59, and in 1927 he slugged 60 homers). Prior to the 1920s, the Texas League home run record was 22, set by San Antonio first baseman Frank Metz in 1911. The next season Metz hit 21 homers, but until the 1920s no other Texas Leaguer had ever hit more than 18 home runs.

The Texas League wasted little time in joining the power parade. Scores went up dramatically, as did batting averages and, of course, ERAs. The leading team batting averages during the previous decade had ranged from .240 to .270, but in seven of the ten seasons of the 1920s the team batting average leaders hit over .300,

51

WICHITA FALLS SPUDDERS, WICHITA FALLS, TEXAS — 1921
Front row, left to right: H. Rothfuss, o.f.; Frank Rose, p.; Dannie Gross, s.s.; Danny
Clark, i.f.; Jake Miller, o.f.; George Bischoff, c.; A. D. (Buddy) Tanner, i.f.; W. C.
Comstock, i.f. and o.f.; Charles (Tex) McDonald, i.f. and o.f.; Back row: Adolph
Ruth, p.; Oscar (Idaho) Anderson, p.; Pierce Works, 1B; Leo Mangrum, p.; W. M.
Marshall, p.; Walter Salm, mgr.; Frank Kitchens, c.; Abe Bowman, p.; Jim W. Sewell,
p.; L. S. McElwee, o.f. and i.f.; Floyd Kroh, p.; Clarence Darrough, p.

and in 1927 the Waco Navigators established a league record .316
team mark. A record 3,778 extra base hits were pounded out
around the league in 1925, and 7,044 runs were scored that year. In
1926, 1,024 home runs were hit, and in 1929 Texas League batters
rapped out a record 12,711 base hits. In 1921 "Hack" Eibel, a
strong Shreveport first baseman who, like Babe Ruth, also was a
lefthanded pitcher, blasted 35 home runs (and led the circuit in triples) to set a new Texas League record. But the mark did not last
for long.

   During the next three seasons, the home run leader was Fort
Worth first sacker Clarence Otto "Big Boy" Kraft. The veteran
slugger hit 32 homers in 1922 and 1923, then poled 55 in 1924 —
the highest total in organized baseball that season and a record
which would stand for 32 years in the Texas League. Kraft retired

after the 1924 season, but his place on the Fort Worth roster was capably filled by longtime major leaguer "Big Ed" Konetchy, who led the Texas League in 1925 with 41 roundtrippers and 166 RBIs. By this time every team in the circuit was on the prowl for sluggers, and hitting exploits continued through the decade. Indeed, in 1929 an all-time total of 17 players scored 100 or more runs during the season.

For the first six years of the 1920s, the Fort Worth Panthers dominated the Texas League with an awesome combination of power hitting and overwhelming pitching. The architects of the most sustained team success in league history was a management trio: two men who became part owners in 1916, W. K. Stripling (team president, 1917–1929) and Paul LaGrave (team secretary and business manager — equivalent to a modern general manager — in 1916–1929), and Jake Atz (field manager, 1914–1929). Stripling and LaGrave collected fine players and paid them so well that they stayed in Fort Worth, even after stellar performances brought offers to play in higher classifications. Of course, independent minor league owners were under no obligation to sell outstanding players, which is a major explanation for the Texas League dynasties of the period.

An infielder by trade, Jake Atz found himself in Fort Worth in 1914 as a 35-year-old player-manager. He did not manage a complete season until 1917, when he won 91 games for a second-place finish. He brought the Panthers (soon they were being called "Jake Atz's Cats") in second again in 1918, and the next season won the most games — 94 — but lost in the playoffs to Shreveport. Then Atz's Cats hit their stride, winning six consecutive Texas League pennants. Atz's victory totals during his string of championships were: 1920 — 108; 1921 — 107; 1922 — 109; 1923 — 96; 1924 — 109; 1925 — 103. The 109 wins in 1922 and 1924 set an all-time Texas League record.

In each of the six years, Fort Worth far outdistanced the closest challengers. Although each season except 1923 was split (a ploy to create playoff competition), Fort Worth won both halves every year. The only playoff the Panthers had to face occurred in the second half of 1925, when Fort Worth tied with archrival Dallas. But Atz's Cats triumphed over Snipe Conley's Steers in three straight, and Fort Worth had won the second half as well as the first half, thus guaranteeing their sixth straight flag without a playoff series. In 1923, with no split season, Fort Worth finished thirteen and a half games ahead of second-place San Antonio.

Five players were on the Panther roster during all six championship seasons. Lefthander Joe Pate was a 20-game winner in each of the six flag years, and in 1921 and 1924 he won 30. Paul Wachtel, the righthanded spitballer, also was a six-time 20-game winner for the Panthers (he won 21 in 1919 and 19 in 1923). Pate and Wachtel won 26 apiece in 1920 to start the pennant run, and over the six years they made a combined contribution of 292-121.* Ponderous Possum Moore caught for Fort Worth from 1919 through 1926; his best seasons were 1921 (.298) and 1924 (.311). Ziggy Sears, who spent 11 seasons in Texas League outfields, hit .304 in 1922, .323 in 1924, and .321 in 1925. Dugan Phelan, a five-year National League veteran, played 13 seasons in the Texas League; with Fort Worth he was a third baseman and pinch hitter who batted .300 in 1922.

Pate and Wachtel had impressive pitching support throughout the string. In 1920 and 1921 there were four 20-game winners on the staff: Pate and Wachtel won 26 each in 1920, while curveballing Buzzer Bill Whitaker was 24-6 and control artist Dick Robertson was 20-7; in 1921 Pate won 30, Wachtel 23, Whitaker 23, and southpaw Gus Johns won 20. There were three 20-game winners — Pate, Wachtel and Johns — in 1922, and in 1923, when Wachtel "slumped" to 19 victories and Pate won 23, Ulysses Simpson Grant "Lil" Stoner took up the slack with a 27-11 season (then he went directly to the major leagues). In 1925 Pate, Wachtel, and Johns won 20 or more, and southpaw Jim Walkup was 19-7. It was the greatest pitching staff in Texas League history.

The Panthers' leading slugger was Big Boy Kraft. He played seven seasons in Fort Worth (1918–1924), and in 980 Texas League games his batting average was .317. In 1921 he won the batting title with a .352 percentage, and he also led the league in at bats, runs, and hits.** Kraft established the Texas League lifetime records for the most consecutive years scoring 100 or more runs, most years scoring 100 or more runs, making 200 or more base hits,

---

* Pate's and Wachtel's records are detailed in the cities section under Fort Worth.

** Kraft's hitting records are detailed in the cities section under Fort Worth.

Fort Worth Panthers, 1925, the sixth consecutive pennant winners. Top row, left to right: Possum Moore, Billy Mullen, Stormy Davis, Ziggy Sears, Roy Storey, Stump Edington, Wayne Windle. Middle row: Jim Walkup, Dugan Phelan, Eddie Palmer, Lou North, Gus Foreman, Gus Johns, Ralph Head, Joe Pate, Paul Wachtel, Jake Atz, Big Ed Konetchy, Doc Smith, Jacinto Calvo.
— Courtesy Baxter Photo, Marshall, Texas

making over 100 RBIs, leading in extra base hits and home runs. His finest season was 1924, when he hit .349 and belted 55 homers and an all-time record 196 RBIs.

The dominance of Fort Worth for the first six years of the decade overshadowed various heroics by players on other teams. Twenty-six-year-old Ike Boone, a six-foot, 200-pounder with three years' experience as a minor leaguer, signed on with San Antonio for 1923. It was to be his only year in the Texas League, but Boone had an unforgettable season, leading the league in batting average (.402), runs (134), hits (241), doubles (53), triples (26), RBIs (135) and total bases (391 — the next year Big Boy Kraft established an all-time record 414 total bases). Boone also pounded 15 home runs and hit safely in 37 consecutive games — still the longest hitting streak in Texas League history. Boone finished the season with the Boston Braves, but he had enjoyed the most productive offensive

Jake Atz (1879–1945), was a mediocre minor league infielder who found his niche as a manager, most notably at Fort Worth (1914–1929 and 1934). Jake Atz's Cats dominated the Texas League from 1920 through 1925, winning a record six consecutive pennants. He also managed Dallas (1930), Shreveport (1931), Tulsa (1934), and Galveston (1936), as well as teams in other leagues.
— Courtesy Baxter Photo, Marshall, Texas

year in modern Texas League play. Two seasons later San Antonio fans watched infielder Dan Clark flirt with .400 before finishing at .399. Wichita Falls Spudder fans cheered four batting champs during the decade: Red Josefson (.345 in 1920), Homer Summa (.362 in 1922), Arthur Weiss (.377 in 1924), and Tom Jenkins (.374 in 1926). Waco produced back-to-back batting champs: former major leaguer Del Pratt (.386 in 1927, plus a league-leading 32 home runs) and outfielder George Blackerby (.368 in 1928, plus a home run championship the next year).

A notable team exploit of the 1920s was Wichita Falls' impressive 1922 winning streak. On July 21 Victor Keen outdueled Snipe Conley and the Dallas Steers, 2-1 in 17 innings. Then the Spudders returned to Wichita Falls for a four-week home stand. During the streak Keen won seven games (he went 13-4, then finished the season with the Cubs), while Floyd "Rip" Wheeler also won seven (he

---

ONE WAY TO WARM UP

Dick "Mutt" Williams was a 20-game winner in 1921 for Dallas and San Antonio, but he had a fondness for John Barleycorn which kept him from advancing to the big leagues. For San Antonio he hurled an iron-man doubleheader triumph over Jake Atz's championship Fort Worth club. But as a precaution Mutt was sometimes locked inside a San Antonio ticket booth a couple of hours before a scheduled start. Occasionally, Mutt would arrive at the ball park moments before game time, order the batboy to bring him a piece of paper and a match, then ceremoniously pass the burning paper under his pitching arm and announce that he was "warmed up" and ready.

---

was a 22-game winner in 1922 and again in 1923), including complete game victories in both halves of a doubleheader against San Antonio on August 3. On August 12 Keen squared off against Snipe Conley again. By the middle of the game spitballer Conley was complaining of burning lips, and soon his lips and tongue were so swollen that he could not talk. One of the Spudders — an aggregation notorious for their addiction to practical jokes — had applied colorless creosote to the game balls, and as Conley wet his fingers throughout the contest he severely burned his mouth. The Spudders won the game, 4-3, for their twenty-fifth consecutive victory. Spudder hopes of surpassing Corsicana's 27 straight in 1902 were thwarted the next day, when Roy Mitchell (who had beaten Wichita Falls the day before the streak started) pitched the Steers to a win. Dallas protested the Conley loss, however, and when the league upheld complaints over the "Creosote Incident," the official total stood at 24 consecutive victories — the second longest skein in Texas League history. But even after winning 24 in a row, the Spudders still trailed mighty Fort Worth by half a game. At season's end the Spudders were 94-61 — good for second place to Fort Worth's 109-46 record.

A significant innovation of the 1920s was the Dixie Series, which became the most popular baseball event in the South for nearly four decades. As far back as the 1890s, Texas sportswriters had urged a post-season playoff series between the champions of the Texas League and the Southern League, forerunner of the twentieth-century Southern Association. But the Southern Associ-

Smead Jolley, a legendary minor leaguer (.366 lifetime for 2,231 minor league games, and .305 in 473 American League games). During his only full season in the Texas League, at Shreveport in 1923, he was 2-8 as a pitcher. Switched to the outfield, he hit .331 and terrorized pitchers for two decades.
— Courtesy Bill McIntyre, *Shreveport Times*

ation was more advanced in classification than the Texas League and had nothing to gain and a great deal of prestige to lose by such a series. In 1920, however, when Fort Worth and Little Rock clearly dominated their respective leagues, Paul LaGrave contacted R. G. Allen, president of the Little Rock club, and reached an agreement for a seven-game series after each team wrapped up its regular schedule. Little Rock, managed by Kid Elberfeld (who had played the 1896 season for Dallas en route to the major leagues), did not officially represent the Southern Association — which proved convenient for the association, since the powerful Panthers won the series. But the seven games had attracted 36,836 ticket-buyers and nearly $50,000 in gross receipts, and the opportunity for future profit was obvious.

In 1921 the Texas League was elevated to Class A status, and the two now-equal circuits made formal arrangements for the Dixie Series. Fort Worth prevailed again, this time over Southern Asso-

Hall of Fame outfielder Al Simmons, in his second year as a professional (1923), hit .360 for Shreveport and was in the American League the next year.
— Author's Collection

ciation winner Memphis, and the next year Panther fans chartered a "Dixie Special" and brought along a Dixieland band, cowbells, and raucous enthusiasm. Fort Worth lost to Mobile in 1922, but during the next three years Jake Atz's Cats beat New Orleans, Memphis, and Atlanta in succession. By this time the Dixie Series had attained the status of a "little World Series," and was avidly followed across the South and Texas.

In 1926 Fort Worth's long monopoly over the Texas League championship finally was ended by archrival Dallas. Panther ace Joe Pate at last went up to the major leagues, while Paul Wachtel, now 38, slipped to 16-19 (Wachtel could not advance to the majors during the 1920s because the spitball, his most effective pitch, had been outlawed). The league did not declare a split season, and the resulting 156-game pennant race proved to be the closest since before World War I. Galveston had dropped out of the Texas League in 1924, replaced by Waco, and the eight member cities in 1926

THE TEXAS NEGRO LEAGUE

Another interesting innovation of the 1920s was the creation of the Texas Negro League. The circuit included clubs such as the Austin Black Senators, the San Antonio Giants, and the Galveston Crabs, and such teams often played in Texas League parks when the hometown white club was on the road. Texas Negro League teams also traveled frequently into Mexico for games with Mexican pros who had no reluctance in playing blacks. One of the finest players to come through the Texas Negro League was Giddings native Hilton Smith, who shut down the Austin Black Senators while pitching an exhibition game for a Brenham town team. The Black Senators promptly signed Smith, and eventually he went up to the famous Kansas City Monarchs, where many considered him an even greater money pitcher than Satchel Paige.

drew 1,159,906 paid admissions — an attendance record that stood for two decades.

Dallas attracted 286,806 of those fans. Snipe Conley had become a playing manager during the 1925 season, and in 1926 he pushed his team relentlessly toward a pennant. Snipe no longer pitched regularly, but 6'6" Slim Love (21-10) and southpaw Dick Schuman (17-5) led a solid mound corps, while R. L. Williams (.369), E. J. Woeber (.330 and 25 home runs), J. N. Riley (.329), and Charles Miller (.321, 30 homers and 118 RBIs) added lethal bats. Dallas battled for the lead throughout the year, but when Fort Worth dropped a late-season doubleheader, Conley's Steers took a stranglehold on first place. Then the Steers went on to beat New Orleans in six games for a Dixie Series triumph.

During league meetings preceding the 1923 season, circuit executives determined to follow the example of the rest of organized baseball and eliminate spitball pitching. Like the majors and other minor loops, the Texas League permitted current spitball practitioners to continue business as usual. Nine spitballers were sanctioned by the Texas League: Snipe Conley, Paul Wachtel, Slim Love, Ed Hovlik, Dana Fillingim, Hal Deviney, Larry Jacobus, Tom Estell, and Oscar Tuero. Most of these men were veterans nearing the end of the line; Estell and Tuero pitched until 1932, the last pitchers to *legally* throw a loaded baseball in the Texas League.

The Dallas Steers won the pennant and Dixie Series in 1926 and posed for this photo at Steer Stadium in the spring of 1927. Player-manager Snipe Conley stands at far right. Tall Slim Love (standing in the middle) was 21-10 in 1926, and Dick Shuman (kneeling at left) was 17-5. Charles Miller (standing at left) hit .321 with 30 homers for the champs, and R. L. Williams (standing fourth from right) hit .369.
— Courtesy Dallas Public Library

Edward Hock, who spent nine years in the Texas League, usually as a third baseman, was at shortstop for Houston when the Buffs lined up against Dallas on May 5, 1927. In the bottom of the third Dallas outfielder Rhino Williams walked. Fred Brainard dropped a sacrifice bunt, but both runners were safe when the ball was bobbled. Then Jodie Tate lashed a line drive up the middle. Moving to his left, Hock speared the ball, stepped on second for out number two, then chased down Brainard as he tried to scramble back toward third. It was the second unassisted triple play in Texas League history, following Roy Akin's unique effort from third base in 1912. Overall, there were six triple plays during the 1927 Texas League season.

Another remarkable fielding performance of the 1920s was turned in by Frankie Fuller, who played second base for San Antonio from 1920 through 1924 and for Houston in 1925. In each of the

A group of early-day Texas Leaguers gathered in Dallas for a 1926 old-timers' game.
— Courtesy Dallas Public Library

six seasons he led all pivot men in double plays, participating in a total of 531 double plays during the six years. Twice, Fuller took part in more than 100 double plays per season, and in 1922 he led the league in starting double plays — the only time a second baseman has surpassed all shortstops in that category.

The Wichita Falls Spudders proved to be the class of the league in 1927. The Spudders won their opener, and never relinquished the lead during the season. Third baseman Walter Swenson hit .300; second sacker Pete Turgeon, the Spudder leadoff man, hit .305, scored 115 runs, hit 31 doubles, 11 triples, 18 homers with 94 RBIs; center fielder Howard Chamney, an ex-University of Texas great who averaged .308 in 1,129 Texas League games from 1924 to 1932, hit .306; right fielder Lyman Lamb hit .314; even the utility man, Stanley "Rabbit" Benton, hit .322. But the offensive star of the team was left fielder "Tut" Jenkins, the defending champ (.374 in 1926) who hit .363 with 25 homers, 147 runs scored, and 129 RBIs.

Spudder pitching matched the explosive attack. At 23-9, old pro George Washington Payne led the league in victories; Frederick Fussell led the league in winning percentage (.724) at 21-8; Joe Kiefer was 20-9; spitballer Tom Estell was 16-7; and Milton Steengrafe was 15-6.

This powerful club overwhelmed the Texas League, finishing 102-54 (second-place Waco was 88-68), then swept New Orleans in four straight in the Dixie Series to complete a splendid season. It was the only time during the first 16 years of the classic that a team from either league took the Dixie Series in four games.

During the Texas League meeting in February 1928, it was decided to divide the season at mid-summer; 1928 would be the first time the league had ever determined beforehand to have a split season. Houston ran away with the first half, opening a lead of seven and a half games by June 29. Right fielder Red Worthington (.353 on the season) and catcher-manager Frank Snyder (.329) led the attack. "Pancho" Snyder had just finished a 16-year major league career, and he expertly handled a superb pitching staff that boasted no fewer than four 20-game winners: James Lindsey (25-10), Wild Bill Hallahan (23-12, with a league-leading 244 strikeouts and 2.25 ERA), Ken Penner (20-8), and Frank Barnes (20-9).

In the second half Wichita Falls aggressively defended their title. Although some of the big guns of 1927 had moved up, Tut Jenkins (.348 with a league-leading 27 homers, 121 runs scored, and 122 RBIs), Rabbit Benton (.324) and catcher Pete Lapan (.324) generated considerable offense, while Milt Steengrafe (22-8) and big league veteran Mike Cvengros (21-8) headed a pitching staff that was not up to the previous year's overall quality. But the Spudders dominated the second half, finishing with a margin of seven and a half games over second-place Houston. It seemed as though Wichita Falls would provide yet another dynasty for the 1920s.

In the best-of-five playoffs the Buffaloes won the first game in Wichita Falls, then dropped a decision to the Spudders. In the opening contest at Houston, Hallahan beat Cvengros, 1-0, on a two-hitter, and the Buffaloes wrapped up the series the next day. Having regained early-season form with their first flag since 1914, Houston downed Birmingham in the Dixie Series.

Competition was fierce throughout the Texas League in 1929. Fort Worth led in team batting (.303), but finished fourth; Waco

Carl Hubbell completed 20 of 21 starts for last-place Beaumont in 1928 and was bought at mid-season by the New York Giants.
— Author's Collection

led in home runs (188), but ended up fifth. During the year, Paul LaGrave died, and longtime Fort Worth president W. C. Stripling and the LaGrave estate sold their interests in the Panthers. Jake Atz, the brilliant field general who had served since 1914, including the past 13 consecutive years, left the team. The splendid management combination that had fashioned the Panther dynasty was dissolved before season's end.

Dallas, sparked by the explosive bats of outfielder Randy Moore (.369) and Simon Rosenthal (.339), took the first-half championship by merely a half game over Shreveport. Bridesmaid Shreveport finished second again in the last half, this time to Wichita Falls. The Spudders were led by George Washington Payne, who pitched in 55 games and finished at 28-12. As usual, Wichita Falls fans enjoyed a number of fine hitters: left fielder Fred Bennett (.368 and 145 RBIs); catcher Pete Lapan (.367); infielder Rabbit Benton (.327); and almost everybody else in the lineup.

The race for the batting title went down to the last day of the

Beaumont's Stuart Stadium seated 7,500 and opened in 1929.
— Courtesy Mrs. Dutch Lorbeer, Beaumont

season. Randy Moore won by a single percentage point and established an all-time league record for base hits (245). Fort Worth center fielder Eddie Moore, a speedy ball hawk and baserunner, set the all-time mark for triples (30). Texas League fans enjoyed the aggressive baserunning of Houston outfielder Pepper Martin, who led the league in stolen bases both years (1927 and 1929) he played for the Buffs.

Wichita Falls ended 1929 with the best record in the league, but the Spudders lost out to Dallas in the playoffs. Although Payne pitched in three of the four games, the Spudder ace ironically could not gain a playoff win. The Dallas Steers, with their second title in four seasons, were defeated in the Dixie Series by Birmingham — snapping a six-year losing streak inflicted by the Texas League on their Southern Association opponents.

By the time the season closed, the New York stock market had begun to wobble toward its disastrous collapse. The 1920s had been a period of unparalleled fan interest and attendance. The decade had exhibited great teams, a number of admirable pitching performances, and, above all, unprecedented hitting. It was the most exciting, explosive baseball that had yet been played in the circuit. But the 1930s would bring the Great Depression to the cities and ball parks and club offices of the Texas League.

1930-1939

Depression Decade

The Depression Decade opened with a familiar champion, Fort Worth, and the Panthers would win three titles during the ten-year period. But in contrast to the stability of the 1920s, the troubled 1930s brought financial strain and failed franchises to the Texas League. The shift of Galveston's club to Waco in 1925 was the sole franchise change of that decade. But during the 1930s, even though Beaumont, Dallas, Fort Worth, Houston, and San Antonio sustained their clubs without interruption, the other three franchises were shifted among eight different cities. Texas League clubs rapidly embraced a revolutionary device that would salvage sagging attendance and, purists would insist, permanently damage the quality of play throughout baseball: night games performed under artificial light. At the National Association meeting in the winter of 1929, Des Moines of the Western Association announced its intention to play the first night game in organized baseball. But Des Moines opened on the road, and a Western Association rival, Independence, Kansas, beat the Iowa club four days by playing under makeshift arclights on April 28, 1930.

Longtime Waco president Charles Turner perceptively recognized a good way to restore lagging attendance for his losing club, and floodlights were installed at Katy Park during the first half of the 1930 season. On Friday night, June 20, Fort Worth's Panthers

were trounced, 13-0, by the Navigators under the lights in Katy
Park. It was the first championship game at night in the Texas
League, although there had been exhibition games under makeshift
lights as early as 1892 in Galveston. There would be no night ball
in the major leagues until 1935 (at Cincinnati's Crosley Field, on
May 24), but the Texas League, like most minor leagues, eagerly
adopted the innovation. During the second half of 1930, Houston,.
San Antonio, and Shreveport equipped their ball parks with lights.
By the end of the season 116 night games had been recorded; during 1931, 309 of 645 Texas League games were played at night, and
only two parks, at Beaumont and Wichita Falls, remained une-
quipped with lights.

Attendance unquestionably was improved by night ball. At
first Texas League fans were attracted by the novelty of baseball
under lights. The author's father and grandfather, who regularly
rode an interurban line to games in Dallas and Fort Worth, drove
140 miles round trip over a gravel road to attend the Texas
League's inaugural night game. But it proved more convenient for
working people to go to night games, although one of the delicious
pleasures of baseball had been — and remains — slipping away
from the job to play hooky at a ball park. Also, in the blistering
summer heat of Texas, the opportunity to patronize baseball in the
relative cool of the evening provided a marked spur to attendance
— until the spread of air conditioning in the 1950s.

It has long been argued that night games, especially under inferior minor league lighting, render fastballs more difficult to see
and hit. Players' daily schedules also become highly irregular when
day games follow night games, or vice versa, and athletes' performances are affected by fatigue. Indeed, throughout the decade, day-
time batting averages were far higher than those compiled under
the lights, while night strikeout figures were much higher. Various
other problems can be suggested regarding night ball, but the improvement in attendance has made games under the lights a neces-
sity, and professional baseball players of the 1930s simply had to
make the adjustment. "In the 1930s," said Carl Hubbell, "we had
the Depression, and you sure as hell didn't want anybody to get
your job. There were millions of people in breadlines, and you
didn't want to go back to that."

In 1929 the Texas League had scheduled eight regular season

doubleheaders per team, resulting in a 168-game schedule. Certain single-season records — such as Randy Moore's 245 base hits — were asterisk-style marks set in the Texas League's longest schedule. The lengthy season had proved to be unwieldy, and in 1930 the league returned to a simple 154-game schedule, with scheduled doubleheaders only on July 4 and Labor Day.

Wichita Falls bolted to the first-half championship. The Spudders had a lethal attack led by first baseman Irving Burns (who hit .336 with 29 homers and promptly went up to the parent club St. Louis Browns), outfielder Jack Kloza (.347 with 28 home runs), and the season's home run champ, Larry Bettencourt (.320, 43 roundtrippers, and a league-leading 145 RBIs). During the first half, on June 13, 1930, veteran Lil Stoner pitched the first night no-hitter. Stoner walked one man, who was doubled up, and faced the minimum 27 batters as Fort Worth beat San Antonio, 2-0.

The second half featured an extremely tight race and numerous outstanding performances. On August 8, under the lights at Katy Park, Waco came to bat in the eighth inning, trailing Beaumont, 6-2. The Navigators brought 21 men to bat, scoring an astounding 18 runs on 16 hits, five homers, six walks, two errors, and a wild pitch. Most incredibly of all, three of the homers were hit by one player, 5'6" left fielder Gene Rye. Leading off the inning, the stocky Rye powered a solo shot over the left field fence. His second home run of the stanza brought in two teammates ahead of him. When he came up for the third time the bases were loaded, and Rye blasted a grand slam over the shallow right field wall. Gene Rye's three home runs and 12 total bases in one inning are all-time records for organized baseball, and were instrumental in beating Beaumont, 20-7.

Also in August, a loud-mouthed, fastballing rookie came up to Houston from St. Joseph. Nineteen-year-old Dizzy Dean, 17-8 for St. Joseph's weak Saints, was promoted by the St. Louis Cardinals to the Buffs. Dean's first Texas League contest was a night game in San Antonio, and his fastball proved to be a blur under the primitive lights of 1930. He struck out 14 and beat San Antonio, 12-1. The brash, colorful righthander won his first six games before being stopped by Fort Worth, then fashioned an 8-2 record with 95 strikeouts in 85 innings, and finished the season by winning a game

Dizzy Dean had a high leg kick before "foggin' 'em in." Texas Leaguers who hit against him said that his younger brother, Paul, had as good a fastball, but Diz had pinpoint control, an excellent curve (Paul's curve "broke" only an inch or two), and a devastating change. Diz pitched for the Houston Buffs in 1930 (8-2) and 1931 (26-10 with 303 strikeouts), then went up to the St. Louis Cardinals.
— Author's Collection

for the Cardinals. Clearly a future star, Diz would be enjoyed by Texas League fans in seasons to come.

Beaumont outfielder Ox Eckhardt, a University of Texas baseball and football star who would become a minor league legend by averaging .367 in 1,926 games, led Texas League hitters in 1930 with a .379 mark. Gene Rye batted .367, and, among many other fine offensive performances around the league in 1930, Joel Hunt provided Houston fans with an exciting season. Hunt was a quarterback standout at Texas A&M who had not played college baseball, but his splendid athletic abilities had carried him into his third Texas League season. He hit .324 with 16 homers, 106 RBIs, and a league-leading 55 stolen bases.

Fort Worth battled its way to the second-half title. The Panthers were managed by Frank Snyder, who had led Houston to the 1928 pennant and Dixie Series triumph. Snyder had an excellent

The incomparable Grover Cleveland Alexander pitched the last five games of his professional career for Dallas in 1930 at the age of 43.
— Author's Collection

defense and the only 20-game winners in the league, Dick McCabe (20-7) and Dick Whitworth (20-11), as well as Stoner (14-6). Whitworth toiled in three Texas League cities for 13 seasons, 1926–1938, and his 453 games pitched established the loop record. Another 13-year veteran, 42-year-old Paul Wachtel, hurled his last innings in 1930, finishing with 443 games pitched.

Wichita Falls, pennant winners in 1927, had reached the playoffs in the succeeding three seasons, but Spudder hopes of winning another flag in 1930 were dashed by the Panthers. The last three games of the five-game playoff were decided by one run, but Fort Worth outlasted the Spudders, then went on to beat Memphis in the Dixie Series.

The 1931 season belonged to Houston. In a time when such arrangements were frowned upon, Houston had become the Texas League's first "farm club" when Branch Rickey, general manager of the St. Louis Cardinals, quietly purchased a part interest in 1920. It was years before the affiliation was made public, but as

---

DOUGHNUTS FOR DONDERO

During the off-season San Antonio inexplicably traded Leonard Dondero, who had led second basemen in fielding and hit .296, to Dallas for a dozen doughnuts, which were promptly eaten by the owners of the Missions and Steers. This whimsical swap was disallowed by baseball's stern czar, Judge Kenesaw Mountain Landis, but Dondero disappeared from San Antonio and the Texas League.

---

former Texas Leaguer Rickey built the prototype farm system — 40 minor league clubs eventually were in the chain — for the Cardinals, Houston became one of the most important clubs owned by St. Louis and a funnel for athletes on their way to the big leagues.

Dizzy Dean started 1931 with the Cardinals, but he saw no action and was sent down to Houston on May 2. Diz blanked Wichita Falls, 6-0, on three hits in his opener; it was the first of a league record of 11 shutouts. The late start prevented him from joining the Texas League's exclusive club of 30-game winners, but he went 26-10, striking out 303 in 304 innings, allowing just 210 hits and 90 walks, and carving a stingy 1.53 ERA. He completed 28 of 32 starts, and worked nine relief appearances. Diz was a fine hitter and baserunner, as well as a gifted bench jockey and eager brawler. His talent and color brought fans in droves to ball parks all around the league. Diz led not only the Texas League but all minor circuits in victories, strikeouts, and ERA — the only time one hurler has dominated the pitcher's triple crown throughout the minors.

George Washington Payne, who had moved from Wichita Falls to Houston in 1930, went 23-13 for the Buffs, while future Cardinal Tex Carleton (from Comanche, Texas) was 20-7 with a 1.89 ERA. Another future member of the Gas House Gang, outfielder Ducky Medwick, hit .305 with 19 homers in his first year as a Buff. Left fielder Homer Peel (.326) and second baseman Carey Selph (.322) also swung big bats for the 1931 champs.

Houston was challenged by Beaumont in the first half. Although Dizzy Dean pitched and won a doubleheader from Fort Worth (12-3 and 3-0) two days before the first half ended, Beaumont managed to tie the Buffs. But Houston won the first-half tiebreaker series, then breezed to the championship in the second half with a brilliant 108-51 season record. Despite the Depression, over 229,000 fans had turned out to watch the Buffs. The Dixie Series went seven games, but Houston lost to the Birmingham Barons, despite a shutout by Dean. The Texas League had won nine of the first 11 Dixie Series, but the Southern Association now recovered respectability with four consecutive triumphs.

The worst year of the Great Depression was 1932, and it proved to be a season of trial for the Texas League. Roster size was trimmed from 20 to 17, and salary limits were lowered. It had been planned not to split the season, but when attendance lagged despite a close race, a divided schedule was declared following the games of June 28.

Wichita Falls was the smallest city (40,000) in the Texas League, and prior to the start of the season the St. Louis Browns had received permission from the league to move the franchise. Although there still were good crowds for games with rival Fort Worth, Athletic Park at Wichita Falls was unlighted and attendance of just a few hundred spectators became increasingly common. Although the Browns started 1932, on May 20 the franchise was shifted to Longview, a center of new business activity from the fabulous East Texas oil field.

Two weeks earlier, Shreveport's ball park was destroyed by fire. The team played to a good crowd in Longview — which had been duly noted by Browns' officials — and to another in Tyler. When Shreveport owners decided not to rebuild, the franchise was transferred to Tyler on May 15 — and the league became an all-Texas circuit for the first time since 1914. In June, League Park in San Antonio also fell to flames, but the Missions shifted operations to local high school fields and stayed in Alamo City.

The Dallas Steers, led by burly ex-major leaguer George Murray (24-15) and Oscar Fuhr (21-7), won the second half. But the first-half victors, Detroit affiliate Beaumont, boasted a colorful, scrappy club and the Texas League's Most Valuable Player. Exporter first baseman Hank Greenberg hammered out a league-leading 39 home runs and 131 RBIs with a .290 batting average, then went up to the majors and a Hall of Fame career. Outfielder Pete Fox chipped in a .357 average and 19 homers in just 115 games, and Fox, too, went up to Detroit and a long career in the big leagues. Catcher Frank Reiber, also Detroit-bound, hit .315, while another future Tiger, Luke Hamlin, went 20-10. But the team's best pitcher was Lynwood "Schoolboy" Rowe, a 6'4½" fireballer

In 1932 Hank Greenberg hammered 39 homers, hit .318 with 131 RBIs, and scored 123 runs for Beaumont. Voted the Texas League MVP, the next year he began a Hall of Fame career with Detroit.
— Author's Collection

who was 19-7 with a circuit-leading 2.24 ERA; although he went on to enjoy a fine major league career, the Texas League would see him again.

Beaumont roared to three straight victories over Dallas in the playoffs and snagged their first Texas League pennant. Other notable performances in 1932 came from Ducky Medwick (.354 and a batting title) and his Houston teammate, Homer Peel (.337), a legendary Texas Leaguer from 1924 to 1942, with periodic trips to the majors. In his 14 seasons and 1,430 Texas League games, Peel established the highest lifetime batting average (.325) for 10 or more years, and hit over .300 a record eight seasons.

After the shaky 1932 season, Texas League offficials adopted another innovation designed to improve attendance: the Shaughnessy Playoff Plan. Frank "Shag" Shaughnessy was a longtime International League executive who persuaded his struggling circuit to adopt a postseason playoff plan for 1933. There would be a semifinals series pitting the first-place finisher against the fourth-place team, at the same time that the second-place and third-place clubs were playing each other. The winners of the semifinals then would engage in a series for the championship. Under this plan, fan interest during the regular season would be sustained even by a race for fourth place, and in the future there would be hotly contested, well-attended one-game playoffs between clubs that had tied for fourth. Teams participating in a number of playoff games stood to benefit by perhaps 50,000 to 100,000 additional paid admissions, which might well mean the difference between a profit or loss, especially in a Depression year.

National Association president William G. Bramham objected to the Shaughnessy Plan on the grounds that it cheapened the accomplishments of teams that finished first in a long schedule, then lost a brief playoff series. But circuits like the Texas League would give separate designations to regular season champions and playoff winners. The International League ignored criticism from purists and announced adoption of the Shaughnessy Plan for 1933, and the Texas League followed suit. The plan proved immediately successful, stimulating fan interest during the season, attracting full houses to five- and seven-game playoff series, and luring most other minor leagues into the Shaughnessy fold in future years.

After the 1932 season the St. Louis Browns arranged to move their Longview franchise to San Antonio, while the league decided not to continue play in Tyler. The two East Texas franchises were replaced by clubs in Oklahoma City and Tulsa. With several new stadiums in the league, ball parks were generally larger and home run production would fall to the lowest level since 1920.

Although roster and salary limits again were reduced in 1933, the Shaughnessy Plan kept teams hustling for fourth place throughout the season, and attendance improved over 1932. In the semifinals of the first Shaughnessy Playoff, fourth-place San Antonio surprised first-place Houston by taking three straight (for years to come Houston would vehemently oppose the Shaughnessy Plan), while second-place Galveston outlasted Dallas, 3-2. Then San Antonio properly concluded the Shaughnessy Cinderella story by winning the finals from Dallas in six games.

The race for the batting title went to the last day between Dallas first baseman Zeke Bonura and San Antonio's veteran left-

The 1933 Galveston Buccaneers, clad in the dark uniforms which were popular for a time during the 1930s, made it to the playoff finals. The Bucs are posed in front of the grandstand at Moody Stadium.

— Courtesy Rosenberg Library, Galveston

handed outfielder, Pid Purdy. During the traditional season-ending Labor Day doubleheader, Purdy had a hitting spree in the first game and sat out the nightcap. Bonura thus lost the batting title and a triple crown by one point, .357 to Purdy's .358. Bonura led the Texas League in home runs, RBIs, runs scored, total bases, extra bases, and received the most walks, and he was voted the Most Valuable Player of 1933.

The Texas League retained the same eight clubs for 1934. Again the Shaughnessy Plan stimulated competition and attendance, as the league entered the last two weeks of the season with every team except Oklahoma City and Fort Worth in the running for a playoff berth. Galveston finished first by a percentage point over defending champion San Antonio. The Buccaneers beat fourth-place Dallas in the semifinals, while San Antonio's Missions squeaked by Beaumont, courtesy of a 1-0 victory in the fifth game by a budding Texas League star, Ash Hillin. For the second year in a row the finals pitted Galveston against San Antonio, but this time the Buccaneers were the winners in six. In the 15 playoff games attendance totaled nearly 100,000, a significant addition to club coffers.

The Galveston Buccaneers won an outright championship in 1934. Second baseman Charles English (front row, left) hit .326 and was voted MVP. When owner Shearn Moody (inset) died in 1936, Roy Koehler (standing, far left) handled the club for two years, then the Moody family sold the franchise to Shreveport.
— Courtesy Rosenberg Library, Galveston

In 1935 there were two remarkable pitching performances. On August 12, Fort Worth fireballer Lee Grissom hurled an iron-man shutout, blanking Houston 1-0 and 3-0 in a doubleheader. But even more memorable was a virtually flawless pitchers' duel on July 10 in Galveston between Eddie Selway of Tulsa and Buccaneer Eddie Cole. Cole, a righthander in his first of seven Texas League seasons, pitched the first perfect game in the history of the circuit. But Selway yielded just four hits and no runs until two were out in the bottom of the ninth, when Buccaneer first baseman Bill McGhee cracked a dramatic solo homer to win the classic contest, 1-0.

At the age of 21, Arthur Weis had won the batting championship in 1924 with a .377 mark for Wichita Falls. He had played part of four seasons with the Chicago Cubs, but spent 1935 in right field for Fort Worth. He took the 1935 batting title with a .331 average, and became the only man in Texas League history to win two batting crowns (although Shreveport's Grant Dunlap shared the 1951 title and won the next year). A slugging young Detroit prospect, Rudy York, was voted Most Valuable Player after leading the league in home runs (32) and RBIs (117) while batting .301.

Beaumont now was the only club in the Texas League without a lighted park — the parent club, Detroit Tigers, did not have lights, and refused to allow their minor leaguers to play at night. Night games outnumbered 1935 day contests 432 to 208, and Galveston unsuccessfully proposed that a 15 percent penalty on receipts be imposed for day games. To further increase revenue, the league expanded the schedule to 161 games, including numerous doubleheaders. Fans were treated to even more double bills as rain forced 84 postponements during the season.

Oklahoma City fought off Beaumont for first place, turning back the Oilers late in the season in a well-remembered series in Oklahoma. Then the Indians again defeated Beaumont in the Shaughnessy finals for Oklahoma City's first Texas League flag. The Indians went on to end a four-year drought for the Texas League by winning the Dixie Series from Atlanta in six games.

A popular innovation of 1936 was the Texas League All-Star Game. The contest was held in Dallas on July 25 and called the Centennial Game (because Texas had won its independence from Mexico in 1836). The North squad was piloted by Bert Niehoff, of the defending champion Oklahoma City Indians, while the South team quite appropriately was led by the great Jake Atz, now managing Galveston — and Atz generaled the South to the first All-Star victory.

Tony Rensa, who caught 130 games for Dallas, demonstrated a cannon for an arm throughout the 1936 season, gunning down 57 of the 100 runners who tried to steal on him. His batterymate, Hugh Fullerton, who came to the Texas League in his 16th minor league season, was the league's only 20-game winner (20-8). Steer second baseman Les Mallon led his position in fielding and the league in hitting (.344), and he was voted Most Valuable Player of 1936.

Bolstered by the league's best pitcher, catcher, and MVP, Dallas sailed through the season in first place, then beat fourth-place Oklahoma City in the opening round of playoffs. But in the finals the Steers dropped the first two games to Tulsa, fought back to even the series after six, then lost the seventh and deciding contest,

Dutch Lorbeer in 1936, when the Beaumont Exporters first sported red uniforms. Lorbeer caught for Beaumont (1931), served as field manager (1934–1936), and was owner and club president (1940–1945). Note the arm patch which celebrated the Texas Centennial.
— Courtesy Mrs. Dutch Lorbeer, Beaumont

7-5. The triumphant Oilers, with their momentum now at full steam, swept the rain-plagued Dixie Series from Birmingham in four straight.

In 1937, for the fifth year in a row, the Texas League lineup of cities remained unchanged. Beaumont still was the lone holdout against night ball, but the league played a record 461 games under the lights. Oklahoma City, paced by pitcher Ash Hillin and second baseman Stanley Sperry (.355), won 101 games to finish in first place. Hillin enjoyed one of the most remarkable seasons ever posted by a Texas League hurler: working in 62 games and 302 innings, he was 31-10 with a league-leading 2.34 ERA. In addition to 21 complete games in 27 starts, the rubber-armed Hillin established a new record with 35 relief appearances. From 1927 to 1941, Hillin pitched 11 seasons in the Texas League for Wichita Falls, Oklahoma City, and Fort Worth, toiling in more than 40 games during seven seasons, 50 or more in three of those years, and, of

---

OPENING DAY

During the heyday of the minor leagues, Opening Day was a community-wide celebration. Governors and other high-ranking public officials were in demand to throw out the first ball of each Texas League season; cities came to a halt to participate in grand parades worthy of the occasion. (In the early years of the Texas League, there were daily parades from hotels to ball parks as players in uniform were displayed in the streets to lure fans to afternoon games. Clubhouses usually had facilities only for the home team, and for decades visiting players suited out in their hotel rooms, then returned after the game to bathe.)

April 16, 1937, in Beaumont offered a typical Opening Day schedule of events. Festivities began at noon in the Rose Room of the Hotel Beaumont, and there was avid competition for the 150 available places. In addition to players, club officials, booster club president W. E. "Buttermilk" Kelly and the mayor of Beaumont, the state attorney general and state treasurer were present. Governor James V. Allred had attended Beaumont openers before, and after a 1937 Opening Day in another city, he returned in 1938 to throw out the first ball. City Hall closed at 1:00, the schools at 2:00, and the parade started from Beaumont High School. Opening Day ceremonies at Stuart Stadium were held at 3:15 and the game began at 3:30.

---

course, establishing a record of 62 pitching appearances in 1937. He was voted the league's Most Valuable Pitcher in 1934 when he was 24-12, he went 23-10 in 1938, and was named Player of the Year for his outstanding 1937 performance. Only Al McFarland, who was 34-12 in the Neanderthal season of 1895, ever won more games in the Texas League.

But Oklahoma City was derailed in the Shaughnessy finals by third-place Fort Worth. Player-manager Homer Peel enjoyed the finest season of his long career. He was the batting champ with a .370 average, blasting out 48 doubles, seven triples, 15 homers, and a league-leading 118 RBIs, and stealing 25 bases on 34-year-old legs. Peel then guided the Panthers to a Dixie Series triumph over Little Rock. Fittingly, the next year he became the only man to appear both as a player and manager in a Texas League All-Star Game.

The Texas League celebrated its 50th anniversary in 1938. Galveston sold its franchise to Shreveport. The business manager of the new club was J. Walter Morris, who had first appeared in the Texas League as second baseman for Corsicana's spectacular Oil-

Homer Peel, the Ty Cobb of the Texas League. In a playing career that spanned 1923–1946, Peel spent all or part of 14 seasons in the Texas League. Playing for Houston (1924–1926, 1928, 1930–1932), Fort Worth (1936–1938), Shreveport (1939–1940), and Oklahoma City (1941–1942), he hit .325 in 1,430 games, including a league-leading .370 in 1937. Peel also managed Fort Worth, Shreveport, and Oklahoma City, and he was named to the All-Star team four times. Today he regularly attends Shreveport games.

— Courtesy Bill McIntyre, *Shreveport Times*

ers of 1902. But Shreveport's guiding spirit was club president Bonneau Peters, who would serve as chief executive longer than any other man in the history of the league.

It proved to be a year for pitchers: batting champ Harlin Pool of Dallas hit just .330; Tulsa's Stanley Schino, the home run leader, got merely 25 roundtrippers, and only two other players in the league hit 20; and only three men hit 100 or more RBIs (Schino led with 118). But Texas League pitchers demonstrated why the hitting was so weak. Tulsa southpaw Max Thomas (23-14) and Ash Hillin (23-10) of Oklahoma City led the league in victories, while Thomas posted the lowest ERA (1.98). Future Cardinal star Mort Cooper of Houston set the pace in strikeouts (201), while the San Antonio Missions boasted 20-game winners in William Trotter (22-9)

Spring exhibition games between Texas League and major league teams long were
important gate attractions. A large crowd gathered at LaGrave Field for a 1937 exhibition pitting the New York Yankees (at bat) against the Fort Worth Cats.
— Courtesy Fort Worth Public Library

and Jack Kramer (20-11). Beaumont ace Dizzy Trout completed
24 of 27 starts and rang up an impressive 22-6 record en route to a
long major league career.

Because of the hot Texas sun, the Texas League long was a favorite circuit for aging pitchers and big leaguers with lame arms
trying to rejuvenate ailing muscles and joints. The 1938 season featured two stars of the 1934 World Series, Schoolboy Rowe and Paul
"Daffy" Dean, who had been standouts for the Detroit Tigers and
St. Louis Cardinals. Both men had pitched in the Texas League on
their way to the majors, later locked horns in the 1934 series, then
had developed arm troubles. Sadly, Dean could only manage an 8-
16 record for Houston and Dallas in 1938. After intermittent appearances in the majors, Dean enjoyed a 19-8 mark with a 2.05
ERA for Houston in 1942, but he could never regain his old effectiveness on the big league level. Rowe, however, was razor sharp in
1938, going 12-2 for Beaumont, and he resumed his major league

Tony York in 1937 at Tulsa's Texas League Park. From June 24 to June 27, York reached base a record 14 consecutive times, collecting five doubles, seven singles, and two walks. A shortstop, York also established various fielding records, and he made the Texas League All-Star team in 1940 and 1941. During 24 years in the minor leagues (and part of a season with the Cubs), York played with Dallas, Tulsa, and Shreveport, 1934–1937 and 1940–1942.
— Courtesy Mariana York, Hubbard, Texas

career with considerable success. Paced by Rowe and Dizzy Trout, Beaumont finished first in the regular season and won the playoffs, but player-manager Al Vincent's Exporters fell to the Atlanta Crackers in the Dixie Series.

During the 1939 season, Texas Leaguers, like everyone else in organized baseball, sported a uniform patch commemorating the proclaimed centennial of the national pastime. At mid-season, for their initial success in four tries, the North won its first All-Star Game. The pennant race was one of the tightest in Texas League history, as six teams were in the playoff chase until late in the season. Tulsa faded when batting champ Lou ("The Mad Russian") Novikoff moved up to the Pacific Coast League after blistering the ball at a .368 clip in 110 games. Texas's four largest cities — Houston, Dallas, San Antonio, and Fort Worth — eventually secured the

Rube Stuart, owner and president of Beaumont from 1927 through 1939. Behind Uncle Rube, left to right, are outfielder Barney McCoskey (who averaged .307 in 311 games for the Exporters, 1936–1938), Jack Zeller (Detroit farm director), and Exporter player-manager Al Vincent.
— Courtesy Mrs. Dutch Lorbeer, Beaumont

playoff spots. Late in the season Houston won 17 of 18 games to take first place, but, in a repeat of 1933 (when they lost to fourth-place San Antonio in the opening round of playoffs), the Buffaloes were dumped by Fort Worth, three games to two. The Dallas Rebels took five games to defeat San Antonio in the first round, which pitted two bitter rivals in the finals.

Fort Worth was led by a trio of fine pitchers: the one-two ERA leaders, veteran Ed "Bear Tracks" Greer (22-11) and former big leaguer Ray Starr (18-7), and another longtime major leaguer, Firpo Marberry (13-9). A future big leaguer, Murray Dickson, added 20 relief appearances to his 31 starts and went 22-15 for Houston, while another Buff (and future Cardinal star) Harry "The Cat" Brecheen was 18-7, including four consecutive shutouts. On September 7 Ray Starr pitched and won a doubleheader against Tulsa, and on May 31 he worked 18$^{1}/_{3}$ scoreless innings in

Beaumont's 1938 champions, seated in front of the Stuart Stadium grandstand. Top row, left to right: Dixie Howell (.298), Frank Secory (.323), Pat Mullin, Dixon Parsons (.320), Ed Selway, Schoolboy Rowe (12-2), Dizzy Trout (22-6, MVP), John Tate, Lloyd Dietz, Dingle Croucher, Les Fleming (.296). Bottom row: Cloyd Stith, Mickey DeJonghe (.309), Barney McCoskey (.302), Dutch Lorbeer (bus. mgr.), Al Vincent (mgr.), Rube Stuart (pres.), Boyd Perry, Jack Tighe, Marvin Garner (.323).

— Courtesy Mrs. Dutch Lorbeer, Beaumont

relief to take the victory in a 20-inning decision, 4-3, over Oklahoma City.

In the Shaughnessy finals Greer, Starr, and Marberry each pitched a shutout as Fort Worth downed Dallas, then went on to defeat Nashville in a seven-game Dixie Series. Nashville would appear in four consecutive Dixie Series under manager Larry Gilbert, who had already served as field general for New Orleans in five previous Dixie clashes. Gilbert won five of his nine Dixie Series for the Southern Association, and his nine series appearances are the greatest total for managers from either league (Jake Atz, who led Fort Worth into the first six Dixie Series, heads Texas League managers).

By the time the 1939 season closed, the attention of the world was focused on Europe, where war erupted in September. The Texas League, displaying remarkable flexibility and durability,

Al Vincent entered the Texas League in 1930 with Shreveport. He began playing for Beaumont in 1934 and was appointed player-manager in 1937. One of the best-known of all Texas League field generals, Vincent also managed Dallas, Tulsa, and Fort Worth.

— Courtesy Mrs. Dutch Lorbeer, Beaumont

had responded successfully to the problems of the Depression Decade. The quality of Texas League baseball during the 1930s was excellent, and fans were treated to performances by numerous past and future major league stars. But even as the Texas League rose steadily out of the Depression doldrums, a new decade ominously posed the uncertainties of another world war.

Vernon "George" Washington played professional baseball from 1931 through 1950. A feared left-handed line-drive hitter, he batted .350 for Shreveport-Tyler in 1932 and .325 for Fort Worth the next year. His next Texas League stint was in Shreveport, 1939–1942. The bat sailed out of his small hands so regularly that the Sports would raise a net in front of the first base grandstand when he came to the plate. At the age of 39 he led the East Texas League with a .404 average in 1947. The slugging outfielder split his last season between the Dallas Eagles (.278 in 36 games) and Gladewater of the East Texas League (.352). His lifetime average for 1,793 minor league games was .347.

— Courtesy Mrs. Vernon Washington, Linden, Texas

Joe Vitter, the best utility man in Texas League history. Playing for Shreveport (1938–1942), he handled every infield and outfield position and was named to the All-Star team in 1938, 1940, and 1941.

— Courtesy Mariana York, Hubbard, Texas

The Fort Worth Panthers and Nashville Vols lined up at LaGrave Field at the opening of the 1939 Dixie Series. Fort Worth won the seven-game series, but Nashville went on to win the next three in a row.

— Courtesy Jess Cummings, Corsicana, Texas

A 1938 instructional school conducted in Fort Worth by Panthers Jerry Moore (standing at far right), Jim McLeod (next to Moore), and Ed "Bear Tracks" Greer (next to McLeod). Among the hopefuls was Jess Cummings (seated third from right), who became a longtime high school baseball coach.

— Courtesy Jess Cummings, Corsicana, Texas

PLAYERS – 1939   NASHVILLE

1940-1949

Another World War — And Another Heyday

The avid fan interest of the late 1930s did not carry over into the new decade. Attendance lagged as World War II increasingly overshadowed all other concerns of the American public. After the United States entered the conflict, the Texas League took a unique stance unprecedented in other wars or by other leagues. But during the postwar years, the Texas League enjoyed more than its share of the greatest popularity yet lavished upon professional baseball.

Houston, with a steady flow of quality ballplayers from the massive Cardinal farm system, won the most games (105) in 1940 for the second season in a row. The Cardinal chain boasted a regiment of upward-bound pitchers, and the deep Buff staff was led by southpaw Howie Pollett (20-7) and Howard Krist (22-9, with a league-leading 1.71 ERA). An equally potent one-two mound combination proved to be Bill Newlin (23-8) and Bob Muncrief (22-9), who was voted the Most Valuable Player of 1940. Newlin and Muncrief were instrumental in a second-place finish by San Antonio. But Houston took first place to stay on May 1, and finished sixteen and one-half games ahead of the Missions. Buffalo dominance of the race was a major factor in an attendance dip of 260,000 across the league. Houston at last shrugged off its Shaughnessy hoodoo and won the flag outright, but Nashville's Vols took the Dixie Series in five games.

These 1940 Detroit Tigers each had played at Beaumont under Uncle Rube Stuart. Back row, left to right: Rudy York (an Exporter, 1933–1935), Hank Greenberg (1931–1932), Rube Stuart, Schoolboy Rowe (1932, 1938), Dizzy Trout (1938), Barney McCoskey (1936–1938), Johnny Gorsica (1939). Front row, left to right: Hal Newhouser (1939), Ed Selway (1938), Del Baker (1930–1932), Birdie Tebbetts (1935–1936), Pat Mullin (1937–1939), Frankie Croucher (1935–1936, 1938).

— Courtesy Beaumont Golden Gators

On September 19, 1940, shortly after the close of the regular season, the ball park at Dallas was devastated by fire. A new stadium soon was under construction, but the 1941 Rebels had to play their first three "home" games in Waco's Katy Park before the new Dallas stadium was ready. Manager Wally Dashiell's Rebels barely made the playoffs, but Dallas had good hitting, with batting champ Grey Clarke (.361) and outfielder Heinz Becker (.319), while veteran righthander Sol Gliatto enjoyed his best season (21-10).

For the third year in a row Houston finished first, posting 103 victories and another margin of 16½ games. The Buff pitching staff boasted three 20-game winners who soon would be in St. Louis: Freddie Martin (23-6 with a 1.54 ERA), Ted Wilks (20-10), and the superb Howie Pollett (20-3), league leader in winning percentage (.870), strikeouts (151), and ERA (1.16). Other spectacular

Eddie Lopat pitched with little effectiveness in the Texas League for four seasons (Shreveport, 1939–1940 and Oklahoma City, 1941–1942), but he later became a star for the New York Yankees.

pitching performances of 1941 included Tulsa's Hank Wyse (20-4) and Fort Worth veteran Earl Caldwell (22-7 with a 1.57 ERA).

Although Houston dominated an unusually rainy season (there were 85 postponements due to wet weather, and attendance again dropped), hard-hitting Buff infielder Danny Murtaugh was sold to the Phillies at mid-season, and Pollett was promoted to the Cardinals before the playoffs began. Suffering its customary Shaughnessy hex, Houston dropped the first round of playoffs to Dallas as Sol Gliatto won two games. The Rebels went on to defeat Tulsa in the finals, only to fall to Nashville in the Dixie Series in four straight.

On February 10, 1942, Lieutenant Gordon Houston of the Army Air Corps was killed during a training flight near Tacoma, Washington. Houston, an Oklahoma City outfielder in 1938, was the first professional baseball player to die in the Second World War.

By the time the 1942 season opened, Pearl Harbor was four

SHREVEPORT 1942 TEXAS LEAGUE CHAMPIONS. First Row, left to right: Zeke Trent, cf; Francis Parker, manager and 3B; Tony York, ss; Floyd Speer, p; Jo-Jo Vitter, lf; Jack Brillheart, p. Second Row, left to right: Al Bronkhurst, p; Tom Jordan, c; Chuck Baron, 1B; Herb Crompton, c; Stanley Sonnier, 2B; Joe Cavosie, utility fielder. Third Row, left to right: Charles Harper, bat boy; Ralph Hamner, p; Vernon Williamson, p; George Washington, rf; Theo Hoemann, p; Gordon Maltzberger, p; Doyle Lade (in inset), p.

— Photo by Gasquet
— Courtesy Mariana York, Hubbard, Texas

months in the past and the Texas League faced its third war. The Spanish-American War season of 1898 had lasted only a few weeks, while the Texas League staggered along until July 7 in 1918, the second year of America's participation in World War I. But Texas League officials determined to maintain operations during the first season of the Second World War, although several steps were taken to support the war effort. It was decided not to award the traditional President's Cup for the opening day attendance winner; instead, the victorious city would forward a $100 cash award to a designated defense organization. The All-Star Game also was eliminated, but each league city was asked to stage a "Franklin Roosevelt Appreciation Day," with receipts to go to the Red Cross.

Roster turnover was constant during 1942, as young players left for the service, but there nevertheless were a number of fine sustained performances. Beaumont right fielder Dick Wakefield, who just one year earlier had been signed for a then-sizeable bonus, fielded brilliantly and led the league in hitting (.345), and was voted Most Valuable Player. Hank Wyse again won 20 games for

Francis James "Salty" Parker, a colorful player-manager in the Texas League from
the 1930s through the 1950s. Parker entered the league as a Beaumont infielder in
1933, and later in the decade he played for Shreveport and Dallas. He managed
Shreveport (1941–1942, 1946–1951) and Dallas (1957).
— Courtesy Bill McIntyre, *Shreveport Times*

Tulsa, while teammate "Jittery Joe" Berry went 18-8 with a 1.88
ERA. Paul Dean found enough life remaining in his right arm to
win 19 games for Houston.

Beaumont, still the only club in the Texas League to play without lights, finished first in a tight race that featured 74 extra-inning
games. Prior to the start of the season, Houston registered its annual protest against the Shaughnessy Plan, and the Texas League
conceded that each playoff series should be decided on a best-four-
of-seven basis (past opening series, of course, had been on a best-
three-of-five basis). Beaumont beat fourth-place San Antonio in six
games, while Shreveport and Fort Worth (managed by Hall of
Famer Rogers Hornsby) battled it out for the full seven games. In
the fifth game Shreveport outlasted the Cats, 4-3, in a 19-inning
marathon at Fort Worth, but the Sports dropped a 1-0 decision in
the sixth game. Shreveport, managed by third baseman Salty Parker, won the last game with Fort Worth at home, but dropped the

Shreveport's 1942 Sports celebrating the second pennant in club history.
— Courtesy Joe Vitter, Carthage, Texas

first two finals contests to Beaumont before disappointed home crowds. Falling behind three games to one, the Sports incredibly shut out the Exporters in the last three games to seize a rare pennant. Gordon Maltzberger, who had pitched much of the year for Dallas, hurled two of the shutouts in three days, while Porky Lade (18-7 with a 1.80 ERA during the regular season) pitched the other whitewash. But the Sports ran out of miracles in the Dixie Series, as Nashville won for the third year in a row.

At the annual Texas League meeting in November 1942, held in Dallas, general sentiment existed to continue operations in 1943. However, attendance in 1942 had been just 490,165 (in 1939 attendance had been over 844,000, dropping to 583,106 in 1940 and 436,187 in 1941). Attendance in Oklahoma City had been less than 37,000 in 1942, but a new ownership was being organized. Each of the eight cities that held franchises desired to keep playing, although there was considerable pressure to reduce the schedule. The regular schedule meeting was set for Shreveport in February 1943. In December, however, each club sent representatives to the Na-

Shreveport program cover of the 1942 Dixie Series.
— Courtesy Joe Vitter, Carthage, Texas

A VINTAGE PERFORMER

Aside from Hank Wyse, the only other 20-game winner in 1942 was old Earl "Teach" Caldwell, who went 21-13 for Fort Worth. A native Texan from Sparks, Caldwell interspersed eight major league seasons with an equal number of Texas League seasons, during a career that lasted nearly three decades. Pitching for Waco, Wichita Falls, San Antonio, and Fort Worth, he was a Texas League 20-game winner in 1929, 1934, 1941, and 1942. He was 13-4 for the White Sox at the age of 41, and he last pitched in the big leagues when he was 43. Caldwell won 20 games for Harlingen and led the Gulf Coast League in ERA when he was 47. With his son, Earl, Jr., as a batterymate, he led the Evangeline League with a 2.07 ERA in 1953, and the next season, his last, he was 12-4 in the Big State League at the venerable age of 49.

tional Association meeting in Chicago, where there was widespread talk of transportation difficulties and discontinuation of many leagues. National Association President W. G. Bramham requested that any circuits intending to suspend operations should do so by February 25, so that players could be notified prior to the March 1 contract deadline. There had been 41 minor leagues in 1939, but the number dropped to 31 in 1942, and the 1943 season would witness only 10 junior circuits in operation.

At the Shreveport schedule meeting on February 13 and 14, 1943, there was deep concern over the recent announcement by the War Department Manpower Commission that all men, ages eighteen to thirty-eight, would be reclassified without regard to dependents unless employed by essential industries. Aware of the chaos caused to the Texas League by the "work or fight" mandate of 1918, club officials envisioned the impossibility of maintaining quality of play for any length of time. There also was a growing feeling that it was unpatriotic to use needed gasoline, food, hotel rooms, and able bodies for a game — and owners realized that these commodities would become increasingly difficult to obtain. Every club except Fort Worth and Oklahoma City became inclined to suspend play, and it was decided to reconvene on February 24.

The highly respected J. Alvin Gardner, Texas League president from 1930 through 1953, continued to poll club officials over the telephone, and on February 24, 1943, he collected a vote by telegram which determined, six to two, to suspend operations. Gardner commented that the leagues which intended to continue play were primarily concerned with protecting their investments. Texas League owners, Gardner declared, "believed it was more important that men build planes and tanks and work on the farm" than play baseball. "We would have taken up space in hotels, used transportation facilities needed in other lines, and added to the food rationing problem." And if further justification were needed, Gardner correctly insisted that "many people who love baseball wouldn't want us to continue play while their sons were risking everything in foreign fields."

Texas League officials determined to remain as active as possible in organized baseball, so that operations could be resumed whenever conditions permitted. Annual dues were regularly paid to the National Association, thereby insuring protection of the Texas

League's territorial rights. The Texas League office was maintained in Dallas, and even though President Gardner declined his
salary during the inactive years, he steadfastly manned his post,
along with the league secretary. Gardner conducted annual meetings, and he and the owners participated actively in National Association conventions. Although Texas League officials hoped to
play ball in 1944, wartime conditions prevailed, and expectations
for 1945 were similarly thwarted.

    When club owners convened in the Texas League office on
August 25, 1945, peace was in sight and it was unanimously agreed
to resume play. Details were hashed out at a meeting in August, in
December at the National Association convention, and in January
1946 at the schedule meeting. The National Association was adding a AAA classification (the number of minor leagues exploded
from 12 in 1945 to 42 in 1946), and the Texas League requested and
received its present AA designation. The Texas League had progressed from Class D (1902–1906) to C (1907–1910) to B (1911–
1920) to A (1921–1935) to A1 (1936–1942), and finally AA (1946–
present).

    In response to the annual assault upon the Shaughnessy Plan,
postseason activities were renamed the Texas League Playoff Plan,
and the Jake Atz Trophy would be awarded annually to the club
which finished first in the regular season. It was decided not to attempt an All-Star Game in 1946. The first official photographer of
the Texas League was secured — George W. Harlan of Houston —
and after a myriad of other matters were taken care of, the Texas
League resumed play for the first time since 1942.

    Postwar fans, starved for baseball and in a festive mood,
flocked to the ball parks in unprecedented numbers. Four franchises set attendance records in 1946, and a total of 1,592,567 fans
jammed Texas League stadiums, breaking the 1926 attendance
mark by more than 400,000 admissions. And the 1946 season was
an artistic as well as a popular success.

    The Texas League long had been known as a pitchers' circuit,
and pitchers continued to dominate hitters after the war. Just four
players hit home runs in double figures, and Dallas's first baseman, Robert Moyer (24 homers, 102 RBIs) was the only Texas
Leaguer who managed to hit more than 13 roundtrippers or 90
RBIs.

19-year-old Duke Snider played for Fort Worth in 1946, and by 1947 had advanced to Brooklyn. He returned to the Texas League as a manager in the 1960s.
— Author's Collection

Hawaiian Hank Oana led the league in victories at 24-10. The first 13 seasons of Oana's 23-year career were spent mostly in the outfield, but in 1942 he was 16-5 for Fort Worth with a 1.72 ERA, and during his last decade as a professional he split his time between the mound, first base, and the outfield.

But Fort Worth, now a farm club of the Brooklyn Dodgers, boasted the finest pitching staff of 1946. John Van Cuyk was 18-8 and led the league in shutouts, strikeouts, and ERA with a brilliant 1.42 mark, while Ed Chandler was 20-6 and Willard Ramsdell was 17-7. The Cats won 101 contests and coasted into first place with a 10-game lead, then beat Tulsa in four straight in the opening round of playoffs. But in the finals the Dallas Rebels stunned the Cats, winning four out of five. In the Dixie Series the Rebels, superbly led by Al Vincent, swept Atlanta in four games. The Texas League had enjoyed a splendid comeback in 1946.

Prior to the next season, the Texas League completely revised its constitution and by-laws, basing most changes on successful practices of other circuits, and the basic player limit was set at 19. It was decided to resurrect the All-Star Game in a different format: the club in first place after July 4 would host all-stars from the other seven teams.

Houston led the Texas League through most of the season, and on July 9 hosted the All-Star Game. The Buffs lost to the All-Stars, but drew a record 11,333 fans into beautiful Buff Stadium. Paced by an impressive pair of hurlers, Clarence Beers (25-8) and Al Papai (21-10), Houston outlasted Fort Worth by half a game through the regular schedule.

The Most Valuable Player was Al Rosen, a future star of the Cleveland Indians wearing the 1947 uniform of the Oklahoma City Indians. Rosen led the circuit in batting (.349) and RBIs (141), and the third sacker added 25 home runs in one of the most productive offensive seasons ever enjoyed by a Texas Leaguer.

In the opening round of the 1947 playoffs Houston brushed by Tulsa in four games, while archrivals Fort Worth and Dallas squared off in one of the classic postseason series in Texas League history. Fort Worth again had an excellent mound staff, headed by Willard Ramsdell (21-5) and the league's leading pitcher, southpaw Dwain Sloat (17-7 and a 1.99 ERA). But Al Vincent's Rebels played above their heads. The Dallas-Fort Worth series lasted seven games: two went into extra innings; the highest-scoring contest was a 5-3 Dallas victory; three games were 2-1 decisions, two were 3-1, and the seventh game was a 1-0 win for Dallas.

Houston won the finals in six games. Beers pitched two shutouts against the Rebels, including a 1-0 victory — his 28th — in the decisive contest. The Buffs closed out a memorable season with a Dixie Series triumph over Mobile.

Shortly before the opening of the 1948 season, oilman Dick Burnett completed negotiations to purchase majority ownership of the Dallas franchise (and by the next year he had bought 100 percent of the stock). Burnett, an experienced baseball man who already had owned clubs in smaller leagues, would prove to be a flamboyant promoter of the team he renamed the Dallas Eagles. But Burnett's first Dallas entry finished next to last in a season dominated by Fort Worth and Tulsa.

Baseball popularity continued to reach new heights in the Texas League as well as in most of the rest of the country. Texas

League attendance soared to an unprecedented 2,041,043, and third-place Houston welcomed a one-team record 401,383 fans. Houston's 1947 record All-Star attendance lasted exactly one year, as 12,636 fans jammed into Fort Worth's LaGrave Field for the 1948 All-Star Game.

Fort Worth edged Tulsa by one and a half games during the regular season, even though the Oilers boasted the Texas League's leading hitter in outfielder Tom Tatum (.333) and the Pitcher of the Year, southpaw Harry Perkowski (at 22-10 the only 20-game winner of 1948), who also was the best pinch hitter of 1948 (an overall .281 in 71 games). But Fort Worth had the Most Valuable Player of 1948, slick-fielding left fielder Irv Noren (.323). Cat player-manager Bobby Bragan also enjoyed the services of other future big leaguers, such as first baseman Dee Fondy (.328) and righthander Carl Erskine (15-7).

Fort Worth and Tulsa disposed of their opening round playoff opponents, then locked horns in the finals. The Cats and Oilers battled the full seven games, but Fort Worth pitchers twirled four shutouts — including two by Dwain Sloat, the leading pitcher of 1947 — and won the outright championship. The Cats faced Birmingham's Barons in the Dixie Series, but dropped four out of five games, the first loss by the Texas League since the postwar resumption of the series.

Fort Worth took up in 1949 where they had left off in 1948. The Cats, still managed by hard-hitting catcher Bobby Bragan, rolled to a 100-win season and a 10-game lead over Tulsa, which finished second to Fort Worth for the second year in a row. Just as Houston had enjoyed a succession of quality players and high finishes when Branch Rickey built the superb Cardinal farm system, Fort Worth similarly benefited in postwar years by becoming part of the Rickey-led Dodger organization (the "Mahatma" had moved from St. Louis to Brooklyn in 1942).

Early in the season Fort Worth faced a formidable adversity when fire swept LaGrave Field, collapsing the grandstand roof and claiming 10,000 seats. All that remained of one of the showplace parks of the minor leagues were the fences and about 3,000 bleacher seats. The next day 3,000 fans turned out amid blackened ruins of the grandstand and twisted girders to see the Cats play San Antonio. A few "home" games had to be staged out of town (the

CARL ERSKINE

Carl Erskine was 15-7 in 1948 when Brooklyn called him up from Fort Worth. Back
with the Panthers in 1949, he was 10-4 at mid-season when the Dodgers brought
him up again. He was 8-1 the rest of the year in Brooklyn and became a National
League star.

— Author's Collection

Cats set a Texas League season record for most victories on the
road), but the debris was cleared away and new construction commenced. Fort Worth even managed to host the All-Star Game, winning 2-1 to delight a commendable crowd of 8,442.

Carl Erskine quickly won 10 games for the Cats, half of them
shutouts, before being called up to Brooklyn (he was 8-1 for the
Dodgers in the remainder of the season). Joe Landrum picked up
the slack, leading the league in victories at 19-11. With no 20-game
winners in the circuit, offense dominated play in 1949. Fort Worth
boasted six regulars who hit over .300, paced by third sacker Bob
Bundy (.350) and outfielder Cal Abrams (.337).

The best power in the league was displayed at Dallas's Burnett
Field. Outfielder Buck Frierson hit .322 with 19 homers and 116
RBIs; outfielder Ben Guintini batted .306 and blasted 32 roundtrippers in just 129 games; and third sacker Bill Serena hit 28 home
runs and 110 RBIs. But the most exciting slugger of 1949 — or al-

most any other Texas League season — was Eagle first baseman Jerry Witte. At first it seemed that the veteran right-handed power hitter would threaten Clarence Kraft's record of 55, but Witte settled for 50 home runs — still the third highest total in Texas League history — and 141 RBIs. There was little pitching to go with all this power, however, and even though the Eagles won 16 of their first 17 games, the club soon sagged to the second division and did not even make the playoffs.

All of those home runs, however, brought 404,851 fans jostling into Burnett Field, and the Dallas spectators were privileged to see the courageous Pete Gray play his final season. As a boy Gray (his real name was Peter Wyshner) had lost his right arm in an accident, but he persisted with baseball, banging out line drives, chasing down outfield flies and quickly transferring his glove under the stub of his right arm, then throwing powerfully with his left. He led the Southern Association with 68 stolen bases in 1944 and spent the next season with the St. Louis Browns. Thirty-two years old at that time, he played 45 games for Burnett's Eagles, but hit just .214 and retired.

In the first round of playoffs Fort Worth easily dispatched Shreveport. Tulsa faced archrival Oklahoma City, and the Indians were led by batting champ Herb Conyers (.355). Conyers, a first baseman, thus claimed his third straight batting crown and his sixth title in three leagues. But Tulsa had ace manager Al Vincent and Russ Burns (.340 with 27 homers and 153 RBIs — he was the Texas League RBI leader in 1948, 1949, 1952, and 1953), and outlasted Oklahoma City. Then the Oilers and the Cats battled through 11 innings of the seventh game before Tulsa took the finals in Fort Worth. Nashville was the defending Dixie Series champion, but the Oilers beat the Vols in seven games to end the 1940s on a triumphant note for the Texas League.

1950–1959

Up and Down During the Fifties

The 1950s began spectacularly for the Texas League, with one of the most flamboyant and successful promotions in the history of minor league baseball. It seemed to reassure the indefinite continuation of the avid fan support of the postwar years. Soon, however, a combination of adverse conditions drastically affected the minor leagues, eliminating large numbers of franchises and circuits from organized baseball. By the end of the 1950s the Texas League had dropped to six teams and attendance had nosedived to a little more than half a million.

Such atrophy seemed inconceivable on opening day of 1950. Dick Burnett decided to go after the Texas League opening day attendance record of 16,018, set by Fort Worth in 1930. Indeed, Burnett had hopes of establishing an all-time minor league *attendance* mark (Jersey City had sold 61,164 tickets as a civic promotion, but that number far exceeded the ball park capacity). Burnett obtained permission to stage the Dallas opener in the Cotton Bowl on the State Fair Grounds, then he recruited an extraordinary all-star team. Ty Cobb was the first baseball great to sign up, then Burnett quickly rounded up eight other famous players, including Tris Speaker, Dizzy Dean, and Charlie Grimm (a hard-hitting third baseman during his playing days, "Jolly Cholly" had just completed 13 seasons as manager of the Cubs — and Burnett had as-

The famous old-timers team used by Eagle owner Dick Burnett to lure more than 53,000 fans into the Cotton Bowl on opening day of 1950, left to right: Dizzy Dean, Mickey Cochrane, Charlie Gehringer, Tris Speaker, Ty Cobb, Charlie Grimm, Duff Lewis, Home Run Baker, Travis Jackson.

— Courtesy Dallas Public Library

tounded the Texas League by signing Grimm for the unprece-dented sum of $30,000 to manage his Dallas Eagles). Burnett actually intended to start his galaxy of old-timers against Tulsa, then place the Eagle regulars on the field. The lineup (with Eagle regulars in parentheses):

DALLAS EAGLES	4-11-50	
Frank "Home Run" Baker (Billy Klaus)		3B
Duffy Lewis (Lew Morton)		LF
Charlie Grimm (Heinz Becker)		1B
Tris Speaker (Vernon Washington)		RF
Charlie Gehringer (Bob Collins)		2B
Travis Jackson (Clyde Perry)		SS
Ty Cobb (Jim Kirby)		CF
Mickey Cochrane (Dick Aylward)		C
Dizzy Dean (Tom Finger)		P

The stunt was ballyhooed far and wide, and an enormous number of tickets were sold, including 15,100 by the First National Bank for distribution to high school students. To alleviate traffic jams, an autographed ball was offered to the fan who arrived earli-

Dizzie Dean and Mickey Cochrane before the record-setting 1950 opener in the Cotton Bowl.

— Courtesy Dallas Public Library

est in each seating section. At three o'clock in the afternoon the old-timers headed a parade from West Commerce, in downtown Dallas, to the Cotton Bowl. J. G. Spinks of *The Sporting News* was among 53,578 who watched the celebrities take batting practice and Governor Alan Shivers throw out the opening ball. Dizzy Dean walked Tulsa leadoff batter Harry Donabedian, then the old-timers surrendered the Cotton Bowl diamond to the Eagle regulars. Donabedian batted again, stroked a single, and the Oilers went on to a 10-3 victory.

The sensational crowd provided a fifth of Dallas's season attendance, as Charlie Grimm's Eagles proved to be a disappointing sixth-place team. Houston's performance also was a great disappointment, providing the first last-place finish in the history of the franchise, although Jerry Witte walloped 30 homers in just 99 games as a Buff.

Beaumont, now a Yankee affiliate, was led to first place by Rogers Hornsby and the Texas League MVP, future New York star

Gil McDougald played second base for Beaumont in 1950. He hit .336, knocked in 115 runs, and was voted MVP. The next year, as a New York Yankee, he was voted A. L. Rookie of the Year.

— Author's Collection

Gil McDougald (.336 with 115 RBIs). But fourth-place San Antonio stunned Beaumont with a four-game sweep of the playoff opener. Although Fort Worth took second place by winning a record 39 one-run games, the Cats were polished off by Tulsa in the first round. The Missions, just 79-75 in the regular season but paced by batting champ Frank Saucier (.343), upended Tulsa, then beat Nashville in a seven-game Dixie Series.

Despite an exciting season, Texas League attendance dropped by more than 350,000. There were more rainouts (40) than usual, but there was another drop of over 300,000 the next year, and this depressing trend continued through the decade and into the 1960s. By the 1950s television had begun to captivate the American public, severely affecting the movie industry and minor league baseball — and most other activities that required people to pry themselves away from the flickering tubes in their living rooms. Little league baseball also took a heavy toll on the minor leagues, as parents found themselves accompanying peewee players to practice or games so often that few nights remained for a family outing to a professional ball park. Another severe influence on minor league baseball in Texas, as well as other southern and western states, was the widespread use of air conditioning. On hot summer nights, local newspaper ads urged fans to cool off in the evening breezes at the baseball park. But air conditioning, of course, made it far more comfortable to stay at home and watch TV — and increasingly fans in minor league cities happily viewed telecasts of major league games.

These and other factors severely reduced minor league support. In 1949, the peak of minor league baseball, there were 464 teams in 59 leagues with a total attendance of nearly 42,000,000. But minor league attendance dropped more than 7,000,000 in 1950, and another 7,000,000 the next season. By the end of the decade there were only 21 minor leagues and attendance was just a little over 12,000,000. The Texas League staggered under these blows, but at least the historic circuit did not fold.

Texas League officials nervously regarded the Korean War, which had broken out in October 1950, but the nation's first no-win conflict did not greatly add to the increasing number of afflictions facing minor league baseball. Texas League fans were treated to a succession of fine pitching performances in 1951. A trio of hurlers struck out 200 batters: Bullet Bob Turley, 20-8 for the San Antonio Missions, whiffed an even 200; Oklahoma City's Harry Markell registered 211 K's; and Vinegar Bend Mizell struck out 257 in 238 innings and posted a 1.96 ERA for Houston. The Buffs' staff also boasted Al Papai (23-9), Octavio Rubert (19-5), and ace reliever Richard Bokelman (10-2 with an 0.77 ERA).

Veteran slugger Jerry Witte (38 homers) supplied the power as Houston, stung by its only last-place finish, roared all the way to first place. The Buffs then downed Beaumont in the playoff opener and seized an outright pennant with a four-game sweep of San Antonio, before finally faltering in the Dixie Series to Birmingham.

In 1952 the Texas League finally joined the integration of baseball (a process begun when ex-Texas Leaguer Branch Rickey brought Jackie Robinson to the Brooklyn Dodgers). Dick Burnett broke the Texas League's color line with Dave Hoskins, a fine right-handed pitcher who also batted well enough from the left side

Banquet preceding an exhibition game between the Dallas Eagles and New York Yankees. Dizzy Dean, by this time a famous sportscaster, sits in the foreground.
— Courtesy Dallas Public Library

to be the Dallas Eagles' top pinch hitter. Hoskins led the league in victories at 22-10, while stroking out a .328 average in 62 games. Hoskins and black athletes in ensuing seasons were not allowed to compete in Shreveport, a circumstance blamed on club president Bonneau Peters but actually attributable to the state laws of Louisiana. The Texas League conceived an awkward rule permitting teams with black players to take white substitutes into Shreveport.

The only other 20-game winner of 1952 was also on the Eagles' staff, Harold Erickson (20-14). The most notable pitching exploit of 1952 occurred on July 15. Johnny Vander Meer had electrified the baseball world in 1938 when he hurled back-to-back no-hitters for Cincinnati. Following a long major league career, Vandy, now 37, pitched the 1952 season for second division Tulsa, where he was 11-10 with a 2.30 ERA. Working against Shreveport, the team which eventually won the flag, Vandy once again summoned a no-hit performance from his left arm, blanking the Sports, 12-0.

Shreveport, led by batting champ Grant Dunlap (.333) and

Southpaw Wilmer "Vinegar Bend" Mizell led the league in strikeouts with 257 in 238 innings as a Houston Buff in 1951.

— Author's Collection

outfielder Harry Elliott (.321), took third place and swept Fort Worth in the first playoff round. Dick Burnett's Eagles finally rewarded his financial backing and promotions with a first-place finish, only to fall to fourth-place Oklahoma City in the opening series. Shreveport then defeated the Indians for a rare title, but dropped the Dixie Series to the Memphis Blues.

There was an important changing of the Texas League guard. J. Alvin Gardner, who had been a bat boy for Beaumont of the South Texas League in 1903 and 1904, had become a successful oilman — like many another Texas League executive. Gardner was one of the first stockholders of the Wichita Falls Spudders in 1920. He sold his interests in the Spudders in 1929, but soon was elected Texas League vice-president, actually running the circuit during the fatal illness of J. Doak Roberts, league president for 1904–1906 and 1921–1929. After Roberts died on November 25, 1929, Gardner was elected president of the Texas League for a five-year term. Popular and efficient, he stayed in his Dallas office until 1953, the

Bob Turley was 20-8 for San Antonio in 1951, with 200 strikeouts. Bullet Bob finished the season with the St. Louis Browns, and soon was a star with the New York Yankees.

— Author's Collection

longest tenure of any Texas League president. John L. Reeves was league president in 1954, then the amiable Dick Butler assumed office, serving from 1955 to 1963.

In 1953, for the second consecutive season, L. D. "Dutch" Meyer guided Dallas to first place. It was a sub-par year for pitching — Eagles' righthander Red Murff led the league in victories with a 17-13 record. But Howard Judson went 11-0 for Tulsa before being called up to Cincinnati, and San Antonio's bespectacled Ryne Duren — who unnerved hitters by uncorking his explosive fastball to the screen in warmups — mowed down 212 Texas Leaguers in 202 innings. Duren had a blazing fastball with a wicked hop, but he also fired a "fastball" that dropped. Players understood that Duren sometimes loaded up and threw old-fashioned spitters.

Dallas had a trio of .300 hitters: third baseman Buzz Clarkson (.330), center fielder Eddie Knoblauch (.304), and right fielder

Hal "Moose" Erickson, 20-14 for the Dallas Eagles, receiving the Pitcher of the Year Award on September 3, 1953.
— Courtesy Dallas Public Library

Willard Brown (.310, with 23 homers and 108 RBIs). The Eagles soared past Tulsa and Oklahoma City in the playoffs to capture an outright championship for Dick Burnett, then triumphed over Nashville in the Dixie Series.

Dallas followed an oft-repeated Texas League trend by plunging to last place in 1954. Championship teams in the minor leagues were commonly gutted by promotions of the best young players to higher classifications, or by outright sales of promising athletes for sums that added to the profits of a winning season. So Dallas, like many another Texas League champ, defended its crown by rebuilding from the bottom.

Shreveport surged to first place in 1954, entering the most successful period in franchise history. The Sports had won the playoffs in 1952, and Bonneau Peters — steadfastly maintaining the only Texas League club to remain independent of major league affiliation — had put together a fine club under the generalship of player-manager Mel McGaha. The pitching staff featured "Long John"

For years a "Miss Texas League" was selected annually. The five "Miss Dallas Eagle" candidates of 1952 are on display in a convertible at Burnett Field, to the obvious delight of two Eagle players.

— Courtesy Dallas Public Library

Andre, who tied for the lead in victories at 21-9, and ex-major leaguer Freddie Martin, who was 9-3 in relief with a 1.67 ERA.

There were many other fine pitching performances around the league, including another blistering strikeout season from San Antonio's Ryne Duren. The nearsighted speedballer recorded 224 K's in 220 innings, but Duren yielded his strikeout crown to a Fort Worth southpaw, Karl Spooner, who was 21-9 with 262 strikeouts in 238 innings. Both Duren and Spooner would be throwing their bullets in the big leagues by the end of the season, and Houston's Willard Schmidt, 18-5 with 186 strikeouts, soon would be hurling for the parent Cardinals.

First baseman Les Fleming was a native Texan who had spent seven seasons in the majors after playing for Beaumont in 1937 and 1938. Now 38, Fleming had returned to the Texas League and, splitting the 1954 season between Beaumont and Dallas, he hit a sizzling .358 to lead the circuit. San Antonio first baseman Frank

**Flamboyant Dick Burnett embraces two of his Dallas Eagles, including slugging
first baseman Joe Macko (24).**
— Courtesy Dallas Public Library

Kellert hit .316 with 41 homers and 146 RBIs, while Buzz Clarkson, playing for Beaumont and Dallas, batted .324 and blasted 42 home runs with 135 RBIs.

In all, 11 hitters drove in 100 or more runs, and 13 players walloped more than 20 home runs. Despite the decline in attendance, the quality of ball in the Texas League had never been better. There still were many career minor leaguers in the high minors, men with experience and sometimes spectacular playing skills, although a weakness in one area or another kept them out of the big time. Of course, there were many former major leaguers whose talents still were formidable, and who provided invaluable instruction (aside from the managers, there was little coaching available in the minors) to the large numbers of young players on the way up.

Fred "Dixie" Walker had spent 18 years in the big leagues, but in 1953 he had signed on to manage Houston. In 1954 Walker's Buffs battled Shreveport throughout the season, finally settling for second place by the margin of one game. But Houston beat Okla-

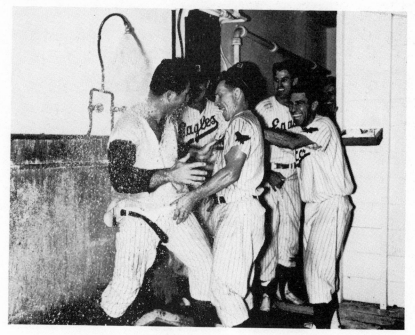

The first-place Eagles celebrate in the shower room.
— Courtesy Dallas Public Library

homa City in the playoffs, while Al Vincent led fourth-place Fort
Worth to victory over Shreveport. Houston won the finals in five
games, but lost a seven-game Dixie Series to the Atlanta Crackers.

Despite the splendid power hitting of 1954, the Texas League
proved that it was still a pitchers' circuit in 1955. Perhaps the finest
one-two mound combination in the postwar Texas League era
pitched Dallas to first place. Pete Burnside, a southpaw with a
blazing fastball, was 18-11 for the Eagles and led the Texas League
with 235 strikeouts. Red Murff, a tall, 34-year-old righthander who
had spent his entire career in the minors, flirted with a 30-victory
season. Murff finally settled for a 27-11 record, but he led the Texas
League in wins, ERA (1.99), starts (35), complete games (28), innings pitched (303), and he even made eight relief appearances. One
of the highlights of the season was a doubleheader in Dallas (attended by the author) in which Burnside sizzled to a victory in the
seven-inning opener, then Murff worked nine in the nightcap to
notch another win. Murff was given a trial by the Milwaukee

Dallas manager Dutch Leonard and Tulsa manager Joe Schultz exchange lineup cards prior to the 1953 finals. Dallas defeated the Oilers, 4-1, for an outright championship.
— Courtesy Dallas Public Library

Braves in 1956 and 1957, but he proved too old to begin a major league career.

Red Murff's magnificent season overshadowed several other excellent performances. Mel Held was 24-7 for San Antonio, while Al Papai had another fine year for Oklahoma City, completing 22 of 29 starts, adding 14 relief appearances, and posting a 23-7 record. Shreveport's Jim Atkins was 22-8, Al Widmar was 18-8, mostly in relief, for Tulsa, Harry Hoitsma was 13-3 in 56 relief appearances for Houston, and Fort Worth's Fred Waters was 7-1 in a record 77 relief appearances.

Southpaw Don Ferrarese was sent down to San Antonio after a 3-7 start with Oakland of the Pacific Coast League. On August 10 he shut out Tulsa on two hits, 1-0. Four days later he blanked Oklahoma City, 4-0, on four hits. On August 18 Ferrarese pitched a 7-0 four-hitter against Beaumont. And on August 24 he yielded four hits in a 13-0 win over Houston. His four consecutive shutouts

Tulsa manager Joe Schultz takes on an umpire during the 1953 finals. Joe had just turned 14 in 1932 when his father, Joe Schultz, Sr., let him have a turn at bat for the Houston Buffs. Father and son each played and managed in the Texas League, and both enjoyed long major league careers.

— Courtesy Dallas Public Library

tied a record set by Harry Brecheen with Houston in 1939 and equalled by Jim Blackburn with Tulsa in 1950. Ferrarese's scoreless string reached $38^2/_3$ innings before Houston finally tallied against him, leaving Tom Gorman's 1951 record — 42 scoreless stanzas with Beaumont — intact. In just over two months of Texas League ball, Ferrarese was 9-0 for the Missions, striking out 99 batters in 79 innings and compiling a 1.48 ERA.

Eddie Knoblauch brought his long minor league career to a close in championship fashion in 1955. Turning pro in 1938, the speedy outfielder played the 1942 season in Houston, spent three years in the service, then returned to Houston. In 11 Texas League seasons with Houston, Shreveport, Tulsa, Dallas, and Beaumont, Knoblauch hit over .300 eight times, but he saved the best for last. Still fleet enough at 37 to play center field, he started the season at Beaumont but was traded to Dallas after 40 games. In all, Knob-

Shreveport youngsters receiving tips from the Sports.
— Courtesy Bill McIntyre, *Shreveport Times*

lauch played 157 games and hit .327 to claim his first Texas League batting title — then he retired at the top of his game.

The Eagles not only had Knoblauch, Murff, and Burnside. Third baseman Ozzie Virgil (.295 with 17 homers) and first sacker Bill White (.295 with 22 homers) soon would reach the big leagues. Ray Murray, a tall catcher with a rifle arm, had played four seasons with Oklahoma City, 1946–1949, before going up to the American League. In 110 games with Dallas in 1955 he hit .329 and blasted 25 home runs, and he would be an important Texas League figure for years to come. The field general of the Dallas Eagles was fiery John "Red" Davis, who was given the first Texas League Manager of the Year Award in 1955, and repeated the same honor the next year.

Dallas edged San Antonio by half a game for first place, but the fifth-place club was only seven and a half games out. Houston had to beat Tulsa, 2-1, in a one-game playoff for fourth place, but then the upstart Buffs downed Dallas in the opening series. Shreveport, in the playoffs for the third time in four years, beat San Anto-

Prior to an exhibition game between the Dallas Eagles and New York Yankees, big leaguers as well as minor league players instructed boys in the fine points of baseball.

— Courtesy Dallas Public Library

nio in the first round. The finals went the full seven games, but Mel McGaha's Sports repeated 1952 and won the playoff championship. Apparently exhausted by the playoffs, Shreveport lost the Dixie Series to Mobile in four straight.

Beaumont finished last in 1955, with a miserable 51-110 record and an attendance of just 60,375. There had not been a franchise change in the Texas League since 1937, but Beaumont was forced to sell out to Austin, which fielded its first Texas League club since 1914. Now that the stability of nearly two decades was disturbed, there would be a flurry of franchise shifts.

Shreveport dropped to seventh place in 1956 but acquired an outfielder who would electrify the entire Texas League. Although Ken Guettler wore thick eyeglasses, in 11 seasons as a minor leaguer he had won seven home run titles in four different circuits. In 1955, playing for Portsmouth of the Class B Piedmont League, Guettler hit 41 home runs — his previous career high. But in the

In his only full season in the Texas League (1956 with Shreveport), Ken Guettler boomed a record 62 home runs. Here he hands an autographed ball to a young admirer.

— Courtesy Bill McIntyre, *Shreveport Times*

Texas League he ripped into Class AA pitching with a vengeance. He played in just 140 games, but led the league with 115 runs scored, 143 RBIs — and an incredible 62 home runs. Big Boy Kraft's record of 55 in 1924 had been seriously threatened only once, by Jerry Witte in 1949, but the Texas League now had a new home run king, and Guettler's record probably will never see a serious challenge. Sadly, 1956 was Guettler's last good season — he played three more years, but never hit more than .232 or five home runs. He retired at the age of 32.

Dallas had another strong team under Red Davis in 1956. Tall righthander Murray Wall was 16-7, Bert Thiel was 18-11, Tommy Bowers was 17-7, reliever Hisel Patrick was 13-4, and Freddie Rodriguez led the league with a 2.33 ERA, while first baseman Joe Macko slugged 36 homers. Fort Worth's power hitters — Don Demeter (40 HRs, 128 RBIs) and Jim Gentile (40 HRs, 115 RBIs) — led the Cats to a third-place finish behind Dallas. The batting

The Texas League still tries to cultivate the support of young fans. Here a large group of youth leaguers are gathered to watch the instructions of Midland Angels.
— Courtesy Midland Angels

champ was diminutive outfielder Albie Pearson, who hit .371 for last-place Oklahoma City and who, like Demeter and Gentile, soon would be in the big leagues.

Houston had a new manager, Harry "The Hat" Walker, younger brother of Dixie and, like Dixie, a longtime major league star. Harry The Hat hit .328 in 82 games for the Buffs, and most of his regulars — such as center fielder Herb Adams (.333), first baseman Pidge Browne (.328 with 29 homers and 105 RBIs), third sacker Ben Valenzuela (.314 with 18 homers), and right fielder Bobby Gene Smith (.299 with 21 homers and 109 RBIs) — triggered an explosive offense. (The remote fences at Buff Stadium had been moved in after the 1952 season.) The Buffs finished first after a close race with Dallas, then beat Tulsa in the opening series in five games. Houston also took the finals from Dallas in five and won the Dixie Series in six games with Atlanta.

The 1957 season featured another rematch between Houston and Dallas. The Eagles, now managed by Salty Parker, once more

Slugger Ken Guettler returning to the Shreveport dugout after walloping one of his 62 home runs in 1956. It was the eighth time Guettler had led a minor league in homers.

— Courtesy Bill McIntyre, *Shreveport Times*

had an excellent pitching staff. Murray Wall again was 16-7, with a league-leading ERA of 1.79 and a no-hitter against Fort Worth (which he lost — the Cats beat him 1-0 in the 13th inning after he yielded three hits in extra innings). Tommy Bowers was 20-8 (the league's only 20-game winner), while Ernie Broglio was 17-6 and Art Fowler was 13-5. The Eagles took first place with a 102-52 record.

Harry Walker's Buffs were close behind with 97 victories. Pidge Browne and Ben Valenzuela were back to drive in runs (80 and 90 respectively), and Harry The Hat put himself in 62 games and hit .288. Phil Clark (16-6), Howard Nunn (16-7), Tom Hughes (14-4), and Billy Muffett (14-6) headed a mound staff almost as strong as that of the Eagles.

In the playoffs, defending champ Houston took seven games to defeat San Antonio. Fourth-place Tulsa boasted the league's batting champion, Jim Frey (.336), but fell to Dallas in six games. The finals pitted Houston against Dallas for the second year in a row,

Catcher Les Peden hit 23 home runs for Shreveport in 1956. Later he managed the Sports in the Southern Association.

— Courtesy Bill McIntyre, *Shreveport Times*

and for the second year in a row Houston won, this time in seven games. The Buffs then went on to win their second consecutive Dixie Series over the Atlanta Crackers, 4-2.

Houston would return to the playoffs in 1958 for their fifth straight year. The Buffs finished first and won the playoffs in 1951, then repeated the double title in 1956. Houston finished second in 1954 and 1957 but won the playoffs each year; four of the seven seasons from 1951 through 1957 were championship years for the Buffs.

In 1957 Shreveport dropped to last place, after finishing next-to-last the year before. Attendance in 1957 had totaled a meager 40,919, and the Louisiana law banning interracial competition caused increasing problems as black players proliferated around the Texas League. Shreveport left organized baseball for the 1958 season, although the city obtained a Southern Association franchise the next year. Oklahoma City also had fallen upon hard times, sharing the bottom of the standings with Shreveport. The Indians

Albie Pearson, a diminutive Oklahoma City outfielder, won the 1956 batting title with a sizzling .371 average.
— Author's Collection

were last in 1956 with a miserable 48-106 record, and next-to-last in 1957, and attendance in both seasons was barely above the 50,000 level. Oklahoma City also left the Texas League after the 1957 season, later reemerging in the Class AAA American Association.

Corpus Christi and Victoria were the new franchise cities of 1958. Victoria's Rosebuds, inheriting Shreveport's moribund club, finished last, but Corpus Christi roared into the playoffs. Ray Murray was the manager, and the 38-year-old catcher hit .357 and cracked 19 home runs in just 93 games. Corpus Christi led the Texas League in hitting behind Murray, batting champ Eric Rodin (.320 with 20 homers), and home run king Mike Lutz (.313 with 39 roundtrippers and 111 RBIs).

There were no 20-game winners in the league and the best ERA was an inflated 2.96, posted by Tulsa reliever Don Erickson in 72 games. But Dallas, as usual, had a good pitching staff, headed by Joe Kotrany (19-10), strikeout leader Jim Tugerson (199 K's)

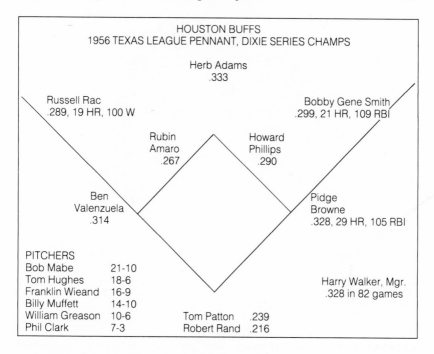

HOUSTON BUFFS
1956 TEXAS LEAGUE PENNANT, DIXIE SERIES CHAMPS

Herb Adams
.333

Russell Rac
.289, 19 HR, 100 W

Bobby Gene Smith
.299, 21 HR, 109 RBI

Rubin
Amaro
.267

Howard
Phillips
.290

Ben
Valenzuela
.314

Pidge
Browne
.328, 29 HR, 105 RBI

PITCHERS
Bob Mabe   21-10
Tom Hughes   18-6
Franklin Wieand   16-9   Harry Walker, Mgr.
Billy Muffett   14-10   .328 in 82 games
William Greason   10-6
Phil Clark   7-3   Tom Patton   .239
                                 Robert Rand   .216

and Dave Hoskins (17-8, and still a good pinch hitter). Fort Worth also enjoyed good pitching from Marcelino Solis (15-2) and eight-year big leaguer Harry Perkowski (12-4).

The Cats finished first in a generally lackluster field, but were swept in four games by the fourth-place Austin Senators when the playoffs opened. Player-manager Harry Walker brought the Buffs in second, but lost to Corpus Christi. Ray Murray then directed Corpus Christi to a first-year playoff championship in a seven-game series with Austin, although Birmingham won the Dixie Series in six games.

Attendance was down all across the league, dipping well below a million for the second year in a row. Three franchise changes in two years were indicative of the depression the Texas League suffered, but worse was in store for 1959. Three charter members — Houston, Dallas, and Fort Worth — moved up to AAA, switching to the American Association. San Antonio was the sole charter member remaining in the circuit, and Tulsa was the only other team with a recent Texas League tenure dating back more than two seasons. Amarillo was the only replacement city that could be re-

Brooks Robinson played second, short, and third for San Antonio in 1956 and 1957 en route to becoming the premier third baseman in the game as a Baltimore Oriole.
— Author's Collection

cruited, so President Dick Butler joined his six-team circuit with the Mexican League in an unusual arrangement called the Pan-American Association.

The Mexican League also consisted of six teams: the Mexico City Reds and Tigers, Monterrey, Nuevo Laredo, Poza Rica, and Vera Cruz. The 146-game schedule included 36 intra-league contests: each member of the Texas League would play three games in the home park of each member of the Mexican League, and vice-versa. At mid-season an All-Star Game was played in Mexico City before an enthusiastic crowd of 19,089, as the Mexican League All-Stars defeated the Texas Leaguers, 9-3. The Texas League abandoned the historic Dixie Series to participate in the best-of-seven Pan-American Series. The Southern Association — which would disband after the 1961 season — had won 17 Dixie Series, while the Texas League had won 19 times.

Corpus Christi dropped to last place in 1959, while Victoria, last in 1958, surged to first under Pete Reiser. Rosebud righthander

Big Frank Howard ripped Texas League pitching for a .356 average and 27 home runs in just 63 games for the Victoria Rosebuds in 1959. On June 8 he blasted three home runs in three consecutive innings.

— Author's Collection

Carroll Beringer led the Texas League in victories at 19-5. The home run leader also was a Rosebud, Carl Warwick, who hit .331 and whacked 35 roundtrippers. Towering Frank Howard, a 6'6" slugger headed for the big leagues, batted .356 and blasted 27 home runs in just 63 games for the Rosebuds. In a game in Austin on June 8, Fabulous Frank hit homers in three consecutive innings. In the fifth, Howard came up with two on and drove a pitch over the 400-foot center field fence. In the sixth, again with two on, he hit a shot over the right field wall. With two aboard in the seventh, he unloaded a rocket that struck two-thirds up a light pole in left-center, nearly 400 feet from the plate. Counting an RBI in the first inning, Howard drove in 10 runs in a 19-4 rout of the Senators.

The light, arid atmosphere of Amarillo proved to be a haven for hitters. Batting champ Al Nagel (.357, 27 homers, and a league-leading 123 RBIs) was one of four Amarillo players who were among the top 10 batters in the league. As the Texas League expanded into West Texas (and, for nearly a decade, into Albuquerque), the longtime reputation of the circuit as a pitchers' league faded amid a profusion of home runs, rising batting averages, and ballooning ERAs.

Despite the availability of just six teams, the Texas League held a four-team playoff — best two of three in the opening round, best three of five in the finals — to determine the Pan-American Series representative. Victoria and Tulsa fell in two games to San Antonio and Austin, respectively, then the Senators swept the Missions in three straight. Austin took on the Mexico City Reds and won, 4-1. The highlight of the series was a 1-0 no-hitter by the southpaw ace of the Senators, Charles Gorin (16-7 in the regular season).

With only six teams in operation, Texas League attendance took a precipitous fall in 1959, down to 559,438 — the lowest since 1942. Last-place Corpus Christi drew only 61,501, and dropped out of the circuit before the next season. As the 1950s ended, the Texas League was in a perilous condition, with attendance continuing to decline and increasing difficulty in keeping stable franchises. President Dick Butler faced grave problems in guiding the Texas League into a new decade.

1960–1969

Texas League Slump

The 1960s was a turbulent era for American society. Even though the Texas League did not have to face political assassinations, a war in Vietnam, or racial upheaval, the problems that confronted the circuit were severe and seemingly unrelenting. Weak attendance and franchise shifts persisted throughout the decade, and a development in 1966 would permanently change the caliber of play throughout the minor leagues.

Corpus Christi was replaced in 1960 by the "Rio Grande Valley" franchise, a club centered in Harlingen and the surrounding area. The move south to the border was logical, considering the continuing Texas League relationship with the Pan-American Association. Ray Murray stayed on as manager of the franchise, and he led the Giants to first place. Murray had at his command the league's batting champ, Charley Hiller (.334), and ERA leader Gaylord Perry, as well as Manny Mota (.307) in the outfield — all future major leaguers.

On April 29 Rio Grande Valley locked horns with San Antonio in Mission Stadium before a modest but typical Texas League "crowd" of 820. The game lasted five hours and 42 minutes — and 24 innings — before the Giants scored two runs to win, 4-2. The Giants used 15 players, including just three pitchers, while the Missions employed 19 men, including six hurlers. The marathon con-

Gaylord Perry pitched for Corpus Christi in 1959 and Rio Grande Valley in 1960, winning the ERA title in the latter season.

— Author's Collection

test eclipsed a 50-year-old Texas League record, set in 1910 when San Antonio and Waco dueled 23 innings to a 1-1 tie.

The All-Star Game was played in San Antonio, and the Texas League won, 7-2. Each of the 1960 playoff series was to be decided on a best-three-of-five basis, and each series became a three-game sweep. In the opener Rio Grande Valley was dumped by Victoria, while Tulsa swept San Antonio. Tulsa beat the Rosebuds in the finals, then took the Pan-Am Series from the Mexico City Tigers, 4-1.

Attendance fell to just 489,547 during the 1960 season, but the same six Texas League teams started 1961. The Victoria Rosebuds, however, soon were in deep financial trouble, and the franchise was transferred to Ardmore on May 27. Ardmore's only previous Texas League entry had occurred in 1904, when Paris had moved its franchise to the Oklahoma city for the rest of the season. But Victoria was not through with Texas League baseball in 1961. On June 10 Ray Murray's Giants were shifted from Harlingen to Victoria, although the total attendance in both cities was just 43,184 (the biggest crowd in the history of the Rio Grande Valley franchise was 3,381 on May 21, 1960). Attendance across the league bottomed out at 468,181 for the year. Amarillo had two managers during the season, while San Antonio tried a total of four field generals.

There were two 1961 All-Star Games, one on each side of the border. At Mexico City, 13,850 *aficionados* attended an 8-3 Mexican League victory, while just 3,850 came to the game in San Antonio to view another Mexican League triumph, 13-3.

Amarillo's lineup bristled with five of the top 10 hitters in the league, including future Yankee star Joe Pepitone (.316 with 21 homers) and batting champ Phil Linz (.349). The Sonic pitching staff also was strong: lefthander Harold Stowe (14-1), Tom McNulty (14-5), Jim Bouton (13-7) and Robert Lasko (11-4). The Sonics orbited to first place, six games ahead of Tulsa.

Austin righthander Larry Maxie (17-7 with a loop-leading 2.08 ERA) pulled off a spectacular feat: on June 14 he no-hit the Victoria Giants for a 2-0 victory; a month later Maxie hurled a second no-hitter as the Senators defeated Poza Rica, 5-0. Alex Dupree, pitching for Fort Worth in 1906, is the only other Texas Leaguer to twirl two no-hitters during a single season.

Austin had to beat Victoria, 4-3, to secure the fourth-place playoff spot. Then the Senators defeated Amarillo in five games, only to fall by a three-game sweep to San Antonio in the finals. The Missions went on to defeat Vera Cruz, 4-2. It was to be the last year of the Pan-American Association, and the Texas League had been victorious in all three Pan-Am Series, winning 12 games to just four for the Mexican League representatives. The Mexican League, however, had won three out of four All-Star Games.

The Texas League and the Mexican League mutually decided to terminate the Pan-American Association at the end of the 1961 season. But only Austin, San Antonio, Amarillo, and Tulsa were prepared to field teams in 1962. El Paso and Albuquerque agreed to join the Texas League, which had to operate under the limitations of a six-team circuit. A 140-game schedule was set up, but there was considerable travel involved, and each club only had five opponents to display before the home fans.

For the players the schedule came to mean long, tedious bus trips, since passenger trains no longer were feasible and planes were out of the question financially. "You'd play in Albuquerque,"

El Paso's first Texas League entry roared to a first-place finish. The explosive 1962
Sun Kings featured Jesus Alou (.343) seated in the second row, second from right.
Standing in the back row (from the left, fourth, ninth, and tenth, respectively) are
batting champ Charlie Dees (.348), RBI champ and MVP Cap Peterson (.335, 29 HR,
130 RBI), and home run king Jerry Robinson (.289, 36 HR, 125 RBI).
— Courtesy El Paso Diablos

recalled Austin infielder Paul Snyder (who hit .312 in 1962), "then
after the game get a box of chicken and take off. You'd try to sleep
on the bus. That was a pretty messy bus by the time you got
home." Texas Leaguers always had been hardy, however. "It
would test you a little," admitted Snyder. "But we didn't know any
better. We didn't complain about it."

El Paso's 1962 Sun Kings hit .310 as a team, and boasted four
of the top hitters in the league: Felix Maldonado (.326), Charles
Peterson (.335 with 29 homers and 130 RBIs in 136 games), Jesus
Alou (.343), and batting champ Charles Dees (.348 with 23 homers
and 115 RBIs). On August 3 the Sun Kings beat Amarillo, 11-3,
and Dees, a left-handed slugger, sent four home runs sailing out of
Dudley Field in consecutive at-bats. Cheering El Paso fans threw
$79 onto the diamond in appreciation of the four-home run explo-
sion.

Hard-hitting El Paso was knocked out of the playoffs by Austin,
however, (3-2), while Tulsa swept Albuquerque. Following their final
victory over El Paso, the Senators boarded a bus and made an all-
night trip to Tulsa. There was a problem over hotel payment, so the
Senators moved into the local YMCA. No home games could be

played in Austin because a rodeo had been booked for Disch Field. And not surprisingly, the Senators lost to Tulsa, 3-1.

Although Austin (41,057) and Amarillo (52,257) drew poorly in 1962, the other four clubs brought in more than 100,000 fans each, and the overall attendance was 659,851 — up more than 200,000 from the year before. Beginning in 1962 there was a gradual upswing in fan support toward healthier levels.

In 1963 the El Paso Sun Kings again led the Texas League in team hitting (.284, down from .310 in 1962) and once more produced the batting champ, catcher Dick Dietz (.354 with 35 homers and 101 RBIs). Other dangerous Sun Devil hitters included Jose Cardenal (.312 with 36 homers) and home run-RBI champ Arlo Engle (.320 with 41 homers and 126 RBIs). But the MVP Award was won by Tulsa outfielder Jim Beauchamp (.337 with 31 homers and 105 RBIs), who led the Oilers to a playoff title.

San Antonio finished first and battled El Paso five games before winning the opening series. In the meantime Tulsa, enjoying an attendance of over 200,000, beat Austin in the opener and took San Antonio in the finals.

San Antonio, with another fine team in 1964, would again face Tulsa in the playoff finals. Amarillo, last place finishers in 1963, dropped out, but the franchise went to Fort Worth. Fort Worth's Cats had spent 1959 in the American Association, then united with Dallas as a twin-city franchise. Dallas-Fort Worth operated in the American Association for three seasons, then spent 1963 in the Pacific Coast League. After a year in the PCL, Fort Worth interests determined to find competition closer to home by rejoining the Texas League, but the new Cats finished last and drew fewer than 100,000.

Albuquerque had five of the top nine hitters of 1964, including batting champ Mel Corbo (.339), as well as the league's strikeout kings, Charles Spell and Jim Ward, who each mowed down 224 batters. But this combination could produce only a third-place finish for the Dukes. Tulsa took second place, with outfielder Joe Patterson becoming the first Texas Leaguer to lead the circuit in stolen bases three seasons in a row (31 in 1962, 54 in 1963, and 67 in 1964).

First-place San Antonio rippled with power, speed, and pitching. Righthander Chris Zachary was 16-6 with 188 strikeouts to

San Antonio second baseman Joe Morgan was the 1964 MVP, after hitting .323 with
90 RBIs, 47 stolen bases and a league-leading 113 runs. Morgan went on to win
back-to-back MVP awards in the National League with Cincinnati in 1975 and 1976.
— Author's Collection

head a good mound staff, while first baseman Chuck Harrison led
the Texas League in home runs with 40. The MVP Award went to
future big league star Joe Morgan, who hit .323, knocked in 90
runs, scored a league-leading 113 runs, and flashed his magnificent
fielding skills at second base. San Antonio hosted the All-Star
Game, pitting the best Texas Leaguers against the Lone Star
State's first major league team, Houston's Colt .45s — and the All-
Stars beat the big leaguers, 8-7.

San Antonio and Tulsa defeated El Paso and Albuquerque, respectively, in the first round of playoffs, then faced each other in a
rematch of the 1964 finals. This time San Antonio won, 3-1, to
claim an outright title.

There were significant changes in 1965, as the gentlemanly
Hugh Finnerty, former general manager at Tulsa, was elected
Texas League president. Defending champion San Antonio, a
charter member of the Texas League, dropped out, while Amarillo,
following a one-year absence from baseball, returned to the circuit.

Dallas had spent 1964 in the Pacific Coast League, then resumed its twin-city arrangement with former archrival Fort Worth as a Texas League franchise. A new ball park, Turnpike Stadium, was constructed, and Whitey Lockman was hired as manager. The innovation was a box-office success, as the Dallas-Fort Worth Spurs attracted 329,294 fans. Another innovation was the separation of the Texas League into East-West divisions: the Eastern Division contained Dallas-Fort Worth, Austin, and Tulsa, while the Western Division was made up of Amarillo, El Paso, and Albuquerque. Division winners would engage in a best three of five playoff to determine the Texas League champion.

The 1965 All-Star Game pitted the Texas League stars against the Colt .45s at Turnpike Stadium, and nearly 11,000 fans watched the big leaguers win, 5-1. Turnpike Stadium also was the site on June 17 of a 25-inning marathon between the Spurs and the Austin Braves, finally won, 2-1, by the Braves after five hours and ten minutes. The former longevity record of 24 innings, of course, had been set in 1960 by San Antonio and Rio Grande Valley. The Amarillo Sonics were the 1965 home run champs, but from July 26 to August 2 Sonic bats were silent. The Sonics were successively shut out by the Spurs, 5-0 and 2-0, then by the Braves, 2-0, 1-0 and 2-0, and finally by Tulsa, 8-0. In all, the Sonics were scoreless for 58 consecutive innings, erasing the old mark of 43 innings unwillingly set by Beaumont in 1955.

Albuquerque easily won the Western Division, but Dallas-Fort Worth and Tulsa battled to the end of the regular schedule, closing with identical 80-60 records. Tulsa had the league's top two hitters, Dave Pavlesic (.344) and Walter Williams (.330), and the strikeout king, Larry Jaster (219 K's in 210 innings) — and second baseman Ike Futch (.290), who set an all-time Texas League record by striking out just five times in 594 plate appearances. Tulsa beat Dallas, 2-0, in a playoff game, but lost three out of four finals contests to Albuquerque.

The Texas League — and all other minor circuits — took on a different roster makeup in 1966. The Free-Agent Player Draft, first employed in June 1965, would be conducted annually in January and June. At each session clubs in organized baseball would select players, thereby acquiring the exclusive negotiating rights to each athlete. With National and American league franchises alternating,

the major league teams would draft in reverse order of their standings the previous season. Major league teams would select just one
player during each phase of each session, while Class AAA clubs
would be permitted two selections apiece, Class AA teams four
each, and each Class A team as many as it wanted. But since almost every minor league franchise has a major league affiliation, in
effect all selections are made by parent organizations. This movement toward major league control of the minors was solidified by
the Player Development Contract, which went into effect in 1967.

With minor league emphasis now strictly on developing players for the parent clubs, career minor leaguers became virtually ex-
tinct, and no more would longtime major leaguers finish out their
careers with a few seasons in the high minors. The Texas League
would no longer showcase veteran players with extensive big league
backgrounds, and young players would not have the benefit of tute-
lage from old pros. For young Texas Leaguers, informal instructions from veteran teammates would be replaced to some degree by
increased coaching staffs. At its best, the Texas League had featured a balance between talented youngsters and experienced veterans, but teams no longer would be seasoned by career minor leaguers and ex-big leaguers. From then on, most Texas Leaguers
would be in their early- or mid-twenties, rendering their quality of
play less polished. Few young men would remain in the Texas
League longer than two or three seasons, which meant that lifetime
marks compiled by hitters and pitchers over eight or ten or twelve
seasons would never be threatened.

Tulsa moved up to the Pacific Coast League in 1966, but the
Arkansas Travelers of Little Rock rounded out another six-team
Texas League. The Eastern–Western Division format was
scrapped in favor of a 140-game race with a four-team postseason
playoff. The All-Star Game again featured Houston in Turnpike
Stadium, and again the Texas Leaguers fell, 7-6.

The Arkansas Travelers finished atop the standings their first
year in the league, while Amarillo, with a fine pitching staff— Don
Wilson (18-6 with a 2.21 ERA and 197 strikeouts in 187 innings)
and George Gerberman (12-2) — came in second. But both Arkansas and Amarillo were knocked off in the best-two-of-three playoff
openers. Fourth-place Austin beat Albuquerque in the first game of

the finals, but when rains continued relentlessly, the Senators were declared playoff champions.

Playoff attendance had been miserable, the seven games attracting a total of just 4,751. For 1967 the Texas League Playoffs were abandoned. The same six clubs returned from 1966, and the team with the best record after 140 games would become the 1967 champion.

Albuquerque, managed by Duke Snider (a Fort Worth Cat in 1946), edged Amarillo by two games for the pennant. Snider's club had six of the top eight hitters in the Texas League, including batting champ Luis Alcaraz (.328). The Dukes combined this explosive attack with the league's best pitching staff: righthander John Duffie led the circuit in victories, complete games and innings pitched (16-9, with 22 complete games in 29 starts and 229 innings); southpaw Mike Kekich (14-4); and strikeout leader Ed Everitt (15-13 and 200 K's). The Dukes were legitimate champions in 1967.

The Dixie Series enjoyed a brief revival in 1967. When the Class AA Southern League was organized in 1964, Dick Butler opened discussions about resuming the Dixie Series, and in 1967 the Southern League agreed with the Texas League to pit their respective champions in a seven-game Dixie Series reprise. Birmingham defeated Albuquerque, 4-2, but the Southern League played to a straight championship, while the Texas League decided to resume its playoff series. Because of the time lapse occasioned by the Texas League's longer season, it was decided not to renew the Dixie Series. Even though the Texas League lost the 1967 series, the loop retains what apparently will be a permanent edge, with 19 series victories to 18 series losses.

Although the Austin Braves disbanded after the 1967 season, the Texas League expanded to eight teams in 1968, for the first time since 1958. San Antonio came back to the fold, after a three-year absence, and established a first by moving into the ball park on the St. Mary's University campus. No professional team had ever played its regular schedule on a college campus, and the Missions' general manager was Elmer Kosub, athletic director and baseball coach at St. Mary's. Shreveport, missing from the circuit since 1957, left the Southern League to rejoin the Texas League. "We're back where we belong," declared Shreveport's Bonneau Peters, "we never did belong in the Southern." Memphis, formerly a stalwart franchise of the defunct Southern Association, rounded out the eight-team circuit for 1968.

With eight teams, the Texas League returned to the East-West Division scheme. The eight-team, Eastern Division–Western Division alignment, would prove to be permanent (except for the Dixie Association experiment of 1971), after a decade of juggling various six-team arrangements. But four of the eight clubs were from outside Texas; the Texas League never again would offer a predominantly Lone Star State flavor. For 1968 Arkansas (Little Rock), Dallas-Fort Worth, Memphis, and Shreveport would make up the Eastern Division, while Albuquerque, Amarillo, El Paso, and San Antonio would be grouped in the Western Division.

For the fourth straight year, the All-Star Game was held at Turnpike Stadium. The Spurs were a last-place team in 1966, 1967, and 1968, but Dallas-Fort Worth was the most attractive Texas League market. Texas League All-Stars had won the first three contests against the Colt .45s, but Houston — now the Astros — prevailed in 1965, 1966, and 1967. The last encounter between Houston and the All-Stars was in 1968, when the All-Stars won, 8-7. The Texas Leaguers took four out of seven All-Star games from Houston. In 1969 and 1970 the Eastern Division All-Stars played against the best from the West. The 1968 All-Star manager was Chuck Tanner of El Paso, who would later earn distinction in the major leagues. Charley Lau, soon to become a guru of hitting instruction, managed Shreveport in 1968, and future Giant manager Roger Craig was the 1968 field general at Albuquerque. Not only did the Texas League feature a constant parade of future big league players — the circuit also was a training ground for major league managers.

By 1968 statistics graphically illustrated the shorter 140-game schedule, a changed style of play, and the increased tendency of parent clubs to call up players from the high minors who were playing well. Rarely would players piling up impressive statistics be allowed to put together a complete, stellar season in the Texas League, and even those who did would not measure up statistically with old-time Texas Leaguers who participated in 154 to 160-plus games of past seasons. For years, too, hitters had swung from the heels as even slightly built infielders sacrificed batting averages for

Chuck Tanner managed losing teams in El Paso in 1965 and 1966, then guided the Sun Kings to the 1968 pennant.

— Courtesy El Paso Diablos

home runs. Five-man starting rotations also became common, replacing four-man rotations — which had replaced the three-man rotations that had prevailed until the 1920s. For years, batting averages had sunk lower and lower. In 1968, for example, only four players hit above .300, and 1967 had produced just three .300 hitters. The 1966 RBI leader, Tom Hutton of Albuquerque, knocked in just 81 runs, and few Texas League sluggers now would be able to exceed 100 RBIs or 30 home runs in a season. Shreveport's Ev Joyner was the last Texas Leaguer to collect 200 hits — three decades ago in 1956! The 20-game winner became unknown in the Texas League (Bill Larkin, who pitched for Albuquerque in 1966, is the only 20-game winner since 1957) and totals for innings pitched, games started, strikeouts, etc., have likewise declined. In 1968 six Texas League hurlers shared the Texas League lead in victories — with just 13 each. But three Texas League pitchers hurled no-hitters during 1968: Albuquerque's Richard Armstrong, and Robert Watkins and Paul Doyle, both from Dallas-Fort Worth.

At the age of 18, Dusty Baker played his first professional baseball in the Texas League for Austin. Two years later, in 1969, he played for Shreveport. Baker has been a major league star since the early 1980s.
— Courtesy Bill McIntyre, *Shreveport Times*

The Arkansas Travelers won the Eastern Division in 1968, while El Paso took the Western Division. Chuck Tanner then directed the Sun Kings to the pennant, winning three games and losing just one to Arkansas in the playoffs. Sun King first baseman Jim Spencer (.292 with 28 homers and 96 RBIs) shared the MVP Award with Albuquerque third sacker Bill Sudakis (.294, 16 home runs, 75 RBIs).

There was a shift in alignment for 1969. Dallas-Fort Worth and San Antonio switched divisions: the Spurs went to the Western Division, while San Antonio, located 285 miles south (and slightly west) of Dallas, moved into the Eastern Division. Among the 1969 Texas Leaguers who would be future big league stars were Bobby Grich and Don Baylor (Dallas-Fort Worth), Charlie Hough and Steve Garvey (Albuquerque), Al Hrabosky (Amarillo), and Oscar Gamble (San Antonio). Shreveport produced the 1969 home run champion, Adrian Garrett (24 roundtrippers), who repeated in

1970 with 29 homers. For the second year in a row, two players would share MVP honors: shortstop Bobby Grich (.309) and batting champ Larry Johnson (.337) — both from Dallas-Fort Worth.

President Bobby Bragan instituted a commendable innovation. Ejection fines cost the offending player an automatic $25 — no small sum on a meager minor league salary. Bragan announced that a player could work off the fine at $12.50 credit for each public appearance on behalf of baseball. Out of 35 ejections, all but two players worked off their fines with PR appearances for their clubs. The next season 37 out of 39 ejected players chose to work off their fines.

Amarillo won the 1969 Western Division, while Memphis was the only team in the East with a winning record (66-65). Surprisingly, however, the Blues swept Amarillo in the playoffs in three games.

Attendance was up for the third year in a row — 828,268. Following eight years as a six-team circuit with frequent franchise shifts, the Texas League had been set at eight clubs for two seasons. Major League support of each franchise was solid, and the circuit had just appointed as president Bobby Bragan of Fort Worth, a former big leaguer and Texas League player and manager. As the Texas League prepared to enter a new decade there was a general feeling that the worst was over and that improvement could only continue.

1970–1979

Texas
League
Comeback

The Texas League continued to struggle during the 1970s. There were more franchise changes, and in 1971 the Texas League identity blurred with the Dixie Association improvisation. Attendance went up and down during the decade, dropping below 600,000 in 1976. But in that same year the circuit elected a president who would provide a long-lasting, firm, congenial leadership. Another instrumental move occurred in 1973, when a promotional genius took over El Paso and began to carry the circuit to a new level of fan enticement. By the end of the decade the Texas League enjoyed stability and an optimistic view of the future.

The 1970s began with the same alignment that had ended the 1960s. Memphis again was the only club in the East with a winning record (69-67) and was paced by Arsenio Diaz, who hit .310 and led the league with 102 RBIs. Also in the East, Jose Cruz (.300 with 21 homers and 90 RBIs) of Arkansas dominated the skills that would make him a longtime National League star.

But the season belonged to Albuquerque. The Dodgers hosted the All-Star Game (won by the West, 8-2) and enjoyed the highest attendance in the league (177,747). Four Dodgers hit above .300, Travis King (12-9) led the league in shutouts (6), and righthander Jim Flynn (19-4) was the leader in victories, starts, complete games, innings pitched, and winning percentage (.826). After win-

142

ning the Western Division by six and one-half games over El Paso, Albuquerque downed Memphis, 3-1, for the outright championship.

In 1971 El Paso dropped out of the Texas League. Like the Texas League, the Southern League also could field only seven clubs, so the two circuits merged into an unusual three-division arrangement called the "Dixie Association." The Eastern Division was made up of six Southern league teams. Birmingham of the Southern League joined Arkansas, Memphis, and Shreveport in the Central Division, while Albuquerque, Amarillo, Dallas-Fort Worth, and San Antonio comprised the Western Division. Central Division clubs would play each other and members of both the Eastern and Western divisions, but teams from the East and the West would not meet during the regular schedule because of the immense distances involved. A postseason playoff involving four teams — the three division winners and a "wild card" — was devised. Texas League All-Stars played the San Diego Padres in Albuquerque at mid-season, dropping a 4-3 decision to the big leaguers.

Dallas-Fort Worth, managed by Cal Ripken, boasted the best hitter and pitcher from a Texas League team in 1971. First baseman Enos Cabell, soon to be a major league star, was the circuit's leading batter (.311) and the Texas League MVP. Righthander Wayne Garland (19-5) led the league in victories, complete games (20 in 25 starts), winning percentage, shutouts, innings pitched, and ERA (1.71).

But Dallas-Fort Worth could not win the Western Division. Amarillo proved to be the best in the West, but the Sonics were swept in two games by Central Division champs Arkansas in the playoffs. Wild card Ashville was downed, 2-1, by the Eastern Division winner, Charlotte. In the Dixie Association finals Charlotte beat the Travelers in three game straight.

The Dixie Association ceased to exist in 1972 when both circuits expanded to eight teams. El Paso returned to the Texas League, but Albuquerque and Dallas-Fort Worth (which at last attained an American League franchise) moved out of the loop. Alexandria and Midland made their first appearances in the Texas League to round out the circuit.

The return to a self-contained Texas League apparently

Bobby Bragan, Texas League president (1969–1975). Bragan also served as catcher-manager at Fort Worth (1948–1952). In 1949 he caught 111 games, hit .295 — and did not allow a single passed ball! In five seasons Bragan also threw out more than half the runners who tried to steal against him.
— Courtesy Bill McIntyre, *Shreveport Times*

helped at the turnstiles: total attendance (848,877) was the highest of the decade. San Antonio somehow led the league in attendance with an impressive 253,139 paid admissions, despite having the worst record (53-87, .379) of 1972. The All-Star Game, played at Alexandria, matched the new Texas Rangers of Dallas-Fort Worth against the Texas Leaguers, and the Rangers won, 4-3. When Dallas-Fort Worth joined the American League in 1972, Rangers' owner Bob Short agreed to pay $40,000 for violation of territorial rights to each remaining member of the Texas League, and to play the TL All-Stars without charge.

Managed by Duke Snider, Alexandria posted the best record of the year. Snider had at his command the Texas League's leading hitter, outfielder Randy Elliott (.335 with 19 homers and a league-leading 85 RBIs), as well as the finest pitcher, righthander Dave Freisleben (17-9), the leader in victories, innings pitched, complete games, and ERA (2.32). El Paso won the Western Division with an unheralded cast — then swept Alexandria in three games to claim the playoff.

In 1973 El Paso picked up a gifted southpaw, Frank Tanana (16-6 with a league-leading 197 strikeouts), who would finish the season with the parent California Angels. El Paso also acquired from Shreveport outfielder Morris Nettles, who led the league in hitting (.332) and stolen bases (41). But El Paso finished 13¹/₂ games off the pace in the West, while Alexandria took the not un-usual tumble all the way to last place.

San Antonio completely dominated the Western Division, emerging with a huge lead and the only winning record in the West. Rick Sawyer (18-5) led a fine San Antonio pitching staff. In the East it was all Memphis, despite good seasons by future big lea-guers Hector Cruz (.328 with a league-leading 30 homers and 105 RBIs in just 114 games) of Arkansas and Shreveport's Sixto Lez-cano (.293 with 18 homers and 90 RBIs). Memphis and San Anto-nio had a memorable postseason series, battling the full five games before the Blues took their third playoff title since 1969.

Memphis advanced to the Class AAA American Association in 1974, but Bobby Bragan reenlisted Victoria to fill the gap. A New York Mets affiliate, Victoria posted the best record in the league, but drew only 49,020 paid admissions. Three other teams attracted even fewer fans, and despite good races in each division, total attendance was just 584,619 — the smallest since 1961.

San Antonio's Dennis Eckersley led the circuit in strikeouts (163 in 167 innings) and tied for the lead in wins (14-5), then vaulted directly from the Texas League to an impressive rookie sea-son with Cleveland in 1975. Jerry Mumphrey, from Tyler, Texas, hit .290 for Arkansas and finished the year with the St. Louis Car-dinals. Midland infielders Jerry Tabb (.263, 29 HRs, 105 RBIs) and Wayne Tyrone (.265, 29 HRs, 108 RBIs) were hitting twins who shared the home run crown.

Explosive hitting already had become the trademark of El Paso teams, whose batters benefited from the light air of far West Texas. The 1974 Diablos had the top three hitters in the league — first baseman Dave Collins (.352), second sacker Gerald Remy (.338), and third baseman Ronnie Jackson (.328) — plus a pitching staff headed by southpaw Isidro Monge (14-5). The team led the league in hitting with a .305 average, the first time since 1962 that a team batting mark reached .300 (and in 1962 it was El Paso that had rapped out a .310 clip). For seven consecutive seasons, 1972–1978, El Paso carried on its lead in team hitting, yielding to Midland in 1979, then winning the team title in 1980. After dropping to third in team hitting in 1981, the El Paso team started another string of five straight seasons, 1982–1986 — and no one would be surprised to see the skein extended in 1987. El Paso produced six straight batting champs, 1973–1978, then provided the titlist in five of the next eight seasons. Surprisingly, however, when Western Division champion El Paso met Victoria in the 1974 finals, Victoria swept the Diablos in three straight to claim an outright title.

El Paso not only enjoyed considerable success on the diamond — the turnstiles at old Dudley Field had begun to whirl in record numbers. The 1973 attendance had been just 63,000, and the club sank $52,000 into the red. A hometown boy, Jim Paul, bought the team — and the debts — on borrowed money, then commenced a phenomenal turnaround. Attendance nearly doubled in 1974, and by 1978 it exceeded a quarter of a million. In many seasons only a few Class AAA franchises could outdraw Paul's Diablos. Paul was voted the Texas League's Executive of the Year three years in a row; *The Sporting News* named him Class AA Executive of the Year two years running; he twice won the McPhail Trophy, the highest award offered an individual by minor league baseball; in 1984 he was designated the State of Texas's Small Businessman of the Year; and in 1986 the franchise won the National Association President's Trophy, the highest award offered an organization by minor league baseball.

Paul claims to know — or care — little about the game of baseball: "Pure baseball in the minors puts more people to sleep than Seconal." But nobody goes to sleep in the "Dudley Dome," because Paul stages a nonstop series of promotions, and the fans are lured into participating as much as the players. Each spectator entering the gates is issued a Kleenex, to be used when opposing pitchers are knocked out and the crowd waves tissues and sings, "Bye bye, Baby, bye bye." Cheerleading banners are run up throughout the game, and anyone who fails to take part is singled out by the P.A. announcer. Between games of a doubleheader, Paul will stage a milking contest or a softball game or a world-record banana split (concessionaires will build a banana split four inches

Jim Paul, a promotional wizard, transformed El Paso baseball in the 1970s and became a major force in popularizing minor league baseball.
— Courtesy El Paso Diablos

wide by 120 feet long, and 200 kids armed with plastic spoons will devour it within moments). The crowds are large and excited — baseball has become the thing to do on summer nights in El Paso.

From a low attendance total of ten million in 1963 (the Texas League hit bottom in 1961), minor league baseball has nearly doubled. Aggressive, imaginative promotion by owners and general managers has been the key to the growth which significantly accelerated during the 1970s, and Texas Leaguer Jim Paul has been one of the leaders of the movement. Indeed, Paul initiated a three-day seminar for minor league club officials interested in improving promotions and attendance, and the El Paso Seminar has contributed significantly to the progressive direction of minor league baseball. Today Texas League franchises are directed by bright, innovative men whose energetic promotions have attracted flourishing crowds throughout the circuit. And in recent years major league general managers — who once scorned "bush league" gimmicks — have

Jack Clark hit .303 with 23 homers as a third baseman for the Lafayette Drillers, 1975 co-champs. For the past decade Clark has starred for San Francisco and St. Louis.
— Author's Collection

begun to look to successful minor league operations for methods to improve their fan support.

Although Amarillo had enjoyed a winning season in 1974, the Sonics only drew 45,691, and Victoria, despite a first-place finish, brought just 49,020 fans to the park. Both teams dropped out for 1975, but new franchises were located at Jackson, which would become one of the most important on-field forces in the Texas League, and at Lafayette. With only three Texas clubs now in the circuit, Shreveport joined El Paso, Midland, and San Antonio in the Western Division, while Alexandria, Arkansas, Jackson, and Lafayette made up the East.

Lafayette celebrated its first year in the league by winning the Eastern Division. Jack Clark (.303 with 23 homers), a third baseman for Lafayette but soon to be switched to the outfield in the National League, and outfielder Gary Alexander (.329 with 23 homers) paced the Drillers in hitting and tied with Shreveport's Mitchell Page for the home run title. Midland won the West, then

Groups such as San Antonio's Dodger Dollies add scenery and charm to Texas League games.

— Courtesy Angela Ploch, San Antonio

split the first four games of the playoff with Lafayette. When heavy rains prevented completion of the fifth and deciding contest, Bobby Bragan declared Midland and Lafayette co-champions.

Bragan, league president since 1969, resigned after the 1975 season. Texas League owners elected Carl Sawatski, former major league catcher and longtime general manager of the Arkansas Travelers, to succeed Bragan as league president, and Sawatski moved the Texas League office to Little Rock. He is now entering his twelfth year as president — the second longest tenure in Texas League history. Only J. Alvin Gardner (1930–1953) served longer, and Sawatski has provided continuity and stability of leadership.

Amarillo returned to the Texas League in 1976, replacing Alexandria, which had drawn fewer than 48,000 fans in 1975. Shreveport went back to the Eastern Division, and the West again became an all-Texas aggregation. The All-Star Game was played in San Antonio, but the Texas Leaguers were walloped, 18-4, by the Texas Rangers.

The 1974 co-champs, Lafayette and Midland, dropped to last place in their respective divisions. As usual, El Paso had a prolific offense, dominated by future big leaguer Willie Aikens (.317, 30 HRs, 117 RBIs), who led the Texas League in homers, RBIs, total bases, and runs scored. But Amarillo, paced by outfielder Don Reynolds (.333) and first baseman Eugene Delyon (.331), edged El Paso for the Western Division title. Shreveport won in the East (but drew only 47,930 fans), then went to the final playoff game before losing the championship to Amarillo.

Lafayette, with fewer than 36,000 paid admissions, dropped out of organized baseball, but Tulsa rejoined the Texas League after a stint in the American Association. The old split-season plan was resurrected and applied to the divisional arrangement. Division winners would be determined at the end of the first and last half of the 130-game regular schedule. Each pair of division winners would play a best-of-three opening round, and the two victors then would play a best-of-three series to determine the champion. Although occasionally a team would win its division in both halves of the season, this scheme is especially relevant in an era when a minor league team that is off to a strong start loses key players at mid-season to the parent club. This playoff arrangement has proven so suitable that it has been maintained through the current season.

El Paso's offense was especially torrid in 1977, with a .310 team batting average. Batting champ Thomas Smith (.366) was backed up by slick-fielding third baseman Carney Lansford (.332 with 18 homers and 94 RBIs), and outfielders Steve Stroughter (.336 with 24 homers and a league-leading 116 RBIs) and Gilbert Kubski (.324). The Diablos won both halves in the Western Division, and compiled the best record of the year.

In the East, Tulsa, Jackson, and Shreveport were neck and neck during the first half. Shreveport's Rick Honeycutt was the 1977 ERA leader, but Jackson had the best mound staff in the league, including strikeout king Juan Berenguer and victory leader Mike Scott. During the season the Jackson staff pitched three no-hitters. But Tulsa, led by future big leaguers Billy Sample (.348) and Danny Darwin (13-4), won the first half title, although Tulsa's Drillers (33-29) had fewer victories than second-place Jackson (34-32), while Shreveport (33-33) was right behind. Last place Arkansas surged atop the East during the second half, then beat Tulsa in two games for the division title. Now with a full head of steam, the

Travelers sailed past El Paso, also in two games, to seize the 1977 flag.

The alignment would remain unchanged through 1982. For the next three years, 1977 through 1979, the All-Star Game would be played at Little Rock's Ray Winder Field, and in each contest the All-Stars would defeat the Texas Rangers. The 1977 All-Star shortstop was Steve Macko, son of longtime Texas League first baseman and manager Joe Macko. Steve hit .302 for Midland, went up to the parent Cubs, then died tragically in the first stages of a promising major league career. Many brothers have played in the Texas League, but there have been relatively few father-son combinations.

Once more hard-hitting El Paso won both halves in the West and posted the best season record for 1978. Batting champ Danny Goodwin (.360) and home run-RBI king Robert Clark (.316 with 31 homers and 111 RBIs) sparked the potent Diablo offense.

Again there was a dogfight in the East. Big Leon Durham (.316), second baseman Tommy Herr (.293), outfielder David Bialas (.315), and righthander Dan O'Brien (12-3) led defending champion Arkansas to the first-half title. In the second half, Jackson's Mets followed another strong mound corps to first place. Righthander Jeff Reardon (17-4) paced the Texas League in victories and winning percentage (.810), Neil Allen led in ERA (2.09), Larry Prewitt (11-6) led in shutouts (5), and Scott Holmes (11-5) rounded out a strong staff.

But the year's finest pitching performance was turned in by Tulsa fireballer Dave Righetti. On July 16, Righetti hurled nine innings against Midland and fanned 21 Cub batters for a Texas League record. At one stretch he whiffed seven in a row, and he mowed down the side in the second, third, eighth, and ninth innings. Southpaw Righetti left the game after nine innings and a 2-2 deadlock, and Midland went on to win, 4-2, in extra innings. The old record of 20 strikeouts had been set in 1909 by San Antonio's Willie Mitchell against the Galveston Sandcrabs. In 1978 Righetti fanned 127 hitters in just 91 innings, and within a few seasons he would be a regular for the New York Yankees.

In the playoff Jackson defeated Arkansas, 2-1, for the Eastern Division crown. In a best-of-five finals series, El Paso took three straight from the Mets to win the 1978 pennant. And during the year, over 250,000 fans paid to cheer the Diablos on to the flag.

Despite the efforts of home run-RBI king Mark Brouhard (.350 with 28 homers and 107 RBIs), the Diablos slumped to last place during the first half of 1979, even though Jim Paul's shenanigans boosted the year's attendance at the Dudley Dome to 266,475. San Antonio edged Midland for the Western Division title. The Dodgers were led by outfielder-first baseman Ron Roenicke (.302), shortstop Gary Weiss (.321), and outfielder Elgardo Santos (.318). During the second half, Midland asserted itself with a ferocious hitting performance, averaging .312 as a team for the season and spotlighting batting champ Jim Tracy (.355), along with outfielders Brian Rosinski (.331) and Carlos Lezcano (.326). There were four no-hitters during the year, but only one against a Western Division team.

In the East, Arkansas won the first half behind All-Star first baseman Joe DeSa (.317) and pitchers Hector Eduardo (10-4) and David Johnson (10-5). Shreveport took the second half, but drew the smallest attendance (47,333) in the league. Shreveport first sacker Jose Barrios (.324), a 6'4" right-handed slugger, walloped five grand slam home runs during the season. Barrios blasted his fifth grand slam on July 9, but fell one short of the Texas League record of six, set by Roy Ostergard of Galveston in 1923.

Shreveport fell to Arkansas in two games in the opening round of playoffs. San Antonio beat Midland, 2-1, for the Western Division championship. Arkansas, with the best record in the league, defeated San Antonio in three straight for the 1979 pennant.

As the 1970s came to a close, hitting increasingly dominated play in the Texas League. Imaginative, professional leadership had come to characterize the circuit, along with strong support from major league parent clubs. Total attendance had risen steadily during the past four seasons, and Texas League officials looked forward to a new decade with cautious but confident expectations.

1980–1987

Centennial Decade

During the 1980s, professional as well as amateur athletes have endured a troubled period. Drugs, player strikes, astronomical salaries, greedy agents, exorbitant ticket prices, recruiting violations, under-the-table payments, doctored transcripts — a lengthening list of shabby practices has tarnished the image of sports. But not the Texas League.

Player strikes are unknown in the minor leagues, and salaries — perhaps $1,200–$1,500 a month in the Texas League — are so low that drugs are virtually unaffordable. But Texas League ticket prices are eminently affordable: children's tickets cost $1.00 to $2.00, general admissions range from $2.50 to $3.00, and box seats are just $4.00 to $5.00. It is cheaper to take a family to the ball park than to the movies. In 1980 Texas League attendance passed one million for the first time since 1956, and paid admissions have bounded well over the million mark in each season of the 1980s. Enthusiastic crowds are turning out for Texas League baseball, which so often played to empty ball parks in recent decades. Urban fans of the 1980s seem to be emulating the legions of fortunate spectators in larger cities who can be seen on TV rooting wildly for major league clubs. For the past few seasons, Texas League ball parks have been filling with fans who imitate the "wave" and generally enjoy wholesome, affordable family entertainment.

153

The Chicken regularly entertains large crowds at Texas League ball parks.
— Courtesy Baxter Photo, Marshall, Texas

Since the old pros of earlier years have disappeared from the minors, modern Texas League fans witness baseball talent in an early stage of development. But enthusiasm runs high on Texas League diamonds, as young athletes hungry for promotion to the majors play with a reckless zest for the game that is seldom seen in modern big league parks. Major leaguers, lionized by the media and paid fortunes to perform, pamper their injuries and often do not seem to go all-out for playoff money that represents a mere fraction of multi-year contracts.

Texas League players, on the other hand, are usually in their third, fourth, or fifth year of professional ball. Signing bonuses probably have been spent, and young Texas Leaguers on meager salaries and meal money risk life and limb to make plays which might bring promotion to Class AAA or to the parent club. Night games are played every day except Sunday, so players sleep until noon, become expert at pinball machines and video games, then report to the ball park to compete with the same abandon as the men who wore handlebar moustaches and double-breasted uniforms be-

Colorful mascots like Midland's Homer McFly roam Texas League grandstands visiting with young fans.

— Courtesy Midland Angels

fore the turn of the century. "Every player in a 'bush' league has an ambition to gratify," declared a 1910 Texas baseball observer. The same can be said today, with the result that modern Texas League fans can enjoy a vigorous brand of play that is closer to baseball's golden age than anything that can be seen in today's streamlined major league parks.

Hitting has continued to dominate Texas League diamonds in the 1980s, although from time to time the decade has witnessed brilliant mound performances. The most remarkable pitching feat of the 1980s occurred on May 5, 1983, when Shreveport righthander Dave Wilhelmi faced the Arkansas Travelers and did not allow a baserunner in winning a 7-0 decision. It was only the second perfect game in Texas League history (Eddie Cole of Galveston beat Tulsa, 1-0, on July 10, 1935).

El Paso's Daryl Sconiers (.370) won the 1980 batting championship, while Diablo Mike Bishop (.325 with 33 homers and 104 RBIs) led in home runs and RBIs. But even though El Paso, as

First baseman Mike Marshall hit .321 for the San Antonio Dodgers in 1980. When the right-handed slugger went up to Los Angeles, he was switched to the outfield.
— Courtesy Angela Ploch, San Antonio

usual, won the team batting and home run titles (143 roundtrippers — no other team hit more than 91), the Diablos finished last in the West during both halves.

San Antonio edged Amarillo by one game to finish atop the West in the first half of 1980. The Dodgers featured first baseman Mike Marshall (.321) and outfielder Dale Holman (.344). Curveballer Orel Hershiser was used as a reliever, and Fernando Valenzuela (13-9), a chunky southpaw who spoke little English, developed a screwball during the season and led the league in strikeouts (162 K's in 174 innings). Amarillo took the second half, paced by first sacker Gary Ashby (.342) and DH Frankie George (.330 with 17 homers and 102 RBIs).

The Arkansas Travelers, boasting stars like catcher Frank Hunsaker (.325) and ERA leader Benny Joe Edelen (13-5), drew more than 216,000 fans, and won the first half in the East. But Jackson, behind Tim Leary (15-8) and a lineup of unspectacular but steady hitters, beat Arkansas by 10 games in the second half.

Orel Hershiser pitched for San Antonio in 1980 and 1981 en route to becoming one of the best righthanders in the National League a few seasons later.

— Courtesy Angela Ploch, San Antonio

Jackson's Mets would prove to be a dynasty during the 1980s, appearing in the playoffs every season to date, finishing with the league's best record in 1983, winning the Eastern Division five out of six years (1981 and 1983 through 1986), and taking the playoff championship in 1981, 1984, and 1985.

The Mets, however, fell to Arkansas in the 1980 playoff opener, losing the first two games to the Travelers. San Antonio also won in two games over Amarillo, but lost three straight to Arkansas in the finals.

Jackson came right back the next season and won the first half under the leadership of manager Davey Johnson, who would guide the New York Mets to the 1986 World Championship. Johnson's greatest strengths at Jackson were All-Star catcher Mike Fitzgerald (.312) and a solid pitching staff. Jackson fell to 29-39 in the second half as Tulsa surged to first place. The Drillers' mound staff featured future major leaguers Walt Terrell (15-7) and a rookie named

Steve Sax hit .346 with San Antonio and was named the Texas League's MVP for 1981.
— Courtesy Angela Ploch, San Antonio

Ron Darling, who flashed signs of greatness by pitching two shut-outs in his four victories.

The Western Division was a repeat of 1980, as San Antonio again won the first half and Amarillo took the second half. San Antonio had the best hitting team in the Texas League, starring batting champ Steve Sax (.346), home run king Greg Brock (.295 with 32 homers and 106 RBIs), and outfielders Dale Holman (.333) and Mark Bradley (.316). The Dodger pitching staff was anchored by Tom Niedenfuer (13-3, 1.80 ERA), Richard Rodas (14-6), and Orel Hershiser, who led the league in saves. Amarillo also boasted a fine pitching staff, with southpaw Dave Dravecky (15-5), who tied for the lead in victories and posted the most shutouts, complete game leader Andy Hawkins (11-10), ERA champ Tim Hamm (2.27), and lefthander Mark Thurmond (12-5); all but Hamm soon would be major league regulars. Rookie outfielder Tony Gwynn came up from Class A late in the year to murder Texas League hitting at a .462 clip in 23 games.

As a rookie in 1981, 18-year-old Tom Niedenfuer went 13-3 for San Antonio, striking out 95 in 90 innings and posting a 1.80 ERA. He finished the season by going 3-1 for the Los Angeles Dodgers.

— Courtesy Angela Ploch, San Antonio

For the second year in a row, San Antonio won the Western Division by defeating Amarillo, while Jackson took the East, downing Tulsa (2-1). Davey Johnson's Mets swept San Antonio in the finals to add a pennant to the one posted in 1978.

El Paso led the league in hitting (.303) and victories (76-60) in 1982. Diablo outfielder Randy Ready ripped out a .375 average, the highest mark in over half a century, since Ox Eckhardt hit .379 for Beaumont in 1930. Outfielder Steve Michael (.345) and Dion James (.322) also did more than their share to fuel a potent offense. There was another scoring machine in Midland, led by future major leaguer Carmelo Martinez (.334 with 27 homers and 98 RBIs), and switch-hitter Dave Owen (.316). Cubs' pitching was led by righthander Jon Perlman (13-7) and Doug Welenc (13-10), who tied for most victories with Tulsa's Brad Mengwasser (13-6).

Jackson once more got off to a fast start, winning the East in the first half. The Mets finished last in team hitting (.252), but

Jon Perlman pitched for the Midland Cubs from 1979 to 1982. He was 13-7 in 1980 and again in 1982, and he finished the latter season hurling for Chicago.

— Courtesy Jon Perlman, Carthage, Texas

slender outfielder Darryl Strawberry (.283 with 34 homers and 97 RBIs) was the 1982 home run champ and MVP. Jackson's pitching staff boasted ERA leader Doug Sisk (11-7, 2.67 ERA) and strikeout king Jeff Bittiger (12-5 with 190 K's in just 164 innings). Tulsa, mired in last place during the first half, suddenly exploded behind righthanders Brad Mengwasser and Allen Lachowicz (12-8), and hard-hitting outfielder Tom Dunbar (.323). The Drillers beat Jackson in the playoff opener, then swept El Paso, victors over Midland, in three straight to claim the 1982 pennant.

El Paso hit 162 home runs during 1982, and three other teams — Midland (140), San Antonio (132) and Amarillo (129) — averaged about one roundtripper per game over the 136-game season. It made for exciting, high-scoring baseball, and fans responded. El Paso attracted 326,000 paid admissions, and Arkansas, despite a .500 team, drew over 213,000 fans. Six clubs brought in over 100,000 fans during the season.

Amarillo (51,812) was one of two teams (Shreveport was the

Sid Fernandez was 13-4 with San Antonio's Dodgers in 1983. He pitched with the world champion Mets in 1986.

— Courtesy Angela Ploch, San Antonio

other) that suffered at the gate in 1982. The Gold Sox owner was Ted Moor, who had grown up enjoying Beaumont Exporter baseball, and in 1983 he brought his franchise to his home town. It was the first Texas League baseball in Beaumont since 1955, and 1983 would offer a fairy tale finish for 129,000 ticket buyers. Good hitting — switch-hitter Mark Gillaspie (.333 with 24 homers and a league-leading 122 RBIs) and outfielder John Kruk (.341) were the best — led the Golden Gators to a first half finish in the Western Division.

El Paso was more explosive than ever at the plate, establishing a remarkable .314 team average behind batting champ Earnest Riles (.349), first baseman Carlos Ponce (.348 with 21 homers and 111 RBIs), third sacker William Max (.336 with 28 homers and 112 RBIs), and outfielder James Paciorek (.326). Diablo righthander Rene Quinones (12-4) led the pitching staff, but the circuit's best pitcher in 1983 was southpaw Sid Fernandez. Fernandez, who began the season with the Los Angeles Dodgers (and who would be

The 1984 Olympic baseball team played an exhibition game against the San Antonio Dodgers.

— Courtesy Angela Ploch, San Antonio

a member of the notable 1986 New York Mets' starting rotation), paced the Texas League in victories (13-5), ERA (2.82, the only ERA below 3.00), and strikeouts (209 K's in merely 153 innings). Of course, the finest pitching performance of the season was Dave Wilhelmi's perfect game for Shreveport.

Jackson, behind the hitting of third baseman John Christensen (.333) and outfielder LaSchelle Tarver (.316), won the first half in the East, then dropped to last place as Arkansas took over in the second half. Shreveport ran up the best season record in the Eastern Division (72-64). The Captains were bettered in the regular schedule only by El Paso (74-62), but finished second in each half and stepped aside in the playoffs to three teams with inferior season records.

Jackson downed Arkansas in two straight to win the Eastern Division, while Beaumont defeated El Paso in three games to claim the Western title. The Golden Gators then won three in a row over the Mets to bring a championship to Beaumont in its first year back in the Texas League in nearly three decades.

In 1984 the prolific hitting parade abruptly halted. El Paso

Shortstop Mariano Duncan led the league in doubles and stole 41 bases for San Antonio in 1984. The next year he became the starting shortstop for the Los Angeles Dodgers.

— Courtesy Angela Ploch, San Antonio

again won the team batting crown, but at .285 the Diablos had dipped far below their .314 clip of the previous year. Furthermore, six clubs in 1984 hit *below* the .266 team average that put Tulsa in last place in 1983. Tulsa had led the league in 1983 with 155 home runs, and a total of five teams had blasted more than 100 four-baggers. But in 1984 Midland led with a comparatively modest 103 home runs, and only two other clubs managed 100 home runs. Attendance stayed up, however, as Shreveport was the only franchise which failed to reach 100,000 paid admissions.

Beaumont and Jackson rendered the split season unnecessary for 1984. The Golden Gators continued their 1983 success by finishing ahead of El Paso in each half, with a margin of six and a half games in the first half and a 10-game margin in the second half. Mark Gillaspie (.274) was not as spectacular for the Golden Gators as in his MVP year of 1983, but first baseman Patrick Casey (.305) and batting champ James Steels (.340) produced plenty of fire-

Action at second base in Midland between the Angels and the Jackson Mets.
— Courtesy Midland Angels

works. Other fine Western Division performers included flashy
Midland shortstop Shawon Dunston (.329) and El Paso's hard-hitting James Paciorek (.366).

Jackson's Mets dominated the East, winning by a 12-game
spread in the first half and a seven-game margin in the second, and
posting the only winning record in the division in each half. Righthander Calvin Schiraldi (14-3) was the Pitcher of the Year, and
Sam Perlozzo was voted Manager of the Year.

With no opening playoff rounds to be staged, a best-of-seven
match was announced between Jackson and Beaumont. The
Golden Gators, playoff champs in 1983, had the best season record
in 1984, but lost the postseason series to Jackson, 4-2.

The Arkansas Travelers temporarily broke Jackson's stranglehold on the Eastern Division by winning the first half of 1985. But
the Mets bounced back in the second half behind All-Star catcher
Barry Lyons (.307 with 108 RBIs), outfielder Mark Correon
(.313), first baseman Randy Milligan (.309), and third sacker
David Magadan (.309).

El Paso dominated the West, winning both halves and finishing first in the composite standings with an 86-50 record — 13

The Jackson Mets, 1985 Texas League champions. The Mets have made the play-offs in each of the seven seasons of the 1980s, winning three pennants and five Eastern Division titles.

— Courtesy Jackson Mets

games ahead of second-place Jackson. The Diablos as usual led the league in batting, featuring home run champ Joe Meyer (.304, 37 HRs, 123 RBIs) and a hard-hitting outfield trio, David Klipstein (.333), Alan Cartwright (.314) and Glenn Braggs (.310, 20 HRs, 103 RBIs). But the best hitter on the team was All-Star first base-man Billy Joe Robidoux (.342, 23 HRs, 132 RBIs), who was named Most Valuable Player after leading the league in batting, RBIs (the highest total since Ken Guettler's 143 in 1956), runs scored, dou-bles, and total bases.

For the third year in a row, Jackson won the Eastern Division crown, defeating Arkansas in two games. El Paso, idle during the opening round, lost momentum, and the Mets swept four straight games to win their second consecutive pennant. For the second year in a row, every team in the circuit except Shreveport drew over 100,000 fans, while El Paso and Little Rock brought in more than 200,000 spectators apiece.

But in 1986 Shreveport abandoned one of the Texas League's historic ball parks, now-decrepit Spar Stadium, and moved into one of the showplaces of the minors, Fair Grounds Field. A splen-did concrete and glass structure that seats 5,200, on opening night Fair Ground Field hosted a standing-room-only crowd in excess of 7,200. And with a playoff-bound club to display, Shreveport more than tripled its total attendance to 183,560. Captain mound ace George Ferran won his first 15 decisions and took the pitcher's tri-ple crown, leading the Texas League in victories (16-1), ERA (2.29) and strikeouts (146 in 153 innings), as well as winning per-

Texas League family photo, taken at the league meeting the morning of the 1986 All-Star Game in Shreveport. Top row, left to right: Charles K. Webb, Con Maloney (Jackson owner), Matt Perry (Midland assistant GM), Bill Davidson (Midland GM), Jay Cicero (Shreveport official), Elizabeth Denham (Shreveport assistant GM), Chuck Lamson (Tulsa assistant GM), Jon Long (Shreveport GM), Lou Valentic (Beaumont GM), Ethan Blackaby, Steve Ford (San Antonio GM), Scott Hale, Mike Feder (Jackson GM), Ted Moor (Beaumont owner). Bottom row: B. Bernard Lankford (Midland owner), Joe Preseren (Tulsa GM), Hugh Finnerty (past president), Carl Sawatski (league president), Taylor Moore (Shreveport owner), Bill Valentine (Arkansas GM).

— Courtesy Photography by Crews, Shreveport

The 1986 East and West All-Star squads mixed together for a group photo.

— Courtesy Photography by Crews, Shreveport

Four Texas League presidents throw out the opening balls at the 1986 All-Star Game, left to right: Bobby Bragan (1969–1975), Dick Butler (1955–1963, 1965, 1969), Carl Sawatski (1976–present), Hugh Finnerty (1966–1969). Sawatski had a knee operation in the summer of 1986.

— Courtesy Photography by Crews, Shreveport

centage (.953). In the first century of Texas League baseball, Dizzy Dean is the only other hurler to win the pitcher's triple crown.

Defending champ Jackson insured its perennial playoff slot by winning the first half in the East. Standouts on the Mets included second baseman Keith Miller (.329), first sacker Randy Milligan (.316), and pitchers Reggie Dobie (13-7) and Kyle Hartshorn (11-4). Shreveport won the second half, while the other playoff club was El Paso, which repeated its 1985 feat of dominating the West in both halves. The Diablos again led the league in team hitting (.302) and showcased the batting champ, first baseman Steve Stanicek (.343). Other hitting support came from outfielders Lavell Freeman (.322), Alan Cartwright, (.321) and Todd Brown (.319), while Dan Scarpetta (15-6) and Pete Kendrick (14-6) provided pitching support.

Midland produced the home run king, DH Kevin King (.301 with 30 four-baggers), and other notable hitters such as first baseman James Randall (.331 with 22 homers) and outfielder Paul Tovar (.320). In the East, Beaumont also had a hard-hitting team, including second baseman Joey Cora (.305). But following a June 21 game in San Antonio, Cora was stabbed in a near-tragic incident, and he missed almost two months before returning to action. Beaumont also lost a large section of outfield fence in a tropical storm, and suffered other damage to lovely Vincent-Beck Stadium. Wind gusts in Midland blew down portions of the outfield fence,

The 1986 Texas League All-Star Game was held at Shreveport's new Fair Grounds Field.

— Courtesy Photography by Crews, Shreveport

forcing cancellation of a game and sending home a big Memorial Day crowd.

Threatening weather conditions in Beaumont in 1985 inclined El Paso manager Terry Bevington not to waste a starting pitcher. Left-handed outfielder John Gibbons volunteered for mound duty, twirled five innings of perfect ball, and was credited with a victory when Chris Bosio completed the shutout. Gibbons was called on twice more for relief duty; in a total of eight innings he allowed just three hits and no earned runs. Among the unusual games of 1986 was a June 7 doubleheader at Little Rock between the Travelers and Tulsa's Drillers. The second contest was delayed by rain nearly an hour and a half, starting at 11:07 P.M., June 7, and ending at 1:07 A.M., June 8. A few days later, on June 13, El Paso annihilated Midland's Angels at the Dudley Dome. The Diablos built a 29-0 lead by the fifth inning, battered seven pitchers for 26 hits, and coasted to a 31-5 victory.

In the rain-plagued 1986 playoff opener, Shreveport won the

El Paso Diablos, 1986 champions. Stars included MVP and batting champ Steve Stanicek (.341 — middle row, third from right); 1985 MVP Billy Joe Robidoux (middle, fifth from left); Lavell Freeman (.322 — front, third from right); Charlie O'Brien (.324 — top, fourth from left); Alan Cartwright (.321 — middle, fourth from left); Dan Scarpetta (15-6 — middle, second from left); and Pete Kendrick (14-6 — front, third from left).

— Courtesy El Paso Diablos

first game against Jackson, 7-0. But the Mets rallied to take the next two games by identical scores of 5-1, and sewed up their fourth consecutive Eastern Division championship. El Paso would not be denied in 1986, however, and swept the finals in four games.

At baseball's Winter Meeting in December 1986, the National Association awarded the President's Trophy to Jim Paul's El Paso franchise. It was the first time the President's Award had been granted to a Class AA club, and "special acknowledgement of El Paso's definite influence on minor league operations" was made. Earlier in the year, Midland was recognized as having the finest infield in the minor leagues. Bill Davidson, in his first two years as general manager, broke Midland attendance records successively in 1985 and 1986, despite a depressed economy in the Permian Basin. Named Texas League Executive of the Year for 1986, he also was selected by *The Sporting News* as the Double-A Executive of the Year.

As the Texas League enters its 100th year — and 92nd season — in 1987, the circuit anticipates continued high attendance, along with an accustomed change. The Texas League, like any minor league, must periodically adjust to franchise shifts. Ted Moor of Beaumont, troubled with declining attendance in a depressed economic area, reluctantly sold the majority ownership of his club to Larry Schmittou, and in 1987 the team will play as the Wichita Pilots.

The immaculate infield at Midland is maintained like a golf green by the crew which tends the adjacent municipal golf course. In 1986 the National Association proclaimed Midland's diamond the best in the minors.

— Photo by Faye O'Neal

A charter city of 1888, San Antonio, prepares for its 83rd year in the circuit, more than any other Texas League community. El Paso's Diablos will play to 200,000 or 300,000 — or 400,000 — laughing, cheering, tissue-waving fans in the Dudley Dome. In Midland, baseballs will skim lightly over the minor league's most beautifully manicured infield, while hitters will rocket shots through the light West Texas air. In 1987 the Texas League will move for the first time into Kansas, where the Wichita Pilots will join a trio of Lone Star teams in the Western Division.

In the East, Driller spectators will be seated by a veteran corps of ushers who fondly remember Dizzy Dean, Joe Adcock, and Johnny Vander Meer playing in Tulsa uniforms. Shreveport fans will continue to support the remarkable renaissance of baseball fortunes at splendid Fair Grounds Field. Baseball thrives on character and tradition, and Little Rock's legions of supporters will enjoy both at historic Ray Winder Field. And Jackson's automatic playoff machine will gear up for an eighth straight postseason appearance.

The Texas League has progressed through 100 years and 38 cities since its founding in 1888. Venerable by baseball's calendar, the historic circuit has evolved vigorously throughout its existence. A large number of baseball's greatest players have performed in the Texas League, most on their way up, some on their way down. As the Texas League proceeds into its second century, the circuit's fans will continue to witness the major league stars of tomorrow and all of the changes and developments of the subtle, ritualistic, graceful game that can still be called the National Pastime.

Nicknames

Athletes always have attracted a wealth of nicknames, and Texas Leaguers have accumulated a remarkable share of colorful or insulting sobriquets from fans and fellow ballplayers. "Terrible Dan" Tipple, Louis "The Mad Russian" Novikoff, "Walloping Willie" Handboe, "Kilo" Watt, "Bad News" Galloway, "Cannon-ball" Weyhing, "Dandy Dave" Danforth, "Pecker" Bobo, "Teat" Tolar, "Hobo" Carson, "Snookums" Cowan, "Climax" Blethen, "Goober" Crawford, "Swampy" Thompson, "Steamboat" Struss, "Available" Jones (whose 1-13 record made him imminently available), "Angel Sleeves" Jones, "Lovey Joe" Bratcher, and "Handsome Harry" Smith are only a few of the Texas Leaguers who provided ammunition just through their nicknames to countless leather-lunged fans and bench jockeys, as well as newspaper reporters and radio announcers in search of a touch of color for their stories and broadcasts.

By far the most common nickname through the years has been "Red." Scores of red-headed Texas Leaguers have been identified by the fiery shade of their hair. From Red Cox before the turn of the century to the superb Dallas pitcher of the 1950s, Red Murff, every decade has known numerous "Reds." A Fort Worth pitcher of the 1920s was not a carrot top, but inescapably he was branded "Red" Bird.

172

The second most popular nickname was "Lefty." Most of these athletes, of course, were southpaw pitchers, but Lefty Houtz and Lefty Nagle roamed the outfield for Galveston's 1899 club. Another popular sobriquet, especially in the early years of the Texas League when many players were recruited locally, was "Tex." A dozen or more Texas Leaguers — usually unsophisticated, youthful types — were known as "Babe," while an approximately equal number were called "Chick." Several light-headed athletes have been known as "Cotton" or "Whitey."

The animal kingdom exerted a strong influence over Texas League nicknames, either because of sometimes unkind physical resemblances or because of quickness and speed. Seven or eight fleet players were called "Rabbit," and Charles C. Robertson, a 1928 Dallas pitcher headed for the majors, was known as "Racehorse." Less charitable appellations included: "Possum" Moore and "Possum" Bill Taff; "Piggy" French, "Piggy" Page and "Piggy" Word; "Hog" Kinnear; "Hippo" Hodge and "Hippo" Vaughn; "Duck" Quiesser, "Duck" Smith, "Ducky" Medwick, "Ducky" Swann, and "Ducky" Tillman; "Mule" Haas and "Mule" Watson; "Flea" Clifton; "Monk" Edwards; "Squirrel" Reynolds; "Sparrow" Morton; and "Goat" Anderson. There were the curiously tagged "Reindeer" Bill Killifer and "Sea Lion" Hall. And big, powerful players received appropriate nicknames: "Ox" Eckhardt and "Ox" Miller; "Bear" Allday and "Bear" Garcia; "Bull" Wagner; and "Moose" Woeber.

In the earliest years of the Texas League, nicknames tended to be unsubtle, blunt: "Dumb Henry" Cote, "Tub" Welch, "Slow" King, "Quick" Gettman, "Heavy" Blair, "Crazy" Schmidt, "Win" Mercer, "Wild Bill" Mercer, "Scrappy Bill" Joyce, "Voiceless Tim" O'Rourke, "Icicle" Reeder, "Spitball" Stricklett, and "No Use" Chiles. "Home Run" Duffee was a New Orleans slugger in 1888, "Globetrotter" Earle had barnstormed around the world with A. G. Spalding's All-Stars in 1888–1889, and Texans of the 1880s and 1890s felt that "Mikado" Flynn's mustache lent an oriental look to his countenance.

From time to time there was a hint of royalty around the Texas League. "King" Joseph Brady reigned from Dallas's mound in 1915, and there were also "King" Bader, "King" Bailey, and the regal pitcher "King" Carl Hubbell, as well as San Antonio's slugging first baseman in 1920, "King" Lear. "Count" Weber was at New Orleans the year the league was founded and proved to be a stellar hitter for a number of other seasons, but he was killed in an altercation in Beaumont in 1914. "Baron" Poffenberger and "Baron" Ozee had their innings, as well as "Duke" Riley, "Duke" Dillinger, and the superb Edwin Donald "Duke" Snider. "Prince Ben" Shelton was a 10-year Texas Leaguer beginning in 1899; a first baseman, he was being favorably compared to the slickest-fielding first sacker of the day, the innovative and gifted major leaguer, "Prince Hal" Chase.

During the first few decades of the Texas League it was common practice for veterans to label callow youngsters fresh off the farm either "Rube" or "Cy." Not only were eight or ten players known by each of these nicknames: even more direct were the so-briquets for "Farmer" Ray, "Farmer" Works (a noted hitter of the 1880s and 1890s), and pitcher "Country" Davis.

Ballplayers who had attended college for a year or two were regarded as more sophisticated. University of Mississippi star Edward H. Marshall was only one of a dozen "Docs" in the Texas League. George "A&M" Smith signed a contract with Galveston when he graduated from Texas A&M in 1907. Hatton Ogle was a tall, smart right-handed pitcher (1909–1915) whom everyone called "Professor," and Jay "Doc" Andrews (1909–1910) had actually been a physician.

It was a time of insensitive racial references. The famous catcher J. J. Clarke (25 years as a professional, eight home runs in one game for Corsicana in 1902) was only one of several players called, for one reason or another, "Nig." Nearly a score of men with Germanic names (Schliebner, Schwind, Hoffman, Dietz, etc.) were known to everyone as "Dutch," while eight or ten others were called "Heinie." An Austin pitcher of 1889 is remembered only as "Sauerkraut" Kraus, and San Antonio infielder Lloyd Otto Krueger was known to his 1898 contemporaries as "Oom Paul."

Places — often where a player hailed from — provided many nicknames. For example, fastballer "Vinegar Bend" Mizell proudly acknowledged his rural hometown, Vinegar Bend, Alabama. "Chicago" Cheatham, "Broadway" Flair, "Idaho" Andersen, "Frisco" Edwards, "Klondike" Davis, and "Klondike" Kane were among those who brought a hint of faraway places to Texas ball parks. "Dixie" Carroll and the great "Dixie" Walker were, of course, Southerners, as were "Rebel" Adams, "Rebel" Oliver, and "Rebel" Russell — but "Yank" Davis and "Yank" Yerkes provided a little balance for the North.

Characteristics of physique or movement determined many a sobriquet. "Big Boy" Kraft, "Big Boy" Guthrie, "Big Mike" O'Connor, "Big Ed" Konetchy, "Muscles" Mole, "Tiny" Osborn, and "Tiny" Owens were, of course, large, strong men. "Slim" Love, "Skinny" Adrian, "Pudge" Gautreaux, "Fat" McDonald, "Smiling George" Blackburn, "Curley" Maloney, "Specs" Meadows and "Nose" Nolly were known for obvious features of appearance, while "Jittery Joe" Berry, "Shaky" Kain, "Preacher" Dorsett, "Parson" Perryman, "Silent" Whitehead, and "Stormy" Davis were identified by their temperament.

Other colorful nicknames abounded from club-to-club and era-to-era. "Howdie" Grosskloss, "Bear Tracks" Greer, "Seacap" Christensen, "Coaster" Connally, "Tomato" Daly, "Bananas" Benes, "Yo-Yo" Epps, "Slippery" Ellam (who was an infielder, but whose last name preordained a sobriquet in honor of slippery elm), "Dynamite" Dunn, "Coo-Coo" DiMaggio, "Wheezer" Dell, "Dodo" Schultz and "Dodo" Pennell, "Dingo" Restelli, "Trapper" Longley, "Sled" Allen, "Scudder" Bell, fastballer Virgil "Fire" Trucks, "Whistling" Wade, "Buzzer Bill" Whitaker, "Kettle" Wirts, "Yam" Yaryan, "Peaches" Nelson, "Iron Joe" Martina, "Pinches" Kunz, "Cowboy" Harrell, "Jinx" Harris, "Shags" Horan, "Long Tom" Hughes, "Shovel" Hodge, "Moon" Harris, "Satchel" Henson — and "Ug" Robertson. Students of nomenclature can find no richer resource than the nicknames of Texas Leaguers.

The
Ball
Parks

Baseball stadiums are the only athletic facilities called "parks." The national pastime is still that, a pastime, which intersperses moments of brilliant individual plays with time to relax and contemplate player shifts on the field, anticipated developments such as a tiring pitcher or a sacrifice bunt, and similar nuances of the game. The leisurely pace of baseball is in direct contrast to the fanatical violence of football and the frenetic pace of basketball. A major part of the charm of baseball is following the home team through a long season, becoming familiar with each player, enjoying the camaraderie of fellow fans — all at a friendly park which becomes a home away from home during six months of play.

Baseball's roots reach far back into the nineteenth century; indeed, Texas League fans of the late 1800s would feel at home in El Paso's Dudley Dome or Little Rock's Ray Winder Field, and, unlike a football spectator from a century ago, he would be able to follow a game that remains relatively unchanged in rules or play. The first Texas League games were conducted on hard-scrabble diamonds in front of plank grandstands and unpainted bleachers. Scoreboards were operated by hand and sometimes there were no outfield fences. In the larger Texas League cities, amateur and semi-pro baseball was played all over town, and a professional club might lease a playing field for the season.

A semi-pro team at El Paso's Dudley Field shortly after it was opened in 1924. Before the advent of night baseball, the grandstand was equipped with a huge venetian blind (upper right) to protect fans from the scorching afternoon sun.
— Courtesy El Paso Diablos

Baseball parks possess features of delightful irregularity and individuality. Dudley Field in El Paso, for example, has a noticeable rise in front of the center field fence — because a canal lies just beyond the fence, and an overflow would flood the entire outfield without the levee effect. The center grandstand at Dudley Field dates back to 1924, and surely it is the only one existing professional ball park that is constructed of adobe bricks. Beaumont's old Magnolia Park had a right field fence so short — about 260 feet — that a line was drawn well toward right center, and any ball hit over the fence between the line and the foul marker counted only as a double. When Albuquerque Sports Stadium opened in 1969, there was a drive-in area overlooking left and center fields to accommodate more than 100 vehicles.

The first Texas League Stadium — and one of the first in organized baseball — to install lights was Katy Park in Waco, which began playing night games on June 20, 1930. Before season's end, every park in the league had lights, except Wichita Falls and Beaumont, and the latter city held out through 1942. The early lighting plants were primitive and inadequate, a boon to fastball pitchers and a deterrent to high batting averages. In time it would be im-

At El Paso's Dudley Field, there is a rise in deep center — because a canal just beyond the fence sometimes overflows and would flood the outfield if it were not for
the levee effect.

— Photo by Faye O'Neal

possible to savor the delicious feeling of playing hooky that comes
from attending a baseball game during a workday afternoon, but
night ball boosted attendance and saved many franchises.

In 1911 the Fort Worth Panthers moved into a new park on
the west side of North Main. With a seating capacity of 4,600, this
facility was the first steel and concrete stadium ever built in the
Texas League, and it had the first turnstiles and reserved seats in
the circuit. Houston's 14,000-seat Buff Stadium was termed "the
finest minor league plant" when it opened in 1928. The same ac-
colade was granted Fort Worth's rebuilt LaGrave Field in 1950,
and streamlined Fair Grounds Field in Shreveport in 1986 — and
the same surely will be said in El Paso when the Diablos move into
their new $6 million stadium in 1989 or 1990.

Since 1968 San Antonio has been at home on the campus of St.
Mary's University at V. J. Keefe Memorial Stadium. This arrangement marked the first time a college campus had become the home

Albuquerque Sports Stadium opened in 1969 with the unique capability of accommodating 102 vehicles in the outfield drive-in terrace, 28 feet above the playing surface.

— Photo by Faye O'Neal

of a professional baseball club. The facility has been greatly expanded and improved, and a similar affiliation was made by the Beaumont Golden Gators from 1983 through 1986. The Golden Gators markedly upgraded Vincent–Beck Stadium, although a tropical storm badly damaged the fence and clubhouse in 1986.

Storms and fires have caused many ball park disasters throughout Texas League history. In June 1915 the Trinity River flooded, causing considerable damage at Panther Park in Fort Worth. A tropical storm on August 15, 1915, severely ravaged the stadiums at Galveston and Houston, and it was necessary to utilize parks in Austin, Brenham, and Corpus Christi during the remaining weeks of the season. During a game at Wichita Falls' Athletic Park on June 22, 1922, a discarded cigarette started a blaze that consumed the grandstand. The 3,000 Spudder fans filed out with no injuries, although more than 50 parked automobiles were damaged or destroyed. A new grandstand was thrown together within

The view from the right field drive-in terrace at Albuquerque Sports Stadium.
— Photo by Faye O'Neal

two weeks, but it burned following the final game of a home stand on June 3, 1924. Once again Athletic Park was rebuilt by the time the Spudders returned from a road trip. On July 19 of the same year, the ball park in Dallas was destroyed by fire immediately following a Steers game.

Another year which saw two parks destroyed by fire was 1932: on May 4 Shreveport lost its stadium after a game with Galveston, and the franchise soon transferred to Tyler; after a San Antonio game on June 18, League Park burned, but the team found new quarters and stayed in town. Just after the 1940 season, on September 19, Dallas lost another ball park to fire. LaGrave Field, Fort Worth's big, comfortable stadium, burned on May 15, 1949, and the next day torrential rains set off another Trinity River flood that caused further damage. But by the following season LaGrave Field had been rebuilt and expanded. On April 3, 1977, the wooden grandstand at Tulsa's Texas League Park collapsed during an exhibition game between two major league clubs, and 17 fans fell 20

A 1985 night game at Midland. Night baseball has been a major aspect of Texas League attendance since the 1930s.

— Courtesy Midland Angels

feet to the ground. Several fans were badly injured, but no one was killed.

Many ball parks that survived fires were razed when a new stadium was built or when the franchise was transferred. In many cases buildings or parking lots were constructed on ball park sites and no trace of the old arenas remain. But in Fort Worth there is a grassy lot where LaGrave Field stood, and in Corsicana and Temple it is likewise possible to walk across vacant fields where Texas League baseball once was played. In Wichita Falls only the concrete base of the reserved seat sections remain to mark the site of Athletic Park, while the light standards and clubhouse outline Austin's Disch Field.

For Western history buffs, there is no keener pleasure than walking the streets of Tombstone, Arizona, or prowling around the vacant buildings of a deserted mining town or cavalry fort. Historical architecture is one of our most tangible links with the past, and old ball parks offer an evocative nostalgia trip for baseball buffs.

The Spanish-style entrance to Houston's Buff Stadium, a minor league showplace
when it opened in 1928. Note the buffaloes above the tile roof.

— Courtesy Baxter Photo, Marshall, Texas

Texas League fans can still imagine the scent of hot dogs and the
crack of bat on ball at Alexandria's intimate Bringhurst Park, at di-
lapidated SPAR Stadium in Shreveport, at Amarillo's decaying
Memorial Park, and at Waco's historic, deteriorating Katy Park.

The Dudley Dome (1924) and Ray Winder Field (1932) are
handsomely maintained and today provide a direct connection with
baseball's past, while Tulsa County Stadium, Jackson's Smith-Wills
Stadium, and brand-new Fair Grounds Field in Shreveport represent
the latest in modern concrete and fiberglass facilities. Today's stadiums feature carpeted clubhouses, private skyboxes, spacious rest
rooms, beer gardens, and comfortable seating.

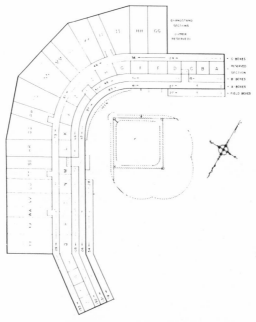

Seating diagram of Fort Worth's LaGrave Field, before the 1949 fire.
— Courtesy Fort Worth Public Library

Disch Field was built in 1947 for $250,000. Located just south of the Colorado River, the park had a seating capacity of 5,500.
— Courtesy Austin History Center, Austin Public Library

The Amarillo Gold Sox played through the 1983 season at Memorial Park, which had a seating capacity of 5,400.

— Photo by Faye O'Neal

Vacant Memorial Park in Amarillo boasts a classic old grandstand with the press box on the roof.

— Photo by Faye O'Neal

All
in the
Family

Dizzy Dean associated with the Houston Buffs during the 1930 season, striking out 14 in his first Texas League game and going 8-2 by the end of the year. The next season Diz was a spectacular 26-10 for Houston, and his younger brother, Paul (soon dubbed "Daffy" by the press) also pitched in the Buff games. The brothers went on to star for the St. Louis Cardinals, then developed arm troubles and returned to the Texas League to try to revive their major league careers. Paul pitched for Houston and Dallas in 1938 (8-16) and for Houston in 1942 (19-8), while Diz finished his career in Tulsa in 1940 (8-8). Joe Macko was a slugging first baseman for Dallas, Tulsa, and Fort Worth during the 1950s, and was player-manager for Amarillo in 1963. In 1978 his son, Steve Macko, hit .302 for Midland and made the All-Star team as a shortstop.

Modern families are advised to do things together. Countless fathers and sons have played catch with each other, brothers play ball in neighborhood games, and, in recent decades, fathers regularly coach their sons in youth baseball programs. Not surprisingly, there have been a great many brothers who have played in the Texas League, as well as a number of father-son combinations.

Mort and Walker Cooper, pitcher and catcher respectively, were batterymates for the Buffs in 1938 before becoming Cardinal stars. Catcher Sled Allen and his younger brother Roy also were

185

Houston batterymates, in 1914, and each played several other seasons in the Texas League. "Pep" Hornsby was a Texas League spitballer from 1906 through 1915, and his teenaged brother, Rogers, had a cup of coffee with Dallas in the spring of 1914. Rogers Hornsby, of course, piled up a lifetime batting average of .358 during a Hall of Fame career, but after his playing days he managed Oklahoma City, Fort Worth, and Beaumont — where he gave his son advice in 1950 to seek a career in another field.

During the Texas League's inaugural season, Galveston featured a battery of T. Stallings and his brother, George Tweedy Stallings, who became a noted major league manager, leading the "Miracle Braves" of Boston to a world championship in 1914. A twin-brother battery for Fort Worth in 1934 was Claude and catcher Clarence "Bubber" Jonnard, each of whom played six years in the big leagues and several seasons in the Texas League. John Henry Van Cuyk led the Texas League in strikeouts while hurling for Fort Worth in 1946, and his brother, Chris Van Cuyk, pitched for the Panthers from 1948 through 1950, leading the league in shutouts in 1948. Wally Schang, who caught in the American League for 19 years, played for Shreveport-Tyler in 1932 when he was 42; his younger brother Robert, who caught in the National League for four seasons, played for Houston in 1926 and 1927, Dallas in 1937, and Fort Worth in 1939.

Bobby Bragan, a National League catcher-infielder for seven years, was player-manager at Fort Worth from 1948 through 1952, where his brother James, a second baseman, played 20 games in 1951. Bobby Bragan, of course, went on to serve as Texas League president from 1970 through 1975. Pitcher-outfielder Claud Longley played in the Texas League for five years during the 1890s, while his brother, the graceful outfielder Trapper Longley, played from 1904 through 1908. The versatile C. B. Douglas played for six Texas League teams during the 1890s, including Sherman, where he teamed with his brother, player-manager "Klondike" Douglas, in 1895. Willie Kitchens, an infielder for six Texas League teams, played in 1905, 1906, 1910, and 1911, while his brother Frank was a catcher and manager for seven teams in 1906, 1911–1914, 1919–1923, and 1934; Frank also was a Texas League umpire in 1934 and 1942.

Oyster Joe (also Iron Joe) Martina was a legendary minor leaguer whose career included 10 seasons in the Texas League (28-13 with Beaumont in 1919), and his brother, infielder S. Martina, teamed with him at Beaumont in 1912. Gus Mancuso (17 years in the National League) and his younger brother Frank (four years in the American League) were native Texans and catchers; Gus played for Houston and Beaumont in 1926 and 1929, then was a Texas League manager after World War II, while Frank caught for San Antonio in 1942, 1950, and 1951. Louis and Otto Drucke from Waco formed a college battery at Texas Christian University, then played for Dallas in 1909; Louis went 14-4 in the Texas League and moved up to the New York Giants, while his brother caught for Waco and Oklahoma City in 1910 and 1911. Catcher Joe Frantz and his brother Walter were Austin batterymates in 1914, and the likeable Walter spent a total of six years in the Texas League as a pitcher, first baseman, and manager.

"Hammerin' Hank" Greenberg was the Texas League MVP at Beaumont in 1932 before proceeding with his Hall of Fame career in Detroit, while his younger brother, Joe, played third base for Fort Worth and Shreveport in 1937, 1940, and 1941. Infielders Roland (Houston, 1950–1952) and Charles (Shreveport, 1951–1952) Harrington played against each other for two seasons. Carl and Charles Littlejohn were on the Houston pitching staff together in 1928; each brother saw action in other Texas League seasons, and Charles also played with the Cardinals. Ham and Billy Patterson played together for three seasons (1918–1920) in Dallas, where Ham was half owner. Ug Robertson and his brother, Jackie, were batterymates at Beaumont in 1926 and 1927, and both played Texas League ball in other seasons.

There have been nearly four dozen brother duos in the Texas League, but only three trios. The first brother trio included: Cotton Knaupp, a Beaumont infielder in 1924 at the end of his career; A. Knaupp, a catcher with San Antonio, Fort Worth, and Waco in 1906 and 1908; and Chick Knaupp, a noted infielder with Houston, San Antonio, and Shreveport from 1912 through 1920. Another set of three brothers spent one season each with the Texas League Cardinal farm club: Cloyd Boyer (Houston — 1953, 4-2 following four years with the Cards); Ken Boyer (Houston — 1954, .319 with 21 homers and 116 RBIs as a third baseman, and on to the Cards the next year); and Len Boyer (Arkansas — 1968, .250,

and 1970, .230 after 24 games when Traveler manager Ken Boyer
sent Len down to Modesto). The most recent brother trio played in
the outfield for Arkansas, then went on to the big leagues: Jose
Cruz (1969, .273, and 1970, .300 with 21 homers); Cirilo Cruz
(1972, .266, and 1973, .230); and Hector Cruz (1973, .328 with 30
homers and 105 RBIs).

Charles Rose, the splendid southpaw (26 victories in 1913, 24
in 1914, 21 in 1912) who spent 10 years in the Texas League, broke
in with Austin in 1908. On the same staff was his brother-in-law,
Ernie Albert, just beginning a seven-year Texas League record.
Dennis Burns, who pitched for four Texas League clubs from 1922
through 1930, was the father-in-law of Hank Wyse, a 20-game-win-
ner in 1941 and 1942 and a six-year Texas Leaguer. In 1922 and
1923 Wilcy Moore pitched for Fort Worth, later spent six seasons
with the Yankees and Red Sox, then, in his early 40s, played for
Oklahoma City in 1938 and 1939. His nephew, Wilcey Cash
Moore, was a hard-hitting Dallas outfielder from 1952 through
1957.

Fred N. Ankenman, Sr., played for Austin in 1908 and was
president of the Houston Buffaloes from 1926 through 1942; his
son, Fred, Jr., was a player-manager at Houston in 1934 and at Oklahoma City from 1946 through 1948, interspersed with three years
in the National League. Eugene Moore, Sr., was a superb southpaw who spent 12 years in the Texas League, 1907 through 1919,
with part of three seasons in the National League. He tried to make
a pitcher of his son, Eugene Jr.; Gene spent three years with Dallas,
1928–1930, was converted to the outfield, enjoyed a fine year with
Houston in 1933 (he hit .334 in a total of 287 Texas League games),
and had a 14-year career in the big leagues. Ziggy Sears spent 11
years (1918–1928) roaming the outfields of the Texas League (he
played left throughout Jake Atz's Fort Worth dynasty), then six
more (1929–1934) as a league umpire, before going up to the National League as an arbiter; his son, Kenneth Sears, was a catcher
for San Antonio (1946–1947).

Joseph Aloysius Mowry, Sr., was a speedy outfielder for Houston during eight seasons from 1906 through 1915, and he saw his
son, Joe Jr., lead Texas League center fielders in fielding while
playing for Dallas in 1937. Joseph Charles Schultz, Sr., played outfield for Houston in 1923 in the midst of an 11-year National

League career, then was player-manager for the Buffs from 1930 through 1932. In the latter year his 13-year-old son, Joe Jr., served as team manager and was allowed one turn at bat by the manager! In 1939, however, Joe Jr., returned to the Buffs as a fine young catcher destined to spend nine years in the big leagues, and from 1952 through 1954 he managed Tulsa. Other Texas League namesake combinations have included: Wilbur Goode, Sr. (1926) and Jr. (1937–1938); Harry Joseph Ragone, Sr. (1920) and Jr. (1946); Carl Grady Ray, Sr. (1908) and Jr. (1948–1949); and Texas League umpires Ulysses E. Welch, Sr. (1921, 1933–1934) and Jr. (1935–1939). Howard Wakefield, a catcher who spent three years in the American League and part of 1911 in San Antonio, did not name his son after him, but he taught him baseball skills so well that the young man was signed by Detroit as one of the first "Bonus Babies." Dick Wakefield played left field for Beaumont in 1942, was the Texas League batting champ (.345), and went on to a successful big league career, thanks to Dad.

The
Media

When the Texas League was founded, Texas newspapers did not have sports sections, but local games were reported, usually with box scores. Most official scorers were newspaper reporters who liked baseball and covered the games as part of their regular assignments. The dean of Texas League sportswriters was Fred Mosebach of the *San Antonio Express,* who covered baseball from 1892 until the late 1940s and who attended games from 1888 until his death in 1951. John Trentem of the *Houston Post* covered Texas League baseball from 1888 until he died in an accident in 1906; during his last few years he wrote sports exclusively and probably was the first specialized sports editor on a Texas newspaper. Pop Boone began writing about Texas League baseball for the *San Antonio Express* in 1903 and covered the circuit for more than half a century while working for a number of newspapers, most notably the *Fort Worth Record* and *Press.*

Of equal longevity and greater service to the Texas League was William B. Ruggles, an Austin native born in 1891 and a baseball fan from boyhood. Ruggles was sports editor of the *Houston Post* from 1910 to 1916, the *Galveston News* from 1916 to 1917, and — following a tour of duty in France as an infantry lieutenant — the *Dallas News* from 1919 to 1925. At the latter paper Ruggles received promotions and became editor in 1943, with time out for duty in

the South Pacific as a staff colonel. In 1920 he accepted appoint-
ment as statistician for the Texas League, an assignment he performed diligently for decades. He meticulously accumulated statistics and personnel records for the pre-1920 period, contacting
numerous old players and officials in the effort. Ruggles also served
as Texas League secretary for 1921–1925 under President J. Doak
Roberts, and when Roberts fell into a fatal illness in 1929, Ruggles
filled in as league president from February to October, 1929. During that period Ruggles conceived of an historical volume about the
circuit, and after two years' work *The History of the Texas League* was
published in 1932. Periodically, Ruggles produced rich statistical
booklets about the league, and in 1951 he published an updated
History of the Texas League. The following year he published a *Roster
of the Texas League,* a collection of brief sketches and facts about
nearly 6,300 players, managers, and umpires who had appeared in
the circuit from 1888 to 1952. His lifelong devotion to the Texas
League ("a labor of love," he confessed) preserved an invaluable
mine of materials about the first seven decades of the loop.

In the early decades of the Texas League there was widespread
gambling activity on baseball games, as well as passionate fan interest in the national pastime. Western Union offered an "every-
pitch service" over ticker tape or Morse wire, and lines were connected to Texas League press boxes so that inning-by-inning scores
from other games could be announced or posted on the scoreboard.
As early as 1889, Galveston's Beach Park boasted "Houlahan's
tally board" in right field, an elaborate scoreboard which kept fans
informed of each Texas League game by the inning. Elsewhere in
Galveston there were several establishments which kept running
telegraph scores of Texas League and big league games for the use
of gamblers.

Young Howard Basquette, a combination office boy-newspa-
per vendor for the *Waco Times-Herald* climbed a ladder to tend the
scoreboard suspended from a telephone pole outside the newspaper
building at Fifth and Franklin. When the Navigators were out of
town on a Sunday afternoon, as many as 200 spectators would sit in
the shade of Tom Padgett's saddle shop and watch the progress of
the game as the score came in over Western Union every inning.
Results of other Texas League games also were posted, inspiring
Basquette to play a practical joke on a man known to bet heavily on

the games. Basquette climbed the ladder and prankishly put up the wrong score. "That gambler almost died because he thought he'd lost his bet," reminisced Basquette, and the angry gambler tried to have the boy fired. The *Times-Herald* also ran the scoreboard at Navigator home games, and Basquette handled that assignment as well. Later, the *Waco Morning News* installed an electric scoreboard in a vacant lot adjacent to the newspaper building on Franklin, providing folding chairs for interested fans. On the last day of the 1916 season, when the Navigators played a doubleheader in Dallas with their third consecutive pennant on the line, 350 straw-skimmered men filled the lot to watch the progress of the games.

In Fort Worth in 1906, 19-year-old Ray McKinley installed a 12- by 20-foot scoreboard over the city's first movie theater at Third and Main. There was room in the middle of the board for inning-by-inning scores of each Texas League game, surrounded by ad space. The enterprising McKinley paid $9 a week for telegraphic reports of the games and collected $175 a month for the ads. Men lined up shoulder to shoulder across the street to watch the afternoon scores. The *Houston Chronicle* installed an elaborate scoreboard which indicated the position of baserunners by means of lights on a diagram of a diamond. Office boys were sent in relays to keep office-bound fans informed of the progress of Buff games, and during the World Series crowds of onlookers often blocked Texas Avenue.

Silent movie theaters often featured the every-pitch service for important games, and baseball fans would pay admission to hear a gong strike once for a single, twice for a double, etc. On June 15, 1922, Al Parker of Wichita Falls was present in a Galveston theater when an enthusiastic crowd "heard" their out-of-town team hit a record-setting five home runs in one inning against the Spudders. Sandcrab Scrappy Moore walloped a home run, then the next batter, Harvey Hendrick, legged out an inside-the-park homer. As the gong sounded, "I watched those Sandcrab fans start smashing chairs against the floor," recalled Parker. After Hank Eibel, Tom Connolly, and Frank Witry had sailed balls out of the park during the same inning, "not many chairs remained intact."

During the 1920s, radio broadcasts began to render telegraphed accounts of ball games obsolete. There were relatively few radio stations in the United States when the *Fort Worth Star-Tele-*

gram went on the air with WBAP on May 2, 1922. On Wednesday afternoon, August 30, 1922, Jake Atz's Panthers hosted the Wichita Falls Spudders in a five-game series that had great bearing on the Texas League championship. Fort Worth had won the first-half title, but Wichita Falls came to town with a slight lead in the second half (44-19, .698 to 46-20, .697 for the Panthers). WBAP sent a man to Panther Park who relayed play-by-play information to an announcer in the downtown studio. Fort Worth won, 6-2, and the next afternoon WBAP once more broadcast a relay as the Panthers won again, 7-3. There was an overwhelming reaction from radio listeners, prompting WBAP to send an announcer directly to Panther Park for Friday's game.

Harold Hough, talking into a telephone transmitter connected by 8,000 feet of wire to the studio in the *Star-Telegram* building, planted himself on an orange crate in the press box and announced a 5-0 Panther shutout. There was no broadcast of the first game of Saturday's doubleheader, which the Spudders won, 8-2, but Hough was back on his orange crate to broadcast a 4-0 Panther triumph in the second game. Although the Panthers clinched their third straight pennant, WBAP did not broadcast the Dixie Series with Mobile because the station went off the air while replacing its original 20-watt transmitter with a new 500-watt transmitter. KDKA in Pittsburgh had carried a game between the Pirates and Phillies on August 5, 1921, the first live baseball broadcast, but WBAP can be credited with the first sportscast in the South.

During the 1923 season, Hough would grab a microphone and head for Panther Park whenever he felt like an afternoon of baseball. Late in the season WBAP acquired "the supersensitive microphone" used by President Warren G. Harding during a speech from St. Louis early in the summer. This engraved microphone was used by Hough during the Dixie Series between the Panthers and the New Orleans Pelicans. When the series moved to New Orleans, a direct wire and Western Union operator were stationed in the studio for relay broadcast.

For years WBAP continued its haphazard broadcast schedule. In 1926 WRR of Dallas, the state's first radio station (founded in 1920), began irregular broadcasts of Steers road games. Two years later, Zack Hunt began regular broadcasts of Wichita Falls games. A controversial topic at Texas League meetings was the harmful ef-

Joe Vitter (left) and Jerry Bozeman, celebrating Shreveport's 1942 championship
by brandishing the commemorative bat of the 1919 Shreveport Gassers. Bozeman
was the popular play-by-play announcer for radio station KWKH in Shreveport from
1938 through 1942.
— Courtesy Joe Vitter, Carthage, Texas

fect of broadcasts on attendance, and during the 1930s broadcasts
of home games were banned for a time. But by the 1940s there were
live broadcasts of almost all Texas League games, and the author
remembers listening to Jerry Doggett describe Dallas Eagle contests over KLIF in the 1950s.

The first televised baseball was a Dodger-Red doubleheader
beamed from Ebbets Field to a few primitive TV sets on August 26,
1939. Texas's first television station was WBAP-TV, which went
on the air in the fall of 1948. On Saturday afternoon, April 2, 1949,
WBAP-TV televised the spring exhibition game between the Fort
Worth Cats and the parent Brooklyn Dodgers — the first baseball
telecast in the South. WBAP-TV offered the first Texas League
telecast from LaGrave Field on Sunday afternoon, April 17, 1949,
as the Tulsa Oilers took on the Cats. The television camera and
other equipment were set up in a booth in the stands just beyond

third base, with a tarpaulin rigged as a sunshade. Home games were telecast on Sundays, Tuesdays, Wednesdays, and Thursdays.

On May 15, 1949, the big grandstand at LaGrave Field was ravaged by fire. The blaze was stopped just short of the television booth, although the tarpaulin was consumed. Makeshift seating arrangements were thrown together, and games — as well as telecasts — continued from Fort Worth. During the off-season LaGrave Field was rebuilt to be bigger (13,005 seats) and better than ever. The main press box, 100 feet long and 12 feet wide, was located on the roof line behind home plate, and suspended below was a smaller television booth with room for three cameras. New La-Grave Field was the first baseball stadium ever designed with special video facilities.

In 1951 KPRC-TV began to telecast Houston games, but by this time televised major league games helped cause the beginning of a serious decline of interest in minor league ball. Television never became a Texas League fixture, and during the lean years of the 1960s and 1970s many markets lost their radio broadcasts. In recent years, however, baseball broadcasts again have become regular features in all Texas League cities. Indeed, young play-by-play announcers, like their Texas League counterparts on the playing fields, strive through hard work and enthusiasm to work their way up to the major leagues.

Texas League Cities

With the 1986 move of Beaumont's franchise to Wichita, Kansas, a total of 38 cities in eight states have hosted Texas League teams. In Texas alone, 101 cities — more than in any other state — have held minor league franchises. The following circuits were Texas-based minor leagues: Texas Association, East Texas League, Rio Grande Valley League, Panhandle-Pecos Valley League, Texas Valley League, Southwest Texas League, Southwestern League, Middle Texas League, Central Texas League, South Central League, Texas-Oklahoma League, Sophomore League, Gulf Coast League, Longhorn League, Big State League, Lone Star League, and, of course, Texas League. Many Texas League cities, at one time or another, placed teams in the other circuits, and Texas League clubs frequently had working agreements with franchises in lower classifications.

There have been only 15 years in which the Texas League has had an exclusively Texan makeup throughout the season: 1889–1890, 1892, 1896–1899, 1902–1903, 1905–1907, and 1912–1914. The 13 out-of-state cities which have participated in the Texas League have also participated in numerous other minor leagues, in which they have been associated cumulatively with scores of other minor league cities. The direct and indirect associations of Texas League teams reach throughout a considerable portion of the minor league world.

Albuquerque
(Dukes, Dodgers)

Albuquerque played Texas League baseball for a decade, making the playoffs in most seasons and introducing the most unique ball park in circuit history. The Albuquerque Browns, a railroad team, played the city's first inter-city baseball, traveling throughout the territory in 1882 and never losing a game. The Browns played on a diamond near Traction Park in Albuquerque's Old Town. In the late 1920s another Santa Fe Railroad team persuaded local Santa Fe officials to donate lumber and ties for Albuquerque's first real stadium, Rio Grande Park, located on the site of an earlier diamond, Stover Field. Then in 1932 the city received a $10,900 grant from the Public Works Administration to erect adobe-based, 3,180-seat Tingley Field, and the Albuquerque Dons entered the Class C Arizona-Texas League.

On opening day the Dons trounced El Paso, 43-15. Unfortunately, 1932 was the worst year of the Great Depression, and Albuquerque's first venture into professional ball abruptly halted when the league folded late in July. The Arizona–Texas League resumed play in 1937, and a year earlier the Work Projects Administration had restructured Tingley Field with steel and expanded the seating capacity to 5,000. The Albuquerque Cardinals won the pennant in 1937 and played through 1941.

In 1942 the Albuquerque Dukes entered the new Class D West Texas–New Mexico League. During a brawl, manager Dixie Howell was clobbered over the head with a chair by a combative fan, but a deadlier war was on and the league disbanded in July. After World War II, the Dukes resumed play in the revived Class C West Texas-New Mexico League. Albuquerque stayed in the circuit through 1955, winning flags in 1948, 1949, and 1953. In 1956 Albuquerque stepped up to the Class A Western League, but after three second-division finishes the debt-ridden club dropped out of organized baseball.

Wealthy oilman Tom Bolack took over the franchise, however, with intentions to advance to the high minors. Bolack absorbed the club's debts in 1958, reorganized during the 1959 season, then played in the Class D Sophomore League in 1960 and 1961 under a working agreement with Kansas City. In 1961 Bolack almost captured Tulsa's Texas League club, then he bought Ardmore's last-place franchise for $35,000.

Albuquerque's Dukes made the playoffs in their first season in the Texas League, finishing third but losing three straight postseason games to Tulsa. More than 133,000 Albuquerque fans turned out to see Class AA ball and such fine players as James Small (.317 with a league-leading 109 walks) and righthander Jose Santiago (16-9), who led the Texas League in victories. The next season Bolack arranged an affiliation with Los Angeles, and the Dukes became the Dodgers. Albuquerque finished fifth in 1963, but then the connection with the fine Dodger organization began to pay off.

The Albuquerque Dodgers led the Texas League in team batting in six of the next eight seasons. First baseman Mel Corbo (.334) took the 1964 hitting title, while Tom Hutton (.340) and Luis Alcaraz (.328) won in 1966 and 1967. In both of the latter two seasons Willie Crawford led the Texas League in runs scored, and Corbo hit the most triples in 1967. The 1964 Dodgers formed the first of four consecutive playoff clubs, finishing third but losing in five games to Tulsa during the postseason opener.

In 1965 the Texas League aligned into two three-team divisions, and Albuquerque won the Western Division. Although Corbo and most of the other big hitters of 1964 were gone, Richard McLaughlin (.307) and Raynor Youngdahl (.295 with 20 homers) paced a league-leading offense. The best pitcher was rookie Don Sutton, who went 8-1 in the California League, then was promoted to Albuquerque. The 20-year-old Sutton had 21 starts during what was left of the season and went 15-6 — and the next year commenced a long major league career that as of this writing has produced 310 victories. Remarkably, the 1965 Dodgers won half of their 82 victories in the last three innings, aided greatly by relievers Jack Billingham and Kenny Page. Albuquerque defeated Eastern Division titlist Tulsa, 3-1, for the playoff championship.

The nucleus of this fine team again promoted out of Albuquerque, but the Dodger organization restocked the franchise for 1966 with another strong group of prospects. Batting champ Tom Hutton was the best of the newcomers, proving himself the league's best fielder at first base, as well as leading another high-powered offense. Veterans around for at least part of the season included

Corbo (.322 in 33 games), shortstop Cleo James (.308), and out-fielder Raynor Youngdahl (.293). The pitching staff featured the Texas League's last 20-game winner to date, righthander Bill Larkin (20-8). The Texas League had returned to a four-team playoff: third-place Albuquerque beat Amarillo two games to one in the opener, lost the first game of the finals to Austin, then saw rainouts halt play and hand the crown to the Senators.

Dodger great Duke Snider, who had played with the Fort Worth Cats in 1946, was given the managerial reins for 1967. He was given considerable talent as well. Albuquerque dominated the All-Star team: batting champ Luis Alcaraz was at second, switch hitter Bill Sudakis (.293) was at third, the shortstop was Don Williams (.297), Willie Crawford (.305) was in the outfield, and the top two pitchers were John Duffie (16-9) and Mike Kekich (14-4). Leon Everitt also pitched well (15-13), and Mel Corbo (.297) was back to man first base. No playoff series was scheduled for 1967, but the talented Dodgers won the pennant after a tight race with Amarillo and El Paso.

The Texas League expanded to eight teams in 1968, with two divisions. The Dodgers still had Sudakis (.294) at third base, and the newcomers included Michael Budd (.315) and Roger Craig, who had ended a 12-year major league career in 1966. But the pitching staff was weak — Craig even started a game himself, and he once had to bring in Sudakis in relief (the All-Star third baseman was shelled, and wound up in the stats with an 81.00 ERA) — and Albuquerque did not make the playoffs.

Del Crandall was the new manager in 1969. Albuquerque led the Texas League in hitting, but the pitching staff finished last in ERA — and the team finished last in the West. But attendance shot up by 75 percent, to more than 176,000 paid admissions. This miracle was wrought by the opening of the most unique ball park in the minor leagues. Located adjacent to I-25, Albuquerque Sports Stadium was built to accommodate 10,610 fans — and 102 vehicles. An outfield parking terrace 28 feet above the playing surface was built to permit drive-in baseball. At one dollar per adult, automobiles, vans, motorcycles, pickups, and motor homes pulled in to watch Dodger games, additionally serviced by a mobile chuck wagon and radio play-by-play. Over one-third of the grandstand seats were theater-style chairs, the Stadium Club offered a glass-enclosed restaurant and bar, the clubhouse, press box, and women's rest rooms were carpeted, and lovely Dodgerettes ushered fans to their seats. In 1970 and 1971 the Texas League All-Star Game was held at this splendid facility. Outfield dimensions — 360 feet down the left field line and 340 in right — reduced home run totals but encouraged high batting averages.

Del Crandall returned as manager for 1970, and he guided the Dodgers to the best record in the league. The home fans enjoyed an All-Star team led by Dodgers: Ron Cey (.331) at third base, Larry Eckenrode (.303) at second, catcher Joe Ferguson (.305), outfielder Bob Gallagher (.336), and pitchers James Flynn (19-4) and Bruce Ellingsen (12-5). Gary Moore (.328) also contributed to an offense that averaged over five runs per game. In the playoffs Albuquerque won another Texas League flag, defeating Memphis in three out of four games.

The 1971 season was the year of the three-division Dixie Association experiment with the Southern League. Albuquerque led the Texas League in hitting and drew over 165,000 fans. For several years club president Tom Bolack had sought a Class AAA franchise. Albuquerque's excellent stadium and sustained high attendance at last resulted in a Pacific Coast League berth for 1972. During its years in the Texas League, Albuquerque had represented New Mexico with the only professional team in the state, and the club had fashioned the best playoff/championship mark of any city during the 1962–1971 period.

Year	Record	Pcg.	Finish
1962	70-70	.500	Third — lost playoff opener
1963	67-73	.479	Fifth
1964	75-65	.536	Third — lost playoff opener
1965	77-63	.550	First — won Western Division and playoffs
1966	74-66	.529	Third — won playoff opener, lost finals
1967	78-62	.557	First — pennant
1968	70-69	.504	Fourth
1969	67-69	.493	Fifth
1970	83-52	.615	First — won Western Division and playoffs

Alexandria (Aces)

Alexandria had a team in the Gulf Coast League in 1907 and 1908, and the Louisiana city eagerly supported clubs in the lower minors whenever opportunities arose. There was the short-lived Louisiana League in 1920, the Cotton States League from 1920 through 1925, and a long tenure in the Evangeline League. Alexandria was a charter member of the Class D circuit in 1934 and was around until the "Vangy's" final season — now in Class C — of 1957.

In 1972, when the Texas League reorganized after the Dixie Association season, Alexandria tried its luck in Class AA with the backing of Pete Tattersall. Tattersall spent $36,000 on improvements of Bringhurst Park, the tidy stadium in the large city park in west Alexandria. Incredibly, he had trouble obtaining a lease, but finally signed a five-year agreement for an accelerating park rent of $1,000, $1,500, $2,000, $2,500, and $3,000, plus utilities.

The Alexandria Aces would be managed by the great Brooklyn Dodger outfielder — and former Fort Worth Cat — Duke Snider. The Aces secured an affiliation with San Diego and obtained several promising players from the Padres' strong Class A farm club, Lodi.

Alexandria began its Texas League tenure with a fine, balanced aggregation that was first in team pitching and second in hitting and fielding. Left fielder Randy Elliott (.335) led the circuit in batting, doubles, total bases, and RBIs. Righthander Dave Freisleben (17-9 with 18 complete games in 25 starts, 163 strikeouts in 190 innings, and a 2.32 ERA) paced the loop in victories, complete games, innings pitched and ERA — and he even hit a grand slam home run! Center fielder John Grubb led all outfielders in fielding, while Freisleben, catcher Joe Goddard, and third baseman Dave Hilton also were the best in fielding at their positions.

The Aces completed the best record of 1972 and won the Eastern Division. In the championship playoff the Aces fell to hard-hitting El Paso in three straight. But paid admissions totaled more than 123,000, second only to San Antonio, and the season had been a resounding success. One of the high points of the year was the All-Star Game, held in the first-place city. Ivie, Hilton, Grubb, El-

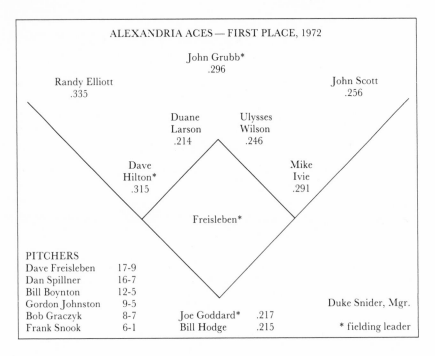

ALEXANDRIA ACES — FIRST PLACE, 1972

John Grubb*
.296

Randy Elliott
.335

John Scott
.256

Duane
Larson
.214

Ulysses
Wilson
.246

Dave
Hilton*
.315

Mike
Ivie
.291

Freisleben*

PITCHERS
Dave Freisleben   17-9
Dan Spillner   16-7
Bill Boynton   12-5
Gordon Johnston   9-5
Bob Graczyk   8-7   Joe Goddard*   .217
Frank Snook   6-1   Bill Hodge   .215

Duke Snider, Mgr.

* fielding leader

liott, and Freisleben started for the All-Stars, but the Texas Rangers won, 4-3, and only 2,930 fans turned out at Bringhurst Park.

Repeatedly in the Texas League the first-place team, gutted by promotions to outstanding players, would plummet to last place the following season. Snider and most of the quality players were gone in 1973. Jackie Brandt, a big league outfielder for 11 seasons, was the new manager, but he had little to work with. John Scott (.295) was back to anchor the outfield and lead the team in hitting. Joe Goddard returned behind the plate, and Duane Larson again ranged across the infield. But the Aces finished last in team batting (.243) and home runs (60), and no pitcher was able to post more than nine victories. The 1973 Aces finished last at 59-77, while attendance plunged to 70,507.

Brandt returned for 1974 but was replaced by Ken Bracey during the season. John Turner, a left-handed outfielder, hit .326 with 18 homers and made the All-Star team. Infielder Wayne Wilson was back for a third season and hit .276 — his highest average with the Aces. But another third-year infielder, Duane Larson, batted just .222. The Aces again finished last in team batting; next-to-last in pitching. Righthander Frank Snook began his third season with the Aces, pitching a 3-0, seven-inning no-hitter against the Victoria Rosebuds. But his performance earned a promotion, and for the second year in a row no Ace pitcher won in double figures. Alexandria again finished last, and paid admissions sank to 44,083.

For 1975 the Padres placed Pat Corrales, a future big league manager, in charge of the Aces. Frank Snook (4-6) again turned up on the mound staff, but for the third consecutive year no Ace hurler could win in double figures. Joe Goddard returned for a fourth year behind the plate, but he hit an anemic .113 in just 39 games. Infielder Marc Rhea also was back for his fourth season, and Alexandria fans had watched him improve as a hitter: .217 in 1972, then .203, .267, and finally a robust .308 in 1975, to lead the team. Switch-hitting catcher Gerard Slone hit .285, while first baseman Scott Brown and outfielder Mike Dupree led the Texas League in fielding at their respective positions. But the Aces finished last in the Eastern Division, and attendance was below 48,000.

Alexandria really was too small for an AA franchise, and the club was moved to Amarillo for 1976. But the Aces of 1972 had been the best in the circuit, and when local teenagers play ball today in Bringhurst Park, a few onlookers recall memories of four Texas League seasons.

Year	Record	Pcg.	Finish
1972	84-66	.600	First — won Eastern Division, lost finals
1973	59-77	.434	Eighth
1974	49-85	.366	Eighth
1975	58-72	.446	Seventh

Amarillo
(Sonics, Gold Sox)

Amarillo's first game in organized baseball came in 1922 during the West Texas League season opener. In typically arctic spring Panhandle weather, Amarillo blasted out a 23-21 victory as official scorer Tex Keirsey went about his chores in an overcoat and gloves. That contest set the tone for Amarillo baseball — harsh weather conditions (including occasional cancellations due to dust storms) and high-scoring games.

In 1923 Amarillo helped form the four-team, Class D Panhandle-Pecos Valley League. The circuit lasted just one season, and Amarillo next fielded a team in the venerable Western League in 1927 and 1928. But after two years of Class A ball, Amarillo did not have another professional team until joining the Class C West Texas-New Mexico League in 1939. The circuit disbanded in 1942, but after World War II Amarillo became part of a rejuvenated West Texas-New Mexico League from 1946 until the loop disbanded for good in 1955. In 1949 Bob Crues hit .404 and blasted 69 home runs in 140 games. Eight of his homers were grand slams, and he walloped an all-time record 254 RBIs. Five times Amarillo teams slugged over 200 home runs in league play: 208 in 1947, 214 in 1948, 216 in 1952, 210 in 1943, and 207 in 1955. In 1956 Amarillo again found a place with the Western League, playing through 1958.

The Texas League lost three of its eight teams in 1959 — Houston, Dallas, and Fort Worth, three mainstays of the circuit. Amarillo was recruited to fill out a six-team Texas League for 1959, and the Panhandle city would spend a total of 21 seasons in the AA loop. Memorial Stadium at the Tri-State Fair Grounds had large dimensions (350 feet down the left field line, 425 in center, and 340 in right), but light air and high winds meant explosive offensive production in Amarillo. Amarillo led the Texas League in team batting its first three years in the circuit, and again in 1966 and 1968. During the inaugural season of 1959, Al Nagel won the hitting title (.344); other Amarillo batting champs were Phil Linz in 1961 (.349) and Bob Taylor in 1968 (.321). Leo Posada was the home run king in 1965 as Amarillo led the Texas League with 119, and two years later Nate Colbert was the leader in home runs *and* stolen bases. Not surprisingly, no Amarillo pitcher ever led the league in ERA.

In addition to batting champ Nagel, the first Amarillo club featured the hitting of Angelo Dagres (.336), William Lajoie (.319), and Jerry Adair (.309). The team had a winning season but finished fifth — the Pan-American Association arrangement with the Mexican League fattened Texas League records and kept Amarillo out of the playoffs. In 1961, however, Amarillo finished first with

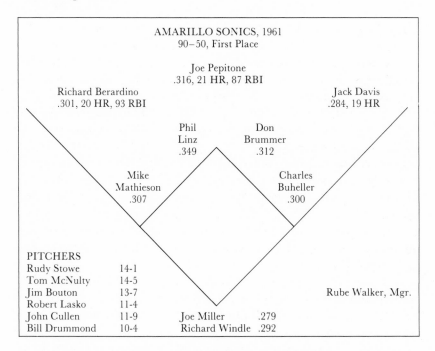

AMARILLO SONICS, 1961
90–50, First Place

Joe Pepitone
.316, 21 HR, 87 RBI

Richard Berardino
.301, 20 HR, 93 RBI

Jack Davis
.284, 19 HR

Phil Linz .349

Don Brummer .312

Mike Mathieson .307

Charles Buheller .300

PITCHERS
Rudy Stowe   14-1
Tom McNulty   14-5
Jim Bouton   13-7
Robert Lasko   11-4
John Cullen   11-9
Bill Drummond 10-4

Joe Miller   .279
Richard Windle .292

Rube Walker, Mgr.

the best Texas League record (90-50) the franchise would ever compile. Rube Walker, an 11-year National League catcher, was the manager, and he had excellent hitting and pitching.

Although Walker returned as manager in 1962, Amarillo dropped to last place and stayed there in 1963 under the leadership of former Texas League slugger Joe Macko. Attendance lagged and Amarillo dropped out in 1964. Amarillo returned to the Texas League the next year, and in 1966 the Sonics made the playoffs with a second-place finish. Righthanders Don Wilson (18-6 with a 2.21 ERA) and George Gerberman (12-2) led a good pitching staff, while future big leaguers Leo Posada (.317) and Doug Rader (.290) were the best hitters. In the opening round of playoffs, however, third-place Albuquerque defeated Amarillo, 2-1.

Amarillo enjoyed another first-place title in 1969, although attendance was a disappointing 68,045. The mound staff led the Texas League in ERA and Miguel Puente twirled a no-hitter against Shreveport on August 15. Puente (13-7), Bill Frost (16-6), Gary Ryerson (13-12), and Hal Jeffcoat (12-4) formed the heart of a fine pitching corps, while first baseman James Mallon (.318) led the hitting attack. But again Amarillo was stymied in the playoffs, losing in three straight games to Eastern Division champ Memphis.

Repeating the pattern of 1962, the first-place Amarillo club was gutted by player promotions and dropped to last in 1970. Attendance, of course, fell too, and by 1974 totaled merely 45,691, even though the club had managed a Western Division title during the Dixie Association season of 1971. Amarillo again dropped out of the Texas League but returned resoundingly in 1976 with another third-place finish. The Gold Sox lineup bristled with dangerous hitters: outfielder Don Reynolds (.333), first baseman Eugene Delyon (.331), and Eugene Mences (.312). The manager was Bob Miller, a veteran of 17 years as a major league pitcher, and he guided the Gold Sox to a thrilling victory over Eastern Division titlist Shreveport, 3-2. It was Amarillo's only outright championship as a Texas League team.

True to club history, Amarillo dropped to the cellar in 1977 and stayed there for three seasons. First baseman Broderick Perkins (.345) and outfielder Ivan Murrell (.342) were fine hitters in 1977, and second baseman Tim Flannery had an excellent year in 1979, but their supporting casts were weak. Improvement came in 1980, when Gary Ashby (.342) and Frankie George (.330 with 102 RBIs) sparked the Gold Sox to a second-half title, although San Antonio prevailed in the opening round of playoffs. The Gold Sox came right back in 1981, led by future San Diego Padres Dave Dravecky (15-5) and Mark Thurmond (12-5). But again San Antonio was the spoiler, winning the opening round, 2-1.

Despite continued good hitting — Gerald Davis (.353 in 95 games), Jeff Ronk (.326), James Steels (.318 in 86 games) — the Gold Sox plunged to last place for the eighth time since 1959. In an effort to boost attendance, free tickets to the next home game were placed under windshield wipers of cars parked outside Memorial Stadium, but admissions totaled only 51,812. Ted Moor of Beaumont had operated the Gold Sox since 1981, and after the 1982 season he received permission to move the franchise to his home town. Memorial Stadium stands vacant now, but memories of more than two decades of hard-hitting Texas League teams fill the old park.

Year	Record	Pcg.	Finish
1959	75-71	.514	Fifth
1960	68-78	.466	Sixth
1961	90-50	.643	First — lost playoffs

1962	56-84	.400	Sixth
1963	57-83	.407	Sixth
1965	60-80	.429	Second
1966	77-63	.550	Second — lost playoff opener
1967	75-64	.539	Second
1968	67-71	.486	Third
1969	80-55	.592	First — won Western Division, lost playoffs
1970	57-78	.422	Fourth
1972	71-68	.511	Second
1973	64-75	.460	Fourth
1974	69-62	.527	Second
1976	81-54	.600	First — won playoffs
1977	56-74	.431	Fourth
1978	44-89	.331	Fourth
1979	54-82	.397	Fourth
1980	77-59	.566	First — lost playoff opener
1981	77-59	.566	Second — lost playoff opener
1982	61-74	.452	Fourth

Ardmore

The southern Oklahoma city of Ardmore twice has finished out a Texas League season for franchises that failed. In 1904 the Texas League had four teams. Corsicana, Fort Worth, and Dallas had winning clubs in the first half, but Paris stayed mired in last place with a dismal 13-40 record. During the second half, the team continued to lose, and Paris finally disbanded on August 4. Ardmore, located just 100 miles north of Dallas and Fort Worth, was known to have a crack semi-pro team. When Texas League President Doak Roberts contacted the Ardmore club, H. B. Bracy and William Hughes agreed to field a team that would replace Paris for the rest of the season.

Hughes, as a nonplaying manager, took two pitchers, two outfielders, and one infielder from the Paris roster. None of these men were noted Texas Leaguers, playing just two or three seasons in the loop. The remainder of the Ardmore team was made up of local talent: one outfielder, three infielders, two catchers, and five pitchers. The season lasted just 11 days after Ardmore entered play, and the Oklahoma boys won three and lost seven in their turn as pros.

Ardmore continued to field semi-pro teams, and in 1911 through 1914 reentered Class D ball with the Texas-Oklahoma

League. Ardmore also played throughout the 11-year existence
(1947-1957) of the Class D Sooner State League. Then in 1961 the
Class AA Texas League called again for help. This time the Victoria franchise was in trouble, and the club was moved to Ardmore
on May 27. (Oddly, when Harlingen folded two weeks later, the
franchise was moved to Victoria for the rest of the year.) The manager from Victoria was George Staller, and the franchise was affiliated with the Baltimore Orioles. But the team was weak — last in
pitching and next-to-last in hitting and fielding — and, as in 1904,
finished last, 33 games out of first.

Ardmore fans — nearly 36,000 attended after May 27 — had a
few good players to watch. Second baseman Dennis Loudenback
and left fielder Al Nagel each banged out 20 home runs. Shortstop
Mickey McGuire hit .281 and played with the Orioles in 1962,
while outfielder Pete Ward batted .307 in 73 games and went on to
a nine-year major league career. Righthander Buster Narum, despite a 4-16 record, managed to pitch all or part of five seasons in
the American League. The 1961 season was the last year of the
Pan-American Association, so Oklahoma fans had the novel experience of watching Mexican League teams come into town for
three-game stands. The Texas League carried on without Ardmore
in 1962, but the Oklahoma community doubtless is ready once
again to step in at mid-season whenever needed.

Year	Record	Pcg.	Finish
1904	3-10	.300	Fourth
1961	57-83	.407	Sixth

Austin (Senators, Braves)

In December 1887 Austin was the site of the meeting which
launched the "State Base Ball League," and the Texas capital had
one of the charter franchises. Playing at a diamond between the
State Capitol and The University of Texas campus, Austin could
finish no higher than third during the first three Texas League
campaigns. Austin did not field a team in 1892, which meant that
the city had no professional baseball from 1891 through 1894.

When Ted Sullivan revived the Texas League in 1895, Austin's Senators reentered the professional ranks. It was a mediocre

The Stacy Hicks Cigar Company provided uniforms and equipment for the H-I-X semi-pro club, an excellent Austin team of 1886 which whetted the local appetite for professional baseball.
— Courtesy Austin History Center, Austin Public Library

team, however, one of four which failed to finish the 1895 season. "The Senators played like they were dead men," complained a newspaper reporter following a doubleheader loss to Fort Worth. "The home team should get a move on themselves and play ball or go off into the wilderness and die." But the 1895 Senators had one superb player, outfielder-manager Algie McBride. Playing in 94 of the 95 Senators' games, McBride hit .444, the highest batting average in Texas League history. He is the only batting champ produced by Austin in 28 Texas League seasons, and no Austin hitter ever won the home run title.

In 1896 the Senators, now under the ownership of the Austin Baseball and Athletic Association, moved to "one of the best baseball parks in the south" on property leased from the Austin Dam and Suburban Railway Company. The field was located just south of the Tenth Ward School and already had a grandstand, rented by circuses that came to town. The grandstand and bleachers were enlarged, 150 reserved chairs were installed for a ladies' section, a ticket booth was erected, the railway company provided transportation for fans, and a clubhouse for the home team was built — containing a shower, 12 lockers, and "two air tight sweat boxes and water basins." But the 1896 team was no more successful than other Senator clubs had been. Austin struggled on to the end of the decade, finishing last in 1899.

The Texas League did not resume play until 1902, but Austin would not field another team until 1905. The next season the Senators played in the South Texas League during that circuit's final year. Houston won the first half, but Austin took the second half, largely because the Senators played last-place Lake Charles 27 times, while Houston and Lake Charles were matched in just 14 games during the same period. Austin won four of the first eight playoff games but protested because Houston had employed star players from Dallas and Galveston. The protest was upheld, Houston's games were forfeited, and Austin was declared 1906 champion of the South Texas League.

The South Texas circuit merged with the Texas League in 1907. Most of the 1906 champions were back in Austin, and the Senators boasted a magnificent pitching staff: tall lefthander Bill Bailey (22-11 with a league-leading 234 strikeouts), southpaw Rube Sutor (23-13 with 226 K's), and righthander Parson McGill (15-4 with the league's best winning percentage and a .333 batting average). Austin won the pennant, and many of the players were sold for profitable sums. The Senators sank to last place in 1908, then dropped out of baseball for the next two seasons.

In 1911 T. S. Iglehart of Austin bought the Shreveport franchise. The Senator pitching staff was led by Wiley Taylor (22-14) and diminutive control artist Jack Ashton (21-12), and the offensive stars were first sacker Rube Gardner (.297) and outfielder Red Downey, who led the league in doubles (49) and stolen bases (48). The 1911 Texas League was unusually well balanced, but Austin blew open a tight pennant race with 22 consecutive victories and claimed another title.

Iglehart lost more than $2,000 at the gate with his pennant winners, but he recouped by selling players. As a result the next three Austin teams were second-division clubs, and the 1914 Senators were the most hapless aggregation in Texas League history. The new owner, W. E. Quebedeaux, began trading players in May. Quebedeaux was called before a league meeting, but he asserted his

The entrance to Disch Field, home of Austin's Texas League Senators and Braves from 1956 through 1967.

— Courtesy Austin History Center, Austin Public Library

right to do whatever he pleased with his club, and before the season ended 70 players and two managers had worn Senators' uniforms. "We tell 'em hello in the morning and kiss 'em goodbye at night," grumbled spitballer Ross Helm. Helm was 5-19, while James Wainwright was 3-22. Austin lost 31 consecutive games and finished 31-114 for a .214 "winning" percentage — all Texas League records for futility.

Quebedeaux sold out to Shreveport interests after the season. In 1915 Austin entered the Middle Texas League, but the franchise was shifted to Taylor in mid-season. Another Class D circuit, the Texas Association, featured an Austin club from 1923 through 1926. Otherwise, Austin baseball fans had to content themselves with sandlot ball and semi-pro clubs until 1947, when the Austin Pioneers joined the Class B Big State League.

The Pioneers played in a new ball park, Disch Field, built just south of the Colorado River with money raised and invested in war bonds prior to World War II. Ed Knebel, founder of 7-Up Bottling Company and a baseball enthusiast, was responsible for the fund drive, construction of Disch Field, and organization of the Pioneers. But in nine seasons (1947–1956) the Pioneers never won a Big State League pennant.

When the Texas League again beckoned in 1956, however,

Uncle Billy Disch played professional baseball from 1900 to 1907, including five Texas League seasons for Fort Worth and Galveston. He was baseball coach at Austin's St. Edward's University from 1900 to 1910, then at The University of Texas from 1911 to 1939. He won 15 of the first 16 Southwest Conference baseball titles and established one of the outstanding baseball programs in the United States at U.T.

— Courtesy Austin History Center, Austin Public Library

Austin jumped eagerly into Class AA with the familiar Senators emblem on their uniforms. In 12 more Texas League seasons, the Senators finished as high as second just twice, but from 1958 through 1966 Austin teams entered the playoffs six times, missing only in 1960, 1964, and 1965. Five times — in 1958, 1959, 1961, 1962, and 1966 — the Senators won the first round. In 1963 Austin lost in the opening round of playoffs to Tulsa, the only time a Senators club failed to advance to the finals. The 1961 Senators tied for fourth place with Victoria, but Austin prevailed, 4-3, in a postseason game to determine which team would enter the playoffs.

The 1959 Senators finished second, beat Tulsa in the playoff opener, then swept San Antonio in three games to win a pennant. The Texas League and Mexican League combined in the Pan-American Association for three years, 1959 through 1961, and Austin represented the Texas League in the first Pan-American Series against the Mexico City Reds. On September 20 Charles Gorin (16-7) pitched a 2-0 no-hitter against the Reds, and the Senators were victorious in the series.

Gorin was the 1959 Texas League strikeout leader, and the next season future big leaguer Denny Lemaster (14-6) also was the strikeout king. Other future major league stars who played for the Senators included Phil Niekro (4-4 in 51 games as a reliever in 1961) and Rico Carty (.327 with 27 homers and 100 RBIs in 1963). Larry Maxie never became a big league star, but in 1961, en route to a 17-7 record, he hurled a 2-0 no-hitter over Victoria on June 14, then twirled a 5-0 no-hitter against Poza Rica on July 15. Peanuts Lowrey, a 13-year National League player, was the most famous baseball figure to manage the Senators, and he took Austin to the 1958 finals.

Hub Kittle managed Austin in 1966 and 1967. His '66 club finished fourth with a losing record, but beat first-place Arkansas, 2-1, in the opener, then defeated Albuquerque in the first game of the finals. Rains then delayed further play, and President Hugh Finnerty declared Austin the 1966 champions.

Austin had another fourth-place team the next year, but there was no playoff series in 1967. Attendance was just 61,000, down from a high of 117,000 in 1958. The 1959 season (102,000) was the only other year in which Austin drew 100,000, and only 41,000 attended in 1962. Austin dropped out of organized baseball after the 1967 season, but the growing city sometimes is mentioned for another Texas League franchise. The University of Texas Longhorns, however, boasting a magnificent stadium and one of the most successful college baseball programs in the United States, would offer almost insurmountable competition to a minor league operation, and to date there has been no revival of the Austin Senators.

Year	Record	Pcg.	Finish
1888	25-21	.543	Third
1889	50-46	.521	Third
1890	13-18	.317	Sixth
1895	32-63	.543	Sixth
1896	60-70	.462	Fifth
1897	53-54	.495	Sixth
1898	18-11	.621	Second
1899	31-45	.408	Fourth
1905	17-22	.436	Fifth

1906	77-47	.621	Second — awarded South Texas League pennant over Houston
1907	88-52	.629	First — pennant
1908	49-95	.340	Eighth
1911	84-62	.575	First — pennant
1912	66-79	.455	Fifth
1913	70-82	.461	Fifth
1914	31-114	.214	Eighth
1956	72-82	.468	Sixth
1957	71-83	.461	Fifth
1958	77-76	.503	Fourth — won playoff opener, lost finals in seven games
1959	80-66	.548	Second — won TL playoffs and Pan-Am Series
1960	73-71	.507	Fifth
1961	69-71	.493	Fourth — won playoff opener, lost finals
1962	69-71	.493	Fourth — won playoff opener, lost finals
1963	75-65	.536	Second — lost playoff opener
1964	63-77	.450	Fifth
1965	70-70	.500	Third
1966	67-73	.479	Fourth — won playoff opener and finals
1967	69-71	.493	Fourth

BEAUMONT GOLDEN

Beaumont (Blues, Millionaires, Orphans, Oilers, Exporters, Navigators, Roughnecks, Golden Gators)

When the South Texas League was organized in 1903, the Beaumont Blues became one of four charter teams. The Blues finished last, then tried to buy a winner with high salaries and ten-dollar bonuses for victories. The Beaumont "Millionaires" finished second in 1905, but the next season produced a loser and the "Orphans" finished the year in Brenham, then Austin and San Antonio. The Beaumont Oilers had a winning season in 1906, but when the South Texas and Texas leagues merged the next year, Beaumont returned to semi-pro ball.

Stuart Stadium under construction in Beaumont. Club president R. L. Stuart spent $120,000 on the 7,500-seat facility, which opened in 1929.

— Courtesy Mrs. Dutch Lorbeer, Beaumont

Beaumont played part of the 1908 season in the Gulf Coast League, but the Oilers returned to the Texas League in 1912. The Oilers played at Magnolia Ball Park, located on Magnolia Avenue between Hazel and Long streets. Built in 1903, the old park had a deep left field fence, but the right field foul line was so short that a home run marker was located far down the fence. Any balls hit out to the right of the marker were counted merely as doubles. (Mrs. Sol Elisha lived on Magnolia next to the park, and balls fouled over the grandstand landed on her roof or lawn or flower beds. She kept every ball she found and campaigned relentlessly to have the park moved, but she died two years before a new stadium was built.)

The Oilers finished last three of their first four years in the Texas League, then had losing teams the next two seasons. In May 1917 Galveston dropped out, and the league pressured Beaumont into withdrawing to even out the schedule. Beaumont agreed, on condition that the league protect its playing rights. The franchise was dormant through the war-shortened 1918 season, then returned in 1919 with a third-place team led by "Oyster Joe" Martina (28-13) and Bill Bailey (24-21 with 277 strikeouts). Martina and Bailey led the league respectively in victories and strikeouts, and set an all-time Texas League record by hurling 378 innings each. The tall, slender Bailey repeated as strikeout leader (216) in 1920, while Martina went 20-14. Oyster Joe pitched for Beaumont from 1912 through 1920, with occasional detours to other clubs.

Beaumont was usually a second-division team during the 1920s, finishing last in 1925 (108 losses), 1927, and 1928 (106

The 1940 Beaumont Exporters took the playoff opener from San Antonio in four straight, but lost the finals to Houston. The Exporters, clad in red uniforms, are arranged outside Stuart Stadium.

— Courtesy Mrs. Dutch Lorbeer, Beaumont

losses). In 1928 a promising southpaw screwballer, Carl Hubbell, somehow went 12-9, completing 20 of 21 starts for the hapless Exporters. A turnaround already was in progress, however, as Uncle Rube Stuart, a stockholder since 1913, bought controlling interest for $20,000 in 1927 and began a 13-year stint as club president. Uncle Rube spent $120,000 to build Stuart Stadium, a 7,500-seat concrete and steel facility on Avenue A with a trolley car line just beyond the left field wall.

Stuart Stadium opened in 1929, the same year that Uncle Rube began a farm club arrangement with the Detroit Tigers. A parade of future major leaguers began honing their skills at Stuart Stadium, and Beaumont entered its baseball heyday, making the playoffs seven times in the 12 seasons from 1931 through 1942. Since Detroit had no lighting system at Navin Field (soon renamed Briggs Stadium), day baseball was mandated for Beaumont, even as the rest of the Texas League went to a predominantly night schedule during the 1930s.

The 1931 Exporters lost a five-game playoff with Houston for the first-half championship, but Beaumont won the pennant the next season. Home run champ and MVP Hank Greenberg (.290 with 39 homers and 131 RBIs), RBI titlist "Pound 'em Paul" Easterling (.278 with 36 homers and 134 RBIs), and tall Schoolboy Rowe (19-7, and a .293 batting average in 47 games) led Beaumont to 100 regular season victories. The Exporters swept Dallas in three post-season games to win Beaumont's first Texas League championship, although the Chattanooga Lookouts took the Dixie Series.

In 1933 Beaumont dropped back to the second division. But the next year Dutch Lorbeer, an Exporter catcher in 1931, became manager and led Beaumont into the playoffs in 1934 and 1935. First baseman Rudy York was the slugging star of these teams, leading the league in home runs (32) and RBIs (117) in 1935.

Al Vincent, an aggressive Exporter second baseman in 1934 and 1935, returned to Beaumont as player-manager from 1937 through 1941. Vincent's 1938 lineup bristled with explosive hitters, and the mound staff starred MVP Dizzy Trout (22-6). Schoolboy Rowe, a Detroit standout for four seasons, was sent down to Beaumont to work a sore arm back into shape in the Texas heat. Rowe responded with a 12-2 record, the best winning percentage of the season, and a .323 batting average. Beaumont finished first and swept Tulsa in three games in the playoff opener. The final series with San Antonio was a classic: the Missions won the opening game in Beaumont, but Rowe pitched a shutout to even the series; in San Antonio the Exporters won only one game and returned to Beaumont trailing, 3-2; the sixth game went 12 innings before darkness — Stuart Stadium still had no lights — halted play; then the Exporters won the seventh and eighth games to capture their second Texas League flag.

Beaumont again lost the Dixie Series, falling to the Atlanta Crackers in 1938. The 1939 Exporters dropped to last place, a common minor league experience as championship players were moved up. But Vincent brought the Exporters into third place in 1940 and advanced to the finals before bowing to Houston. In 1940 right fielder Dick Wakefield (.345), an early bonus baby and the son of former San Antonio catcher Howard Wakefield, won the batting

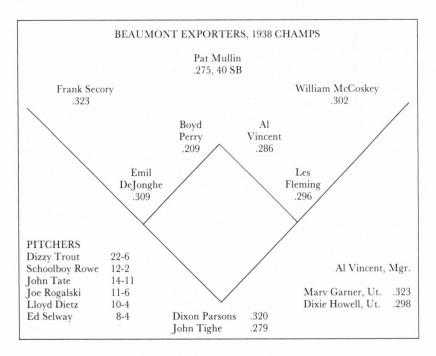

BEAUMONT EXPORTERS, 1938 CHAMPS

Pat Mullin
.275, 40 SB

Frank Secory   William McCoskey
.323   .302

Boyd   Al
Perry   Vincent
.209   .286

Emil   Les
DeJonghe   Fleming
.309   .296

PITCHERS
Dizzy Trout   22-6
Schoolboy Rowe   12-2   Al Vincent, Mgr.
John Tate   14-11
Joe Rogalski   11-6   Marv Garner, Ut.   .323
Lloyd Dietz   10-4   Dixie Howell, Ut. .298
Ed Selway   8-4   Dixon Parsons   .320
                            John Tighe   .279

title and was named MVP. The 1942 Exporters were never out of first place after April 29, beat San Antonio in the playoff opener, won three of the first four final games over Shreveport — then lost the last three games and the playoff title to the Sports.

Following World War II, exhibition games were played in Stuart Stadium, the highlight being an appearance by Bob Feller on October 22 in which the returning veteran struck out 14. A local stock organization backed the new Texas League entry, to be called the "Roughnecks." A working agreement was arranged with the New York Yankees, and lights were installed at Stuart Stadium. After three straight last-place finishes, 1947 through 1949, Hall of Famer Rogers Hornsby was hired as manager. Second baseman Gil McDougald (.336) was named MVP and led the Roughnecks to first place, although the club was swept by San Antonio in the playoff opener. McDougald moved up to New York and Rookie of the Year honors in 1951, but a fine pitching staff — Tom Gorman (12-8 and a league-leading 1.94 ERA), southpaw Harry Schaeffer (19-9), and reliever Richard Mitchell (5-2 with a 2.07 ERA) — hurled the team to the finals of the playoffs.

But the next four years were dismal. The Roughnecks were last or next-to-last each season; the 1955 club was 51-110, finishing 42½ games out of first place. Although 60,000 fans loyally had trooped to the ball park, Beaumont dropped out of the Texas League. The Beaumont Shippers played in the Class B Big State League in 1956 and 1957, but when that circuit died, professional baseball seemed finished in Beaumont. Stuart Stadium was sold in 1958 and demolished. Today a bronze plate marks the site of home plate on a sidewalk in the Stadium Shopping Center. In 1977 a move to form a Class A club for the Longhorn League fizzled when a game between Texas City and Harlingen at Lamar University's Cardinal Stadium drew only 100 Beaumont fans.

But Ted Moor, Jr., a successful insurance executive who had been an Exporter fan as a boy, determined to bring a Texas League team back to Beaumont and the Golden Triangle. Moor purchased the Amarillo Gold Sox in the fall of 1980 and operated the club at a loss in West Texas for two years. In the fall of 1982 Cardinal Stadium was expanded and renovated (and renamed Vincent-Beck Stadium). More than $600,000 was spent on the project by Moor, Lamar University, and the Beaumont Convention and Visitors Bureau. A local contest gathered 1,200 entries for a new team name and Reverend Terry Pierce successfully submitted "Golden Gators" as the label for Beaumont's first professional club in a quarter of a century.

The 1983 home opener brought out 3,767 fans. General Manager Lou Valentic twice lined up appearances by the San Diego Chicken — a standing-room-only crowd of 5,373 showed up in May, while 6,377 turned out in July — and nearly 130,000 paid admissions were recorded for the year. Behind the hitting of outfielders John Kruk (.341) and MVP Mark Gillaspie (.333), the first Golden Gator team won the first half, defeated El Paso for the Western Division championship, then swept Jackson in three games for the Texas League pennant. Tragically, on the return trip from Jackson there was a late-night accident; team members escaped with minor scrapes, but bus driver Wayne Sheppard suffered fatal injuries.

For an encore, the 1984 Gators won both halves in the West and compiled the best record in the Texas League. Behind batting champ James Steels (.340), first baseman Pat Casey (.305), and righthander Bill Long (14-5), the Gators were 51-18 at home and twice posted nine-game winning streaks. In the playoffs, however, Jackson found revenge for 1983, winning four games to two.

Beaumont finished second behind El Paso in both halves of 1985, despite the hitting of outfielders Greg Smith (.315) and Johnny Tutt (.314). The 1985 All-Star Game was held in Beaumont, where Stuart Stadium had hosted the All-Stars in 1941 and 1955. The best Gator hitter of 1986, second sacker Joey Cora (.315) missed much of the season after being stabbed in San Antonio, and a tropical storm damaged Vincent-Beck Stadium during the same troubled season. The team finished fourth, and in the face of a falling economy, Moor reluctantly sold his club. The franchise moved to Wichita, Kansas, for the 1987 season, and once again Beaumont fans lost their Texas League team. Hopefully there will be an economic upswing, and perhaps the future will bring another professional club to the Golden Triangle.

Year	Record	Pcg.	Finish
1903	52-71	.423	Fourth
1904	68-54	.557	Second
1905	41-68	.378	Dropped out
1906	72-50	.690	Third
1912	55-87	.387	Eighth
1913	60-90	.400	Eighth
1914	89-54	.622	Third
1915	61-84	.421	Eighth
1916	66-79	.455	Sixth
1917	19-23	.452	Dropped out
1919	80-69	.537	Third
1920	81-70	.537	Fourth
1921	64-93	.408	Seventh
1922	65-88	.425	Seventh
1923	71-77	.480	Sixth
1924	77-73	.513	Third
1925	42-108	.280	Eighth
1926	76-80	.487	Fifth
1927	56-97	.366	Eighth
1928	50-106	.321	Eighth
1929	72-87	.453	Seventh
1930	68-84	.447	Sixth
1931	94-65	.591	Second — lost playoffs
1932	100-51	.662	First — won playoffs, lost Dixie Series
1933	73-79	.480	Fifth
1934	81-69	.540	Third-lost opener
1935	90-69	.566	Second — won opener, lost finals
1936	69-80	.463	Seventh

1937	82-77	.516	Fifth
1938	99-57	.635	First — won opener, won finals, lost Dixie Series
1939	58-103	.360	Eighth
1940	88-72	.550	Third — won opener, lost finals
1941	58-94	.382	Seventh
1942	89-58	.615	First — won opener, lost finals
1946	70-83	.458	Fifth
1947	60-94	.390	Eighth
1948	61-90	.404	Eighth
1949	55-97	.367	Eighth
1950	91-62	.595	First — lost opener
1951	84-77	.522	Fourth — lost opener
1952	77-84	.478	Seventh
1953	65-89	.422	Eighth
1954	77-84	.478	Seventh
1955	51-110	.317	Eighth
1983	68-68	.500	Second — won Western Division, won pennant
1984	89-47	.654	First — won Western Division, lost finals
1985	69-67	.507	Fourth
1986	60-76	.441	Seventh

Cleburne

Cleburne boasts one of the briefest — and most successful — tenures in Texas League history. In 1906 J. Doak Roberts, beginning his third year as league president, agreed to place a team in Cleburne as part of an effort to increase the circuit from four to six clubs. Roberts appointed Phil Allen to act as club president, and he hired Prince Ben Shelton to play first base and manage the team. Roberts had operated the Temple Boll Weevils in 1905, where Shelton had served as player-manager. From Temple, Roberts and Shelton brought ace pitchers Rick Adams and Hickory Dickson, catcher William Powell, colorful second baseman Mickey Coyle, third sacker Roy Akin, left fielder Dee Poindexter, infielder Zena Clayton, and pitcher-outfielder Cal Lewis. Early in the season Lucky Whiteman (a star of the 1918 World Series) was acquired from Fort Worth and installed in center field, and big, versatile Charlie Moran was brought in from Waco.

Roberts and Shelton demonstrated their feel for new talent by signing two remarkable rookies. Hulking, 21-year-old Dode Criss proved to be an excellent right-handed power pitcher. He hit from the left side of the plate so effectively that he was tried at a variety of other positions, despite glaring deficiencies as a fielder. In 52 games Criss batted .396, although his 192 at-bats did not qualify him for the hitting title, won by Whiteman with a modest .281 average. Twice more, in 1914 (.348) and 1915 (.333), Criss posted the Texas League's highest batting average, but failed to qualify for the hitting crown.

The other rookie was an 18-year-old pitcher from Hubbard, Tris Speaker, who proved to be a flop on the mound. He lost his first seven starts, and in the last game fell behind 24-6. "Stay in there, Tris," shouted manager Shelton. "They haven't gotten a *single* hit off of you yet." Every hit had been for extra bases, Speaker later claimed. But in a day of small rosters, pitchers often filled in at another position, and Speaker exhibited blazing speed on the basepaths and in the outfield. Placed in right field, he stole 33 bases in 84 games and hit .268, the third highest average on the team, after Criss and Whiteman (the next year Speaker would win the Texas League batting title). By the second half of 1906 Poindexter, Whiteman, and Speaker formed one of the slickest fielding units ever to patrol a Texas League outfield.

Cleburne finished the first half of the season in third place, but at 38-24 they were only four games behind the leading Fort Worth Panthers. By this point lagging attendance had caused Roberts to consider transferring the club, but local supporters in Cleburne pledged financial support and the team was not moved. By the second half Criss had joined Adams and Dickson in the usual three-man rotation. Rick Adams and Hickory Dickson won nearly two-thirds of Cleburne's victories. Adams was the 1906 strikeout champion and tied for the league lead in wins with 25. Hickory Dickson was right behind with 24 victories. Walter Dickson acquired his nickname when he fractured his right shoulder and it healed so rapidly that observers decided his bones were made of hickory saplings. Hickory was a control artist: "He was the only man I ever saw," said one admirer, "who could throw a ball into a tomato can all day long."

For Cleburne in 1906 Dickson tuned up with a June 30 no-hitter against Temple, then pulled off two of the most remarkable pitching performances in Texas League history, both times against

Fort Worth. On July 23 Dickson locked into a pitching duel with Alex Dupree, the Panther ace who fashioned a superb 25-7 record in 1906. The two pitchers hurled 19 scoreless innings before darkness ended the game (it was played in less than three hours!). Dickson gave up just six hits, walked two, struck out seven; Dupree allowed nine hits (big Dode Criss, on first that day, went four-for-eight, including a double), walked none, struck out nine. This classic pitchers' duel is the longest scoreless game in the Texas League record book. On the next to last day of the season, September 2, the two clubs played a Sunday doubleheader, with the outcome to determine the second-half champion. Dickson took the mound and beat the Panthers, 2-0, in the first game, then won the second contest by an identical score. Dickson's iron-man shutouts were duplicated in the Texas League only by Harry Ables, pitching for Fort Worth in 1905.

During the last half of 1906 hard-hitting Charlie Moran played almost every position on the field as he was needed, and Dode Criss also frequently lumbered from position to position to take advantage of his powerful bat. The light-hitting infield became a deft defensive combination, and the outfield was magnificent. Cleburne won the second half and defeated Fort Worth in six of their last seven matches. Fort Worth was so intimidated that the players refused to engage in the expected playoff series, and Cleburne was awarded the pennant.

Most of the local guarantors failed to come up with the money they had pledged, and Roberts lost $1,400 on his pennant winner. He pulled out of Cleburne and arranged with Claud Reilly of Houston to sell some of his best players: Coyle, Akin, Wright, Whiteman, and Speaker wore Buffalo uniforms in 1907. W. H. Thacker of Cleburne attended the first Texas League organizational meeting of 1907, but he could not find adequate backing and another club did not materialize. Cleburne placed a team in the Texas-Oklahoma League in 1911, played part of the next season in the South Central League, and in 1921 and 1922 again participated in the Texas-Oklahoma League. When the Class D circuit disbanded during the 1922 season, professional baseball ended in Cleburne.

Five Cleburne alumni graduated to the big leagues: Hickory Dickson went up for five seasons, then came back to set the all-time Texas League ERA (1.06) for Houston in 1916; Lucky Whiteman played for New York and Boston in the American League; Charlie Moran caught for the St. Louis Nationals in 1908; Dode Criss pitched and pinch hit for the St. Louis Americans for four years; and Tris Speaker spent 22 seasons in the American League, hit .344 lifetime, and was one of the first five players inducted into the Baseball Hall of Fame.

Year	Record	Pcg.	Finish
1906	77-49	.611	Third — won championship

Corpus Christi (Giants)

Corpus Christi had considerable experience with baseball in the low minors, starting with the Class D Gulf Coast League in 1926. There were stints in the Texas Valley League (1927–1928, 1938), the Rio Grande Valley League (1931, 1949–1950), and again in the Gulf Coast League (1951–1953), now a Class B circuit. From 1954 through 1957 the Corpus Christi Clippers competed in the Big State League, but the Class B loop dissolved after the '57 season.

Cigar-puffing Jimmie Humphries, president of the Oklahoma City franchise since 1950, had seen barely 50,000 fans pass through the turnstiles in 1956 and 1957. In January 1958 Humphries went to Corpus Christi and met with Bob Hamric, general manager of the defunct Clippers, and Jack Ryan, immediate past president of Corpus Christi's Chamber of Commerce. Humphries said that he could make a profit with an attendance of 125,000, and Hamric assured him that he could expect 150,000 paid admissions and $100,000 in advance ticket sales. A working agreement was established with San Francisco, which led to Corpus Christi's "Giants" nickname.

Ray Murray, who had caught for Dallas in recent seasons and who had previously played for three American League clubs, was engaged as player-manager. Now 38, Murray caught only 69 games for the Giants, but he made 24 pinch hit appearances and blistered the ball all season: .357 with 19 home runs. Murray headed a fine offensive club which led the league in hitting and featured batting champ Eric Rodin (.320 with 26 homers and 95

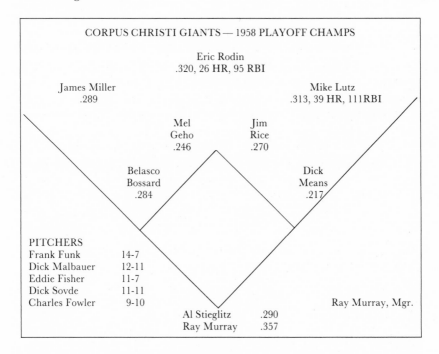

CORPUS CHRISTI GIANTS — 1958 PLAYOFF CHAMPS

Eric Rodin
.320, 26 HR, 95 RBI

James Miller
.289

Mike Lutz
.313, 39 HR, 111RBI

Mel
Geho
.246

Jim
Rice
.270

Belasco
Bossard
.284

Dick
Means
.217

PITCHERS
Frank Funk   14-7
Dick Malbauer   12-11
Eddie Fisher   11-7
Dick Sovde   11-11
Charles Fowler   9-10

Ray Murray, Mgr.

Al Stieglitz   .290
Ray Murray   .357

RBIs) and home run/RBI king Mike Lutz (.313 with 39 homers and 111 RBIs). Rodin had sipped a cup of coffee with the New York Giants in 1954, while pitchers Frank Funk (14-7) and Eddie Fisher (11-7) soon would go up to the majors. Fisher's wicked knuckleball kept him in the big leagues for 15 years, and it was the main reason the 1958 Giants led the league in passed balls. Right-hander Charles Fowler (9-10) twirled a 1-0 no-hit victory over Austin on May 31.

The Giants finished third before a disappointing attendance of 87,774. In the opening round of playoffs the Giants beat second-place Houston, four games to one, then defeated Austin's Senators in a seven-game series to win the Texas League title their first year in the circuit. In the next-to-last Dixie Series, the Birmingham Barons outlasted the Giants, four games to two.

As so often happened in the Texas League, defending champ Corpus Christi saw its best players promoted, and the Giants thudded to last place in 1959. Murray was back, but he limited himself mostly to pinch hitting (.328). Left-handed first baseman Charlie Dees (.303), returning infielder Jim Rice (.296), and center fielder

Johnny Weekly (.277 with 23 homers) hit well, but no one else did, and the Giants plunged to last in team batting. The pitching staff was led by future big league star Gaylord Perry, but he was only 10-11 with the Giants. Attendance dropped with the team's fortunes, to 61,501 — an average of just 854 per game. Of course, conditions were difficult throughout the Texas League. Before the season ended, Corpus Christi fans cheered a familiar face: Eric Rodin returned to the Giants and hit .367 in 24 games.

In February 1960, Texas League owners voted unanimously to approve a move of the Corpus Christi franchise to Harlingen. Humphries took his working agreement with San Francisco, along with Ray Murray, Gaylord Perry, and a few other players, and moved south to form the "Rio Grande Valley Club." Organized baseball returned to Corpus Christi's Cabanis Field in the mid-1970s in the form of the Class A Lone Star League, the only minor circuit with no major league affiliations. The Corpus Christi Seagulls won the 1976 title. There was speculation then that Corpus Christi might soon return to the Texas League, and whenever there is talk of expansion Corpus Christi always is one of the cities mentioned as a potential site for a Texas League club.

Year	Record	Pcg.	Finish
1958	77-75	.507	Third — won opener, won finals, lost Dixie Series
1959	66-79	.455	Sixth

Corsicana (Oilers)

When the Texas League resumed play in 1902, businessman J. Doak Roberts, a native Corsicanan who had managed numerous semi-pro teams, organized a professional franchise for his home town. Backing came from the Oil City textile mill: Corsicana professional clubs would always be dubbed the Oilers, and baseball was played in the Oil City Park in the south end of town. Big Mike O'Connor, who had played and usually managed in the Texas League every season since its formation in 1888, was secured as player-manager. Between O'Connor's practiced eye for talent and Roberts's budding gifts as a baseball executive, a memorable team was assembled.

Rosters were limited to eleven men. The bellwethers of the 1902 pitching staff were Bob White, Belmont Method, and Lucky Wright (who made such an impression that for years most Texas Leaguers named Wright were dubbed "Lucky"). The catcher was a nineteen-year-old Canadian, J. J. "Nig" Clarke, whose professional career would span a quarter of a century, including nine major league seasons. The six-foot-five-inch O'Connor stationed himself at first; he had won the Texas League batting title in 1896 with a .401 average, and Big Mike still hit with authority. The second baseman was Alec Alexander, who occasionally spelled Clarke behind the plate. Walter Morris, a brilliant shortstop, was signed out of amateur ball; he enjoyed a long playing career, then spent the rest of his life as a manager and baseball executive. The third baseman was George Markley, a fine fielder who had broken into the Texas League in 1895. Ike Pendleton was in left field; he was a swift baserunner who filled in at second base when Alexander "donned the mask and pad." The center fielder was James J. "Curley" Maloney, a League fixture since 1889 who could also pitch and play third. Frank Ripley was in right most of the year.

In those days managers set a batting order and stuck with it. A man hit in the leadoff or fifth spot in the order just as he played center field or catcher. The Corsicana order throughout most of 1902 was: Maloney, leadoff; Alexander; Ripley; Pendleton; Markley; O'Connor; Clarke; Morris; and the pitcher. It proved to be a sensational combination.

Opening day in 1902 was April 26. Corsicana ripped the league to shreds, from June 8 through July 5, reeling off 27 consecutive victories. Thirteen of these games were on the road, although the June 15 contest against Texarkana was supposed to be a home game. Corsicana ordinances prohibited Sunday baseball, and the game was transferred to Ennis. The fences at the Ennis field were short, but Corsicana and Texarkana agreed beforehand that any ball hit out of the park would be a home run. C. B. DeWitt, one of the Texarkana owners, took the mound, but the powerhouse Oilers scored six runs in the first inning and turned the game into a rout. The Oilers battered DeWitt for 53 hits, including 16 home runs, and won, 51-3.

There were many hitting standouts in this landmark game, but perfection was reached by catcher Nig Clarke, who came to the

plate eight times and hit eight roundtrippers. Clarke's eight home
runs in a single game set an all-time record for professional baseball. Big Mike O'Connor hit three home runs and went seven for
eight. Two other Oilers besides Clarke went eight for eight, another
was six for eight, and still another was six for seven. Every man hit
safely, and the Oilers stranded just five base runners. Corsicana's
defense did not commit an error and clicked off four double plays.
The 51 runs and 53 hits, Clarke's eight home runs, eight runs
scored, 16 RBIs — these and other marks all are records which still
stand.

During the 27-game winning streak (another all-time record
which the New York Giants matched in 1916), Corsicana outscored
its opponents 287-77, recorded six shutouts, and won five games by
one run. The lineup and batting order went virtually unchanged
during the streak, and Lucky Wright (10 victories, one shutout),
Belmont Method (nine victories, three shutouts), and Bob White
(eight victories, two shutouts) did all of the pitching. On Sunday,
July 6, the Oilers were scheduled to host Waco, but because of Corsicana's blue laws the game was moved to Waco. Lucky Wright
was defeated 3-1 by Dad Ahorn, bringing the incredible streak to a
close.

Corsicana's record was a sizzling 58-9 by July 8. The league
declared a split season to rejuvenate fan interest, but Corsicana
continued to lead the field. Late in July, however, Walter Morris,
Bob White, and George Markley clashed with management and
bolted the club to play independent ball. Hunter Hill, an aggressive, hot-tempered infielder who was a deadly bunter, filled in well,
but the Oilers were not as dominant after their original combination was broken up. The league voted to end play on August 1, a
week ahead of schedule. Corsicana led with a 30-14 mark, and since
the Oilers won both halves, no playoff was necessary. Their complete record was 88-23, for an unequaled .793 season winning percentage, and their first half .866 percentage also still stands un-
matched by any league club in a split season.

Big Mike O'Connor returned as manager in 1903, but Lucky
Wright, Curley Maloney, and Hunter Hill were his only holdover
regulars. W. L. Miller handled the catching chores for the next
three seasons, spelled in 1903 by W. A. "Heavy" Blair, who would
move up to the American League in 1907. O'Connor's best pitchers

in 1903 were Wright and Con Lucid, a 34-year-old Irishman who had spent five seasons in the National League during the 1890s. Bert Hise, who had seen some mound duty in 1902, returned to the pitching staff, and Ike Pendleton moved from left field to second base for the 1903 season. Tony Thebo, a small, speedy Frenchman, was installed in center field, and proved to be a standout in 1903 and 1904. He was an excellent leadoff man and base stealer, a picturesque performer who was popular with Texas League fans. Prince Ben Shelton, a splendid hitter and 10-year-Texas Leaguer who had played a few games for the Oilers in 1902, also was aboard for 1903 and 1904.

Not surprisingly, Corsicana was down in 1903, dropping to last place in a four-team league during the first half. On May 14 Lucky Wright gave up nine home runs — including four to Clyde Bateman — in a 13-7 loss to Paris, but by the next afternoon the left field fence had been moved back to a more hospitable distance. The Oilers rallied during the second half, finishing in second place and claiming first. It seemed that first-place Dallas had hired outfielder Charlie Barrett, but J. Doak Roberts persuaded the league office that the Oilers had a prior claim on his services and that Dallas should forfeit several games to Corsicana. These forfeits would have put Corsicana in first place for the second half. But Dallas and Waco went ahead with a planned playoff series, and Corsicana's claim to playoff status, in the haphazard manner of the day, was ignored. Corsicana finished 1903 with a composite 54-54 record.

In 1904 Roberts organized a triple partnership with Curley Maloney, who would serve as player-manager, and Prince Ben Shelton, who would double as business manager off the diamond. Big Mike O'Connor moved to Paris as player-manager, but Shelton was a superb first baseman. Mickey Coyle, on the roster for a time in 1903, was a wiry, hustling infielder and a colorful crowd-pleaser. Belmont Method, a mound stalwart from 1902, was back, and the outfield was outstanding with Tony Thebo, Curley Maloney, and Trapper Longley, who hit .372 in Corsicana's first 70 games to cop the Texas League batting title.

The 1904 Texas League again was a four-team loop, and Corsicana led through the first two months of the season. On June 26, with the Oilers enjoying a 32-20 record, the season was split. Roberts, who had become president of the Texas League early in the

season, and his partners found themselves losing money despite the
Oilers' winning performance. They sold out at mid-season to a
local stock company headed by C. H. Mills.

During the second half the Oilers faltered, especially after
Tony Thebo and Trapper Longley were lured by higher salaries to
Beaumont of the South Texas League. First baseman Prince Ben
Shelton went to the South Texas League's Austin club, although
burly Walter Salmburger proved a hard-hitting replacement. On
August 1 Curley Maloney was traded to Paris, and Salmburger
(who shortened his name to Salm for the benefit of box scores) took
over as manager. During one roster shuffle no one was available for
mound duty. Jack Bankhead, a bank clerk who had pitched only
amateur ball, was summoned to the Oil City Park — and he responded with a shutout in his sole professional game! Tom Huddleston, a regular member of the mound corps, twirled a no-hitter
for the pitching gem of the season.

Despite a third-place record in the second half, their first-half
finish placed Corsicana in a marathon 19-game playoff with Fort
Worth. With the Oiler roster sadly depleted of the stars who had
opened the season, Corsicana recruited actively for the playoffs.
They hired Harry Ables, pitching ace at Southwestern University
in Georgetown, and they brought Curley Maloney back as a
pitcher for the postseason. Branch Rickey (then in the rookie season of a distinguished career in professional baseball) and Charlie
Moran (later the football and baseball coach at Texas A&M) were
acquired from Dallas to handle catching chores for the series. Indeed, so many Dallas team members were hired that Dallas newspapers urged their readers to root for Corsicana.

The first five games of the series were played in Corsicana, but
the remaining contests were split between Fort Worth (eight) and
Dallas (six). The Oilers won 11 of the 19 games, securing their second Texas League pennant.

In 1905 the veteran pitcher Con Lucid returned to Corsicana
as player-manager. Most members of the championship clubs had
moved up to a higher circuit or had been hired away by rival Texas
League cities. Otto McIver, a fine hitter and baserunner, was the
class of the outfield, while Bruno Block, whose real name was John
Blochowicz and who went up to the American League in 1907, was
an excellent catcher. The rest of the cast was weak, however, and

the Oilers were the poorest of the six teams in 1905. Con Lucid was replaced as manager by a pitcher-outfielder named Mahaffey. On June 6 Mills gave up on a losing proposition, turning the franchise back to the Texas League. The league tried to continue operations, but after a week the 9-29, last-place club was disbanded.

With two Texas League pennants and records that would never be surpassed to their credit, the Oilers reappeared in several professional loops. Corsicana was part of the short-lived North Texas League in 1906, then the Central Texas Trolley League in 1914 and 1915 and the Central Texas League in 1917. The Oilers joined the Texas-Oklahoma League in 1922, the Texas Association, 1923–1926, and the Lone Star League, 1927–1928. Old-timers may recall Jimmy Andrews, star pitcher of the 1920s who went up to Dallas of the Texas League, and the brick Cotton Oil Mill building beyond the right field fence, where a sign on an upper story window read: "Any player who hits a home run through this window wins $25." The last team to play at the historic old ball park was the Corsicana High Tigers of 1958, coached by Jess Cummings (who had a brief stint with the Fort Worth Cats in 1938) to a second-place finish in the state playoffs.

Year	Record	Pcg.	Finish
1902	88-23	.793	First — pennant
1903	54-54	.500	Second
1904	50-51	.495	Third — pennant (defeated FW 11 games to 8) FW 11 games to 8)
1905	9-29	.370	Sixth — X
Composite	212-165	.562	Two pennants (1902 and 1904)

Dallas (Hams, Giants, Submarines, Steers, Rebels, Eagles, Spurs)

The Dallas Hams won the first Texas League pennant in 1888; the nickname did not last for long, but Dallas fielded a team for 69 seasons in the circuit. The Hams played at Oak Cliff Park across the Trinity River from downtown. Later Dallas teams played at

Gaston Park on the State Fair Grounds, about where the Music Hall is today.

When Ted Sullivan revived the Texas League in 1895, he operated the Dallas club. "Sullivan's Steers" hit .305 as a team, won the first half of the schedule, and finished with the best record in the league, but dropped a disputed 13-game playoff with archrival Fort Worth. Dallas led the league in 1898, but the season was halted after just a few weeks of play because of the Spanish-American War, and no pennant was awarded.

Dallas spent the 1899 season in the old Southern League, but rejoined the Texas League when it was reorganized in 1902 after two years of inactivity. The team president was Ernest Bohne, who ran a saloon. The saloon doubled as club "office," and players went there to collect their pay — and sometimes to spend it on Bohne's liquid wares.

In 1903, behind batting champ Harry Clark (.326) and stolen base leader Lon Ury (46 — he repeated the next year with 56), Dallas again finished first and defeated Waco in a 10-game playoff for the flag. Joe Gardner, who had actually operated the 1902 club, was president by 1903 — a position he held through the 1916 season. In 1903 and 1904 Gardner's manager was future Texas A&M football coach Charles Moran, and for the next seven years James J. "Curley" Maloney was player-manager.

In 1919 Gardner moved his Giants from Gaston Park to a new diamond at West Jefferson and Comal in Oak Cliff on the West Side of the Trinity River. Joe Gardner Park adjoined the first ice rink in the South (also owned by Gardner), and streetcar barns were nearby. Out-of-town fans (including the author's father and grandfather) could ride an interurban to a station across the river from the park, then take a streetcar to within walking distance of the stadium. Gardner sold the team after the 1916 season.

Joe Gardner Park burned immediately following a doubleheader with Wichita Falls on July 19, 1924. Riverside, home of black baseball in Dallas, was donated for the next day's game, then the Steers finished their home schedule at the vast State Fair horse-racing arena. The first game staged there was on August 3, against the hated Fort Worth Panthers. The official paid admissions totaled 16,484, which stood as the Texas League attendance record for more than a quarter of a century. Joe Gardner Park was rebuilt across the street and renamed Steer Stadium, a facility seating 8,000 which was destroyed by fire shortly after the close of the 1940 season.

In 1903 the Dallas Giants (John J. McGraw and his New York Giants had deeply impressed Dallas in exhibition appearances) were declared co-champions by a controversial ruling. The Dallas Submarines won back-to-back pennants in 1917 and 1918. Snipe Conley, popular star of the Submarines, led the league in strikeouts and victories in 1917 — his 27 wins included 19 in a row, and a no-hitter over Fort Worth. The right-handed spitballer was a superb fielder and was the control leader for five consecutive seasons. Snipe pitched for Dallas from 1916 through 1927, and he was the manager in 1926 and 1927, winning a flag in 1926. In 1941 Snipe came back as a gate attraction and pitched two games for Dallas.

The Steers won the first half in 1929 and defeated Wichita Falls for another pennant. The Shaughnessy system brought play-off championships in 1941, 1946, and 1953. Dallas teams finished first but lost out in the playoffs in 1936, 1952, 1955, and 1957. Randy Moore was the 1929 batting champ (.369), while first baseman Zeke Bonura was a hitting star in 1932 (.322 with 21 homers and 110 RBIs) and 1933 (.357 with 24 homers and a league-leading 111 RBIs). Other Dallas batting champs were Les Mallon (.344 in 1936), Grey Clarke (.361 in 1941), and veterans Les Fleming (.358 in 1954) and Eddie Knoblauch (.327 in 1955). Jerry Witte pounded 50 home runs in 1949, and Buzz Clarkson led the league with 42 in 1954. Dallas's best pitching combination was the 1955 duo, Red Murff (27-11 and a league-leading 1.99 ERA) and southpaw fast-baller Pete Burnside (18-11 with a league-leading 235 strikeouts). Murff's 27 wins represent the highest total in the second half-century of the Texas League's existence.

In 1949 Dallas fans saw Pete Gray, the remarkable one-armed outfielder who had starred in the Southern Association and played for the St. Louis Browns in 1945. But for the Eagles, Gray hit just .214 in 45 games, and he retired as an active player. Another star was Miss Inez (Inez Peddlie), the lovely organist who became a fixture at Dallas games for 15 years, playing every request with artistry, and convincing generations of fans that no seventh-inning stretch could ever be the same without her melodies. Dick Burnett engaged Miss Inez in 1949; an innovative musician, she became the

Texas League's first organist, and she was so popular that organs soon were installed at other parks around the circuit.

George and Julius Schepps bought into the club in 1922, and in 1938 George purchased a controlling interest, 84 percent of the stock, for $150,000. Schepps rechristened his team the Rebels. A decade later, Schepps sold the Rebels to East Texas oilman Dick Burnett for $550,000 — the largest total ever paid at the time for a minor league club. Burnett, a baseball enthusiast who had owned smaller franchises in East Texas, changed the name of the team to the Eagles and the name of the 10,500-seat stadium to Burnett Field. The free-spending but competitive Burnett rejoiced in his team's triumphs and despaired at defeats, once hurling a typewriter from the press box to the diamond after a particularly excruciating loss. In 1950 Burnett established a minor league attendance record by attracting more than 53,000 fans to the Cotton Bowl with an opening day extravaganza that featured an All-Star team of Dizzy Dean, Ty Cobb, Home Run Baker, Tris Speaker, and other baseball greats. Burnett broke the Texas League color line in 1952, signing righthander Dave Hoskins, who responded with a 22-10 record and a 2.12 ERA, leading the league in victories and 26 complete games in 33 starts. When Burnett suffered a fatal heart attack in 1957 the Texas League lost one of the most flamboyant and innovative independent owners in circuit history.

Burnett had pushed Dallas as a major league site as early as 1948. This enthusiasm was shared by new owners J. W. Bateson and Amon Carter, Jr. In 1959 they moved Dallas up to the Class AAA American Association, and the next year Dallas and Fort Worth combined resources (splitting the home schedule between their respective parks) for an American Association twin-cities franchise. Hopes for a club in the proposed Continental League collapsed when American League expansion killed the new circuit before it came into existence. After three seasons, the American Association disbanded and Dallas-Fort Worth transferred to the Pacific Coast League.

Fort Worth businessman Tommy Mercer bought the DFW franchise, intending to keep Dallas in the PCL and return the Fort Worth Cats to the Texas League, all the while angling for major league status. By 1965 Turnpike Stadium — seating just 10,000 in its initial phase — was completed in Arlington, and the Dallas-Fort

The Dallas Eagles of 1952 romp off the diamond after clinching first place.
— Courtesy Dallas Public Library

Worth Spurs reentered the Texas League. In six seasons there were only two winning teams, but the franchise drew well, and the Texas League All-Star Game was held at Turnpike Stadium in 1966, 1967, and 1968. In 1971 the Spurs participated in the Dixie Association, attracting over 16,000 fans for one July game at Turnpike Stadium. After the close of the season the sale of the Washington Senators to Dallas-Fort Worth was announced, and in 1972 the Texas Rangers at last brought major league baseball to the Dallas area.

Year	Record	Pcg.	Finish
1888	55-27	.671	First — pennant
1889	49-42	.538	Second
1890	22-18	.551	Second
1892	23-30	.434	Fourth
1895	82-33	.713	First — lost playoffs
1896	25-69	.269	Eighth
1897	51-73	.411	Seventh

A crowd at Union Station in Dallas ready to welcome home the first-place Eagles at the end of the 1952 regular season.
— Courtesy Dallas Public Library

1898	13-7	.650	First — but no pennant awarded
1902	60-53	.531	Second
1903	61-47	.565	First — won playoffs
1904	57-46	.553	Second
1905	65-64	.504	Third
1906	80-49	.621	Second
1907	84-55	.604	Second
1908	90-55	.620	Second
1909	75-64	.540	Fourth
1910	83-57	.598	First — co-champs
1911	77-69	.528	Fourth
1912	73-67	.522	Fourth
1913	92-61	.601	Second
1914	67-83	.447	Sixth
1915	73-75	.493	Fifth
1916	61-84	.421	Eighth
1917	96-64	.600	First — pennant
1918	52-37	.584	First — pennant
1919	75-73	.507	Fifth
1920	63-85	.426	Sixth
1921	81-78	.508	Fourth
1922	82-74	.525	Third
1923	78-70	.527	Third
1924	75-79	.487	Sixth
1925	85-36	.563	Third — lost playoff

1926	89-66	.574	First — pennant
1927	74-80	.481	Fifth
1928	66-93	.415	Seventh
1929	91-69	.569	Third — won playoff
1930	58-93	.384	Eighth
1931	83-77	.519	Fourth
1932	98-53	.648	Second — lost playoff
1933	82-70	.539	Third — lost playoff opener
1934	80-73	.523	Fourth — lost playoff opener
1935	71-88	.447	Seventh
1936	93-61	.604	First — won opener, lost finals
1937	55-106	.342	Eighth
1938	65-94	.409	Seventh
1939	89-72	.553	Second — won opener, lost finals
1940	75-83	.475	Sixth
1941	80-74	.519	Fourth — won opener and finals
1942	48-104	.314	Eighth
1946	91-63	.591	Second — won opener and finals
1947	79-74	.516	Third
1948	64-89	.418	Seventh
1949	76-77	.497	Fifth
1950	74-78	.487	Fifth
1951	85-75	.531	Third — lost opener
1952	92-69	.571	First — lost opener
1953	88-66	.571	First — won opener and finals
1954	64-97	.398	Eighth
1955	93-67	.581	First — lost opener
1956	94-60	.610	Second — won opener, lost finals
1957	102-52	.662	First — won opener, lost finals
1958	76-77	.497	Fifth
1965	80-61	.567	Second
1966	59-81	.421	Sixth
1967	62-78	.443	Sixth
1968	60-79	.432	Fourth
1969	75-58	.571	Second
1970	63-73	.463	Third

Denison (Tigers)

Denison's first professional baseball club was sponsored by a local stock company headed by Major L. L. Maugh. He obtained one of eight franchises in the 1896 Texas League. There was continual personnel turnover, which permitted such noted Texas Leaguers as Big Mike O'Connor, Dit Spencer, Wirt Spencer, and Cy Mulkey to don a Denison uniform for part of the season, but the team never had a chance to jell. In early August Denison, with a 41-51 mark, became one of four teams to disband while the season was in progress.

The next year baseball enthusiasts from Denison and Sherman decided that a twin-cities franchise would work, with home games being split between the two communities. As the 1897 season progressed, however, manager Pete Weckbecker decided that it was preferable to play most of his home games in the Denison ball park, which understandably irritated Sherman boosters. Infielder Pierce "No Use" Chiles replaced Weckbecker as manager, but even though the Twin Cities Tigers won more than they lost, the club disbanded in July. Chiles led the players to Waco for the rest of the season, and Denison would not have professional ball for another five years.

When the Texas League reorganized in 1902, Cy Mulkey was practicing law in Denison. Still fascinated with baseball (he ultimately played for 11 Texas League clubs in 12 cities, a league record), Mulkey resurrected the twin-cities concept of 1897. Mulkey acted as club president, managed the team, and took a regular turn on the mound. But Sherman-Denison staggered to a 1-10 record in the first 11 days of the season, whereupon Mulkey promptly packed his team off to Texarkana.

A decade passed before Denison again enjoyed professional baseball. Beginning in 1912 there were Twin Cities franchises in various years in the Texas-Oklahoma League, Western Association, Texas Association, East Texas League, and Big State League. Home site differences were resolved by building Twins' Park between the two cities. The Twins won a Texas Association flag in 1923 and a Big State League pennant in 1948, and there were memorable seasons after World War II. Following the 1952 season in the Class D Center State League, Denison and Sherman gave up minor league baseball, and four years later Twins' Park was flattened by a tornado.

Year	Record	Pcg.	Finish
1896	41-51	.446	Sixth
1897	44-41	.518	Fourth
1898	1-10	.091	Dropped out

El Paso (Sun Kings, Diablos)

In 1884 baseball kranks in El Paso crowded into the grand-stand at the end of the San Antonio Street car line and watched the newly organized Browns take on their first outside opposition, a team from Fort Bliss. The El Paso Browns won, 18-17, and more than a century later, El Paso baseball games still are being decided by inflated scores.

A great deal of baseball was played in El Paso in the fall and winter because of the favorable climate. Many professional teams came through town after the regular season, but in 1915 El Pasoans finally saw their own team play in the Class D Rio Grande League — organized by none other than Honest John McCloskey, founder of the Texas League. A few years later, El Paso participated in the Copper League, an "outlaw" circuit in which the discredited first baseman Hal Chase and several members of the infamous Chicago Black Sox participated. Most of this baseball was played in Rio Grande Park, but in 1924 an adobe grandstand was built around a diamond that soon would be christened Dudley Field. Mayor Tom Dudley saw just one or two semi-pro games before his death, but the expanded "Dudley Dome" still is the home of organized base-ball in El Paso.

In 1930 an El Paso club entered the Arizona State League, and after the season the circuit reorganized into the Arizona-Texas League. El Paso played in this league in 1931–1932, 1937–1941 (there were championships in 1931, 1938, and 1940), 1947–1950, and 1952–1954. After World War II the circuit was elevated to Class C status, and El Paso spent the 1951 season in the Class C Southwest International League. In 1955 El Paso played in the West Texas-New Mexico League, then moved up to Class B with two years in the Southwestern League. By this time the minors were drying up, but El Paso found a berth in the Class D Sopho-more League in 1961.

The following season El Paso's Sun Kings joined the Texas League. El Paso was an immediate success in Class AA, drawing over 148,000 fans and driving to first place behind an explosive of-fense that would become typical of the franchise. The Sun Kings

led the league in batting (.310 — the next closest team, Albuquerque, hit .287), walloped 183 homers in 141 games, and produced
four of the top five hitters: batting champ Charlie Dees (.348),
Jesus Alou (.343), RBI champ Charles Peterson (.335 with 29 homers and 130 RBIs), and Felix Maldonado (.326), as well as home
run champ Gerald Robinson (.289 with 36 homers and 125 RBIs).
The Sun Kings lost a five-game series to Austin in the playoff
opener, but El Paso had witnessed the best baseball in its history.

The Sun Kings dropped to fourth the next year and again were
beaten in the opening round of playoffs. But once more El Paso led
the league in team hitting, blasted 207 home runs, and produced
batting champ Richard Deitz (.354 with 35 homers and 101 RBIs)
and home run/RBI king Arlo Engel (.320 with 41 homers and 126
RBIs), not to speak of future big league star Jose Cardenal (.312
with 36 homers and 95 RBIs).

The next four seasons were not as exciting. In 1964 a mediocre
club again finished fourth and for the second consecutive year lost
to San Antonio in the playoff opener. El Paso did not make the
playoffs the next three seasons, and attendance fell sharply. In
1968, with the Texas League reorganized as an eight-team, two-di-
vision alignment, El Paso won the Western Division. Chuck Tanner was the manager of a powerful club that pounded out 155 home
runs — 50 more than the second best total. The Sun Kings beat
Eastern Division champ Arkansas, to win their first playoff title.

But El Paso failed to make the playoffs in 1969 and 1970. Although Johnny Rivers won the batting title in 1970 (.343), only
37,000 fans came to Dudley Field, and El Paso dropped out of the
league. The Texas League could not find an eighth club for 1971
and entered into the Dixie Association with the Southern League.
In 1972 El Paso agreed to resurrect the Sun Kings, and enjoyed an
excellent season. The team led the league in batting, but hit just 63
home runs to finish last in that category. But the Sun Kings won
the Western Division and swept the playoff with Alexandria, adding to El Paso's growing collection of Texas League titles.

Attendance improved to 108,000, but dropped to 63,000 the
next year as the club failed to make the playoffs, despite another
team batting championship (Morris Nettles hit .332 to capture one
more hitting title for El Paso). Debts mounted as attendance fell.
An electrifying reversal commenced in 1973, however, as Jim Paul

The adobe-based center grandstand at El Paso's "Dudley Dome" was built in 1924. The Diablos' third-base dugout is plainly marked.

— Photo by Faye O'Neal

took over the club. A native of El Paso with no background in professional baseball, Paul changed the name of the team to Diablos and soon proved himself to be a promotional genius. The Dudley Dome, expanded and brightly painted, rapidly became as lively as a circus. Diablo baseball soon was the best show in town, and fans crowded into the old stadium in unprecedented numbers. By 1977 attendance exceeded 217,000, and in 1982 total paid admissions soared over the 326,000 mark.

In addition to Paul's endless stream of promotions and crowd-pleasing activities (described in the chapter on the 1970s), the Diablos played a high-scoring, exciting brand of ball. The 1975 team led the league in batting (.305) and boasted the top three hitters — Dave Collins (.352), Gerald Remy (.338), and Ronnie Jackson (.328). The Diablos won the Western Division, but lost the playoffs to Victoria. The 1975 Diablos had a losing season, but record numbers of fans watched batting champ Francis Alberts (.342) and another high-scoring offense. Although the 1976 club failed to make the playoffs, it was a better team, led by yet another hitting champ, Fred Frazier (.363) and the league's most victorious pitchers, southpaw Bob Nolan (15-3) and righthander John Caneira (15-4).

In 1977 the Diablos won their sixth straight batting title (.310), as Tommy Smith blistered the ball at a league-leading .366 clip. El Paso was victorious in the West in both halves of a split season and posted the best composite record in the league, but lost in the playoffs to Eastern Division winner Arkansas. The next year El Paso repeated as Western Division champ in both halves and again rang up the league's best record and team hitting crown. The 1978 batting titlist was Danny Goodwin (.360), while slugger Bob Clark (.316 with 31 homers and 111 RBIs) led the circuit in home runs and RBIs. Manager Moose Stubing guided a three-game sweep over Jackson and El Paso's first outright championship.

The next three Diablo clubs had losing records and failed to make the playoffs, but attendance totals remained well above the 200,000 mark. The 1980 batting champ was left-handed first baseman Daryl Sconiers (.370), but in 1982 third sacker Randy Ready (.375) rang up the Texas League's highest batting average since Ox Eckhardt (.379) in 1930. Ready, Steven Michael (.345), and Dion James (.322) led the Diablos into the playoffs with the best record in the league. El Paso beat Midland in the opening round, but lost to Tulsa in the finals.

The Diablos again posted the season's best mark in 1983, hitting .314 and averaging more than seven runs per game (of course, the pitching staff allowed over six earned runs per game, finishing last, as usual). The hitting race was tight, between Diablos Earnest Riles (.349) and Carlos Ponce (.348). This potent club lost the opening playoff round to Beaumont, but attendance was more than 4,000 per game, the envy of most Class AAA franchises.

The next year was an off season, but the Diablos roared back in 1985 and 1986. El Paso won both halves of the schedule in both years, led in team hitting each season, and produced batting champs Billy Joe Robidoux (.342 with 23 homers and a league-leading 132 RBIs) in 1985 and Steve Stanicek (.341) in 1986. The 1986 Diablos lost four straight to Jackson in the finals, but the next year provided a happier finish. All-Star first baseman Stanicek was backed by catcher Charlie O'Brien (.324) and outfielders Lavell Freeman (.322) and Alan Cartwright (.321), as well as pitchers

Dan Sarpetta (15-6) and Pete Kendrick (14-6). In the playoff series El Paso won four in a row from Jackson for another pennant.

El Paso has made the playoffs in half of the franchise's 24 years in the Texas League. An El Paso player has won the batting title in 11 of the 14 seasons since 1973, and during that period the Diablos posted the best team average 12 times. In 1986 Diablos management was elated over the award of the prestigious President's Trophy, presented to the top minor league franchise by the National Association. Even greater cause for elation was the passage of a six-million-dollar bond issue to construct a new ball park. The Diablos hope to open play in their new stadium in 1989, and there is also hope that a AAA franchise can be attracted to El Paso. But as the Texas League enters its 100th year, El Paso will be aiming for another hitting crown, another playoff berth, and, of course, another total of 250,000-300,000 laughing, screaming, stomping fans in the Dudley Dome.

Year	Record	Pcg.	Finish
1962	80-60	.571	First — lost playoff opener
1963	68-72	.486	Fourth — lost playoff opener
1964	67-73	.479	Fourth — lost playoff opener
1965	53-87	.379	Sixth
1966	62-78	.443	Fifth
1967	73-67	.521	Third
1968	77-60	.562	First — won Western Division, won playoff
1969	71-65	.523	Third
1970	77-59	.566	Second
1972	78-62	.557	First — won Western Division, won playoff
1973	69-71	.493	Second
1974	76-61	.555	First — won Western Division, lost playoff
1975	62-71	.466	Third
1976	77-56	.579	Second
1977	78-52	.600	First — won Western Division, lost playoff
1978	80-55	.593	First — won Western Division, won playoff
1979	61-75	.449	Third
1980	50-86	.368	Fourth
1981	65-69	.485	Third
1982	76-60	.559	First — won Western Division, lost finals
1983	74-62	.544	First — lost division playoff
1984	72-63	.533	Third
1985	86-50	.632	First — won Western Division, lost finals
1986	85-50	.630	First — won Western Division, won finals

Fort Worth
(Panthers, Cats)

A charter member of the Texas League, Fort Worth was destined to establish the greatest dynasty in loop history. Baseball was being played in Panther City by 1877 (a Dallas newspaper claimed that frontier Fort Worth's rowdy Main Street was "the noonday lair of the panther" — Fort Worth proudly began to call itself Panther City, and the professional baseball team would always be called "Panthers," or "Cats" for short). From 1888 until 1904, the Panthers played at a 1,200-seat ball park just south of the T&P station in an area known as the "Reservation."

The Panthers finished next-to-last in each of the first four Texas League campaigns. In 1895, however, Fort Worth placed second and entered a 15-game playoff with archrival Dallas. Al McFarland, with a 34-12 record and a hot bat, was the Panther leader, but the lineup was bolstered with stars from other teams for the playoffs. When the Panthers took a seven- to six-game lead with the playoffs scheduled to return to Fort Worth, Dallas conceded the championship.

In 1904, 1905, and 1906 the Panthers posted consecutive first-place finishes but realized only one pennant. The 1904 Panthers moved into new Haynes Park, located south of Lancaster (then Front Street) and seating 1,500. In 1904 the Panthers lost a long playoff series to Corsicana, which had liberally fortified its roster with Dallas standouts. Fort Worth took the 1905 flag outright, but the next season conceded the playoffs to a superb Cleburne club. In each of these years Fort Worth was paced by the Texas League's leading pitcher: Charles Jackson (26-8), Walt Chrisman (25 wins), and Alex Dupree (25 wins, tied with Cleburne's Rick Adams).

A dozen lackluster seasons followed, although the fans offered sufficient support to justify the construction of Panther Park, the Texas League's first steel and concrete ball park. It was located just west of North Main between North Sixth and North Seventh streets along the Cotton Belt Railroad. There were 4,000 seats in the grandstand, bleachers that would accommodate 600 more fans, and the first turnstiles, reserved seats, and rain checks in the Texas

League. In June 1915 Panther Park was damaged by a windstorm and floodwaters from the nearby Trinity River.

From 1910 to 1914 J. Walter Morris, who broke into the Texas League with Corsicana's spectacular 1902 club and who would serve as league president from 1916 to 1920, was owner of the Panthers. He also played and managed the team during part of his tenure, and was the only man to serve a twentieth-century Texas League franchise as player-manager-owner. In 1914 Morris had infielder Jake Atz manage the Panthers for part of the season. Atz (who was born John Jacob Zimmerman but who legally changed his name in 1900 after he stood last in a baseball team payline and watched the money run out) also managed for part of the next two years. In 1917 W. K. Stripling, Paul LaGrave, and others purchased the club; for the next decade Stripling as club president, LaGrave as business manager, and Atz as field manager constructed one of the most overpowering dynasties in all of baseball history.

In the first year of the Stripling-LaGrave-Atz triumverate, the Panthers finished second. For the 1918 season LaGrave acquired slugging first baseman Clarence Otto "Big Boy" Kraft, second sacker Dutch Hoffman, slick-fielding shortstop Bobby Stow, left fielder Ziggy Sears, and pitchers Joe Pate, Paul Wachtel, and Buzzer Bill Whitaker. Whitaker was a right-handed curveballer who won 24 games in 1919 and again in 1920, then 23 in 1921, while southpaw Pate and right-handed spitballer Wachtel formed the greatest one-two mound combination in Texas League history.

The 1919 Panthers finished first but lost to Shreveport in the last inning on the last play of the last game of a splendid seven-game playoff series. LaGrave then acquired a fine southpaw, curveballer Gus Johns (a 20-game winner in 1921, 1922, and 1925, the Texas League ERA leader in 1922 and 1925, and later a big leaguer), third baseman Dugan Phelan (a former big leaguer who proved to be a dangerous pinch hitter), and the ponderous but steady catcher, Possum Moore. ("He looked like a possum and he was always talking about eating possum," explained Vince De-Vaney, Panther batboy in the early 1920s and a pitcher for the Cats in 1928 and 1929.) LaGrave solidified his outfield in 1922 with Cuban Jacinto Calvo (a sensational fielder in center who hit .305 lifetime) and Stump Edington (a stocky, powerfully built left-

PATE AND WACHTEL TOGETHER AS PANTHERS

Year		G	W-L	IP	H	SO	BB	ERA
1918	Pate	7	2-2	46	40	20	17	3.13
	Wachtel	10	7-1	74	54	36	18	1.87
1919	Pate	23	15-4	176	119	74	62	1.68
	Wachtel	38	21-15	289	216	150	117	2.40
1920	Pate	41	26*8	314	258	125	52	1.71*
	Wachtel	38	26*10	308	280	110	86	2.43
1921	Pate	52*	30*9	333	329*	108	73	2.70
	Wachtel	44	23-12	317	290	124	102	1.97
1922	Pate	42	24-11	302*	293	107	53	2.70
	Wachtel	43	26*7	280	255	193	95	2.43
1923	Pate	46	23-15	328*	327	158	92	2.88
	Wachtel	40	19-12	257	253	121	108	3.42
1924	Pate	49	30*8	335*	328*	127	93	3.06
	Wachtel	38	22-10	289	258	125	119	2.88
1925	Pate	46	20-12	307*	289	106	59	3.51
	Wachtel	38	23*7	267	275	114	104	3.87

* League leader

Pate, a Texan from Alice, went up to Connie Mack's Philadelphia A's in 1926, making a 9-0 contribution to the American League club. But after an 0-3 start in 1927 he soon returned to Fort Worth, where he went 6-3, then 11-8 in 1928. When he retired after the 1932 season he was 257-134 as a minor leaguer, and he is the only pitcher to win 30 games twice in the Texas League. Wachtel remained in Fort Worth in 1926 (16-19), 1927 (17-14), and 1928 (16-14). He spent 1929 and 1930 with Houston, Dallas, and Waco, then retired with a career record of 317-221, all in the minors.

handed right fielder who hit .319 as a Texas Leaguer and who was one of the greatest leadoff men in loop history).

For the next six seasons, 1920–1925, these Panthers dominated the Texas League. Except for 1923 (95-56), Fort Worth won no fewer than 103 regularly scheduled games per season. In every year except 1923 — when the season was not split — the Panthers won both halves of the split season, thus capturing the Texas League pennant outright in each consecutive championship year.

The Panthers also captured the heart of Fort Worth, as fans reveled in the off-field antics of their heroes. Atz grumbled that his Cats could "drink any brewery dry at night and beat any baseball team the next afternoon." One afternoon southpaw Jimmy Walkup struck out Babe Ruth three times during an exhibition game with the New York Yankees. "I'll tell you one thing," growled the Babe as Fort Worth fans razzed him unmercifully, "I'm in the big leagues and he ain't." But Walkup was happy enough in Fort Worth. He liked to fill a drinking straw with gunpowder, twist it at one end, light the other, and watch his homemade missile take off. When Walkup ignited one of his explosive straws in the direction of a slumbering Possum Moore, the big catcher leaped from his bed stark naked, jammed his foot into a spittoon, and angrily chased Walkup through the hotel.

Another local favorite was Big Boy Kraft. "You always want to get your name in the paper," said Kraft. "If you're walking down the street and you haven't been getting enough publicity, hit someone in the nose." He was better at hitting baseballs, as his phenomenal totals from 1921 to 1924 prove:

Year	G	AB	R	H	2B	3B	H4	RBI	SB	AVG
1921	154	602*	132*	212*	47	12	31	141	18	.352*
1922	140	543	127	184	32	4	32*	131*	17	.339
1923	157	565	129	183	48	3	32	125	21	.324
1924	154	581*	150*	203	36	5	55*	196*	18	.349

* League leader

Following his record-setting 1924 season, the 37-year-old Kraft retired from baseball to purchase an auto dealership in Fort Worth. LaGrave, however, resourcefully filled Big Boy's place in the lineup by acquiring Big Ed Konetchy, who had spent 15 years in the National League. Big Ed batted .345, including 213 hits and a league-leading 41 homers and 166 RBIs.

In 1920, the first season of Fort Worth's six-year reign, the Dixie Series was organized between the champions of the Texas League and the Southern League. The Panthers beat Little Rock, then defeated Memphis in 1921. The next year Fort Worth lost to Mobile, but triumphed in the "minor league world series" the following three seasons. Amon Carter, publisher of the *Fort Worth Star Telegram,* chartered a special train dubbed the "Dixie Special" to take Panther fans to Dixie Series games held out of state. A 32-piece band was hired to enliven the Dixie Special in 1922, and Carter handed out big cow bells to create more racket. For those fans who had to stay in Fort Worth, since 1906 there had been telegraphed inning-by-inning results posted on street scoreboards, which resulted in large afternoon crowds during important out-of-town games. (Indeed, in 1922 WBAP provided the Texas League's first

play-by-play live broadcasts during a key series with Wichita Falls
at Panther Park.)

By 1926 there was a new Panther Park, built a couple of blocks
east of old Panther Park across North Main. One of the show places
of minor league baseball, it was designed to handle the throngs who
swarmed to Panther games, and eventually seated over 13,000. The
facility was renamed LaGrave Field after Paul LaGrave died in
1929.

When the Panthers moved into the new stadium, many members of the championship combination had won promotions to
higher leagues or had retired. In 1929 Jake Atz was replaced at
mid-season, but the next year the Panthers won the first half, beat
Wichita Falls three games to two to take the 1930 pennant, then
whipped Memphis in the Dixie Series.

Six disappointing years passed, but in 1937, behind the
league-leading bat of player-manager Homer Peel (.370), the third-
place Cats emerged from the playoff series to win another flag. The
customary Fort Worth magic prevailed in the Dixie Series as Little
Rock fell in five games. The Panthers dropped to last the next season, but in 1939 a fourth-place finish returned Fort Worth to the
playoffs. There were no outstanding hitters, but the pitching staff
boasted Bear Tracks Greer (22-11, a league-leading 2.29 ERA, and
30 complete games in 35 starts) and former big leaguers Firpo Marberry (13-9) and Raymond Starr (18-7 and soon to return to the
National League). After losing the first two playoff games to Houston, the Panthers took three straight, beat hated Dallas for the pennant, then won the Dixie Series from Nashville in seven games. But
again the Panthers nosedived to last following a pennant, and there
would be no more playoff appearances until after World War II.

Following the war, Fort Worth, now a member of the excellent
farm system organized by Branch Rickey for the Brooklyn Dodgers,
appeared in the playoffs for nine consecutive years. From 1946
through 1949 the Cats finished in first place three years out of four,
and the second-place standing of 1947 was by just half a game. In
1946 the Cats were 101-53, and in 1949 the record was 100-54, but
the 1948 club, although only 92-61 in the regular season, proved to
be the only postwar Fort Worth club to win a pennant. The pitching staff was excellent — Carl Erskine (15-7), Robert Austin (17-7),
Chris Van Cuyk (14-7) — and catcher Bobby Bragan provided tal-

ented leadership as player-manager, but the Cats lost to Birmingham in the Dixie Series.

Early the next season, on May 15, 1949, fire gutted the grandstand at LaGrave Field. Incredibly, makeshift arrangements allowed more than 4,000 fans to view the next day's game with San Antonio, as firemen continued to hose down the smoldering wreckage. Brooklyn toyed with abandoning Fort Worth, then decided to rebuild LaGrave Field. The park, completed during the 1950 season, was better than ever. There were 13,005 seats, and the 100-foot-long press box sported the first television booth in any new baseball park (WBAP-TV had initiated the first Texas League telecasts in 1949).

In 1957 Brooklyn President Walter O'Malley engineered a swap with the Chicago Cubs: the Fort Worth franchise for the Cubs' Wrigley Field in Los Angeles, where O'Malley soon would move his Dodgers. Fort Worth gave the Cubs a first-place finish in 1958, but lost four straight to Austin in the opening playoff round. The next year Fort Worth, Dallas, and Houston joined the American Association, but the next season the AAA circuit cut back from ten to eight teams, and Dallas and Fort Worth formed a joint franchise. In 1964 Fort Worth resurfaced as a separate entry in the struggling six-team Texas League ("The Cats Is Back" proclaimed an outfield fence ad), but the Cats finished last. Dallas-Fort Worth then competed as a Texas League franchise until 1972, when the Texas Rangers entered the American League.

Year	Record	Pcg.	Finish
1888	19-25	.432	Sixth
1889	45-51	.469	Fifth
1890	17-28	.378	Fifth
1892	21-33	.389	Fifth
1895	77-39	.664	Second — won playoff
1896	71-29	.710	First — but not in playoff
1897	60-60	.500	Fifth
1898	9-10	.474	Fifth
1902	48-62	.436	Third
1903	49-59	.454	Fourth
1904	71-31	.696	First — lost playoffs
1905	72-60	.545	First
1906	78-46	.629	First — conceded playoffs
1907	62-78	.443	Fifth
1908	68-74	.479	Fifth
1909	73-71	.507	Sixth

1910	75-63	.543	Fourth
1911	80-67	.548	Second
1912	59-81	.421	Seventh
1913	70-83	.458	Sixth
1914	71-77	.480	Fifth
1915	81-72	.530	Third
1916	71-76	.483	Fifth
1917	91-70	.565	Second
1918	47-39	.547	Second
1919	94-60	.610	First — lost playoff
1920	108-40	.730	First — pennant, won Dixie Series
1921	107-51	.677	First — pennant, won Dixie series
1922	109-46	.703	First — pennant, lost Dixie Series
1923	96-56	.632	First — pennant, won Dixie Series
1924	109-41	.727	First — pennant, won Dixie Series
1925	103-48	.682	First — pennant, won Dixie Series
1926	83-73	.532	Third
1927	77-79	.494	Fourth
1928	83-73	.532	Third
1929	84-76	.525	Fourth
1930	84-69	.549	Fourth — won playoff and Dixie Series
1931	90-70	.563	Third
1932	68-81	.457	Fourth
1933	63-88	.417	Seventh
1934	59-92	.391	Seventh
1935	64-95	.403	Eighth
1936	76-78	.494	Fifth
1937	85-74	.535	Third — won opener, finals, and Dixie Series
1938	61-99	.381	Eighth
1939	87-74	.540	Fourth — won opener, finals, and Dixie Series
1940	52-108	.325	Eighth
1941	78-76	.506	Fifth
1942	84-68	.559	Third — lost opener
1946	101-53	.565	First — won opener, lost finals
1947	95-58	.623	Second — lost opener
1948	92-61	.601	First — won opener and finals, lost Dixie Series
1949	100-54	.649	First — won opener, lost finals
1950	88-64	.579	Second — lost opener
1951	84-77	.522	Fifth — lost playoff for fourth
1952	86-75	.534	Second — lost playoff opener
1953	82-72	.532	Third — lost playoff opener
1954	81-80	.503	Fourth — won opener, lost finals
1955	77-84	.478	Sixth

1956	84-70	.545	Third — lost opener
1925	70-84	.455	Sixth
1925	89-64	.582	First — lost opener
1925	51-89	.364	Sixth

Galveston (Giants, Sandcrabs, Cubs, Buccaneers)

"Oh, pshaw! They have stolen our old game of town ball!"

Sporting fans of Galveston first witnessed baseball as played by Union occupation troops right after the Civil War, and they immediately recognized familiar qualities of the game. Baseball was firmly established in Galveston by amateur teams: Major Burbank's Artillery, Turf Association, Galveston Stars, The News, Athletics, Drummers, Santa Fe, Athletics, Island Juniors, Bricklayers, Cornice Makers, Invincibles, Western Union, Young Joplins, and the Flyaways, a crack Negro team.

When the Texas League was organized, Galveston was the state's leading city and a key franchise. The early home of Galveston baseball was Beach Park, located on Tremont near the beach. A board fence was erected around the field, and grandstands were built — one 80 feet in length, the other 50 feet long — behind each foul line. Down the right field side a special grandstand was put up "especially for the ladies from which they may view the game without being annoyed by the noisy crowd," and on April 11, 1888, a ladies' day was inaugurated — free admission every Wednesday. "Houlahan's tally board" was located on the right field fence, posting scores of all Texas League games, thanks to the telegraph wire at the scorer's table (several dives in town also had wires, for the benefit of gamblers).

Galveston finished fourth in 1888 and 1889, repeatedly turning down a $500 guarantee from the Flyaways, who were frantic to play the white professionals. In 1889 the Galveston Giants, togged out in maroon and blue uniforms, played the opening game of the season in Houston, accompanied by 600 fans who paid $1.50 each to ride an excursion train. Although Houston "downed the Galveston Giants with apparent ease," a bitter rivalry between the two cities had already developed which stimulated attendance and betting activity. In 1890, behind hard-hitting player-manager "Farmer" Works, the Galveston Sandcrabs won the pennant in a shortened season. The next three Sandcrab teams — in 1892, 1895, and 1897 — finished third. The 1895 club was the best, winning 16 games in a row and being paced by pitcher-outfielder George Bristow, who won 16 straight victories in a splendid 30-16 season, 22-game winner Piggy Page, and Will Blakey, who stole an all-time record 116 bases.

In 1897 and 1899 the Sandcrabs won pennants. Outfielder Kid Nance won the 1897 batting title with a .393 average, while infielder Pop Weikart hit .385 the same year. Team president George Dermody also served as Texas League president in 1899. After a lapse of four years, Galveston resumed professional ball with the South Texas League from 1903 through 1906. The Sandcrabs won the second half of the 1903 season, but dropped a long playoff series to San Antonio. The next year Galveston again won the second half, but Sandcrab owner Marsene Johnson refused to participate in postseason play in Houston, where the first-half winners had an unfenced park. All games of the playoff were staged in Galveston, which probably gave the Sandcrabs the winning edge in a 4-3-3 series. In each of these seasons Galveston had the leading hitter and pitcher of the South Texas League: 1903 — outfielder-manager Ed Pleiss (.360) and Baldo Luitich (17-7); 1904 — first baseman-manager Prince Ben Shelton (.352) and John Reuthor (24-7). But in 1905 and 1906 the Sandcrabs suffered losing seasons, going through a record eight managers in 1905.

The 1907 seasons brought a merger of circuits and Galveston's return to the Texas League. But during the ensuing 18 years, Galveston fans enjoyed just four winning seasons. Rarely out of the second division, the Sandcrabs boasted one crowdpleaser in power pitcher Eugene Moore, Sr. (213 strikeouts in 1912, 240 in 1914, 238 in 1915). Fond of the sauce, during batting practice the muscular Moore would deliberately loft flies over the short (260 feet) right field fence of Gulfview Park. A longstanding rule required hitters to retrieve any balls sent over right, and Moore would happily stop by the adjacent Blue Goose Saloon.

Galveston dropped out of the Texas League on May 18, 1917,

while mired in last place, and did not return until 1919. In 1920 the team was last with a miserable 49-100 record. A change of name to the Cubs brought no change of luck, although in 1923 Roy Oster-gaard (.328 with 25 homers) walloped a record six grand-slam home runs. Ostergaard had suffered a broken shoulder and could not make the throw from third base, but Galveston manager Pat Newnam decided he could play first successfully. Galveston owner Nelson Leopold picked up Ostergaard from the White Sox for $500 as damaged goods, then sold him back to the Chicago organization for $15,000 after the 1923 season. But shrewd deals could not offset poor attendance, and following seventh-place finishes in 1923 and 1924, the Galveston franchise was sold for $22,500 to the Texas League, which found a home for the Cubs in Waco.

Six years later, Shearn Moody brought Texas League ball back to Galveston by purchasing the Waco franchise, renaming his team the Buccaneers. Although Moody's Bucs were managed by former big league slugger Del Pratt, the 1931 team finished last with a dismal 57-104 mark, and the 1932 edition rose only to sixth place. But in 1933, under manager Billy Webb, the Bucs finished second behind the play of George Darrow (22-7), third baseman Buck Fausett (.324), and outfielders Wally Moses (.294), Tony Governor (.294) and Beau Bell (.293). In the Shaughnessy playoffs Galveston beat Dallas, three games to two, but lost in six games to San Antonio, despite a shutout by Darrow in the fourth game.

Darrow was gone in 1934, but the hard-hitting outfield and most of the rest of Webb's team returned, and Moody bought pitch-ing help. The Buccaneers squeaked into first place by a percentage point (.579 to .578) over San Antonio. Moses (.316) and Bell (.337) would go up to the American League the next year, and second baseman Charles English (.326) was voted the Most Valuable Player of 1934. In the playoff opener the Buccaneers again beat Dallas, then once more faced off against San Antonio in the finals. Over 9,200 fans crowded into Tech Field to see Galveston win the first game on the road. San Antonio evened the series the next night, but when play shifted to Moody Stadium Galveston took two in a row. Although the Missions won the fifth game, the Bucca-neers clinched an outright championship with a 9-8 triumph back at Tech Field. In their only Dixie Series appearance, Galveston lost to New Orleans in six games.

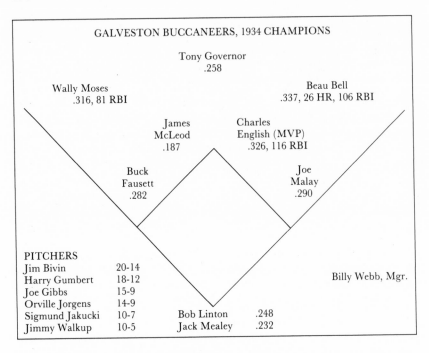

GALVESTON BUCCANEERS, 1934 CHAMPIONS

Tony Governor
.258

Wally Moses
.316, 81 RBI

Beau Bell
.337, 26 HR, 106 RBI

James
McLeod
.187

Charles
English (MVP)
.326, 116 RBI

Buck
Fausett
.282

Joe
Malay
.290

PITCHERS
Jim Bivin	20-14
Harry Gumbert	18-12
Joe Gibbs	15-9
Orville Jorgens	14-9
Sigmund Jakucki	10-7
Jimmy Walkup	10-5

Billy Webb, Mgr.

Bob Linton   .248
Jack Mealey   .232

Most of the 1933–1934 team was gone by 1935, but English (.304 with 104 RBIs) returned for another fine season. The best new players were Max Butcher (24-11 with seven shutouts and 30 complete games in 36 starts) and left fielder Joe Prerost (.316). On July 10 Eddie Cole (15-19) won a 1-0 decision over Tulsa with the Texas League's first perfect game. The Bucs made the playoffs for the third straight year with a third-place finish. Galveston won the first two playoff games in Moody Stadium over Beaumont, then dropped three in a row to the Exporters.

Shearn Moody died unexpectedly in 1936, and the Buccaneers sank to last place. Roy J. Koehler handled the club for Moody's estate, but he was badly injured in an accident, and after a sixth-place finish in 1937, the club was sold to Shreveport for $23,000. It was 13 years before Galveston returned to organized baseball, as the White Caps of the Class D Gulf Coast League. After four seasons Galveston moved up to the Class B Big State League, playing in 1954, then dropping out during the 1955 season.

Year	Record	Pcg.	Finish
1888	41-46	.471	Fourth
1889	50-48	.510	Fourth
1890	31-13	.705	First — pennant
1892	39-44	.470	Third
1895	72-47	.605	Third
1896	69-61	.530	Third
1897	72-44	.621	First — lost playoff
1898	16-17	.485	Fourth
1899	52-26	.667	First — pennant
1903	67-57	.540	Second — lost playoff
1904	82-43	.656	First — won playoff
1905	57-70	.449	Third
1906	58-68	.460	Fourth
1907	59-81	.421	Sixth
1908	59-86	.407	Seventh
1909	53-89	.373	Seventh
1910	64-75	.460	Sixth
1911	50-97	.340	Eighth
1912	59-79	.428	Sixth
1913	67-85	.441	Seventh
1914	86-63	.577	Fourth
1915	67-63	.515	Fourth
1916	73-68	.518	Third
1917	11-29	.275	Eighth — dropped out
1919	63-87	.420	Sixth
1920	49-100	.329	Eighth
1921	68-87	.439	Sixth
1922	79-76	.510	Fourth
1923	68-80	.459	Seventh
1924	61-93	.396	Seventh
1931	57-104	.354	Eighth
1932	67-86	.438	Sixth
1933	88-64	.579	Second — won opener, lost finals
1934	88-64	.579	First — won opener and finals, lost Dixie Series
1935	86-75	.534	Third — lost opener
1936	57-96	.373	Eighth
1937	73-86	.459	Sixth

Greenville (Hunters)

In 1906 Dallas, Fort Worth, Waco, Cleburne, and Temple fielded Texas League clubs, but a sixth team was needed to balance the schedule. Joseph W. Gardner, who had owned the Dallas franchise since 1903, discreetly provided the financing to place the sixth team in Greenville. Gardner's front man in Greenville was Arch "Pie" Bailey, who had begun umpiring Texas League games in 1895. Bailey was named club president, while the manager was Don Curtis, an outfielder who had played under Gardner in Dallas in 1903.

Gardner sent two players to Greenville with Curtis. Billy Doyle had been a Dallas pitcher-outfielder since 1903, while hard-hitting W. R. Jackson had played infield and pitched for Dallas in 1905. The mound staff was bolstered by Tom Huddleston, a mainstay of Corsicana's 1904 pennant winners. Baldy Louden and Heinie Maag, in their first Texas League season, proved themselves expert infielders. Twenty-one-year-old Otto McIver, who had managed Gardner's Dallas club in 1904, was a Greenville native and an understandably popular outfielder-first baseman. Pitcher-outfielder Sam Stovall was an excellent hitter, and catching chores were in the capable hands of Jimmy Stephens.

The Greenville Hunters were explosive. Their finest day came on Wednesday, June 11, when they pounded out 22 hits in a 15-1 victory over veteran pitcher Red Jarvis and an excellent Fort Worth team. But the Hunters were inconsistent, and when the season was split on June 30 Greenville stood fourth in the standings with a 30-30 record. Attendance had been poor, and Gardner decided to bail out. Fifth-place Temple, with a 20-44 mark, also was dropped by the league (Waco, in the cellar at 15-48, kept its franchise), and the second half was played by four clubs.

Billy Doyle, Sam Stovall, and Otto McIver were hired by talent-hungry Waco. Gardner, demonstrating a shrewd eye for talent, brought Jimmy Stephens, Heinie Maag, and Baldy Louden to Dallas — and all three players soon were sold to major league clubs. After a few more seasons as a player, Don Curtis became a Cardinal scout; his greatest coup was signing Dizzy Dean off a San Antonio semi-pro team.

The half season of 1906 proved to be Greenville's only venture in the Texas League, but local fans retained an interest in professional ball. Greenville placed teams in the Texas-Oklahoma League in 1912 and 1922, then participated for the next four seasons in the East Texas League. When minor league baseball reached a peak following World War II, the Greenville Majors joined the East Texas League in 1946, then switched to the Big State League for the 1947, 1948, 1950, and 1953 seasons. In 1947 over 161,000 fans jammed Majors Field, establishing a record for Class C attendance. Greenville's most famous baseballer was Monty Stratton, a pitching ace for the Chicago White Sox until he lost a leg in a hunting accident on his mother's farm near town. In 1946 he made a thrilling comeback, going 18-8 for Sherman of the East Texas League and inspiring a movie which starred James Stewart. Stratton lived on the Greenville farm until his death in 1982 at the age of 70.

Year	Record	Pcg.	Finish
1906	30-30	.500	Fourth — dropped out

Harlingen
(Rio Grande Valley
Giants)

The Pan-American Association was organized in 1959 by two six-team circuits, the Texas League and the Mexican League. This southerly orientation of the Texas League was accelerated by the addition of Harlingen's "Rio Grande Valley" franchise on the border.

Jim Humphries was president of the club. He had moved his team from Oklahoma City to Corpus Christi in 1958, but poor attendance caused him to seek a new home for his Giants. In 1960 he brought a few holdover players and manager Ray Murray, along with his San Francisco affiliation and Giants' nickname, to Harlingen. Murray, a big-league veteran and longtime Texas League catcher, had directed the Giants to a playoff title in 1958. From Corpus Christi he retained a future major league pitching great, Gaylord Perry, who had a disappointing record (9-13) but won the ERA (2.83) title. The mound staff was the best in the league: Murray's old batterymate from the Dallas Eagles, Tommy Bowers (13-8); ace reliever Ray Daviault (13-5 and 113 strikeouts in 111 innings); Ron Herbel (15-4); and Bob Bolin (10-4).

Chuck Hiller, a left-handed batter who soon would be San Francisco's second baseman, led the Texas League in hitting

(.334). Another future big leaguer, Manny Mota (.307), provided offensive help, along with Rafael Alomar (.294), Larry Stubing (.292), and Richard Pawlow (.291).

On April 29 the Valley Giants played San Antonio on the road before 820 fans in Mission Stadium. The game lasted five hours and 42 minutes — and a record 24 innings. The old mark, a 23-inning 1-1 deadlock in 1910 between San Antonio and Waco, had lasted half a century. The record-setting marathon was won by the Giants, 4-2.

Murray's well balanced Giants sailed through the regular schedule, finishing in first place, eight and a half games ahead of second-place San Antonio. But in the opening round of playoffs they were swept in three games by the Victoria Rosebuds.

Despite an excellent season, attendance ominously totaled just 75,291, and the highest turnout for one game was only 3,381 early in the season. Murray was still the manager in 1961, and the pitching was solid, but the only good hitters were lefthanders Jose Tartabull (.304) and Marion Talton (.292). The team did not do well on the field, fewer than 17,000 fans attended during the first two months of the season, and on June 10 the franchise was moved to Victoria. It was a turbulent season: Victoria's franchise had been shifted to Ardmore on May 27, and even though attendance remained low, the Giants finished the season in Victoria.

Harlingen first fielded professional teams in the Rio Grande Valley League (1931) and the Texas Valley League (1938). During the 1950s Harlingen played in the revived Rio Grande Valley League (1950), Gulf Coast League (1951–1953), and the Big State League (1954–1955). Harlingen's Suns provided the latest entry (1975–1976) in organized baseball, competing in the Lone Star League — a baseball enthusiasts' circuit that was the only league in the United States without major league affiliations. Fittingly for the baseball fans of Harlingen, the Valley Giants won a first-place title in their only full season of AA competition.

Year	Record	Pcg.	Finish
1960	85-59	.590	First — lost opener
1961	69-71	.493	Fifth — dropped out

Houston (Lambs, Red Stockings, Babies, Buffaloes, Moore's Marvels, Buffs)

On January 18, 1888, a meeting was held in Houston to finish plans for the "State Base Ball League," and for the next 70 years the Bayou City would be a mainstay of the Texas League. Initially, Houston Texas Leaguers were called "Lambs" or "Red Stockings"; in 1889 the team was known as "Babies"; and in 1905 the charges of catcher-manager Wade Moore were known as "Moore's Marvels." But Buffalo Bayou gave the Houston team the nickname that would prevail for seven decades with sportswriters and fans.

John McCloskey, father of the Texas League, roamed the outfield and managed Houston in 1889, 1890, and 1892. McCloskey's "Babies" won the pennant in 1889, and in 1892, following a year of no play, he put together another club which dominated the Texas League throughout the season. In 1896 Houston was led by 29-game winner John Roach and outfielder Rabbit Slagle, who hit .367, stole 86 bases and scored a record 171 runs in 130 games. Houston earned a playoff spot with Galveston, and the archrivals planned a 30-game postseason series to determine the championship. But the Buffaloes won the first five games, and after Galveston managed a doubleheader sweep, Houston was declared league champion.

Houston was a member of the South Texas League through the four years of the circuit's existence, finishing first the last two seasons. The 1905 champions ("Moore's Marvels") featured southpaw Eddie Karger (24-8) and 23-game winner Peaches Nelson, while the 1906 club — which had to forfeit the playoff series to Austin — boasted Nelson (18-8) and Prince Gaskill, who led the league with 19 victories.

In 1907 and 1908 Houston produced its only Texas League batting champions — future Hall of Famer Tris Speaker (.314) and outfielder-pitcher Bob Edmondson (.391). After the 1908 season, Otto Sens and Doak Roberts (Texas League president, 1904–1906 and 1921–1929) bought the club for $11,000; 11 years later they would sell out for more than $200,000. During their first season, the Buffaloes brought another Texas League pennant to Houston, led by veteran; outfielder-manager Hunter Hill, curveballer Harry Stewart (23-8), 21-game winner Charlie Rose, and 24-game winner Ivy Tevis. The next year Hill apparently won another flag, but a controversial decision to reverse four Buffalo victories resulted in a tainted championship for Dallas in 1910. In August 1911 Hill was fired during the season's final road trip, and six regulars supported the popular manager by refusing to play. But the owners quickly filled the roster, and after one day the "strike" was called off.

Houston began a three-year dynasty in 1912 with teams that stressed pitching, defense, bunting, hit-and-run, and base stealing. The Buffaloes won tight races in 1912 and 1913, but the 1914 season involved more disputed games, and Houston and Waco were declared co-champions. Catcher Sled Allen was with the club in each of these seasons, and so was outfielder Red Davis (65 stolen bases in 1914 to lead the league), pitcher Charlie Rose (21-11 in 1912, 26-7 in 1913, 24-9 in 1914), and speedy first baseman Pat Newnam, who doubled as manager in 1914. Rube Foster was 24-7 in 1912, and Andy Ware was 20-14 in 1913 and 26-8 in 1914.

A long pennant drouth ensued, and Sens and Roberts sold the club in 1919. At some obscure point during the next few years, the St. Louis Cardinals acquired majority interest in the Buffaloes for Branch Rickey's growing farm system. Although some stock remained locally owned, Houston became the first Texas League franchise to be controlled by a major league club. Independent owners objected defiantly to such control, and it was 1925 before the Cardinal acquisition was publicly admitted.

In 1928 Buffalo Stadium was erected on an 18-acre tract on St. Bernard Street (now Cullen Boulevard) beside the interurban tracks. Previously, the Buffs had played at an unfenced park and at centrally located West End Stadium, which seated just 4,000. Buffalo Stadium would seat 14,000, and land and construction costs totaled $400,000. Baseball Commissioner Kenesaw Mountain Landis attended the dedication ceremonies of the "finest minor league plant" in the United States. Buffalo Stadium opened in 1928 with a shutout over Waco by veteran righthander Ken Penner, and hosted a pennant-winner during its first season. Penner was 20-8, Frank

Barnes was 20-9, and Wild Bill Hallahan led the league with 23 victories and 244 strikeouts for a Buffalo team which won 104 games, defeated Wichita Falls in the playoffs, then downed the Birmingham Barons in the Dixie Series.

Buffalo Stadium immediately became known as a pitchers' park. The deep fences (344 feet in left, 434 in center, 323 in right, and 12 feet high) combined with high humidity and southeast winds which blew in from right field, discouraged home run sluggers and incited fine pitching performances. Dizzy Dean was 26-10 with a 1.53 ERA in 1931, Howie Pollett was 20-3 with a 1.16 ERA in 1941, and there was a host of other impressive pitching seasons. In 1953, after August Busch bought the St. Louis Cardinals, the park was renamed Busch Stadium (old-time fans stubbornly persisted in using the Buff Stadium label) and the fences were moved in 20 feet. "We hope to make the contest between pitcher and hitter more even with the move," it was announced, "and to provide a more interesting type of baseball for Houston fans."

Houston fans enjoyed many years of interesting ball before the dimensions were reduced. Fiery Pepper Martin led the league in stolen bases in 1927 (36) and 1929 (43). The irrepressible Dizzy Dean arrived in 1930, struck out 14 in his first game, then led a splendid club to the championship in 1931. During one four-day stretch in 1931 Dean won three games, and before he left Houston for St. Louis he married a local girl.

Outfielder Ducky Medwick hit .305 in 1931 and .354 in 1932. The Buffaloes finished first in 1933 behind Bear Tracks Greer (22-10), Mike Cvengros (21-11), and George Payne (19-11). There were three consecutive first-place finishes beginning in 1939, although only the 1940 club managed to win the playoffs. Howie Pollett was 20-7 in 1940, and Howie Krist was 22-9 with a league-leading 1.71 ERA. The 1940 Buffs won 105 regular season games, and the 1941 team won 103, behind Pollett (20-3), Freddie Martin (23-6), and Ted Wilks (20-10).

After World War II, the 1947 Buffs finished first, won the playoffs, and beat Mobile in the Dixie Series. As usual, there was excellent pitching: Clarence Beers (25-8) and Al Papai (21-10). The next first-place finish came in 1951, when the Buffs took the playoffs but lost the Dixie Series to Birmingham. Papai (23-9) led the league in victories, and Vinegar Bend Mizell was the strikeout

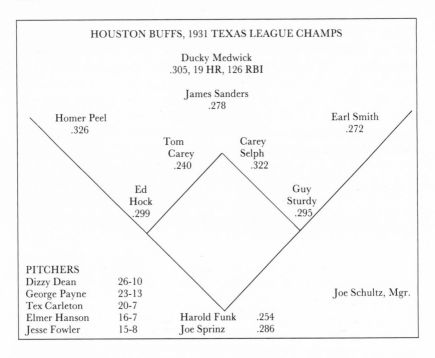

HOUSTON BUFFS, 1931 TEXAS LEAGUE CHAMPS

Ducky Medwick
.305, 19 HR, 126 RBI

James Sanders
.278

Homer Peel
.326

Earl Smith
.272

Tom
Carey
.240

Carey
Selph
.322

Ed
Hock
.299

Guy
Sturdy
.295

PITCHERS

Dizzy Dean	26-10
George Payne	23-13
Tex Carleton	20-7
Elmer Hanson	16-7
Jesse Fowler	15-8

Joe Schultz, Mgr.

| Harold Funk | .254 |
| Joe Sprinz | .286 |

leader (257). The next year Houston suffered the only last-place season during its long Texas League history. But the club rebounded to make the playoffs five years in a row, 1954 through 1958. The second-place Buffs won the 1954 playoffs, then battled seven games before losing the Dixie Series to Atlanta. The remarkable 1955 team had to win a playoff game 2-1 over Tulsa to take fourth place, then beat Dallas in the opening round and took Shreveport to the seventh game before bowing out. The 1956 Buffs finished first and won the playoffs, then beat Atlanta in the Dixie Series, 4-2. In 1957 the second-place Buffs won the playoffs, going seven games in each round, and for the second year in a row took the Dixie Series by beating Atlanta in six games. The 1958 second-place Buffs lost in the opening round, but in the 17 seasons since 1939 Houston had finished first six times, made the playoffs 11 times, and won six playoff titles and three Dixie Series.

Houston moved up to AAA in 1959, playing in the American Association through 1961. In 1962 the Houston Colt .45s entered the National League, playing at Colt Stadium, and two years later moved to the nearby Astrodome — the "eighth Wonder of the

World" (40,000 fans could wash their hands simultaneously without overloading the plumbing!) and the first domed stadium. Meanwhile, old Buff (Busch) Stadium had been sold in 1963 to Sammy Finger for $1 million. Buff Stadium brought $19,750 at auction and was demolished. The Gulf Freeway had replaced the old interurban line, while the vast Finger Furniture Center rose on the site of Buff Stadium. A plaque in the Center marks the spot once occupied by home plate.

Year	Record	Pcg.	Finish
1888	32-42	.432	Fifth
1889	54-44	.551	First — pennant
1890	23-23	.500	Fourth
1892	59-26	.694	First — pennant
1895	26-65	.286	Seventh
1896	81-49	.623	Second — won playoff
1897	60-54	.526	Third
1898	15-15	.500	Third
1899	34-41	.453	Third
1903	57-63	.475	Third
1904	64-61	.512	Third — lost playoff
1905	83-42	.664	First — pennant
1906	78-43	.645	First — forfeited playoff
1907	79-60	.568	Fourth
1908	77-67	.535	Third
1909	86-57	.601	First — pennant
1910	82-58	.598	Second
1911	71-74	.486	Sixth
1912	87-52	.626	First — pennant
1913	93-57	.620	First — pennant
1914	102-50	.670	First — co-champions
1915	68-74	.479	Sixth
1916	74-73	.503	Fourth
1917	77-88	.467	Fourth
1918	38-48	.442	Fifth
1919	87-77	.531	Fourth
1920	50-101	.331	Seventh
1921	92-67	.679	Second
1922	57-95	.375	Seventh
1923	74-75	.497	Fifth
1924	80-73	.523	Second
1925	87-56	.569	Second
1926	75-80	.484	Sixth
1927	85-70	.548	Third
1928	104-54	.658	First — won playoff and Dixie Series
1929	73-86	.459	Sixth
1930	89-65	.578	Second
1931	108-51	.679	First — won playoff and Dixie Series

1932	88-66	.574	Third
1933	94-57	.623	First — lost opener
1934	76-78	.478	Sixth
1935	77-84	.478	Fifth
1936	83-69	.547	Second — lost opener
1937	67-91	.424	Seventh
1938	74-84	.468	Fifth
1939	97-63	.606	First — lost opener
1940	105-56	.652	First — won opener and finals, lost Dixie Series
1941	103-50	.673	First — lost opener
1942	81-70	.536	Fifth
1946	64-89	.418	Sixth
1947	96-58	.623	First — won opener, finals, and Dixie Series
1948	82-71	.536	Third — lost opener
1949	60-91	.397	Seventh
1950	61-93	.396	Eighth
1951	99-61	.619	First — won opener and finals, lost Dixie Series
1952	66-95	.410	Eighth
1953	72-82	.468	Sixth
1954	89-72	.553	Second — won opener and finals, lost Dixie Series
1955	86-75	.534	fourth — won opener, lost finals
1956	96-58	.623	First — won opener, finals, and Dixie Series
1957	97-57	.630	Second — won opener, finals, and Dixie Series
1958	79-74	.516	Second — lost opener

Jackson (Mets)

On the night of June 22, 1978, Jackson Mets' center fielder Mookie Wilson was married to Rosa Gilbert at home plate in Smith-Wills Stadium. In the time-honored tradition of home-plate weddings, Mookie and Rosa marched back to the dugout beneath an archway of bats held aloft by Mets teammates. Wilson — who was back in center field the next night — is just one of nearly a dozen players to have wed girls they met while in a Jackson uniform. The Mississippi capital acquired a Texas League franchise in 1975, and the union has been a happy and successful one.

Victoria, the Mets' Texas League franchise in 1974, won the title but drew only 49,000 fans. Jackson had not enjoyed professional baseball since 1953, when the Senators played in the Class C

Cotton States League out of the old ball park at the fair grounds. Civic leaders organized a campaign to erect a new 5,000-seat ball park, and the Texas League Mets moved to Jackson.

The 1975 Mets opened in Smith-Wills Stadium, even though there were no lights, no roof over the press box, an unpaved parking lot, and a club office temporarily situated in a trailer. John Antonelli, a former Cardinal infielder who had played for Houston from 1938 through 1941, was the first manager for the Mets. Although the Mets were just a break-even team, first baseman Craig Cacek hit .313, and an average of nearly 1,600 fans turned out for each game. The next season was little better, but All-Star outfielder Lee Mazilli went up to the parent club, the first of many Mets to go directly from Jackson to Shea Stadium. In 1977 Bob Wellman succeeded Antonelli. Although Wellman's first year was the only losing season to date in the Mets' Texas League tenure, the burly field general would remain in Jackson through 1980. The 1977 Mets boasted five future big leaguers, including catcher Ned Yost (.309) and pitchers Mike Scott (14-10) and Juan Berenguer (9-8). The mound staff produced three no-hitters during the season.

But there were eight future major leaguers on Wellman's roster in 1978. This nucleus of talent won the second half in the East and beat Arkansas for the Eastern Division title, before losing to El Paso in the finals. Mookie Wilson hit .292, and the pitching staff was the best in the league. Jeff Reardon led the circuit in victories (17-4) and winning percentage (.810), while Neil Allen was the ERA champ (2.10). The 1979 Mets did not make the playoffs and were last in team batting, but All-Star third baseman Hubie Brooks hit .305 and All-Star catcher Jody Davis hit .296. The current general manager, Mike Feder, assumed control of the club in 1979, and he has provided aggressive promotions, high attendance, and consistent winners in the ensuing eight years.

The decade of the '80s would provide a steady succession of playoff teams from Jackson. The Mets have made seven consecutive playoff appearances from 1980 through 1986. The string has included five Eastern Division titles and three playoff championships.

The 1980 Mets boasted fine pitching, leading the Texas League in ERA and shutouts (the 24 shutouts in 136 games more than doubled the total of Shreveport (10), second in that category). Tim Leary was 15-8 and southpaw reliever Jesse Orosco displayed the assortment of pitches that soon would baffle National League hitters. The best pitching in the Texas League was quickly becoming a trademark of the Mets.

Future New York Mets' manager Davey Johnson was the Jackson field general in 1981. Johnson led the Mets to their first Texas League flag, sweeping San Antonio in four straight in the finals. More than 112,000 fans trooped into Smith-Wills Stadium, and Feder and the victorious Mets have kept attendance above the 100,000 mark for six straight years. In 1982 ownership became local when Con Maloney bought the team from the Mets organization. An ardent booster club also adds local support, sponsoring a pre-season "Meet the Mets" banquet, an annual covered supper for the players, summer cookouts, and personalized gifts for each Met and his wife at the end of the season.

The Mets won the first half of a split season for five consecutive years, 1980 through 1984. The 1982 Mets typically finished last in team batting, but provided three of the top four ERA pitchers in the league, including Doug Sisk (11-7 with a league-leading 2.67 ERA) and Jeff Bittiger (12-5), who paced the circuit by whiffing 190 batters in just 164 innings. All-Star outfielder Darryl Strawberry provided offensive fireworks, leading the league with 34 home runs — an all-time Jackson record — and stealing 45 bases.

In 1983 the Mets flashed more offense than usual, primarily through a hard-hitting outfield: John Christensen (.333), LaSchelle Tarver (.316), and Herm Winningham (.354 in 78 games). Third baseman Kevin Mitchell (.299) and catcher John Gibbons (.298) also hit well, as the Mets took the first of four straight Eastern Division titles.

The Mets won both halves in 1984 and hosted the All-Star Game, as a near-capacity crowd of 4,828 gathered to see the best of the Texas Leaguers. Future big leaguers Billy Beane (.281 with 20 homers) and Lenny Dykstra (.275 with 53 stolen bases) produced runs, but as usual the strength of the 1984 club was a pitching staff which already has sent five men to the majors: Pitcher-of-the-Year Calvin Schiraldi (14-3), Rick Aguilera, Roger McDowell, Jay Tibbs, and Floyd Youmans. Beaumont had swept the Mets in the finals to take the 1983 title, and the Golden Gators finished first in

1984. But the Mets turned the tables on Beaumont in the '84 play-offs, winning their second flag in six games. Sam Perlozzo was named Manager of the Year, while Mike Feder was again voted General Manager of the Year, an honor he was first awarded in 1980.

Perlozzo won a second straight championship in 1985. After a poor start the Mets took the second half, while powerful El Paso won both halves in the West and streaked to first place, 13 games ahead of second-place Jackson. Mets Barry Lyons (.307 with 108 RBIs), David Magadan (.309), Randy Milligan (.309), and Mark Carreon (.313) hit impressively, but three Diablos had higher bat-ting averages. The Mets, however, gathered momentum by defeat-ing Arkansas in two games for the Eastern Division crown. Then Jackson won three straight in El Paso, before returning home to take a fourth victory and the Texas League flag at Smith-Wills Sta-dium.

Perlozzo was promoted after his second straight pennant, and new manager Mike Cubbage inherited a young club in 1986. But the Mets won the second-half title, then surprised a strong Shreve-port team by winning two out of three games in Jackson for another Eastern Division title. All-Star shortstop Kevin Elster finished the year playing in the World Series for the parent Mets. El Paso found revenge with a four-game sweep in the finals, but as the Texas League enters its 100th year, Jackson will be seeking its accus-tomed spot in the playoffs.

Year	Record	Pcg.	Finish
1975	65-65	.500	Second
1976	69-66	.511	Second
1977	62-68	.477	Fourth
1978	76-58	.567	Second — won Eastern Division, lost finals
1979	70-65	.519	Third
1980	74-62	.544	Third — lost opener
1981	68-66	.507	Second — won Eastern Division and pennant
1982	68-65	.511	Second — lost opener
1983	69-67	.507	Third — won Eastern Division, lost finals
1984	83-53	.610	Second — won Eastern Division and pennant
1985	73-63	.537	Second — won Eastern Division and pennant
1986	72-63	.533	Third — won Eastern Division, lost finals

Lafayette (Drillers)

Lafayette's first entry into professional ball was with the Gulf Coast League in 1907, and the southern Louisiana city was a long-time member of the Evangeline League, from 1934 through 1942 and from 1948 until the final season of the "Vangy" in 1957. Thus when the San Francisco Giants moved their AA franchise from Amarillo to Lafayette in 1975, it was the city's first participation above Class C. There were three Louisiana cities in the 1975 Texas League: Lafayette, Shreveport, and Alexandria.

Lafayette was managed by Dennis Sommers, and the roster featured a lethal balance of hitting and pitching. Third baseman Jack Clark (.303 with 23 homers) and catcher Joe Martin (.329 with 23 homers) made the All-Star team and tied for the home run title. Outfielders Reggie Walton (.310) and John Yeglinski (.287) also added punch to a lineup which managed a .272 team batting average. The most consistent pitchers were Julio Division (15-6) and Frank Riccelli (14-6). Robert Dressler (5-1 with a 1.96 ERA) pitched six games and was promoted, and Kyle Hypes (6-3) moved up after 10 games. Three Lafayette hurlers combined for a 1-0 seven-inning no-hitter against Jackson on September 1.

Lafayette finished with the best record in the East, winning the division title by a game margin of seven and a half over second-place Jackson. Midland, the Western Division champs, sported a better season record, but Lafayette managed to split the first four games of the playoffs. Then it rained in southern Louisiana, and continued raining, and Texas League President Bobby Bragan finally declared Lafayette and Midland co-champs.

In 1976 Dennis Sommers moved to Midland with the Cubs organization, and the new Lafayette manager was John Van Ornum. Most of the players from 1975 also had moved up, and Lafayette dropped to last place in the league. Wendell Kim, a part-time player in 1975, led the league in fielding at second base in 1976 and hit .305 (Kim would reemerge in the Texas League in 1986 as manager of Shreveport's Captains). Outfielder John Yeglinski also was back and hit .301, but returning outfielder Reggie Walton saw his batting average nosedive to .253 in 1976. The best of the new players were All-Star catcher Dick Bradley (.270) and first baseman-

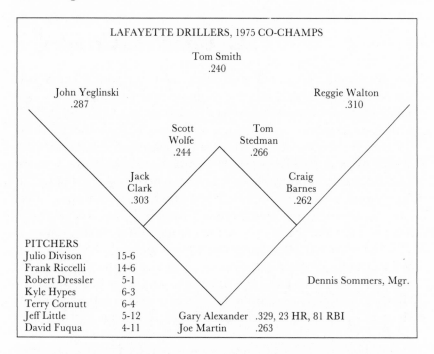

LAFAYETTE DRILLERS, 1975 CO-CHAMPS

Tom Smith
.240

John Yeglinski
.287

Reggie Walton
.310

Scott Wolfe
.244

Tom Stedman
.266

Jack Clark
.303

Craig Barnes
.262

PITCHERS		
Julio Divison	15-6	
Frank Riccelli	14-6	
Robert Dressler	5-1	Dennis Sommers, Mgr.
Kyle Hypes	6-3	
Terry Cornutt	6-4	
Jeff Little	5-12	Gary Alexander .329, 23 HR, 81 RBI
David Fuqua	4-11	Joe Martin .263

outfielder Craig Barnes (.264 with 20 homers). Righthander Jay Dillard (8-5, 2.30 ERA) was named to the All-Star squad and was the ERA champ. There were two good right-handed relievers, Joe Heinan (5-2) and Andy Muhlstock (8-4), but the starting rotation was weak, even though Mike Rowland (5-14) pitched a 1-0, seven-inning no-hitter over Jackson on August 5.

In 1975 there were 72,549 paid admissions for a championship club, but the 1976 total dipped to 35,808. It was unrealistic to expect a city of 68,000 to support a Class AA club, and the Giants shifted their AA franchise out of the Texas League. But local fans can point with pride to the pennant won during Lafayette's highest level of participation in organized baseball.

Year	Record	Pcg.	Finish
1975	72-57	.558	First — Eastern Division champs, Texas League co-champs
1976	58-76	.433	Eighth

Lake Charles (Creoles)

The southern Louisiana city of Lake Charles had a long history in organized baseball, and their first professional club was a member of the six-team South Texas League in 1906. A. C. L. Hill of Beaumont promoted the franchise to round out the South Texas League, then sold the club during the season to a Lake Charles stock company headed by W. H. Simmons. Pitcher-outfielder Ed Switzer was appointed manager, but later gave way to the hard-hitting veteran outfielder Dick Latham, who in turn was replaced before season's end by first baseman Dennis Lyons. Games were played at Athletic Park, just south of the Southern Pacific depot.

The Lake Charles roster boasted a number of players familiar to Texas League fans of the era. In addition to the three player-managers, pitcher Charles Blackburn and first baseman Ellis Hardy were well known around the loop, as were outfielders Casey Horn and Lefty Logan, and eight-year Texas League catcher Foley White.

But the turnover in managers was paralleled by turnovers in the player roster, and the club never jelled. Lake Charles found in its five Texas opponents stiff competition — the Creoles finished last with a dismal 30-94 record. The South Texas League ceased to exist after 1906, when there was a merger with the northern-oriented Texas League.

Undiscouraged by the weak showing of 1906, the Lake Charles Creoles became charter members of the Gulf Coast League. After playing in 1907 and 1908, Lake Charles dropped out of organized baseball but participated actively in the "sawdust circuit," a loose aggregation of semi-pro teams from sawmill towns such as Bon Ami, DeRidder, Fullerton, Leesville, Longville, and Merryville. The keenest rivalry for the Lake Charles semi-pro Athletics was the Patterson Grays, owned by sawmill magnate Harry Williams. He sometimes would secure the services of professional players from Beaumont, Houston, or Galveston for crucial games. Pitching occasionally against the Athletics were such outstanding Texas Leaguers as Oyster Joe Martina, Wild Bill Bailey, and spitballer Stuart Jacobus. Joe Mathes sometimes came over to bolster the lineup at first base, and Williams once showed up with a young slugger named Mel Ott. The Athletics countered on occasion with a future major league pitching star from Texas, Ted Lyons.

In 1920 Connie Mack brought his Philadelphia big leaguers to Lake Charles for spring training. Later in the year, the Southern Pacific reclaimed the site of Athletic Park, but local boosters eagerly raised funds for a grandstand which was the beginning of Legion Field. The new ball park hosted its first professional games when Lake Charles played in the Cotton States League in 1929 and 1930. The Lake Charles Skippers came into existence when the Evangeline League was formed in 1934, playing until the "Vangy" suspended play during the 1942 season. After World War II Lake Charles fielded a team in the Class B Gulf Coast League from 1950 through 1953, then rejoined the Class C Evangeline League from 1954 until the Vangy disbanded after the 1957 season.

Year	Record	Pcg.	Finish
1906	30-94	.242	Sixth

Little Rock
(Arkansas Travelers)

A visit to Ray Winder Field in Little Rock is a visit to all that is best about baseball. The traditions of long participation in two historic leagues, a ball park with personality, enthusiastic fan support, and "the best entertainment bargain in the country," according to general manager Bill Valentine and legions of baseball zealots.

Little Rock was a charter member of the Southern Association in 1901 and played through 1958, with the exception of a 1910–1914 interlude and a few months during a bleak 1956 season. The Travelers won their initial pennant in 1920, then made a significant contribution to Texas League history by agreeing to meet Fort Worth in the first Dixie Series. Although there were other pennants in 1931, 1937, 1942, and 1951, the Travelers more often were at the bottom of the standings. In 1957 the club began calling itself the "Arkansas" Travelers in order to build statewide support.

There was no organized baseball in Little Rock in 1959, but a public stock drive returned a fan-owned Travelers team to the Southern Association for the last two years of the circuit's exist-

Little Rock had a long history in the Southern Association before joining the Texas League. The first-place 1942 Travelers are posed at their home park, now known as Ray Winder Field.

— Courtesy Arkansas Travelers

ence. There was a year of no baseball in Little Rock in 1962, then the Travelers went up to AAA, spending 1963 in the International League and 1964 and 1965 in the Pacific Coast League. The "Boom-Boom Travs" of 1964 blasted a franchise record of 208 home runs, but PCL travel proved too costly to operate successfully.

After the 1965 season Tulsa moved from the Texas League up to the Pacific Coast League, while Little Rock pulled out of the PCL and returned to its accustomed niche in AA ball as a St. Louis Cardinal Texas League farm club. Vern Rapp, manager at Tulsa in 1965, moved over to Little Rock and led the Travelers to first place in their first year in the Texas League. The 1966 Travs stole 121 bases (Albuquerque, second in that category, swiped 88), while first baseman Moose Stubing hit 25 home runs, most in crucial situations. The Travelers were defeated in the opening round of playoffs, but Little Rock fans were elated with the fine start in the Texas League. Late in the season, Travelers Field was renamed Ray Winder Field, in honor of the man who had guided Little Rock baseball from 1931 through 1965. The stadium was built in 1932 in what is now called War Memorial Park, replacing old Kavanaugh Field.

In 1967 the Travs were no-hit in their opening game and went on to finish last in team batting and home runs. Reliever Sal Campisi (11-3) led the league in ERA (2.26), but the Travelers failed to make the playoffs. In 1968, however, Rapp again led the Travs to the best record in the league. The pitching staff had a trio of solid starters, Joe DiFabio (13-6 with a league-leading 2.17 ERA), Phil Knuckles (13-6), and Santiago Guzman (13-8), plus starter-reliever Andy Martin (10-5), and relief specialist Tom Hilgendorf (4-1), as well as Jerry Reuss (7-8). El Paso prevailed in the playoffs, but the Travs drew well over 100,000.

In 1969, for the third year in a row, a Traveler hurler won the ERA title — Ramon Hernandez (10-4 with a 2.40 ERA) — and Reggie Cleveland was 15-6. But the Travs missed the playoffs in 1969 and in 1970, despite the efforts of manager Ken Boyer in the latter season. In the Dixie Association year of 1971, Jack Krol piloted the club to a Central Division crown, although the team batting average was just .236. The Travelers beat Western Division titlist Amarillo, but lost to Charlotte, winners in the East, three games to none.

It would be 1977 before the Travelers could capture another title. All-Star outfielder Hector Cruz (.328) put on quite a hitting show for 1973 fans, leading the league in home runs (30) and RBIs (105), and missing a triple crown by four percentage points. John Denny hurled a no-hitter against Midland on May 17, 1973, while the 1974 pitching staff led the league in ERA and featured ERA champ Randy Wiles and righthander Harold Rasmussen (14-5). The next year, All-Star first baseman John "Duke" Young hit .330, while shortstop Garry Templeton ripped the ball at a .401 clip in 42 games.

In 1976 Traveler general manager Carl Sawatski was elected president of the Texas League, and the new general manager was Bill Valentine, a husky, crewcut former American League umpire who proved to be an intuitive promoter. Duke Young (.321) had another good year in 1976, but the rest of the team was mediocre. In 1977, however, Valentine launched a four-year playoff string. Arkansas won the second half in the East, beat Tulsa two straight for the division title, then took the 1977 pennant with two victories

in a row over El Paso. In the final game, a 4-0 shutout by Joe Edelen, Duke Young ended his playing career with a home run that
sailed over the tall protective screen in right field and cleared Wilbur D. Mills Freeway.

In 1978 manager Tommy Thompson had big Leon Durham
(.316) at first, Tommy Herr (.293) at second, Terry Kennedy
(.289) behind the plate, and Dave Bialas (.293) in the outfield,
while Dan O'Brien (12-3) led a good mound staff. The Travs won
the first half, but mid-season callups decimated the lineup, and the
team was bumped off by Jackson in the opening round of playoffs.
Again managed by Thompson, the 1979 Travelers were led by another hard-hitting first baseman, Joey DeSa (.317) to a first-half
title. Switch-hitter Gene Roof (.303) and second-year shortstop
Gene Dotson (.306) added strong bats to the lineup. The Travelers
beat second-half champ Shreveport in two games, then swept San
Antonio in three straight to win the flag.

For the third year in a row Arkansas won a first-half title in
the East. The 1980 Travelers were paced by ERA leader Benny Joe
Edelen (13-5, 2.63), relief ace Luis DeLeon (7-6 in 76 appearances), catcher Frank Hunsaker (.325), and third baseman Jim
Riggleman (.295 with 21 homers and 95 RBIs). In the playoff
opener the Travs beat Jackson (2-0) then swept San Antonio in
three games for the second consecutive season.

The attendance figures for 1977 through 1980 were 116,000,
then an unprecedented 175,000, 183,000, and finally 216,000. Valentine has since kept the annual attendance comfortably above the
200,000 mark, and El Paso is the only franchise in the Texas
League which consistently rivals the Arkansas totals. Valentine
usually pours most of the profits back into Ray Winder Field.

The Travelers dropped to last place in 1981 (somehow drawing 202,000 fans), and only had a .500 club the next year (with
213,000 admissions). But in 1983 Manager of the Year Nick Leyva,
first baseman Jon Ayer (.313), and a league-leading pitching staff
took the second half in the East before bowing to Jackson in the
playoff opener. And in 1985, managed by former slugging star Jim
Riggleman, the Travelers won the first half. Rod Booker was the
All-Star shortstop, while Tom Pagnozzi (.309 in 40 games) and
Don Stryffeler (.301 in 58 games) added hot bats while wearing
Traveler uniforms. The past decade in the Texas League has pro-

duced more postseason activity for the Travelers than their six decades spent in the Southern Association.

Year	Record	Pcg.	Finish
1966	81-59	.579	First — lost opener
1967	75-64	.539	Third
1968	82-58	.586	First — lost playoff
1969	66-69	.492	Third
1970	67-67	.500	Second
1972	65-74	.468	Third
1973	69-71	.493	Third
1974	75-59	.560	Second
1975	63-72	.467	Third
1976	59-76	.437	Third
1977	63-67	.485	Second — won Eastern Division and pennant
1978	77-55	.583	First — lost opener
1979	76-57	.571	First — won Eastern Division and pennant
1980	81-55	.596	First — won Eastern Division and pennant
1981	52-80	.394	Fourth
1982	68-68	.500	Third
1983	69-67	.507	Second — lost opener
1984	62-74	.456	Third
1985	64-70	.478	Fifth — lost opener
1986	67-67	.500	Fourth

Longview
(Cannibals, Browns)

Longview's first involvement with the Texas League occurred only a few years after the circuit was formed. One season during the 1890s (probably 1895, the first year Shreveport had a franchise) Longview boasted a crack semi-pro team, organized and managed by Bill Maxfield. When the San Antonio Missionaries missed a train connection at Longview, Maxfield quickly arranged a game between the Texas Leaguers and his undefeated semi-pros. Longview hosted the Missionaries at Mobberly Park, triumphing 7-0 behind the shutout pitching of Bill Sharpert. (Sharpert's batterymate was Billy Alexander, who later would catch and manage for the San Antonio team.) Local sportswriter C. B. Cunningham happily reported that "the Longview Cannibals ate up the San Antonio Missionaries here today." Longview baseball teams in the future would be dubbed the Cannibals, with frequent references in sports columns to the "Savages" and "Savs."

The Longview Cannibals were semi-pro aggregations until 1912, when they played with the six-team Class D South Central League. The Cannibals participated in the Class D East Texas League from 1923 to 1926, winning the championship in the latter year, then spent 1927 in the Lone Star League. In 1931 Longview joined an attempt to resurrect the East Texas League, but the loop folded after two weeks. It looked as though 1932 would be equally disappointing for Longview baseball fans, even though the East Texas oil boom had brought an impressive transfusion of population and wealth to the area.

On May 4, however, the Shreveport ball park burned to the ground following a game. Shreveport played their next home game in Longview before a crowd of 3,000, then tried out Tyler. After it was determined that Shreveport would not rebuild, the franchise was shifted to Tyler on May 15. However, the St. Louis Browns had become dissatisfied with attendance at their Texas League farm club in Wichita Falls, and by May 10 it was rumored that the franchise would be transferred to Longview because of the large crowd drawn on short notice for the Shreveport contest. After the Wichita Falls game on May 20, Browns' management decided to move their 16-19 club to Longview.

Hank Severeid, a major league catcher from 1911 through 1926, was the field manager. By 1932 he was a 23-year-veteran who managed to catch 84 games and hit .272 (in 1937, when he was 46, Severeid caught 44 games for Galveston). Former major leaguer Harold "Whitey" Wiltse headed the mound corps with a 2.61 ERA, while Forrest "Tot" Pressnell was 16-11 and Tom Conlan went 14-14.

Veteran center fielder Debs Garms was the team's best hitter, racking up a .344 average and finishing the season with the Browns (he stayed in the major leagues through 1946, batting .293 lifetime). Not another man, however, hit close to .300: right fielder Robert Fuss had the second highest average, .288, and three other regulars hit in the .280s, but no one managed more than nine home runs (Garms) or 79 RBIs (Fuss).

With no power hitters and mediocre pitching, the club finished fifth at 69-83. Added to this lackluster performance was the absence of night ball in Longview, which restricted attendance. Fans and potential backers hoped that the Browns would leave their Texas League franchise in Longview for another season. But the Browns entertained offers from Tyler, Waco, and Wichita Falls, and opened talks with San Antonio, which reportedly had fallen $30,000 in debt. L. C. McEvoy, vice-president of the Browns, hosted a meeting of interested backers in Wichita Falls in January 1933. When McEvoy announced his decision, Longview fans were disappointed — but surely not greatly surprised — that the Browns' franchise would move to San Antonio.

Longview's brief tenure in the Texas League was over, but the Cannibals long remained in organized baseball. For 1933 Longview helped found the Class C Dixie League. They played in the East Texas League, now Class C, from 1936 to 1940. After World War II, Longview spent two seasons each in the Lone Star League, East Texas League, and Big State League, before bowing out of professional baseball following the 1953 season.

Year	Record	Pcg.	Finish
1932	53-64	.453	Fifth

Memphis (Blues)

From 1968 through 1972 the Memphis Blues provided the state of Tennessee with its only member of the Texas League, but the city's overwhelming image in professional baseball history came as the Memphis Chicks of the Southern Association. In 1921, 1924, and 1930 the Chicks played against the Texas League champions in the Dixie Series, losing to Fort Worth in each series. In 1944 the Chicks' outfielder Pete Gray won the Southern Association MVP — fans cheered the one-armed player who stole 68 bases and hit .333.

Memphis pulled out of the Southern Association after the 1960 season, a year before the historic league disbanded. During this period, the Texas League limped along with six teams, but when the circuit increased its membership to eight clubs in 1968, Memphis rejoined Class AA baseball. Chicks Stadium (renamed Blues Stadium) was dusted off, and club management aggressively went after fans. College students, for example, were offered season tickets for five dollars, and more than 141,000 fans — second best total of the year in the Texas League — trooped into the park to watch a fifth-place team. Former big leaguer Roy Sievers was the manager, and future big leaguer Rod Gaspar (.309 with 25 stolen bases) was the star. (The first member of the Blues to go up, Gaspar was the center fielder for the Miracle Mets of 1969.) Southpaw Richard Folkers fashioned a 13-9 record, and on July 21 righthander Steve Renko (who would spend a decade in the majors) twirled a 1-0, seven-inning no-hitter against Albuquerque.

The Blues were much better in 1969. The All-Star Game was played in Memphis before a crowd of 5,579. The East team won, 2-1, and featured Blues outfielder Ken Singleton (.309), shortstop Teddy Martinez, and pitchers Jim Bibby (10-6) and Bob Johnson (13-4). The pitching staff led the league in shutouts with 17, and southpaw Les Rohr pitched a seven-inning no-hitter against San Antonio on April 20. The Blues won the Eastern Division, then took the playoff title by sweeping Western Division champion Amarillo in three games.

Memphis again won the Eastern Division in 1970. John Antonelli, who had managed part of 1969, was at the helm. His best pitcher was Charles Williams (12-5), and the attack was spearheaded by RBI champ Arsenio Diaz (.310 with 102 RBIs) and All-Star first baseman John Milner (.297, 20 homers, and a league-leading 100 walks). A strong Albuquerque Dodger club beat Memphis for the playoff championship, but it had been another fine season at the gate and on the field.

During the Dixie Association year of 1971, Memphis finished last in team hitting with an anemic .229 average. The pitching staff was led by righthanders John Glass (13-6) and strikeout champion Tommy Moore (11-10 with 160 K's), but they could not offset the lack of scoring. In 1972, with Antonelli back as manager, the Blues rebounded strongly, fashioning the third best season record but finishing second in the East behind Alexandria. Again the team batting average was low (.238), but Memphis led the league in fielding, behind All-Stars Terry Deremer at second base and catcher Joe Nolan.

With back-to-back Eastern Division crowns and a playoff title to show for its brief sojourn in the Texas League, Memphis went up to the Class AAA International League. Fans enjoyed watching such future stars as Gary Carter, but Memphis soon gravitated back to Class AA and the Southern League. In 1986 the biggest attraction since Pete Gray came to town: Bo Jackson spent his first few weeks in professional baseball wearing a Chicks uniform, striking out frequently, and now and then hitting the baseball as far as the Chicks' young Ted Kluszewski once had.

Year	Record	Pcg.	Finish
1968	67-69	.493	Fifth
1969	66-65	.504	Fourth — won Western Division and finals
1970	69-67	.507	Third — won Western Division, lost finals
1972	75-64	.540	Third

Midland (Cubs, Angels)

In 1971, when only seven clubs could be lined up for the Texas League, the circuit participated in the Dixie Association, a three-division arrangement with the seven-team Southern League. The next year, even though Albuquerque and Dallas-Fort Worth left the circuit, the Texas League again became an eight-team entity by locating franchises in Alexandria, El Paso, and Midland.

For more than half a century baseball has had a strong following in this West Texas oil city. The Midland Colts played in the Permian Basin League in 1934. In 1937 the Midland Cardinals entered the West Texas-New Mexico League, and the ball park at Illinois on the Andrews Highway was given a new fence and club house (and team officials searched for a dwelling to move to the stadium so that bachelor players would have a place to stay rent-free). The club later changed its name to Cowboys, then Indians, and Midland maintained a franchise in the Longhorn League throughout the nine years of the circuit's existence in Class D (1947–1950) and Class C (1951–1955). Midland next participated in the Class B Southwestern League (1956–1957), then the Class D Sophomore League (1958–1961).

In 1972 the Texas League beckoned. There was discussion about locating the new stadium midway between Midland and Odessa, but the twin-cities concept was scrapped in favor of concentrating on a specific local identity with Midland. Throughout each season West Texas communities are given heavily publicized "nights" in order to promote attendance from outside the immediate area.

Cubs (now Angels) Stadium; was built in the north part of Midland adjacent to the municipal golf course and a summer league baseball-softball complex. An intimate park which seats 3,300, the stadium features the most meticulously manicured field in minor league baseball. The outfield grass would be the envy of the most conscientious yardman, and the infield is groomed like a golf green — indeed, the crew which maintains the next-door golf course is responsible for the superb condition of the diamond.

Open fields are situated beyond the left field fence, which resulted in a locust invasion reminiscent of the grasshopper clouds which descended upon western farms a century ago. Early one evening in 1977 a dark mass of insects flew in over the scoreboard in left center. The grasshoppers swarmed into the grandstand, landing on fans who leaped up, screaming, and sprinted for their cars. Many women became hysterical as insects clustered in their hair, then followed them into their automobiles. In a singular ruling, the game was called because of insects. Hail storms and dust storms also have halted games in Midland.

Although there has been only one grasshopper infestation, Texas League games in Midland are lively and exciting. Between innings the PA system rocks the stadium with Buddy Holley in "Every Day" or the Beatles in "Help," and when a Midland player hits a home run Petula Clark belts out "Downtown." When a foul ball sails into the parking lot the sound of breaking glass tinkles loudly from the speakers. The specialty of the concession stands is jumburritos, with an order of nachos on the side. Fans respond generously when a batting helmet is passed following a home run, sometimes stuffing in as much as $250 for a timely roundtripper. Since pitchers never hit because of the designated-hitter rule, a clubhouse drawing before home games assigns each hurler to a starter — the pitcher gets 25 percent of a home run pot earned by "his" batter, and in turn the hitter gets his own personal batboy and cheerleader. An active booster club hosts postgame parties, barbecues, and covered dish suppers for the players.

The light West Texas air is a boon to home run hitters, and regardless of the deficit on the scoreboard no one is ever out of a

Although Midland trails, 3-0, in the third inning, no lead is safe in the West Texas ball park.

— Courtesy Midland Angels

game. Four-hour slugfests are not uncommon. Once Midland scored 10 runs in the first inning, and once hard-hitting El Paso was defeated 31-5. Every year Midland ranks high in team batting average and home runs, and the pitching staff often finishes last in ERA. Young pitchers up from a successful stint in Class A sometimes have their confidence shattered after being bombed in their first couple of appearances in Midland.

Despite Midland's annual success at the plate, the club's first 15 years in the Texas League have produced just three playoff appearances. In 1975 the Midland Cubs won the Western Division with the best season record of the year. All-Star second baseman Allan Montreuil (.324) and outfielder José Ortiz (.323) led a high-octane offense, while the best pitchers were future big leaguers Donnie Moore (14-8) and Mike Krukow (13-6). In the playoff with Eastern Division champion Lafayette, Midland split the first four games, before rains inundated the Louisiana playing field. Presi-

dent Bobby Bragan declared a co-championship, and Midland
flew its only Texas League flag to date.

The other two playoff appearances came in 1979 and 1982.
The 1979 Cubs, managed by former big leaguer Randy Hundley (a
genuinely intense field general whose strongest profanity is, "Jim-
iny crickets — confound it!"), won the second-half championship
behind a formidable scoring machine. The batting champ was left-
handed Jim Tracy (.355), while outfielders Brian Rosinski (.331)
and Carlos Lezcano (.326), first baseman Gary Krug (.387 in 44
games), second sacker Dan Rohn (.307), catcher Bill Hayes (.300),
and shortstop Jesus Alfaro (.352 in 77 games) helped build an eye-
popping .312 team batting average. But the Cubs were defeated by
San Antonio, two games to one, for the Western Division championship. In 1982 the Cubs met the same fate, winning the second
half, but losing in the opening round of playoffs to West Texas rival
El Paso. Outfielder-first baseman Carmelo Martinez (.334 with 27
homers), outfielder Joe Carter (.319 with 25 homers), and switch-
hitter Dave Owen (.316) paced a typically hard-hitting lineup,
while tall righthander Jon Perlman (13-7) and Doug Welenc (13-
10) tied Tulsa's Brad Mengwasser for most victories.

The only no-hitter hurled by a Midland pitcher in the Texas
League occurred on June 8, 1976, when southpaw Bernie Beckman
beat San Antonio, 5-0, in seven innings. In 1973 righthander Dan
Corder (13-3 with a 2.33 ERA) became the only Midland pitcher to
win the ERA title. Midland stolen base champs have been outfielders Matthew Alexander (38 in 1972) and Henry Cotto (52 in 1982).
In 1974 first baseman Jerry Tabb and third sacker Wayne Tyrone
tied for the home run title, with 29 each, and in 1977 outfielder
Karl Pagel batted .334, made the All-Star team, and hit 28 homers
to lead the league.

The most recent honors for the franchise came in 1986: Bill
Davidson, appointed general manager in 1985, was named Texas
League Executive of the Year and *The Sporting News* Class AA Executive of the Year; and the National Association awarded the immaculate Angels Stadium diamond the highest rating of any infield
in minor league baseball. Although the longtime Cubs' affiliate
switched to the Angels in 1985, club officials recognize that the ex-
traordinarily high quality of the playing field is an important at-

traction for major league teams who want young prospects to play on a near-perfect surface.

Year	Record	Pcg.	Finish
1972	68-71	.489	Third
1973	64-74	.464	Third
1974	65-73	.471	Fourth
1975	81-53	.604	First — won Western Division, declared co-champs
1976	62-74	.456	Fourth
1977	70-60	.538	Second
1978	70-65	.519	Third
1979	76-59	.563	First — lost opener
1980	64-72	.471	Third
1981	62-73	.459	Fourth
1982	67-66	.504	Second — lost opener
1983	63-73	.463	Fourth
1984	52-84	.382	Eighth
1985	59-77	.434	Eighth
1986	62-71	.466	Sixth

New Orleans (Pelicans)

By the 1870s baseball was hugely popular in New Orleans. Amateur baseball thrived in the Crescent City League and numerous other intercity circuits, Tulane University boasted active clubs, and in the 1880s the New Orleans Base Ball Park was built to attract barnstorming professional teams. In 1886 New Orleans and Mobile provided two clubs from each city for a Gulf League, the Crescent City's first venture into professional ball. The next year the New Orleans Pelicans joined the Southern League. New Orleans proved to be the bellwether franchise of the struggling circuit, regularly drawing several thousand fans, even for weekday afternoon games. "Sportsman's Park" was renamed and expanded to seat 5,000, but on Sundays there were standing-room-only crowds.

The Pelicans won the Southern League title in 1887 and had another good team in 1888, but the circuit faltered and disbanded in mid-season. The Texas League, then staggering through its inaugural season, experienced similar difficulties at the same time. Two of the original six Texas League teams folded; by July only Dallas, Houston, Galveston, and San Antonio were sponsoring

clubs. Abner Powell, a longtime player, manager, and club owner
in the Southern League, quickly arranged for the Pelicans to make
a fifth Texas League team. Toby Hart served as president.

It was appropriate that New Orleans participate in the first
Texas League season, because the Crescent City had been "well
represented" in Austin when the circuit was organized in December 1887. In the summer of 1888 New Orleans traveled to Texas to
take on the surviving members, although one of the five teams was
always idle.

Powell played in the outfield, where he was joined by
"Farmer" Works, a powerful hitter who would play four more seasons in the Texas League. Outfielder Frank Behan also would play
later, with Sherman and Galveston. Charles Weber was an outstanding player — a hard-hitting outfielder and a fine pitcher who
played eight years in the Texas League, and who was one of the finest athletes in the circuit during the 1890s.

The original Texas League schedule called for play until October, but Houston and then Galveston folded by early September.
With only Dallas and San Antonio still in operation, New Orleans
realized it was pointless to make another trip to Texas, and it was
mutually agreed to close the season on September 2. New Orleans
had participated in the Texas League a little over 30 days, accumulating a 15-10 record — the second best winning percentage in
the circuit.

New Orleans returned to the tenuous Southern League and
participated in its successor, the Southern Association, from 1901
through 1959. New Orleans represented the Southern Association
five times in the Dixie Series, losing to the Texas League champs in
1923, 1926, and 1927, then winning back-to-back titles over San
Antonio in 1933 and Galveston in 1934.

In the fall of 1986, when Beaumont's franchise was sold to
Larry Schmittou, it was thought that the club would move to New
Orleans. Problems over a playing site developed, however, and the
team moved to Wichita instead. But perhaps some day New Orleans will again join the Texas League.

Year	Record	Pcg.	Finish
1888	15-10	.600	Second

Oklahoma City
(Mets, Indians)

Baseball came to Oklahoma City with the "run" of 1889. The original '89ers nailed together a grandstand of boards and beer kegs from a saloon, but as the growing city expanded, the ball park was shifted from one location to another. Oklahoma City nines such as the Browns and Dudes and Pirates and Statehoods took on various amateur and semi-pro aggregations.

ABSOLUTELY NO PROSTITUTION ON THE GROUNDS

In 1891 the Oklahoma City Pirates played at a ball park east of the Santa Fe depot. There was an eight-foot board fence, a covered grandstand, and a plank backstop designed to allow catchers to field wild pitches on the rebound. There were no gate receipts because there were no gates, but the hat was passed among the fans. The Pirates announced a decorous code of conduct for those attending games:

> No intoxicating liquors allowed on the grounds.
> No profane language allowed.
> Betting strictly forbidden.
> Killing of umpire prohibited.
> Absolutely no prostitution on the grounds.
> Horses and carriages admitted on grounds free of
> charge.
> Admission 25¢ for adults and 15¢ for children.
> Grandstand privileges 10¢ additional.

In July 1899, as the Texas League tottered toward another premature end to the regular schedule, baseball supporters in Oklahoma City were sounded out about promoting a team in the circuit, and similar feelers were extended in other seasons. But Oklahoma City would not enter the Texas League until 1909, after a four-year stint in the Class C Western Association.

R. E. Moist of Oklahoma City bought the Austin franchise, which had finished last in 1908. Shreveport had been required to put up a $75 per game guarantee to visiting teams, even though Texas clubs only posted $50 per game. Oklahoma City, however, was forced to put up $100 per game, a requirement that soon would cause resentment in Sooner baseball circles. Early in the 1909 season, Oklahoma City player-manager George Kelsey had a brawl with his Houston counterpart, Hunter Hill, and the rivalry thus generated was intensified when the two clubs fought it out for the flag. Houston finished first, but James Drohan (21-12) and batting champ Red Downey (.346) led a crowd-pleasing second-place team. Left fielder Downey also stole 30 bases, right fielder Bill McCormick hit .311, and sportswriters called the players "Mets" and "Indians."

Journalists settled on "Indians" by 1910, but Oklahoma City sagged to seventh place, despite the efforts of Downey (.298), now the manager, and Hank Chelette (21-17). The next season brought another seventh-place finish, although Oklahoma City also produced another batting champ, Bill Yohe (.320), who also stole 47 bases and led all third basemen in fielding. Harley Young (18-17) led the Texas League in strikeouts with 245. But Moist had sold the team for $18,000 to banker Abner Davis, who raged at everyone in the league about the $100 guarantee, and who was prone to pull his players off the field. After the 1911 season, Davis sold his franchise to Beaumont.

Oklahoma City reentered the Western Association in 1914, then switched to the Class A Western League in 1918, developing a natural rivalry with Tulsa through the years. In 1926 the two Oklahoma cities applied for admission to the Texas League, but since both were members of the Western League there was no way of surrendering National Association territorial rights. Oklahoma City petitioned the Texas League again in 1931, this time with the permission of the Western League, but no franchises were available. Finally, in 1933, both Oklahoma City and Tulsa were admitted to the Texas League. The Indians' owner was John Holland, a veteran minor league executive who had been a Texas League outfielder in 1897, 1898, and 1899. After he died in 1936, John Holland, Jr., took over the club.

Oklahoma City finished last in 1933 and 1934, but the team roared to first place in 1935. In the Shaughnessy playoff opener, the Indians beat Tulsa in four straight, then polished off Beaumont in five games to claim their first Texas League flag. The club's strength was pitching: Russ Evans (24-8) tied for the lead in wins; southpaw Jack Brillheart (17-11) would become a five-time All-

Star; and John Niggerling (9-2) posted a 1.17 ERA in half a season. Bert Niehoff won a pennant in his first try as a manager, then guided the Indians to a Dixie Series championship over the Atlanta Crackers.

In 1936 outfielder Paul Easterling (.330), a veteran Texas Leaguer, led the Indians to fourth place, but Niehoff's charges lost to Dallas in the playoff opener. James Keesey became manager in 1937 and took the tribe to two more playoffs. Former Texas Aggie star Ash Hillin (11-20 for the 1936 Indians) was magnificent in 1937, going 31-10 in 62 appearances (27 starts) and winning the ERA crown and the Most Valuable Player award. Brillheart was 18-13, infielder Stanley Sperry hit .355, and Keesey batted .317 as his team won 101 games. The Indians beat San Antonio in the first round of playoffs, but lost to Fort Worth in the finals.

The next year Keesey (.304) sparked the attack and relied on another superb pitching staff-Hillin (23-10), Brillheart (19-9), Clay Touchstone (16-11), and Frank Lamanske (14-11). The third-place Indians were swept by San Antonio in the first round of playoffs. The only other playoff representative before World War II was the 1940 club, which finished fourth and lost to first-place Houston in the playoff opener.

During the first six years after the war, Oklahoma City made the playoffs only once, finishing third in 1949 but suffering defeat at the hands of hated Tulsa. First baseman Herb Conyers (.355) won the 1949 hitting crown (he previously had won three other batting titles in lower leagues). Other postwar batting champs were Dale Mitchell (.337 in 1946), Al Rosen (.349 in 1947), Bob Nieman (.324 in 1951), Joe Frazier (.332 in 1953), and Albie Pearson (.371 in 1956). Bob Lemon won the home run crown in 1950 with 39.

Oklahoma City began a three-year playoff string in 1952 under manager Tommy Tatum. The Indians upset first-place Dallas in the opening round of the 1952 playoffs but lost the finals to Shreveport. In 1953 Tatum's tribe again struggled with first-place Dallas in the opener, but lost in the seventh game of a classic series. The 1954 Indians also were defeated in the first playoff round, by the Houston Buffs in five games.

The last three Oklahoma City Texas League teams finished seventh, eighth, and seventh. Despite Albie Pearson's red-hot bat, the last-place 1956 Indians lost 106 games. In 1951 a sixth-place

The Oklahoma City Indians congratulate each other following a 1952 playoff victory over Dallas.
— Courtesy Dallas Public Library

Oklahoma City club drew more than 333,000 fans, but by 1957 attendance had plummeted to 51,000.

Oklahoma City left the Texas League after the 1957 season but would find a new baseball future in Class AAA. In 1962 the Oklahoma City '89ers moved into the beautiful new All Sports Stadium as a member of the American Association. Attendance was just 44,000, but Oklahoma City transferred into the Pacific Coast League, won two championships, then returned to the American Association. In 1985 the '89ers won a division title and set an attendance record of 364,000, and owners Bing and Patty Cox Hampton sometimes talk eagerly about bringing major league baseball to Oklahoma City.

Year	Record	Pcg.	Finish
1909	79-63	.547	Second
1910	63-74	.460	Seventh
1911	71-77	.480	Seventh
1933	62-90	.408	Eighth
1934	54-93	.388	Eighth

1935	95-66	.590	First — won opener, finals, and Dixie Series
1936	79-75	.513	Fourth — lost opener
1937	101-58	.635	First — won opener, lost finals
1938	89-70	.560	Third — lost opener
1939	59-102	.366	Seventh
1940	82-78	.513	Fourth — lost opener
1941	69-85	.448	Sixth
1942	58-95	.379	Seventh
1946	54-98	.355	Eighth
1947	71-83	.461	Sixth
1948	70-84	.455	Sixth
1949	81-72	.529	Third — lost opener
1950	72-79	.477	Sixth
1951	75-86	.466	sixth
1952	82-79	.509	Fourth — won opener, lost finals
1953	80-74	.519	Fourth — lost opener
1954	87-74	.540	Third — lost opener
1955	70-90	.438	Seventh
1956	48-106	.312	Eighth
1957	66-88	.429	Seventh

Paris
(Texas Midland,
Eisenfelder's
Homeseekers)

Paris enjoyed a long history as a baseball hotbed. In 1868 George Thebo organized a "Base Ball Club" which proved so popular that "prominent citizens and even ladies" attended the games. In ensuing years there were numerous amateur clubs: the best was the "Quicksteps" of 1884. In 1896 Russ Steinhoff, who had played in the Fort Worth infield during the 1895 Texas League season, organized a crack semi-pro team in Paris. On June 10, 1896, Sherman abruptly disbanded its unprofitable Texas League franchise, creating an awkward seven-team circuit. League President John Ward, aware of the enthusiasm that Steinhoff's team had created, caught the first train to Paris and within a single day established a stock company of local backers. Most of the investors were railroad men, and the club was nicknamed "Texas Midland."

Steinhoff agreed to be player-manager, and he had to utilize several athletes from his independent club because most of the Sherman veterans wee snapped up by rival Texas League teams. The versatile George Nie, who played catcher, first base, and outfield, proved to be up to Texas League standards by hitting well over .300. Pitcher-outfielder Cy Mulkey, brother of famed Methodist evangelist Abe Mulkey, had played with San Antonio in 1895, and the graceful Dudley Payne had pitched for Galveston and Houston. But there were not enough seasoned pros to win consistently. Texas Midland fashioned a 19-22 record and, with attendance weak, dropped out of the league on August 2.

But the professional baseball bug had bitten deeply at Paris. When the Texas League organized for 1897 in a Fort Worth meeting, baseball enthusiasts Jim Patrick and Sandy Neville attended and brought back a franchise to Paris. A stock company was formed, headed by a local millionaire, Col. E. H. R. Green. In the north end of town a ball park was erected, complete with a grandstand and plank fence. Fans came out on street cars or rode horses or buggies.

A veteran first-baseman-catcher, Duke Jantzen, who had played briefly with the Texas Midland in 1896, was engaged as player-manager. Tall and ungainly, Jantzen could wallop a baseball over the outfielders, but he was an "ice wagon" — too slow to get past third. The hard-hitting George Nie was back, along with infielder Harry Swearingen. Three-year veteran Irwin Isaacs was signed. Isaacs was a popular pitcher who also was a fine hitter, but the best hurler was Jake Thielman, who spent 1905 through 1908 in the major leagues. The team's strongest hitter was an outfielder named Hill, who rapped out a .335 average, while the best infielder was Kid Peeples, a popular figure around the league since 1888. Edward Pabst, a slugging first baseman, had first appeared in the Texas League in 1890.

But overall the Texas Midland team of 1897 was a weak aggregation, consistently in the cellar of the eight-team circuit. Jantzen soon was out as manager, but neither of his successors — catcher Dan Boland nor infielder Robert Burns — could lead Paris out of last place. Although some of the league franchises folded in 1897, financial transfusions from Colonel Green allowed Texas Midland to complete the season.

The last-place finish of 1897 discouraged another professional entry until 1902, when the Texas League reorganized after two inactive seasons. C. W. Eisenfelder put together the club, which featured stellar first baseman Prince Ben Shelton, third sacker Roy Akin, slugger Emmett Rodgers, who had been catching in the league since 1888, and Tony Thebo, a colorful, fleet outfielder who was an outstanding leadoff man and base stealer. The left fielder was Carl "Bones" France, a precise place hitter who could drop Texas Leaguers over the shortstop almost at will. But the pitching staff was weak, and the team could not rise above .400, finishing the year at 44-66. Eisenfelder, losing money, tried to move the team to Houston at mid-season, but local fans put up funds to keep the club in Paris. Attendance was so poor, however, that the team played mostly on the road in the last half of the season, and the club was called "Eisenfelder's Homeseekers."

Eisenfelder moved to Galveston of the South Texas League in 1903, but veteran organizer Ted Sullivan decided to locate a club in Paris. Sullivan managed the team himself and promptly led Paris into first place. Cy Mulkey left his law practice to take the mound for Paris, the fiery Mickey Coyle was a catalyst in the infield, and the offense was explosive. On May 14 Paris played defending champion Corsicana in the Oilers' small ball park. Paris won, 13-7, battering Lucky Wright for nine home runs. Outfielder Sis Bateman walloped four homers and catcher Roland Wolfe added three — and Corsicana moved the fence back before the next day's game!

At the end of the first half Paris was in first place at 32-20, the only one of the four teams to have a winning record. But attendance revenue did not match expenses and Sullivan, lacking the limitless resources of Colonel Green, shifted his club to Waco when the season was split on June 25. Several key players were lost in the move, and Waco finished last in the second half. Representing Paris in a 10-game championship playoff with Dallas, Waco lost, 7-3.

When the Texas League organized for 1904 there were four franchises, one of which was owned by W. H. Miller and George S. Ralls. Miller and Ralls decided to place their team in Paris and secured Big Mike O'Connor, a legendary Texas League first baseman, as player-manager. Cy Mulkey was back for another year, but no one else returned from 1903, and the roster proved mediocre. Paris was the only team in the first half with a losing record

18-year-old Rogers Hornsby played his first professional ball in 1914 with Hugo of
the Texas-Oklahoma League. Opponents Hugo and Paris posed for a photo, previously unpublished. Young Hornsby, who later managed in the Texas League, is
seated second from left.
— Courtesy Aikin Regional Archives, Paris Junior College,
Paris, Texas

(13-40), and Miller surrendered his holdings to Ralls. Late in June,
Ralls announced that he was moving his team to Ardmore, Oklahoma, but local backers pledged financial support — which apparently was what Ralls wanted all along. Local support proved inadequate, however, and in mid-July Ralls turned his franchise back to
the league. The league financed the club for a few more weeks, and
all games were played on the road. Mired in last place with a miserable record of 23-69, Paris disbanded on August 4.

In 1912 Paris organized a club in the South Central League,
then appeared in the Texas-Oklahoma League in 1913, 1914, 1921,
and 1922. The next season Paris won the East Texas League pennant, and there were entries in the Lone Star League in 1927 and
1928. After World War II, the Paris "Red Peppers" were active for
more than a decade in the East Texas League (1946, 1949, 1950),
the Big State League (1947, 1948, 1952, 1953), and the Sooner
State League (1955, 1956, 1957). The great Texas League star,
Homer Peel, played his last season at Paris, hitting .322 in 1946 at
the age of 43. The 1947 club boasted fine batters — Paul Martin

(.371), Frank Carswell (.364), Harry Schmiel (.350), George Sprys (.340), Lloyd Rigby (.334), Joe Weeks (.331), Mike Rollins (.323) — and a 20-game winner, James Walkup. The next year Mervyn Connors hit .373 and Barney White rapped out a .365 average. Pinky Griffin, a second baseman of this era, was married at home plate, and a standing-room-only crowd donated some $300 to the newlyweds.

Today the top level of baseball in town is played by the Paris Junior College Dragons. But the concrete reserved seating area of the last professional ball park still overlooks a diamond, and on a drizzly spring day in 1986 the author watched two area high schools play where the pros had held forth three decades earlier.

Year	Record	Pcg.	Finish
1896	19-22	.463	Fourth
1897	41-82	.333	Eighth
1902	44-66	.400	Fifth
1903	32-20	.615	First
1904	23-69	.250	Fourth

San Antonio (Missionaries, Bronchos, Bears, Indians, Shamrocks, Missions, Bullets, Brewers, Dodgers)

San Antonio has fielded teams in the Texas League during 82 seasons, plus four years in the South Texas League — more than any other city. A charter member of the league, San Antonio's club dropped out in June 1888, but later in that first summer Austin's team was transferred to the Alamo City to finish the abbreviated schedule. San Antonio did not participate in 1889 or 1890, but played through the remainder of the decade. After the 1899 season, San Antonio did not resume professional ball until 1903, when the

Bronchos won the Alamo City's first pennant during the inaugural season of the South Texas League. During a long playoff series with Galveston, the Bronchos won all six games played in San Antonio, the last on a no-hitter by Eddie Taylor.

In 1904 president-player-manager Wade Moore sold the club to Charles Blackburn for $1,000, the first time anyone had seen sufficient business promise in Texas League baseball to put up money for a franchise. After the 1906 season, San Antonio's new owner, Morris Block, was instrumental in a movement to merge the north and south circuits, and in November 1906 the Alamo City hosted a meeting which reorganized the Texas League.

Led by first baseman and home run champ Pat Newnam, center fielder Tony Thebo, who stole 90 bases, and 22-game winner Fred Cook, who threw curve balls from a submarine delivery, the 1908 Bronchos took the Texas League flag. Late each afternoon Block's downtown tobacco shop would be besieged with phone inquiries about the day's game, and Block had to hire an operator just to handle baseball calls. After the championship season, a banquet for the players was held at one of the plushest houses in the West Side red-light district. With the formally gowned madam presiding, a magnificent meal was served and each of the 15 players found a $100 bill under his plate.

It would be a quarter of a century before another Texas League flag would fly in San Antonio, but there were many fine baseball moments. In 1909 Fred Cook won 21 games and led the league with 264 strikeouts. Harry Ables, who posted 259 K's in 1909, was the strikeout king the next year with 325 in 320 innings. The big southpaw could wrap his fingers completely around a baseball, and his 1910 mark remains the all-time standard in the Texas League. In 1953 the nearsighted fireballer Ryne Duren struck out 212 in 202 innings. Other noted San Antonio strikeout champs have included Dennis Eckersley in 1974 and Fernando Valenzuela in 1980.

In 1923 San Antonio's second-place club took the team batting title with a .307 average, and first baseman Ike Boone won the hitting crown with a .402 mark. Two years later, third baseman Danny Clark hit 31 homers, drove in 143 runs, scored 144 times, and led the league with a .399 average. There were back-to-back batting championships in 1933 — outfielder Pid Purdy (.358) —

and in 1934 — infielder Chester Morgan (.342). The latest San Antonio batting champ was second baseman Steve Sax (.346) in 1981.

After the 1914 season, Morris Block sold the club to H. J. Benson. When Benson died in 1924, Mrs. Benson took over the team and started the next season as president. Although her tenure was brief, Mrs. Benson is the only woman who has served as president of a Texas League club. Harry Ables bought her out during the 1925 season. Ables, now 40, pitched (and lost) one game as a gate attraction, and repeated the stunt in 1926. Ables sold his stock to Homer H. Hammond who, in four years as club president, proved to have great enthusiasm but little expertise as baseball management. San Antonio was in danger of losing its franchise in 1933, but the St. Louis Browns bought the club, then watched the fourth-place Missions take a playoff championship.

There were other playoff appearances in 1938 through 1940 and in 1942. San Antonio made the playoffs in the first postwar season, then, led by batting champ Frank Saucier (.343) and outfielder James Dyck (.321), the Missions finished fourth in 1950. San Antonio swept first-place Beaumont in four straight in the playoff opener, beat Tulsa in six games to win the championship, and won a seven-game Dixie Series over Nashville.

The Missions made playoff appearances in 1951, 1955, 1957, 1959, and 1960. In 1961 the third-place Missions beat Tulsa in the opener, swept Austin in the playoff finals, then defeated the Mexican League representative in the last Pan-American Series. As the Bullets, San Antonio finished first in 1963 and 1964, winning the opening round of playoffs each year. In 1963 the Bullets dropped the finals to Tulsa, but won the Texas League pennant over Tulsa in 1964.

Since the Dodgers affiliated with San Antonio in 1968, there have been playoff appearances in 1973, 1980, and 1981. The San Antonio Dodgers were Western Division champs in 1973 but lost to Memphis in the finals. The Dodgers beat Amarillo for the 1980 Western Division title before dropping the finals to Arkansas. The next year San Antonio again won the Western Division by beating Amarillo, but the Dodgers were swept by Jackson in the finals. The Dodger years have produced a parade of future big leaguers: Fernando Valenzuela, Steve Sax, Orel Hershiser, Sid Fernandez, Steve Howe, Mike Marshall, Tom Niedenfuer, R. J. Reynolds, Ron

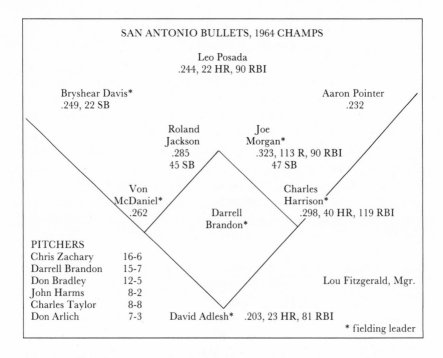

SAN ANTONIO BULLETS, 1964 CHAMPS

Leo Posada
.244, 22 HR, 90 RBI

Bryshear Davis*   Aaron Pointer
.249, 22 SB   .232

Roland   Joe
Jackson   Morgan*
.285   .323, 113 R, 90 RBI
45 SB   47 SB

Von   Charles
McDaniel*   Harrison*
.262   Darrell   .298, 40 HR, 119 RBI
                Brandon*

PITCHERS
Chris Zachary   16-6
Darrell Brandon   15-7
Don Bradley   12-5   Lou Fitzgerald, Mgr.
John Harms   8-2
Charles Taylor   8-8
Don Arlich   7-3   David Adlesh*   .203, 23 HR, 81 RBI

* fielding leader

Roenicke, Sid Bream, Greg Brock, and numerous others. Distinguished alumni from pre-Dodger days include Brooks Robinson, Joe Morgan, Gorman Thomas, Dennis Eckersley, and Ryne Duren.

San Antonio teams have sported many nicknames since 1888. The earliest and best-remembered derived from the five old missions that once provided an outpost of Spanish culture. Early newspaper accounts of Texas League games refer to the San Antonio "Missionaries," and "Missions" was a shortened version which came naturally. But when San Antonio reentered professional baseball in 1903, the club was called the "Bronchos." A few years later that name was abandoned, and San Antonio players were called "Bears," then "Indians." In 1917 Charley O'Leary, who had spent 10 years as a major league shortstop, was hired to manage San Antonio. The Irishman called his charges the "Shamrocks," and uniforms featured green socks and caps and green pinstripes. When L. C. McEvoy, a devout Catholic, became club president in 1933, San Antonio resumed the "Missions" label, and the name stuck until 1963, when the Houston Colt .45s took over the team. A name-selection contest was held: many votes were cast for "Colt .22s," "Colt .38s," and "Bee Bees," but it was decided that the San Antonio "Bullets" would supply ammunition for the Colt .45s in Houston. In 1972, when Milwaukee controlled San Antonio for one season, the team was called the "Brewers." Los Angeles became the parent club in 1977, and San Antonio has been called the "Dodgers" for the past decade.

Early San Antonio baseball was played on various makeshift diamonds, but the first grandstand erected for the sport was at Electric Park, where Tech Field and, currently, the city bus garages were later located. Because of the field's name, strings of incandescent bulbs were hung on one or two occasions for "special night exhibitions." Morris Block bought the club in 1905 and built a fine facility between South Presa and South St. Mary's, where Carolina Street comes into Presa. Block Stadium frequently was used in the spring by major league clubs, including John J. McGraw's New York Giants.

After Block Stadium was abandoned, several ball parks were utilized over the years — and each was groomed by Dick Dunavan, employed as groundskeeper in 1919 and a San Antonio baseball fixture for decades. One park had outfield fences — adorned with the customary advertising signs — which slanted outward at a 45-degree angle, and outfielder Pete Kniseley delighted 1920 fans by acrobatically scrambling up the incline to snag long fly balls. At League Park on Josephine Street, "Tiny" Owens, a hulking right-handed pitcher in 1925 and 1926, hoisted a few too many in the clubhouse, then astounded the crowd by climbing the grandstand wire like an oversized monkey. On June 18, 1933, League Park burned down following a game. San Antonio played the June 19 game at Eagle Field of Breckenridge High School, then finished the home schedule at Tech Field of Technical High School, located near the site of old Block Stadium.

Mission Stadium, a 9,500-seat facility located on Mission Road, was the most famous home of San Antonio's Texas League clubs. An overflow crowd of 12,496 set San Antonio's attendance record on June 1, 1962, but Mission Stadium was demolished in 1974. When San Antonio returned to the Texas League in 1968 after a three-year absence, the parent Cubs made a unique arrangement with St. Mary's University. San Antonio would play at V. J.

San Antonio's 9,500-seat Mission Stadium shortly before it was demolished in 1974. Fans Charles and Gertrude Ploch stand in front.

— Courtesy Angela Ploch

Keefe Memorial Stadium — the first time a professional team secured a permanent home on a college campus. The lighting plant was imported from abandoned LaGrave Field, and seating was expanded to 3,500. Improvements are regularly made at the comfortable, intimate ball park, which teemed with 6,000 fans who saw the Chicken at a 1980 game, and standing-room-only crowds are never unexpected at Dodger games.

Year	Record	Pcg.	Finish
1888	6-27	.182	Seventh
1892	11-20	.355	Sixth
1895	21-72	.226	Eighth
1896	57-71	.441	Seventh
1897	68-44	.607	Second
1898	8-19	.296	Sixth
1899	35-40	.467	Second
1903	69-54	.561	First — won playoff
1904	32-88	.267	Fourth
1905	69-60	.586	Second
1906	57-70	.449	Fifth

1907	81-58	.583	Third
1908	95-48	.664	First
1909	76-63	.547	Third
1910	74-62	.544	Third
1911	77-68	.531	Third
1912	84-57	.596	Second
1913	74-78	.487	Fourth
1914	46-103	.309	Seventh
1915	81-67	.548	Second
1916	66-79	.455	Seventh
1917	76-89	.457	Fifth
1918	43-45	.489	Fourth
1919	60-89	.403	Eighth
1920	79-71	.527	Fifth
1921	60-98	.380	Eighth
1922	76-79	.490	Fifth
1923	81-68	.556	Second
1924	75-75	.500	Fifth
1925	81-64	.559	Fourth
1926	86-70	.551	Second
1927	65-90	.419	Seventh
1928	76-83	.478	Fifth
1929	56-106	.346	Eighth
1930	79-71	.392	Seventh
1931	66-94	.413	Seventh
1932	57-91	.385	Seventh
1933	79-72	.523	Fourth — won opener and finals, lost Dixie Series
1934	89-65	.578	Second — won opener, lost finals
1935	75-84	.472	Sixth
1936	73-77	.487	Sixth
1937	85-76	.528	Fourth — lost opener
1938	93-67	.581	Second — won opener, lost finals
1939	89-72	.553	Third — lost opener
1940	89-72	.553	Second — lost opener
1941	58-96	.377	Eighth
1942	80-68	.548	Fourth — lost opener
1946	91-63	.572	Third — lost opener
1947	75-79	.487	Fifth
1948	75-76	.497	Fifth
1949	70-83	.458	Sixth
1950	79-75	.513	Fourth — won opener, finals, and Dixie Series
1951	86-75	.534	Second — won opener, lost finals
1952	79-82	.491	Fifth
1953	67-87	.435	Seventh
1954	78-83	.484	Fifth
1955	93-68	.578	Second — lost opener
1956	76-78	.494	Fifth

1957	76-78	.494	Third — lost opener
1958	74-79	.484	Sixth
1959	75-70	.570	Fourth — won opener, lost finals
1960	77-68	.531	Second — lost opener
1961	74-64	.532	Third — won opener, finals, and Pan-Am Series
1962	68-72	.486	Fifth
1963	79-61	.564	First — won opener, lost finals
1964	85-55	.607	First — won opener and finals
1968	53-86	.381	Eighth
1969	51-81	.386	Eighth
1970	67-69	.493	Third
1972	53-87	.379	Eighth
1973	82-57	.590	First — won Western Division lost playoff
1974	68-64	.515	Third
1975	50-85	.370	Eighth
1976	63-71	.479	Third
1977	61-67	.477	Third
1978	79-57	.581	Second
1979	69-62	.527	Second
1980	74-62	.544	Second — won Western Division, lost finals
1981	77-57	.571	First — won Western Division, lost finals
1982	68-68	.500	Third
1983	66-70	.485	Third
1984	64-72	.471	Fourth
1985	59-75	.440	Seventh
1986	64-71	.474	Fifth

Sherman

In 1895, following two seasons of inactivity, the Texas League was reorganized. For the first time in league history, there were eight teams in the circuit, and Sherman was one of the last cities to obtain a franchise. A local stock company backed the teams. The infield was solid: Big Mike O'Connor played part of the season at first base; James Driscoll led all second basemen in games, total chances, and fielding percentage; and William Oswald batted over .300. Infielder C. B. Douglas and catcher W. B. Douglas were brothers. Star outfielder William "Kid" Nance was in the first year of a long Texas League career. James "Curley" Maloney was one of the pitchers, along with George Gilpatrick, an excellent Texas League hurler during the 1890s who was on the staff for St. Louis in the National League in 1898. A local youth, Lee Garvin, took a regular turn on the mound, reached the big leagues the next year, and pitched for five teams during seven major league seasons.

Early in August, four clubs dropped out of the Texas League, but Sherman was one of the teams that played on until Labor Day. Sherman managed only a 55-62 record, but local backers were sufficiently encouraged to field another team in 1896. Though Oswald returned to anchor the infield and again hit over .300, he was the only returning player. Attendance was poor. On June 10 the team disbanded abruptly, not even notifying the league office.

The next season Sherman and Denison (Denison had fielded an 1896 club that failed to finish the year) obtained a combined franchise in the Texas League. It was the first of numerous Sherman-Denison twin-city franchises in various circuits. The best player on the club was first baseman William Kemmer, who hit well over .300 for the third season in a row. The colorful Pierce "No Use" Chiles played and managed for part of the season, and Sherman-Denison played better than .500 ball. But fan support was weak, and on July 11, despite a 44-41 record, the Twin-Cities franchise folded.

Sherman-Denison again attempted a joint effort in 1902, when the Texas League reorganized after another two-year hiatus. Cy Mulkey was president, manager, and pitcher for the team. But the Twin Cities club got off to a miserable start, winning just one of its opening 11 games. After the May 5 loss, with attendance understandably poor, Mulkey moved his club to Texarkana.

There was no more professional ball in Sherman-Denison for a decade. Then the Twin Cities placed a franchise in the Texas-Oklahoma League, operating in 1912, 1913, 1914, 1921, and 1922, with three seasons in the Western Association, 1915–1917. In 1923 Otto McIver, a 13-year Texas Leaguer, managed Sherman-Denison to a Texas Association championship, and in 1929 Sherman placed an entry in the Lone Star League. After World War II the Sherman-Denison Twins flourished in the East Texas and Big State Leagues. In 1946 third baseman Donald Stokes won the East Texas League batting title with a .361 average.

But the most remarkable performance of 1946 was delivered by a 34-year-old Twins' righthander. Monty Stratton had gone 15-5 and 15-9 for the Chicago White Sox in 1937 and 1938, but his big league career ended tragically when he shot himself in the leg while

hunting on his mother's farm near Greenville. His right leg was
amputated above the knee. Years later Stratton pitched a few exhibition games, found that his sweeping curve still was effective, and
signed with the Twins in 1946. He completed 20 of 27 starts and
carved out a brilliant 18-8 record. Stratton moved to Waco in 1947,
but Stokes hit .390 for the Twins (he did not repeat as batting
champ — former Texas Leaguer Vernon Washington clubbed out a
.404 mark for Texarkana) and the team batting average was .314
with a league-leading 258 home runs, including 58 by left fielder —
and future Texas Leaguer — Buck Frierson.

The next season brought a Big State League pennant to
Twins' Park, which was located just off the highway between Sherman and Denison. The Washington Senators stocked the Twins
with Cuban players, including shortstop Willie Miranda, who
made the big leagues in 1951. The 1951 season nearly brought another Big State League title to Sherman-Denison, but the Twins
lost in the finals to Gainesville. The final Twins' franchise was a
weak entry in the Class D Center State League. In 1956 old Twins'
Park was destroyed by a tornado.

Year	Record	Pcg.	Finish
1895	53-64	.453	Fifth
1896	25-27	.481	Fourth
1897	44-41	.518	Fourth
1902	1-10	.091	Sixth

Shreveport (Pirates, Gassers, Oilers, Sports, Braves, Captains)

When Ted Sullivan reorganized the Texas League in 1895,
Shreveport was one of eight teams to start the season. Aside from a
brief appearance by New Orleans in 1888, there had never been a
Texas League team from outside the Lone Star State until Shreveport's Pirates. The first Shreveport club was strong, finishing second in the first half of 1895 with a sparkling 42-18 record. But in
July attendance problems plagued several teams. Early in August,

the teams in Austin, Houston, and San Antonio decided to fold, and the league arbitrarily dropped Shreveport's club to keep the schedule balanced and to eliminate travel to Louisiana.

The Pirates played in the Southern Association from 1901 through 1907, then Capt. W. T. Crawford purchased the Temple franchise and Shreveport rejoined the Texas League for the 1908, 1909, and 1910 seasons. But these were undistinguished Pirate clubs which stayed mired in the second division. Captain Crawford sold his franchise and players to Austin interests, and once again Shreveport left the Texas League. In 1915, however, Crawford repurchased the Austin franchise. By this time Galveston had assumed the nickname "Pirates," so Shreveport became the "Gassers."

In 1915 and 1916 outfielder Hyder Barr led the league in triples. The Gassers went into the last day of 1916 needing a double-header victory over Fort Worth to win the pennant. But the Panthers managed a double bill split, and the Gassers finished second to Waco. In 1919 the Gassers won the first half. Even though they dropped to fifth place in the second half, they engaged in a postseason playoff with Fort Worth. The Gassers won the first three games but could not gain the fourth victory until game number seven, held in Shreveport. Before the home fans the Gassers won, 6-5, and Shreveport had its first Texas League flag.

In 1921 first baseman Hack Eibel, a left-handed slugger, hit .337 and led the league in home runs (35 — a new circuit record), triples (18), RBIs (145 — also a new record), and walks (106). In 1908 Shreveport outfielder Tony Thebo stole 90 bases to lead the league, and in 1922 the pacesetter was Gasser infielder Homer Ezell, with 55 thefts. But 1922 saw the first of three consecutive last-place finishes by Shreveport. Local baseball fans during these dismal years found solace in the big league teams which trained in Shreveport. As early as 1903 Detroit brought the Tigers to Shreveport for their spring training camp, and they returned the next spring. In 1914 and 1915 Chicago of the Federal League worked into shape at the State Fair Grounds, where a clubhouse was built beneath the racetrack grandstand. The Cincinnati Redlegs trained at the Fair Grounds in 1916 and 1917, while the next season Shreveport hosted the St. Louis Browns. In 1921 Babe Ruth and the New York Yankees trained at Gasser Park, while the Gassers moved out to the Fair Grounds. The Yankees played 16 games with the Brooklyn Dodgers and 11 contests with the Gassers; the Texas League club actually beat New York twice. The Browns returned in 1923, and that spring local fans also got to see the Yankees, White Sox, and Dodgers in exhibition games. Even after major league clubs stopped training in Shreveport, the city was on the spring exhibition route through the 1940s.

By this time Shreveport's club had a new nickname, the Oilers, but fared little better in the standings. In 1932 the Oilers were off to a miserable 9-21 start. On the night of May 4, following a loss to Galveston, fire consumed the ball park, destroying the grandstands and Oiler equipment and uniforms (Galveston lost only a bag of bats — visiting teams still dressed in their hotels, and Galveston had returned downtown clad in their uniforms). Management announced that the next several games would be played in East Texas while the park was rebuilt. There was an excellent crowd in Longview, however, and even better turnouts in Tyler, and on May 15 the franchise was transferred to Tyler.

But B. A. Hardey, president of the short-lived 1932 club, would not give up, and arranged for the purchase of the ball park site. Six years later, the Galveston club came up for sale. Hardey and a fellow baseball enthusiast, Henry O'Neal, board president of the Shreveport Chamber of Commerce, organized the Shreveport-Texas League Baseball Corporation, which bought Galveston's franchise and players for $23,000. Bonneau Peters long would serve expertly as club president without pay, and groundskeeper A. E. Gaedke was installed in a small bachelor's dwelling just beyond right field. The new stadium, Texas League Park (later renamed Braves' Field, Bonneau Peters Stadium, SPAR Stadium, and informally known as Gaedke's Gardens), was built on the old site and at its peak could — and occasionally did — seat 10,000.

Texas League Park was not quite complete when play opened in 1938, but fans flocked to see the Shreveport "Sports." Although the Sports lost their first nine games and finally finished sixth, Shreveport led the league in attendance. On a hot, muggy Sunday afternoon, Sports' shortstop Salty Parker hit a grand slam home run, and a few minutes later outfielder Merv Connors blasted another grand slam in the same inning. Although the legendary hitter Homer Peel was player-manager in 1939 and 1940, there were two

Al Gaedke, longtime Shreveport groundskeeper, lived in a house in the far right field corner year round. During the off-season, he transformed the outfield into a small golf course, and his domain was known as "Gaedke's Gardens." In the winter of 1938–1939, the owners kept sheep in the ball park, but one morning Gaedke found that dogs had wiped out the flock.

— Courtesy Bill McIntyre, *Shreveport Times*

more second-division finishes. But in 1941, led by slugging right fielder Vernon Washington (.349 in 1941) and utility man nonpareil Jo-Jo Vitter (Texas League All-Star team three years in a row), the Sports reached the playoffs. It was Shreveport's first postseason action since the 1919 pennant. The Sports, now managed by Salty Parker, were eliminated in the first round, suffering three straight losses to Tulsa.

But the Sports were back in 1942. The "Parkermen" faced Fort Worth in the first round, beat the Cats in Fort Worth in a 19-inning marathon, and won the series in seven games. In the pennant playoff, Beaumont took three of the first four games from Shreveport, and the next morning a Beaumont newspaper wished Shreveport a pleasant winter. The Sports responded with back-to-back 3-0 shutouts by George Maltzberger (16-12 during the regular season) and Porky Lade (18-7, 1.80 ERA). Then Maltzberger, working with only one day's rest, hurled Shreveport's third straight shutout, 4-0, and the Sports won their second Texas League crown before the home crowd. In their first Dixie Series, Shreveport lost to Nashville, four games to two.

After World War II, the Sports struggled to two second-division finishes, but Shreveport won the Texas League opening day attendance cup in 1946, 1947, 1948, and 1951 (the uniquely named "Left Shoe Off Club" was a productive booster organization). Salty Parker put the club back in the playoffs in 1948 and 1949, although Fort Worth beat the Parkerman in the first round both years. The next playoff appearance came in 1952, when the Sports were led by batting champ Grant Dunlap (.333) and Harry Elliott (.321 with 104 RBIs). The Sports drubbed Fort Worth in four straight in the first playoff round, then beat Oklahoma City, four games to one, to capture their third pennant. Again the Sports were frustrated in the Dixie Series, losing to Memphis in six games.

The Sports recorded a first-place finish for the first time in 1954, under the guidance of popular player-manager Mel McGaha. First baseman Ed Mickelson hit .335 with 139 RBIs, while Long John Andre went 21-9 and Bob Smith was 13-5 with a league-leading 2.89 ERA. The postseason was anticlimactic, as Fort Worth won in the first round, four games to one. But the following year McGaha put the Sports back in the playoffs, as Pidge Browne hit .304 and paced the league with 33 home runs (one mammoth shot cleared the center field scoreboard in LaGrave Field and sailed more than 500 feet before hitting a house), and 40-year-old first baseman Les Fleming hit .303 with 21 homers. Joe Koppe (1953–1955) was regarded as the best shortstop in the league, while Arnie Atkins headed the 1955 mound staff at 22-8. The 1955 Sports defeated San Antonio in the first round of playoffs in six games, then went the full seven games to edge Houston for the pennant. Mobile swept the Dixie Series in four games, but since 1952 the Sports had twice captured the Texas League flag and finished first another season.

The sensation of 1956 was right fielder Ken Guettler. Although he only appeared in 140 games, Guettler, who wore bottle-thick eyeglasses, hit .293 and led the league with 143 RBIs and 115 runs scored — and an eye-popping 62 home runs, which eclipsed Big Boy Kraft's 55 roundtrippers in 1924 as the all-time Texas League mark. Shreveport fans witnessed 39 of Guettler's blasts clear the 20-foot-high fences at Texas League Park. Despite Guettler's heroics, the Sports sagged to seventh in 1956, then finished last the next year. From 204,231 paid admissions in 1952 the Sports dropped to 40,919 in 1956, and it was decided not to field a club in 1958.

In 1959, 1960, and 1961 Shreveport tried the Southern Association, then dropped out of organized baseball until 1968, when the Atlanta Braves moved their Austin franchise to Shreveport. Then the old ball park — now called SPAR Stadium — was refurbished and Shreveport rejoined the Texas League. "We're back where we belong," commented Bonneau Peters. For three seasons Shreveport was known as the Braves because of their parent club, but Atlanta moved the franchise in 1971. Shreveport acquired the El Paso franchise, and from 1971 to the present the team has been called the Captains.

Since reentering the Texas League in 1968, Shreveport has not enjoyed another pennant, although there were Eastern Division championships in 1976 and 1979. Mitchell Page tied for the league lead in home runs (23) in 1975 and Dan Gladden led the league in stolen bases (52) in 1981. In 1970 Ron Schueler pitched a no-hitter, a feat duplicated by Shreveport hurlers Juan Arias in 1978 and Mike Glinatsis in 1979, while Davie Wilhelmi pitched a perfect game in Little Rock in 1983.

SPAR Stadium, which had badly deteriorated through the years, was last used in 1985. (The author had the pleasure of attending the final game in the historic ball park, along with 1,500 other fans who regularly shook the old grandstand with a "wave.") Beginning in 1986, the Captain's home became Fair Grounds Field, a splendid facility seating 5,200, plus 1,000 more in the beer garden, and boasting an air-conditioned skybox area. On opening night, over 7,200 fans jammed into Fair Grounds Field, the All-Star Game brought in another 4,600, and paid attendance soared past 183,000 as the Caps made it to the playoffs. The parent club Giants stocked the Caps' roster in an obvious effort to help rejuvenate Shreveport baseball, and as the Texas League enters its second century Shreveport is one of the most promising franchises.

Year	Record	Pcg.	Finish
1895	58-38	.604	Fourth
1908	66-78	.458	Sixth
1909	73-68	.518	Fifth

About 1,500 Captains' fans gathered in 1985 for the last game in Shreveport's historic old SPAR Stadium.

— Courtesy Author's collection

1910	75-66	.532	Fifth
1915	62-85	.422	Seventh
1916	84-61	.579	Second
1917	72-90	.444	Seventh
1918	34-50	.405	Sixth
1919	81-59	.579	Second — won playoff
1920	81-66	.551	Third
1921	74-84	.468	Fifth
1922	56-99	.381	Eighth
1923	50-99	.336	Eighth
1924	54-100	.351	Eighth
1925	59-84	.386	Seventh
1926	77-79	.494	Fourth
1927	73-82	.471	Sixth
1928	79-81	.494	Fourth
1929	91-66	.580	Second
1930	86-65	.570	Third
1931	66-94	.413	Sixth
1932	9-21	.300	Eighth — dropped out
1938	69-90	.434	Sixth
1939	86-75	.534	Fifth

1940	72-88	.450	Seventh
1941	80-71	.530	Third — lost opener
1942	83-61	.576	Second — won opener and finals, lost Dixie Series
1946	61-92	.399	Seventh
1947	75-79	.487	Fifth
1948	76-77	.497	Fourth — lost opener
1949	80-74	.519	Fourth — lost opener
1950	63-91	.409	Seventh
1951	63-98	.391	Eighth
1952	84-77	.534	Third — won opener and finals, lost Dixie Series
1953	79-75	.513	Fifth
1954	90-71	.559	First — lost opener
1955	87-74	.540	Third — won opener and finals, lost Dixie Series
1956	69-85	.448	Seventh
1968	78-62	.557	Second
1969	61-75	.448	Third
1970	58-76	.433	Fourth
1972	64-76	.457	Fourth
1973	70-68	.507	Second
1974	59-79	.428	Third
1975	76-52	.594	Second
1976	70-66	.515	First — won Eastern Division, lost playoff
1977	62-68	.477	Third
1978	55-81	.404	Fourth
1979	73-62	.541	Second — lost opener
1980	49-87	.360	Fourth
1981	68-67	.504	Third
1982	62-73	.459	Fourth
1983	72-64	.529	First (best record in division, but second each half)
1984	59-77	.434	Seventh
1985	72-64	.529	Third
1986	80-56	.588	Second — lost opener

Temple (Boll Weevils)

The Temple Boll Weevils participated in the Texas League for three consecutive seasons, 1905–1907. J. Doak Roberts, league president, agreed to head the first Temple club, with the assurance of local backing. Roberts selected Prince Ben Shelton, his classy first baseman in Corsicana the previous two seasons, as player-manager of the Boll Weevils.

Roberts and Shelton rounded up an excellent pitching staff: southpaw Rick Adams, who would go up to the American League before the season ended; Hickory Dickson, starting a professional career that would lead to the big leagues; Red Jarvis, a popular veteran who eventually spent 14 years in the Texas League; and Roy Mitchell, a 20-game winner for Temple who enjoyed seven seasons in the major leagues. There was also Smiling George Blackburn, a league crowdpleaser since 1892 who still displayed versatility on the mound or in the infield or outfield. The catcher was Heavy Blair, a Corsicana Oiler in 1903 and an American Leaguer by 1907. Zena Clayton led the Texas League in doubles and third basemen in games and fielding, and the aggressive Mickey Coyle added experience and hustle to the infield. The outfield was led by slick-fielding Dee Poindexter and Otto McIver, an excellent baserunner.

This talented club found the 1905 Texas League unusually competitive. There were six teams, but Austin and Corsicana dropped out with losing records. Each of the four surviving teams concluded the year with winning marks. But when the Boll Weevils finished their home schedule on August 29, they enjoyed a four-game lead over the second-place Fort Worth Panthers, with seven games remaining on the road. Four of those games were in Fort Worth; the Panthers won a doubleheader on August 30, then swept the series with single victories the next two days. Temple won two out of the last three from Dallas, but Fort Worth copped the pennant by half a game with three straight wins over Waco.

Roberts lost money in Temple and in 1906 backed Cleburne's only Texas League team — where he also lost money. But another Corsicana businessman, J. E. Edens, organized a club in Temple. Early in the 1906 season a local stock company headed by Mayor Fred P. Hammill bought out Edens. Everyone from 1905 had moved on, except for pitching ace Roy Mitchell and infielder-outfielder Wesley Nicholls. When the season was split on June 30 the Boll Weevils were in fifth place with a 20-44 record. Third-place Greenville folded, which forced the league to drop another team to maintain a balanced schedule. Last-place Waco had a miserable record (15-48) but was willing to continue. Since Temple was the most southerly team and presented the greatest traveling expenses for visiting clubs, the league voted to drop the Boll Weevils. Temple backers, who had purchased the franchise and vigorously supported their club, angrily sought an injunction and damages against other team owners.

In 1907 the South Texas and Texas League merged. Seven cities organized franchises, and Prince Ben Shelton agreed to head an eighth club in Temple if the other teams would provide players. The outfield was superb: veterans Otto McIver, Dee Poindexter, Trapper Longley, and speedy Tony Thebo. Pitcher Red Jarvis returned, while Shelton, Mickey Coyle, and Wesley Nicholls were infield returnees. But the team never jelled, and support was poor, in part because the league's cavalier action in 1906 had left a bitter resentment in Temple. During the latter part of the season, Shelton found it necessary to play all of his games on the road. "The strolling players" finished in last place.

Professional baseball was far from dead in Temple. The city held franchises in the Middle Texas League (1914 and 1915), the Central Texas League (1916 and 1917), and the Texas Association (1924, 1925, 1926). Then, after an absence of more than two decades from professional ball, Temple joined the Big State League for seven seasons (1949–1954 and 1957).

Year	Record	Pcg.	Finish
1905	70-59	.543	Second
1906	20-44	.313	Fifth
1907	52-88	.371	Eighth

Texarkana

Texarkana's first professional baseball team was a Texas League entry. In 1902, when the league reorganized after two years of inactivity, there were six clubs. But Denison, whose president, manager, and best pitcher was veteran Texas Leaguer Cy Mulkey, lost 10 of its first 11 games. Attendance was totally inadequate to meet expenses, so Mulkey moved his club to Texarkana and a ball park where the Texarkana Casket Company later was built.

But the roster, weak enough to start with, was raided by other clubs during the transfer, and several local players received their first — and only — professional experience. Nevertheless, Texarkana fans saw a few old pros in action — Mulkey and infielders Dit Spencer and

Harry Tackaberry — and outfielder Don Curtis would play, manage, and umpire in the Texas League for the rest of the decade.

This makeshift crew continued to lose, and Mulkey soon sold out and returned to his law practice in Denison. C. B. DeWitt, who bought Mulkey's interests, pitched and played in the infield. On June 15, a match with the league-leading Corsicana Oilers was moved to Ennis because Sunday ball was not allowed in Corsicana. DeWitt was on the mound, but he proved no match for one of the most dominant teams in Texas League history. DeWitt was pounded for 53 hits, including 16 home runs that soared out of the tiny Ennis ball park. The final score was 51-3 in a game that set many all-time records for a professional contest at any level.

When the first half of the season was declared on July 8, Corsicana was atop the league with a spectacular 59-8 mark, while Texarkana was mired in last place at 20-47. The record since moving from Denison was 19-37, and there was little fan support. Texarkana dropped out of the league, along with Waco.

But Texarkana would rebound strongly in professional ball. The team participated in the Texas-Oklahoma League in 1913 and 1914. A new diamond was erected at Maxwell Park near the State Line: sportswriters happily wrote of home runs hit from Texas into Arkansas! In 1924 the Texarkana Bears, now playing at Lee Park, entered the East Texas League for the next three seasons. The Bears played in the Lone Star League, 1927–1929, the Cotton States League in 1941, and again in the East Texas League, 1937–1939 and 1946. There followed eight seasons in the Class B Big State League, 1947–1953, before organized baseball finally left Texarkana for good.

Year	Record	Pcg.	Finish
1902	19-37	.339	Sixth

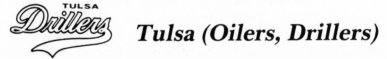

Tulsa (Oilers, Drillers)

"Let's . . . go . . . Tulsa!"

Andy Andrews, an Oilers fan for many years, became a fixture at Tulsa baseball games by slowly bellowing his familiar chant to the cheers of an expectant crowd. Professional baseball has been a going concern in Tulsa since 1905, when the oil boom town of 4,000 fielded a team in the Missouri Valley League. The city's population reached 27,000 by 1920, 141,000 by 1930, and today the metropolitan area totals more than 500,000. Baseball has prospered along with the city.

The Tulsa Oilers played in the Oklahoma-Arkansas-Kansas League in 1907 and the Oklahoma-Kansas League the next year. The Oilers participated in the Western Association in 1910 and 1911, tried the Oklahoma State League in 1912, then returned to the Western Association from 1914 through 1917. In 1919 the Oilers joined the Western League, winning pennants in 1920, 1922, 1927, 1929, and 1932.

The first home of the Oilers was Athletic Park, located on West Archer, a little east of what became Owen Park. Within three or four years the ball park was moved to East Archer, east of the Missouri Valley and south of the Frisco tracks, between First and Archer. Within a few years there was a new park at South Main, where a 1913 exhibition game pitting the New York Giants against the Chicago White Sox featured a pitching duel between Christy Mathewson and Walter Johnson. Johnson, the Washington Senators' ace, hurled a shutout victory over the Giants, but the overflow crowd collapsed the right field bleachers, and a soldier was killed. When the Oilers joined the Western League in 1919, McNulty Park was built in 22 days at 10th and Elgin. McNulty Park was sold to commercial interests in 1929 and demolished, which forced Tulsa to drop out of the league in 1930. Playing on a diamond in front of the old Fair Grounds racetrack grandstand, the Oilers rejoined the Western League in 1931 and 1932.

Tulsa and Oklahoma City entered the Texas League in 1933, intensifying a natural rivalry with a massive brawl that erupted in Tulsa when Oiler pitcher Ralph Birkhofer deliberately hit Ralph Boyle with a pitch. The Oilers finished sixth in their inaugural Texas League season, but in 1934 moved from their makeshift race track diamond to a new wooden park just to the north. (For years a bandstand on the third base side was the home of the Wildcatter Band, which would march through the stands between innings and would allow one child to share the bandstand with them at each game.) First called Tulsa County Stadium, the facility later was known as Texas League Park, then Oiler Park. A legendary Texas

League slugger, "Pound 'em Paul" Easterling (.296 with 29 homers and 105 RBIs), was the 1934 home run champ, and he was ably supported by first baseman Alex Hooks (.340), left fielder Chuck Hostetler (.324 with a league-leading 124 runs scored), and right fielder John Stoneham (.314 with 109 RBIs).

This explosive team barely missed the playoffs, but from 1935 through 1965, the Oilers made 21 playoff appearances in 28 seasons. The 1936 Oilers beat Houston in the playoff opener and outlasted Dallas in a seven-game final series to take the playoff title. Left fielder Murray Howell (.319 with 23 homers and 127 RBIs) sparked the offense, along with center fielder Harold Patchett (.305) and first baseman Bernard Cobb (.304), while the best pitcher was Newell Kimball (16-7). In their first Dixie Series, the Oilers swept the Birmingham Barons in four straight games.

The 1938 playoff club was led by right fielder Stanley Schino (.302 with a league-leading 25 homers and 118 RBIs) and Max Thomas (23-14, with 29 complete games in 34 starts and a 1.98 ERA). Lou "The Mad Russian" Novikoff won the batting title in 1939 (.368), and Gordon Donaldson (.319) won the crown the next year. In 1940 Dizzy Dean came to town, installed his wife in Tulsa's finest apartment complex, the Sophian Plaza, and tried to work his arm back into shape. Enthusiastic crowds turned out to see Diz, but his comeback attempt failed with an 8-8 record.

Following World War II, Texas League Park was spruced up with $100,000 worth of improvements, and the Oilers made five straight playoff appearances. The 1947 club featured infielder Jack Cassini (.319), who led the league in stolen bases (52) and runs scored (116). Several future Oilers would win the stolen base crown: Tommy Tatum in 1948 (also the batting champ at .333); John Temple in 1951; Jim Frey in 1957 (also the batting champ at .336); Jim Beauchamp in 1958 and 1959; Joe Patterson in 1962 (31), 1963 (54), and 1964 (67); Walter Williams in 1965; Ed Miller in 1977 (80); Greg Jamison in 1978 (65); and Nick Capra in 1980 (55). Aside from winning the stolen base title, another Tulsa baseball tradition was the Diamond Dinner, annually featuring the likes of Casey Stengal, Joe DiMaggio, Dizzy Dean, Ducky Medwick, Duke Snider, Bob Feller, Hank Aaron, Satchel Paige, Sandy Koufax, Ken Boyer, Johnny Bench, and Willie Mays.

The star of the 1948 playoff team was southpaw Harry Perkowski (22-10), who also was the club's best pinch hitter (.281 in 71 games), and who went to the National League the next year. Russ Burns, a strapping outfielder "with arms like Popeye," led the league in home runs and RBIs in 1948 (.310 with 26 homers and 113 RBIs) and in RBIs again the next year (.340 with 27 homers and 153 RBIs). Burns and manager Al Vincent led the 1949 Oilers to second place. In the playoff opener, hated Oklahoma City won the first two games in Tulsa, but the Oilers rallied to win four straight. In the finals, Fort Worth won the first two at home, then Tulsa took the next three. Back in Fort Worth, the Panthers won the sixth game, 1-0. The decisive contest was deadlocked in the 11th inning when first baseman Joe Adcock (.298 with 19 homers and 109 RBIs) walloped a three-run homer to win Tulsa's second playoff title. The Dixie Series went seven games before the Oilers lost to the Birmingham Barons.

On July 12, 1952, 37-year-old Johnny Vander Meer, who had pitched back-to-back no-hitters for Cincinnati in 1938, twirled a 12-0 no-hitter against Beaumont while in the twilight of his career in Tulsa. Beginning in 1959, the Oilers made seven consecutive playoff appearances. The 1960 team, led by James Hickman (.323) and Fred Whitfield (.310 with 23 homers), beat San Antonio in the opening round, then won three straight from Victoria to bring another playoff flag to Tulsa.

The Oilers won back-to-back playoff titles in 1962 and 1963. Managed by Whitey Kurowski, the 1962 Oilers did not lose a single playoff game, downing Albuquerque, then Austin, in three straight. Jim Beauchamp (.337 with 31 homers and 105 RBIs) was back in 1963 to pace the Oilers to playoff triumphs over Austin and San Antonio. The 1964 Oilers made it to the finals before losing to San Antonio. The next year batting champ Dave Tavlesic (.344) and Walter Williams (.330 with a league-leading 106 runs and 36 stolen bases), along with pitchers Harold Gilson (11-4) and Donal Hagen (13-6), led the Oilers to Tulsa's only first-place Texas League finish. But the playoff was a disappointment, as Western Division champ Albuquerque won three out of four games.

Oiler president A. Ray Smith, who had bailed out the club financially and put $200,000 into ball park renovations when he took control in 1961, was encouraged to move up to AAA by total attendance exceeding 200,000 for three straight years. Smith placed the

The 1985 Tulsa Drillers. Pitcher Bobby Witt (standing, fourth from left) went on to become a rookie sensation for the 1986 Texas Rangers.

— Courtesy Tulsa Drillers

Oilers in the Pacific Coast League in 1966, and after three seasons transferred to the American Association. Following the 1976 season, frustrated by the city's persistent refusal to build a new stadium, Smith moved his franchise to New Orleans.

But construction executive Bill Rollings, a boyhood fan of the Oilers, and country music star Roy Clark bought the Lafayette franchise (to be called the "Drillers"), poured a vast amount of money into decaying Texas League Park, and arranged an affiliation with the Texas Rangers. The Rangers and Astros played an exhibition game in the 43-year-old stadium on April 3, 1977. A heavy rain broke out, and a section of the stadium collapsed, hurling 17 fans 20 feet to the ground. Although no one was killed, several were seriously injured, and the ensuing investigation revealed that most of the structure was rotten. The wooden stands and roof were razed, replaced by temporary bleachers. The 1977 Drillers won the first half in the East, but lost the division title to Arkansas.

The next year's team had a losing record, and attendance plunged to 46,000. Rollings waged a long fight for a new stadium. His construction company provided much of the work, and the 7,300-seat facility opened in 1981 just east of old Texas League Park. The 1981 Drillers responded by winning the second half in the East, although first-half champ Arkansas prevailed in the playoffs. The following season Tulsa again won the second half, then defeated Jackson for the Eastern Division title. The Drillers swept powerful El Paso in three games to win Tulsa's sixth Texas League playoff title. The 1982 champions featured outfielder Tom Dunbar (.323) and pitchers Brad Mengwasser (13-6) and Allen Lachowicz (12-8). Ron Darling pitched for the Drillers in 1981, and such Texas Rangers as Pete O'Brien, Steve Buechele, Jeff Kunkel, and Bobby Witt have worn Driller uniforms during the 1980s. Young, aggressive Joe Preseren became general manager in 1984. Preseren attracted more than 10,000 fans into Tulsa County Stadium with a magnificent fireworks display at a game on July 4, 1985. The Tulsa franchise is ably led, enjoys a rich baseball tradition, and is one of the cornerstones of the current Texas League.

Year	Record	Pcg.	Finish
1933	65-86	.430	Sixth
1934	77-75	.519	Fifth
1935	82-79	.509	Fourth — lost opener
1936	80-74	.519	Third — won opener, finals, and Dixie Series
1937	89-69	.563	Second — lost opener
1938	86-75	.534	Fourth — lost opener
1939	78-82	.488	Sixth
1940	76-82	.481	Fifth
1941	86-66	.566	Second — won opener, lost finals
1942	76-75	.533	Sixth
1946	84-69	.549	Fourth — lost opener
1947	79-75	.513	Fourth — lost opener
1948	91-63	.591	Second — won opener, lost finals
1949	90-64	.584	Second — won opener and finals, lost Dixie Series
1950	83-69	.546	Third — won opener, lost finals
1951	67-94	.416	Seventh
1952	78-83	.484	Seventh
1953	83-71	.539	Second — won opener, lost finals
1954	78-83	.484	Sixth
1955	86-75	.534	Fifth — lost playoff for fourth place
1956	77-77	.500	Fourth — lost opener
1957	75-79	.487	Fourth — lost opener
1958	71-81	.467	Seventh
1959	77-67	.535	Third — lost opener
1960	76-68	.528	Third — won opener, finals, and Pan-Am Series
1961	83-55	.601	Second — lost opener
1962	77-63	.550	Second — won opener and finals
1963	74-66	.529	Third — won opener and finals
1964	79-61	.564	Second — won opener, lost finals
1965	81-60	.574	First — lost playoffs
1977	68-62	.516	Third — lost opener
1978	57-78	.422	Third

1979	58-75	.436	Fourth
1980	75-61	.551	Second
1981	68-65	.511	First — lost opener
1982	70-66	.515	First — won opener and finals
1983	63-73	.463	Eighth
1984	62-73	.459	Fifth
1985	60-76	.441	Sixth
1986	49-85	.366	Eighth

Tyler (Sports)

Tyler long had been a baseball hotbed when it finally obtained a Texas League franchise. Tyler fielded professional teams in the South Central League, Middle Texas League, East Texas League, and Lone Star League during the seasons of 1912, 1915, 1924–1929, and 1931. There were pennant winners in 1924, 1927, and 1929. But the Depression year of 1931 saw the East Texas League fold after just two weeks of play, and the next year there was no circuit for Tyler to join.

Three weeks after the 1932 Texas League season opened, however, Shreveport's ball park was destroyed by fire. A couple of days later Shreveport played San Antonio before a good crowd in Longview, then shifted to Tyler for the last two games of the series. At first Shreveport management announced plans to rebuild their park immediately, but these plans soon derailed. Fan support in Tyler was promising, and soon it was decided to place the club in the East Texas oil capital for the duration of the season — which meant that the Texas League had an all-Lone Star membership for the first time since 1914.

A public poll was taken, and from hundreds of suggestions it was decided to call the team the Tyler "Sports," the same name used in Shreveport. Opening day in the franchise's new home was May 21. There was a parade through downtown Tyler, a Lone Star flag was brandished in the center of the diamond as a band played "The Eyes of Texas," and Governor Ross Sterling threw out the first ball.

When the Sports came to Tyler, the famous George Sisler was the manager and first baseman. Sisler had compiled a lifetime .340 batting average in 15 big league seasons, including a remarkable .407 in 1920, and he appeared in 70 games for the Sports and hit

.287. There were other notable ex-major leaguers wearing the Tyler uniform: 42-year-old Wally Schang had caught for 19 years in the American league, but hit just .214 in 23 Texas League games; infielder Aaron Ward had spent 12 seasons in the American League, and he batted .264 in 99 games for the Sports. Future major leaguers included outfielders Vernon Washington, who pounded the ball at a .350 clip in 89 games, and Wally Moses, who batted .287 in 41 games, then went on to an American League career that spanned 1935–1951. Outfielder Cy Cashion batted .318 in 58 games, infielder Ray Ater hit .296 in 72 games, and slick-fielding third baseman Gus Whelan hit .283 in 74 games, usually as leadoff man.

Overall, there were too many veterans past their prime to play regularly, and the good young players on the way up only played part of the season. None of the pitchers had a winning record. Sisler, bothered by eye trouble, stepped down, to be followed in turn by Walter Morris and Frank Kitchens. The inconsistency in the lineup and in field managers, combined with a weak pitching staff, produced a last-place 57-93 finish. The initial enthusiasm for Texas League ball lagged as the defeats piled up, and at season's end the franchise was turned back over to the league.

Tyler promptly reentered the lower minors, fielding teams in the Dixie League, West Dixie league, East Texas League, Lone Star League, and Big State League. In 1938 Tyler broke in a new ball park, built by the WPA, with an East Texas League pennant. This fine old field continued to be Tyler's professional home until the last team dropped out of the Big State League in 1955. For years the Tyler Junior College Apaches continued to play there, and amateur teams still use the diamond, although it is deteriorating and in need of repair.

Year	Record	Pcg.	Finish
1932	48-72	.400	Eighth

Victoria (Rosebuds, Giants, Toros)

Victoria made its first appearance in the Texas League in 1958. By the turn of the century Victoria had fielded its first semi-pro team, and in 1905 the semi-pro "Safe Hits" went undefeated.

Future Texas League star Pat Newnam played first base for the Safe Hits, and pitcher C. H. Wilson won 27 straight decisions.

The Victoria Rosebuds, which won the Class D Southwest Texas League pennant in 1910, brought the South Texas city into professional baseball. The Southwest Texas League folded after the 1911 season, but Victoria continued to field excellent semi-pro teams. The Rosebuds spent 1926 in the Gulf Coast League, joined the Guadalupe Valley League in 1940, and won titles in 1940, 1946, 1948, and 1949. In 1956 and 1957 Victoria placed two clubs, the Eagles and Rosebuds, in the Class B Big State League.

The Big State League disbanded after the 1957 season, but if Victoria could support two Class B teams, surely there would be enough backing for one Class AA club. The Rosebuds joined the Texas League for 1958, affiliated with the Los Angeles Dodgers. Lon Rochelli, who had had a cup of coffee with the old Brooklyn Dodgers during World War II, was the manager, but the supply of talent was limited. There were a couple of good pitchers, Carroll Beringer (10-1) and Chris Nicolesi (15-12), and young outfielder Tommy Davis (.304) flashed the talent of a future big league star. Left fielder Jim Miller (.289 with 19 homers and 114 RBIs) and in-fielder Allen Norris (20 home runs in 108 games) supplied power, but there was little other offensive punch, and the rest of the pitching staff was weak. The Rosebuds finished last in the standings and in attendance.

Dallas, Fort Worth, and Houston moved out of the Texas League in 1959, but Amarillo joined the circuit, and the six teams organized the Pan-American Association with the Mexican League. Victoria had a new manager, Pete Reiser, a Brooklyn star of the 1940s whose hell-for-leather style of play cut short his career because of injuries. Reiser had a team that shared his explosive offensive talents. Carl Warwick (.331 with 35 homers and 94 RBIs) led the club in hitting and the Texas League in home runs. Big Frank Howard (.356 with 27 homers and 79 RBIs in just 63 games before being called up) most dramatically showed his big league slugging ability by blasting three home runs in three consecutive innings during a June 8 game in Austin. Other hitting talent on the Rosebud roster included Ramon Conde (.326), Charles Smith (.309), Clint McCord (.298), William Parsons (.296), and Don Miles (.281 with 23 home runs and 88 RBIs in only 81 games). Carroll Beringer (19-5) was back to lead the pitching staff and the league in victories, complete games, and winning percentage. Ford Young (18-14) was right behind in wins and tied Beringer in complete games (18). James Harwell (12-9), Scott Breeden (11-6), and reliever Ed Strichek (8-5) rounded out a strong pitching staff. The Rosebuds finished in first place, six games ahead of second-place Austin, but lost in the opening round of the playoffs to fourth-place San Antonio.

There were many changes in 1960, beginning with a new manager. Johnny Pesky, a career .307 hitter in 10 American League seasons, took over as field general. The only big hitters who returned from 1960 were Clint McCord (.300 in 1960) and Don Miles (.276 with 26 homers), but there were several solid new hurlers, beginning with James Proctor (15-8), who also was a good pinch-hitter (.308). Horace Smallwood (12-10) was another pitcher who could swing a bat (.281); James Raugh (11-4) split his time as a starter (19 starts) and reliever (23 bullpen appearances); and reliever Manuel Montejo (10-8) led the Texas League in games pitched (65). The Rosebuds finished fourth, but swept first-place Harlingen in three games in the playoff opener. The season ended, however, when Tulsa beat Victoria in three straight for the title.

The next season was the last for the Pan-American Association — and for the Rosebuds. Attendance was weak throughout the Texas League, and for Victoria the previous three years had produced admissions of only 79,464, 86,040, and 69,760 — excellent totals for a small city of just 50,000, but hardly enough to maintain a Class AA franchise. By May 27 just 13,000 had turned out to watch a last-place team, and the Rosebuds were moved to Ardmore, Oklahoma.

But Victoria was without Texas League baseball for just two weeks. Harlingen's Rio Grande Valley franchise also was in trouble, and on June 10 the San Francisco farm club was transferred to Victoria. The Victoria Giants were managed by Ray Murray, a former big league and Texas League catcher. There was a solid pitching staff, led by Clark Johnson (14-9) and James Gibson (12-9), but center fielder José Tartabull (.304) and catcher Marion Talton (.292) were the only strong hitters. Victoria and Austin finished the schedule with identical records (69-71) and a fourth-place tie. There was a one-game playoff to determine which team would enter the playoff series, but the Giants lost a 4-3 decision.

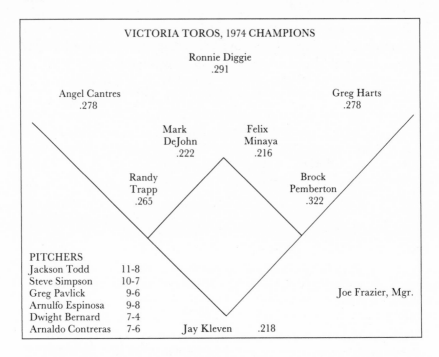

VICTORIA TOROS, 1974 CHAMPIONS

Ronnie Diggie
.291

Angel Cantres
.278

Greg Harts
.278

Mark
DeJohn
.222

Felix
Minaya
.216

Randy
Trapp
.265

Brock
Pemberton
.322

PITCHERS
Jackson Todd   11-8
Steve Simpson   10-7
Greg Pavlick   9-6
Arnulfo Espinosa   9-8
Dwight Bernard   7-4
Arnaldo Contreras   7-6

Joe Frazier, Mgr.

Jay Kleven   .218

Just 26,000 fans had turned out to see the Victoria Giants, and the city lost professional baseball for the next 13 years. But in 1974 the New York Mets moved their AA franchise from Memphis to Victoria. The Victoria Toros had few stars, but manager Joe Frazier juggled his lineup and fashioned a pennant-bound club through teamwork. Jackson Todd (11-8) led the pitching staff and hurled a no-hitter on May 14 against Arkansas. There were two other no-hitters in 1974, and the Toros were victimized both times, by Alexandria on May 20 and San Antonio on June 1. All-Star first baseman Brock Pemberton (.322) was the best Toro hitter, while outfielder Ronnie Diggie (.291) and All-Star third sacker Randy Trapp (.265) also provided talented play.

The Toros had the best record of eight teams and won the Eastern Division. But the Western Division champs, the El Paso Diablos, boasted the Texas League's top three hitters and a team batting average (.305) nearly 50 points higher than that of the Toros (.257). Ignoring the disadvantages on paper, the unimpressive Toros went to work in their businesslike way and beat El Paso in three straight games to claim an outright pennant.

But Victoria would not defend its championship. Attendance in 1974 had been only 49,000, and the Mets moved the team to Lafayette. In five Texas League seasons Victoria had twice finished first, made the playoff series three times, and won the playoffs in their last year. There would be a final fling in Class A with the short-lived Lone Star League, as the Victoria Cowboys in 1976 and — reviving the city's favorite baseball nickname — the Rosebuds in 1977.

Year	Record	Pcg.	Finish
1958	68-85	.445	Eighth
1959	86-60	.589	First — lost opener
1960	77-69	.527	Fourth — won opener, lost finals
1961	69-71	.493	Fifth — lost playoff for fourth place
1974	79-57	.581	First — won playoff

Waco (Tigers, Navigators, Cubs)

Waco entered the Texas League in 1889 and played a total of 27 seasons. Only a trio of flags were collected in more than four decades of Texas League ball, but these pennants came in three consecutive years. Waco fielded one of six teams which made up the Texas League in 1889, and club president Louis Newburg soon became president of the circuit. Undaunted by a last-place finish, Waco tried again in 1890 and 1892. In the latter year Waco joined the league at mid-season, and Ed Grider, a 14-year-old schoolboy pitcher, was signed and worked several turns on the mound.

There was no more professional baseball in Waco until 1897, when the Sherman-Denison Tigers were moved to town by James Drake. Waco baseballers were called the Tigers, a nickname later adopted by the famous Waco High School football squads of coach Paul Tyson. Sunday baseball was not permitted in Waco, but Drake arranged to play in Corsicana and Hillsboro on Sundays.

When the Texas League reorganized in 1902, Waco formed a club managed by Emmett Rodgers, a veteran who had played for Fort Worth, Austin, and San Antonio during the Texas League's inaugural season. Waco dropped out at mid-season, but not before

Rodgers drove in the run that halted Corsicana's record winning streak at 27.

Waco did not start the 1903 season, but Ted Sullivan transferred his club from Paris for the second half. Waco did not play in 1904, but rejoined the league in 1905 for a 15-year stay. Dallas owner Joe Gardner financed Waco's team in 1905 and 1906, but W. R. Davidson headed a local stock company which took control from Gardner. When Davidson was elected Texas League president in 1914, Charles R. Turner became head of the Waco club. During this period, efforts were being made to render the Brazos river navigable from Freeport to Waco, and Waco baseballers now became known as the "Navigators."

In 1911 Davidson hired Ellis Hardy, coach at Texas Christian University, to manage the Navigators. A veteran Texas League first baseman, Hardy had played for Waco in 1897 and 1905. Hardy produced winning teams in Waco for two years, but resigned after the 1912 season. During the next season, Davidson persuaded him to return, and Hardy would stay through 1918, leading Waco to its pinnacle of baseball glory.

The Navigators of 1914, led by tall righthander Eddie Donalds (30-4) and batting champ Robert Clemens (.327), went 102-50 to tie Houston for the pennant after a bitterly disputed race. In 1915 catcher Al Walters (.325) won the hitting crown and Waco won an outright title. The Navigators repeated in 1916, surviving a close chase by Shreveport. For the third year in a row Waco produced the batting champ, right fielder Clarence "Little Bit" Bittle (.335). Righthander Cliff Markle (19-11) led the league in strikeouts (228) in 1915, while southpaw Cliff Hill was the 1916 leader in strikeouts (251) and victories (23-14). Outfielder Bob James was the most consistent hitter (.295, .313, and .303) during the three-year championship run, and a total of 10 players gave Hardy a solid nucleus throughout the Waco dynasty. In addition to James, pitchers Donalds, Hill, and George Sage were aboard during all three seasons, along with catcher Emmett "Turkey" Reilly and a complete infield: first baseman Fred Wohleben, second sacker Walter Malmquist, shortstop Arch Tanner, and third baseman Harvey Grubb.

After third-place finishes in 1917 and 1918 Hardy resigned. The 1919 club was backed by the Young Men's Business League,

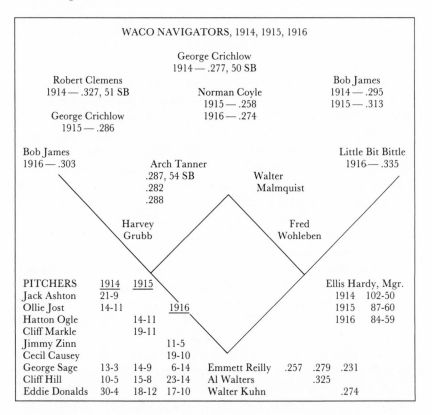

WACO NAVIGATORS, 1914, 1915, 1916

George Crichlow
1914 — .277, 50 SB

Robert Clemens
1914 — .327, 51 SB

Norman Coyle
1915 — .258
1916 — .274

Bob James
1914 — .295
1915 — .313

George Crichlow
1915 — .286

Bob James
1916 — .303

Arch Tanner
.287, 54 SB
.282
.288

Walter
Malmquist

Little Bit Bittle
1916 — .335

Harvey
Grubb

Fred
Wohleben

PITCHERS	1914	1915	1916					Ellis Hardy, Mgr.
Jack Ashton	21-9							1914 102-50
Ollie Jost	14-11							1915 87-60
Hatton Ogle		14-11						1916 84-59
Cliff Markle		19-11						
Jimmy Zinn			11-5					
Cecil Causey			19-10					
George Sage	13-3	14-9	6-14	Emmett Reilly	.257	.279	.231	
Cliff Hill	10-5	15-8	23-14	Al Walters		.325		
Eddie Donalds	30-4	18-12	17-10	Walter Kuhn			.274	

but following a seventh-place season the franchise was sold to Wichita Falls interests. Waco placed a team in the Class D Texas Association in 1923 and 1924. At the end of the 1924 season the Texas League bought Galveston's franchise, and Charles Turner was persuaded to head a stock company that would return Texas League baseball to Waco.

From 1925 through 1930 the Waco Cubs (Galveston had been the "Cubs") were managed by Del Pratt, a 13-year American League infielder with a .292 lifetime batting average. Pratt only managed one winning team in six seasons, but he put on quite a show as a player. Thirty-seven when he came to the Texas League, Pratt kept himself in the lineup as a regular for three years: 1925 (.368, 28 HR, 116 RBI); 1926 (.308, 25 HR, 102 RBI); 1927 (.386, 32 HR, 140 RBI). After winning the triple crown in 1927, Pratt became a spot player, but he hit .287, 299, and .374 over the next three years. A playing-manager until the age of 45, he compiled a lifetime Texas League batting average of .332 over nine seasons and 782 games.

Outfielder George Blackerby was another Waco hitting star during the same period: 1927 (.364, 17 HR, 91 RBI); 1928 (.368, 19 HR, 73 RBI); 1929 (.365, 33 HR, 115 RBI). In three years as a Cub, Blackerby won the hitting title in 1928 and the home run championship the next season. In addition to Pratt and Blackerby, the 1927 second-place Cubs also featured outfielders Max West (.365, 24 HR, 124 RBI) and Randy Moore (.360), who went on to win a batting title with Dallas in 1929.

The home of Waco professional baseball was Katy Park, located just north of old Baylor Stadium and also adjacent to the Cotton Palace Fair Grounds. During the final season of Texas League baseball at Katy Park, the historic stadium was the site of two landmark events. In an effort to stimulate Depression-era attendance, Charles Turner followed a recent minor league innovation and installed light standards at Katy Park. The first Texas League night game was played in Katy Park on June 20, 1930, with Waco downing Fort Worth, 13-0. Other cities soon followed suit, and today most Texas League games are played at night.

On the night of August 6, 1930, Waco trailed Beaumont, 6-2, going into the bottom of the eighth. Waco left fielder Gene Rye, a short, stocky, left-handed slugger who would finish the season with 26 homers and a .367 average, poled a leadoff home run for the Cubs and triggered an offensive explosion. Before the inning ended, Waco had scored 18 runs, and Rye had hammered two more roundtrippers over the tall but close right field fence. Rye's three homers and 12 total bases in one inning, of course, are Texas League records.

Rye went up (briefly) to the Boston Red Sox, and Waco went out (temporarily) of organized baseball. In 1933 Waco helped form the short-lived Dixie League, but the Class D club folded at midseason. For years Katy Park was the site of fine semi-pro ball, as well as Baylor Bears' baseball. During the post–World War II baseball boom, Waco joined the Class B Big State League. The disastrous 1953 Waco tornado badly damaged Katy Park, but the stadium was repaired. The Pirates continued to play through 1956, a year before the Big State League disbanded. Today Katy Park remains basically intact, although in growing disrepair, and it is one of several old stadiums that still stand as former sites of Texas League baseball.

Year	Record	Pcg.	Finish
1889	33-50	.398	Sixth
1890	24-20	.545	Third
1892	16-16	.500	Second
1897	20-17	.541	Fourth
1902	26-35	.426	Fourth
1903	20-36	.357	Third
1905	65-64	.504	Fourth
1906	30-97	.236	Sixth
1907	53-86	.381	Seventh
1908	71-72	.487	Fourth
1909	51-91	.359	Eighth
1910	38-99	.277	Eighth
1911	75-71	.514	Fifth
1912	82-63	.566	Third
1913	81-71	.533	Third
1914	102-50	.670	First — co-champs
1915	87-60	.592	First — pennant
1916	84-59	.587	First — pennant
1917	84-73	.535	Third
1918	45-40	.529	Third
1919	60-86	.411	Seventh
1925	62-86	.419	Sixth
1926	65-91	.417	Eighth
1927	88-68	.564	Second
1928	71-87	.449	Sixth
1929	77-83	.481	Fifth
1930	68-81	.457	Fifth

Wichita (Pilots)

In the 1870s Texas Cowboys drove herds of longhorns to Wichita, Kansas. Texans will return to Wichita in 1986, throwing baseballs instead of lariats. When Beaumont owner Ted Moor, Jr., decided to sell his club following the 1985 season, Larry Schmittou headed a group which purchased the franchise. Searching for the most favorable location for his new team, Schmittou soon settled upon Wichita. The metropolitan area today encompasses a population of nearly 400,000, and the major industry is aircraft manufacture — leading to the team nickname "Pilots."

The Wichita Pilots will be the AA affiliate of the San Diego Padres. Wichita's first professional team was entered in the Class C Western Association (1905–1908). Wichita then served a long stint in the Class A Western League (1909–1933). The Great Depression saw Wichita withdraw from organized baseball, but the city later returned to the Western League (1950–1955). In 1956 Wichita joined the American Association, played three seasons, dropped out for more than a decade, then rejoined the American Association in 1970 and played until 1984.

Kansas' first entry in the Texas League will compete in the Western Division. Steve Smith will move from Beaumont to serve as field manager, and the Pilots will play in Lawrence-Dumont Stadium, an atmospheric ball park built in the 1930s which seats 7,500 and is located beside the Arkansas River in downtown Wichita.

Wichita Falls (Spudders)

The first notable baseball team in Wichita Falls was the semi-pro "Cremos" of 1905, sponsored by The Cremo Cigar Company. The city's first professional club appeared in the Texas-Oklahoma League in 1911, 1912, and 1913. Early baseball was played at a diamond at Scott and Lamar and 13th and 14th streets. A 10-foot board fence surrounded the outfield, and a wooden grandstand at the northeast corner seated fewer than 500. There was a set of bleachers down the left field side, while a double gate provided an entrance for buggies and wagons.

By the fall of 1919 Wichita Falls had grown to 40,000, thanks in great part to a nearby oil boom, and local baseball enthusiasts formed a local stock company to purchase Waco's Texas League franchise. The manager was Walter Salm, whose Texas League playing days had begun with Corsicana in 1903. Right fielder Red Josefson hit .345 to lead the league, and righthander Jimmy Zinn (18-10) pitched a no-hitter against Houston on August 22, and hit .342 in 64 games. The Spudders beat the Dallas Steers, 2-1, on opening day, and went on to finish second in their Texas League debut — indeed, only two Wichita Falls clubs would have losing seasons.

The home of the Spudders, Athletic Park, was built a few

blocks north of the downtown area. The grandstand seated 5,000, and a bleachers section stretched down the right field side. Later, a "Knothole Gang" section was built for young fans. The stadium capacity totaled 8,500, but there were 11,549 paid admissions for the Dixie Series opener in 1927. In 1922 and 1924 fire ravaged the stadium, but both times Athletic Park was rebuilt by the return of the Spudders from a road trip. The press box was perched atop the grandstand roof, while a two-story frame club house was built off the right field area. Downstairs was a shower room and individual lockers, and the upstairs was a dormitory. Most players who attended spring training — especially rookies who had never received a paycheck — stayed in the clubhouse, and so did many single roster members who stretched minor league pay with a free bed. Spring training in Wichita Falls was accompanied by chill winds and occasional snow. Rarely could a major league team be lured to town for a spring exhibition game, but in 1930 the New York Yankees and Babe Ruth came to Wichita Falls, and the Bambino slammed two homers for the Texas fans.

Fort Worth dominated Texas League play during the first six years of the Spudders' existence, and a keen rivalry quickly developed between the two North Texas clubs. Salm, Spudder manager for four seasons, excited the fans with loud quarrels with Jake Atz.

The 1922 Spudders were second only to Fort Worth, and ran off a string of 24 straight victories, all but one before the home fans. The 25th contest, a 4-3 victory over Snipe Conley and the Dallas Steers, had to be forfeited because a Spudder prankster put creosote on the baseball, blistering the mouth of spitballer Conley. Rip Wheeler won 22 games for the Spudders in 1922 and again in 1923, while spitballer Hal Carlson went 20-10 in 1924.

After the 1925 season, J. Alvin Gardner, one of the original club stockholders, purchased the Spudders and set out to build a champion. Although agreements with the Cubs and Pirates had brought several good players to Wichita Falls, Gardner gravitated toward club-owned talent. He paid as much as $5,000 for players who would form the nucleus for the magnificent team which won the pennant and swept the Dixie Series. One of Gardner's most impressive stars was slugging left fielder Tom "Tut" Griffin, who loved the south winds that blew steadily toward the left field fence in Athletic Park, and who averaged .346 in 564 games during five

Babe Ruth and the New York Yankees drew a big crowd at a 1930 exhibition game in Wichita Falls, (left to right): Texas League president J. Alvin Gardner, Ruth, Spudder club president William E. Huff.

— Courtesy Eakin Press, Austin

Texas League seasons. The St. Louis Browns were keenly interested in Jenkins, and Gardner, who had achieved his ambitions for
the club in 1927, agreed to surrender the hard-hitting prospect only
if the Browns would purchase the franchise. Soon the Browns acquired Jenkins and the Spudders, and by 1930 Gardner had been
elected Texas League president, eventually serving longer than any
other chief executive of the circuit.

The 1927 Spudders won 102 games, then overwhelmed New
Orleans in postseason play. After the first two victories in Wichita
Falls, a special train took a high-spirited crowd to New Orleans to
see the Spudders win two more and become the first team to sweep
the Dixie Series. The next year the Spudders won 104 games, including the second half of a split season, but were defeated by
Houston for the pennant.

In 1929 and 1930 Wichita Falls had the best record in the
Texas League, but lost to Dallas and Fort Worth in the playoffs. A

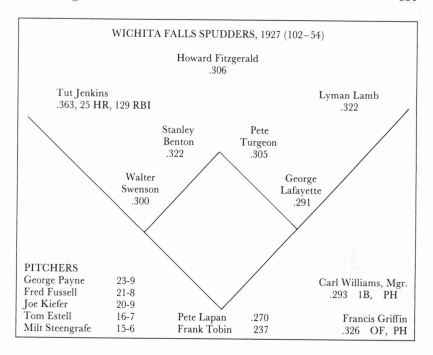

WICHITA FALLS SPUDDERS, 1927 (102–54)

Howard Fitzgerald
.306

Tut Jenkins
.363, 25 HR, 129 RBI

Lyman Lamb
.322

Stanley
Benton
.322

Pete
Turgeon
.305

Walter
Swenson
.300

George
Lafayette
.291

PITCHERS
George Payne	23-9
Fred Fussell	21-8
Joe Kiefer	20-9
Tom Estell	16-7
Milt Steengrafe	15-6

Carl Williams, Mgr.
.293 1B, PH

Pete Lapan   .270
Frank Tobin 237

Francis Griffin
.326 OF, PH

slugging star of the '29 and '30 Spudders was Larry Bettencourt, who demonstrated his powerful arm by throwing the ball from home plate over each outfield fence. During the closing game of 1929, Bettencourt proved his versatility by playing each outfield and infield position. The 1930 Spudders boasted the "$100,000 in-field" — Jack Burns, Lin Storti, Walter Eueller, and Jim Levey, who received national attention by playing together in the Western League, promoting intact to Wichita Falls, then to Milwaukee, then (except for Euller) to St. Louis.

In 1920 the Spudders had wasted no time in establishing a hard-hitting reputation. They produced a batting champ their first year in the league, and four of their first seven seasons. Red Josefson (.345) won the first hitting title for the Spudders in 1920, followed by Homer Summa (.362) in 1922, Art Weiss (.377) in 1924, and Tut Jenkins (.374) in 1926. Each Spudder batting champ was an outfielder and, curiously, Wichita Falls produced no hitting titlist during the 1927–1930 era, when the team led the league in victories for four consecutive years. Two Spudders won the home run title, Tut Jenkins (27 homers) in 1928 and Larry Bettencourt (43)

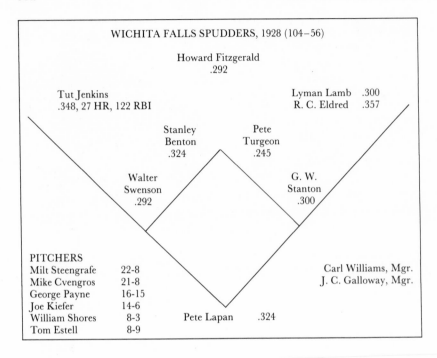

WICHITA FALLS SPUDDERS, 1928 (104–56)

Howard Fitzgerald
.292

Tut Jenkins
.348, 27 HR, 122 RBI

Lyman Lamb .300
R. C. Eldred .357

Stanley
Benton
.324

Pete
Turgeon
.245

Walter
Swenson
.292

G. W.
Stanton
.300

PITCHERS
Milt Steengrafe	22-8
Mike Cvengros	21-8
George Payne	16-15
Joe Kiefer	14-6
William Shores	8-3
Tom Estell	8-9

Carl Williams, Mgr.
J. C. Galloway, Mgr.

Pete Lapan   .324

in 1930. For three years in a row, 1928–1930, the Spudders took
the RBI title — Jenkins (122), Fred Bennett (145 in 1929), and Bettencourt (145). Wichita Falls players who could deliver a game-
winning RBI at home usually were showered with coins from the
stands, while batboys passed a cap for currency. When light-hitting
shortstop Joe Berger hit a home run to win a game before a Sunday
crowd at Athletic Park, he pushed a groundskeeper's wheelbarrow
in front of the grandstand and collected over $60 from the laughing
crowd.

George Payne twice led the Texas League in victories — the
right-handed control artist was 23-9 in 1927 and 28-12 in 1929 (before he retired in 1940 Payne won 348 games in the minors, including 153 Texas League victories). Milt Steengrafe pitched for the
Spudders from 1925 until the club moved to Longview in 1932; the
curveballer pitched and won more games for the Spudders than
any other hurler, and later he spent nine years as a Texas League
umpire. Infielder and leadoff man Pete Turgeon wore a Spudder
uniform from 1924 through 1929, and center fielder Howard Fitz-

Pitcher Milt Steengrafe and second sacker Pete Turgeon were Spudder stars of the 1920s.

gerald, a University of Texas star, also started with the Spudders in 1924 and played for six seasons.

Wichita Falls was the smallest city in its classification. Although the Spudders had attracted 130,000 fans in 1920 and 131,000 in 1927, there were no other 100,000 seasons, and by 1932 the Depression had caused severe attendance problems. On May 20, 1932, the parent club moved the franchise to another oil boomtown, Longview, in East Texas.

For a decade and a half there was no professional baseball in Wichita Falls, but the city became caught up in the postwar boom and joined the Big State League in 1947. The Spudders played in the Class B circuit through 1953, winning one pennant and making the playoffs another season. In 1954 the Spudders tried the Class C Longhorn League, then returned the next season to the Big State League under an affiliation with the Los Angeles Dodgers. Oilman Joe Hale was the primary force behind Spudder baseball during these years, and in 1957 he determined to try independent ownership. But the quality players were monopolized by the major league farm systems, and Wichita Falls failed to last the season. Hale filed an antitrust suit for $2 million against the Dodgers, the National League, and the baseball commissioner's office. Hale settled out of court for $10,000, feeling that he had made his point.

There has been no professional ball in Wichita Falls since 1957 and today only the concrete grandstand base remains of Athletic Park. But during the summers, first-rate amateur teams play hardball on the old diamond, witnessed by baseball fans who fondly remember the Spudders.

Year	Record	Pcg.	Finish
1920	85-63	.574	Second
1921	86-74	.541	Third
1922	94-61	.606	Second
1923	79-72	.523	Fourth
1924	77-74	.510	Fourth
1925	81-68	.544	Fifth
1926	72-84	.462	Seventh
1927	102-54	.654	First — pennant, swept Dixie Series
1928	104-56	.650	Second — lost playoff
1929	94-65	.591	First — lost playoff
1930	95-58	.621	First — lost playoff
1931	76-85	.472	Fifth
1932	16-19	.457	Fourth — franchise moved to Longview

Texas League
Records

ANNUAL STANDINGS

During 31 seasons of Texas League play, the team which compiled the best record over the regular schedule was declared champion. The first post-season playoff for the championship occurred in 1895, and other playoffs were staged in 1896, 1903, 1904, 1919, 1928, 1929, and 1930. Since 1932 playoffs have been held every season at the conclusion of the regular schedule. Playoff devices have included the Shaughnessy Plan, split-season winners and East-West Division winners. * indicates playoff winners. X indicates did not finish season. + indicates joined league after start of season. Co indicates Co-champions. Composite standings year-by-year:

1888

Dallas	55-27	.671
New Orleans +	15-10	.600
Austin-SA	38-29	.559
Galveston	41-46	.471
Houston	32-42	.432
Fort Worth X	19-25	.432
San Antonio X	6-27	.182

1889

Houston	54-44	.551
Dallas	49-42	.538
Austin	50-46	.521
Galveston	50-48	.510
Fort Worth	45-51	.469
Waco	33-50	.398

1890

Galveston	31-13	.705
Dallas	22-18	.550
Waco	24-20	.545
Houston	23-23	.500
Fort Worth	17-28	.378
Austin X	13-18	.317

1892

Houston	59-26	.694
Waco +	16-16	.500
Galveston	39-44	.470
Dallas X	23-30	.434
Fort Worth X	21-33	.389
San Antonio +	11-20	.355

1895

Dallas	82-33	.713
Fort Worth *	77-39	.664
Galveston	72-47	.605
Shreveport X	58-38	.604
Sherman	53-64	.453
Austin X	32-63	.337
Houston X	26-65	.286
San Antonio X	21-72	.226

1896

Fort Worth X	71-29	.710
Houston *	81-49	.623
Galveston	69-61	.530
Sherman-Paris X	44-49	.473
Austin	60-70	.462
Denison X	41-51	.446
San Antonio	57-71	.445
Dallas X	25-68	.269

1897

Galveston	72-44	.621
San Antonio	68-44	.607
Houston	60-54	.526
Den-Sher-Waco	64-58	.525
Fort Worth	60-60	.500
Austin	53-54	.495
Dallas	51-73	.411
Paris	41-82	.333

1898

Dallas X	13- 7	.650
Austin	18-11	.621

336

Houston	15-15	.500
Galveston	16-17	.485
Fort Worth X	9-10	.474
San Antonio	8-19	.296

1899

Galveston	52-26	.667
San Antonio	35-40	.467
Houston	34-41	.453
Austin	31-35	.408

1902

Corsicana	88-23	.793
Dallas	60-53	.531
Fort Worth	48-62	.436
Waco X	26-35	.426
Paris	44-66	.400
Sher-Den-Tex X	20-47	.299

1903

Dallas *	61-47	.565
Corsicana	54-54	.500
Paris-Waco	52-56	.481
Fort Worth	49-59	.454

1903 — SOUTH TX LEAGUE

San Antonio *	69-54	.561
Galveston	67-57	.540
Houston	57-63	.478
Beaumont	52-71	.423

1904

Fort Worth	71-31	.696
Dallas	57-46	.553
Corsicana *	50-51	.495
Paris-Ardmore	26-76	.255

1904 — SOUTH TX LEAGUE

Galveston *	82-43	.656
Beaumont	68-54	.557
Houston	64-61	.512
San Antonio	32-88	.267

1905

Fort Worth	72-60	.545
Temple	70-59	.543
Dallas	65-64	.504
Waco	65-64	.504
Austin X	17-22	.436

Corsicana X	9-29	.370

1905 — SOUTH TX LEAGUE

Houston	83-42	.664
San Antonio	69-69	.586
Galveston	57-70	.449
Bmt-Bren-Orphans	45-82	.354

1906

Fort Worth	78-46	.629
Dallas	80-49	.621
Cleburne	77-49	.611
Greenville X	30-30	.500
Temple X	20-44	.313
Waco	30-97	.236

1906 — SOUTH TX LEAGUE

Houston	78-43	.645
Austin *	77-47	.621
Beaumont	72-50	.590
Galveston	58-68	.460
San Antonio	57-70	.449
Lake Charles	30-94	.242

1907

Austin	88-52	.629
Dallas	84-55	.604
San Antonio	81-58	.583
Houston	79-60	.568
Fort Worth	62-78	.443
Galveston	59-81	.421
Waco	53-86	.381
Temple	52-88	.371

1908

San Antonio	95-48	.664
Dallas	90-55	.620
Houston	77-67	.535
Waco	71-72	.497
Fort Worth	68-74	.479
Shreveport	68-78	.458
Galveston	59-86	.407
Austin	49-95	.340

1909

Houston	86-57	.601
Oklahoma City	79-63	.556
San Antonio	76-63	.547
Dallas	75-64	.540

Shreveport	73-68	.518	Galveston	86-63	.577
Fort Worth	73-71	.507	Fort Worth	71-77	.480
Galveston	53-89	.373	Dallas	67-83	.447
Waco	51-91	.359	San Antonio	46-103	.309
			Austin	31-114	.214

1910

1915

Dallas	83-57	.593			
Houston	82-58	.586	Waco	87-60	.592
San Antonio	74-62	.544	San Antonio	81-67	.548
Fort Worth	75-63	.543	Fort Worth	81-72	.530
Shreveport	75-66	.532	Galveston X	67-63	.515
Galveston	64-75	.460	Dallas	73-75	.493
Oklahoma City	63-74	.460	Houston	68-74	.479
Waco	38-99	.277	Shreveport	62-85	.422
			Beaumont	61-84	.421

1911

1916

Austin	84-62	.575			
Fort Worth	80-67	.548	Waco	84-59	.587
San Antonio	77-68	.531	Shreveport	84-61	.579
Dallas	77-69	.528	Galveston	73-68	.518
Waco	75-71	.514	Houston	74-73	.503
Houston	71-74	.486	Fort Worth	71-76	.483
Oklahoma City	71-77	.480	Beaumont	66-79	.455
Galveston	50-97	.340	San Antonio	66-79	.455
			Dallas	61-84	.421

1912

1917

Houston	87-52	.626			
San Antonio	84-57	.596	Dallas	96-64	.600
Waco	82-63	.566	Fort Worth	91-70	.565
Dallas	73-67	.522	Waco	84-73	.535
Austin	66-79	.455	Houston	77-88	.467
Galveston	59-79	.428	San Antonio	76-89	.457
Fort Worth	59-81	.421	Beaumont X	19-23	.452
Beaumont	55-87	.387	Shreveport	72-90	.444
			Galveston X	11-29	.275

1913

1918

Houston	93-57	.620			
Dallas	92-61	.601	Dallas	52-37	.584
Waco	81-71	.533	Fort Worth	47-39	.547
San Antonio	74-78	.487	Waco	45-40	.529
Austin	70-82	.461	San Antonio	43-45	.489
Fort Worth	70-83	.458	Houston	38-48	.442
Galveston	67-85	.441	Shreveport	34-50	.405
Beaumont	60-90	.400			

1919

1914

			Fort Worth	94-60	.610
Houston-Co	102-50	.670	Shreveport *	81-59	.579
Waco-Co	102-50	.670	Beaumont	80-69	.537
Beaumont	89-54	.622	Houston	87-77	.531

Dallas	75-73	.507	Wichita Falls	77-74	.510
Galveston	63-87	.420	San Antonio	75-75	.500
Waco	60-86	.411	Dallas	75-79	.487
San Antonio	60-89	.403	Galveston	61-93	.396
			Shreveport	54-100	.351

1920

1925

Fort Worth	108-40	.730
Wichita Falls	85-63	.574
Shreveport	81-66	.551
Beaumont	81-70	.537
San Antonio	79-71	.527
Dallas	63-85	.426
Houston	50-101	.331
Galveston	49-100	.329

Fort Worth	103-48	.682
Houston	87-56	.569
Dallas	85-56	.563
San Antonio	81-64	.559
Wichita Falls	81-68	.544
Waco	62-86	.419
Shreveport	59-94	.386
Beaumont	42-108	.280

1921

1926

Fort Worth	107-51	.677
Houston	92-67	.679
Wichita Falls	86-74	.541
Dallas	81-78	.508
Shreveport	74-84	.468
Galveston	68-87	.439
Beaumont	64-93	.408
San Antonio	60-98	.380

Dallas	89-66	.574
San Antonio	86-70	.551
Fort Worth	83-73	.532
Shreveport	77-79	.494
Beaumont	76-80	.487
Houston	75-80	.484
Wichita Falls	72-84	.462
Waco	65-91	.417

1922

1927

Fort Worth	109-46	.703
Wichita Falls	94-61	.606
Dallas	82-74	.525
Galveston	79-76	.510
San Antonio	76-79	.490
Beaumont	65-88	.425
Shreveport	56-99	.381
Houston	57-95	.375

Wichita Falls	102-54	.654
Waco	88-68	.564
Houston	85-70	.548
Fort Worth	77-79	.494
Dallas	74-80	.481
Shreveport	73-82	.471
San Antonio	65-90	.419
Beaumont	56-97	.366

1923

1928

Fort Worth	96-56	.632
San Antonio	81-68	.556
Dallas	78-70	.527
Wichita Falls	79-72	.523
Houston	74-75	.497
Beaumont	71-77	.480
Galveston	68-80	.459
Shreveport	50-99	.336

Houston *	104-54	.658
Wichita Falls	104-56	.650
Fort Worth	83-73	.532
Shreveport	79-81	.494
San Antonio	76-83	.478
Waco	71-87	.449
Dallas	66-93	.415
Beaumont	50-106	.321

1924

1929

Fort Worth	109-41	.727
Houston	80-73	.523
Beaumont	77-73	.513

Wichita Falls	94-65	.591
Shreveport	91-66	.580

Dallas *	91-69	.569		Beaumont	81-69	.540
Fort Worth	84-76	.525		Dallas	80-73	.523
Waco	77-83	.481		Tulsa	77-75	.519
Houston	73-86	.459		Houston	76-78	.478
Beaumont	72-87	.453		Fort Worth	59-92	.391
San Antonio	56-106	.346		Oklahoma City	59-93	.388

1930

1935

Wichita Falls	95-58	.621		Oklahoma City *	95-66	.590
Houston	89-65	.578		Beaumont	90-69	.566
Shreveport	86-65	.570		Galveston	86-75	.534
Fort Worth *	84-69	.549		Tulsa	82-79	.509
Waco	68-81	.457		Houston	77-84	.478
Beaumont	68-84	.447		San Antonio	75-84	.472
San Antonio	60-93	.392		Dallas	71-88	.447
Dallas	58-93	.384		Fort Worth	64-95	.403

1931

1936

Houston	108-51	.679		Dallas	93-61	.604
Beaumont	94-65	.591		Houston	83-69	.547
Fort Worth	90-70	.563		Tulsa *	80-74	.519
Dallas	83-77	.519		Oklahoma City	79-75	.513
Wichita Falls	76-85	.472		Fort Worth	76-78	.494
Shreveport	66-94	.413		San Antonio	73-77	.487
San Antonio	66-94	.413		Beaumont	69-80	.463
Galveston	57-104	.354		Galveston	57-96	.373

1932

1937

Beaumont *	100-51	.662		Oklahoma City	101-58	.635
Dallas	98-53	.648		Tulsa	89-69	.563
Houston	88-66	.574		Fort Worth *	85-74	.535
Fort Worth	68-81	.457		San Antonio	85-76	.528
WF-Longview	69-83	.454		Beaumont	82-77	.516
Galveston	67-86	.438		Galveston	73-86	.459
San Antonio	57-91	.385		Houston	67-91	.424
Spt-Tyler	57-93	.380		Dallas	55-106	.342

1933

1938

Houston	94-57	.623		Beamont *	99-57	.635
Galveston	88-64	.579		San Antonio	93-67	.581
Dallas	82-70	.539		Oklahoma City	89-70	.569
San Antonio *	79-72	.523		Tulsa	86-75	.534
Beaumont	73-79	.480		Houston	74-84	.468
Tulsa	65-86	.430		Shreveport	69-90	.434
Fort Worth	63-88	.417		Dallas	65-94	.409
Oklahoma City	62-90	.408		Fort Worth	61-99	.381

1934

1939

| Galveston * | 88-64 | .579 | | Houston | 97-63 | .606 |
| San Antonio | 89-65 | .578 | | Dallas | 89-72 | .553 |

San Antonio	89-72	.553	Dallas	79-74	.516
Fort Worth *	87-74	.540	Tulsa	79-75	.513
Shreveport	86-75	.534	Shreveport	75-79	.487
Tulsa	78-82	.488	Oklahoma City	71-83	.461
Oklahoma City	59-102	.366	San Antonio	60-94	.390
Beaumont	58-103	.360	Beaumont	60-94	.390

1940

1948

Houston *	105-56	.652	Fort Worth *	92-61	.601
San Antonio	89-72	.553	Tulsa	91-63	.591
Beaumont	88-72	.550	Houston	82-71	.536
Oklahoma City	82-78	.513	Shreveport	76-77	.497
Tulsa	76-82	.481	San Antonio	75-76	.497
Dallas	75-83	.475	Oklahoma City	70-84	.455
Shreveport	72-88	.450	Dallas	64-89	.418
Fort Worth	52-108	.325	Beaumont	61-90	.404

1941

1949

Houston	103-50	.673	Fort Worth	100-54	.649
Tulsa	86-66	.566	Tulsa *	90-64	.584
Shreveport	80-71	.530	Oklahoma City	81-72	.529
Dallas *	80-74	.519	Shreveport	80-74	.519
Fort Worth	78-76	.506	Dallas	76-77	.497
Oklahoma City	69-85	.448	San Antonio	70-83	.458
Beaumont	58-94	.382	Houston	60-91	.397
San Antonio	58-96	.377	Beaumont	55-97	.362

1942

1950

Beaumont	89-58	.615	Beaumont	91-62	.595
Shreveport *	83-61	.576	Fort Worth	88-64	.579
Fort Worth	84-68	.559	Tulsa	83-69	.546
San Antonio	80-68	.546	San Antonio *	79-75	.513
Houston	81-70	.536	Dallas	74-78	.487
Tulsa	76-75	.533	Oklahoma City	72-79	.477
Oklahoma City	58-95	.379	Shreveport	63-91	.409
Dallas	48-104	.314	Houston	61-93	.396

1946

1951

Fort Worth	101-53	.565	Houston *	99-61	.619
Dallas *	91-63	.591	San Antonio	86-75	.534
San Antonio	87-65	.572	Dallas	85-75	.531
Tulsa	84-69	.549	Beaumont	84-77	.522
Beaumont	70-83	.458	Fort Worth	84-77	.522
Houston	64-89	.418	Oklahoma City	75-86	.466
Shreveport	61-92	.399	Tulsa	67-94	.416
Oklahoma City	54-98	.355	Shreveport	63-98	.391

1947

1952

Houston *	96-58	.623	Dallas	92-69	.571
Fort Worth	95-58	.621	Fort Worth	86-75	.534

Shreveport *	84-77	.522
Oklahoma City	82-79	.509
San Antonio	79-82	.491
Tulsa	78-83	.484
Beaumont	77-84	.478
Houston	66-95	.419

1953

Dallas *	88-66	.571
Tulsa	83-71	.539
Fort Worth	82-72	.532
Oklahoma City	80-74	.519
Shreveport	79-75	.513
Houston	72-82	.468
San Antonio	67-87	.435
Beaumont	65-89	.422

1954

Shreveport	90-71	.559
Houston *	89-72	.553
Oklahoma City	87-74	.540
Fort Worth	81-80	.503
San Antonio	78-83	.484
Tulsa	78-83	.484
Beaumont	77-84	.478
Dallas	64-97	.398

1955

Dallas	93-67	.581
San Antonio	93-68	.578
Shreveport *	87-74	.540
Houston	86-75	.534
Tulsa	86-75	.534
Fort Worth	77-84	.478
Oklahoma City	70-90	.438
Beaumont	51-110	.317

1956

Houston *	96-58	.623
Dallas	94-60	.610
Fort Worth	84-70	.545
Tulsa	77-77	.500
San Antonio	76-78	.494
Austin	72-82	.468
Shreveport	69-85	.448
Oklahoma City	48-106	.312

1957

Dallas	102-52	.662
Houston *	97-57	.630

San Antonio	76-78	.494
Tulsa	75-79	.487
Austin	71-83	.461
Fort Worth	70-84	.455
Oklahoma City	66-88	.429
Shreveport	59-95	.383

1958

Fort Worth	89-64	.582
Houston	79-74	.516
Corpus Christi *	77-75	.507
Austin	77-76	.503
Dallas	76-77	.494
San Antonio	74-79	.484
Tulsa	71-81	.467
Victoria	68-85	.445

1959

Victoria	86-60	.589
Austin *	80-66	.548
Tulsa	77-67	.535
San Antonio	75-70	.517
Amarillo	75-71	.514
Corpus Christi	66-79	.455

1960

Rio Grande V.	85-59	.590
San Antonio	77-68	.531
Tulsa *	76-68	.528
Victoria	77-69	.527
Austin	73-71	.507
Amarillo	68-78	.466

1961

Amarillo	90-50	.643
Tulsa	83-55	.601
San Antonio *	74-65	.532
Austin	69-71	.493
Rio G. V.-Vict.	69-71	.493
Vict.-Ardmore	57-83	.407

1962

El Paso	80-60	.571
Tulsa *	77-63	.550
Albuquerque	70-70	.500
Austin	69-71	.493
San Antonio	68-72	.486
Amarillo	56-84	.400

1963

San Antonio	79-61	.564
Austin	75-65	.536
Tulsa *	74-66	.529
El Paso	68-72	.489
Albuquerque	67-73	.479
Amarillo	57-83	.407

1964

San Antonio *	85-55	.670
Tulsa	79-61	.564
Albuquerque	75-65	.536
El Paso	67-73	.479
Austin	63-77	.450
Fort Worth	51-89	.364

1965

EASTERN DIVISION

Tulsa	81-60	.574
Dallas-Ft. Worth	80-61	.567
Austin	70-70	.500

WESTERN DIVISION

Albuquerque *	77-63	.550
Amarillo	60-80	.429
El Paso	53-87	.379

1966

Arkansas	81-59	.579
Amarillo	77-63	.550
Albuquerque	74-66	.529
Austin *	67-73	.479
El Paso	62-78	.443
Dallas-Ft. Worth	59-81	.421

1967

Albuquerque	78-62	.557
Amarillo	75-64	.539
El Paso	73-67	.521
Austin	69-71	.493
Arkansas	63-77	.450
Dallas-Ft. Worth	62-78	.443

1968

EASTERN DIVISION

Arkansas	82-58	.586
Shreveport	78-62	.557
Memphis	67-69	.493
Dallas-Ft. Worth	60-79	.432

WESTERN DIVISION

El Paso *	77-60	.562
Albuquerque	70-69	.504
Amarillo	67-71	.486
San Antonio	53-86	.381

1969

EASTERN DIVISION

Memphis *	66-65	.504
Arkansas	66-69	.489
Shreveport	61-75	.449
San Antonio	51-81	.386

WESTERN DIVISION

Amarillo	80-55	.585
Dallas-Ft. Worth	75-58	.564
El Paso	71-65	.522
Albuquerque	67-69	.493

1970

EASTERN DIVISION

Memphis	69-67	.507
Arkansas	67-67	.500
San Antonio	67-69	.493
Shreveport	58-76	.433

WESTERN DIVISION

Albuquerque *	83-52	.615
El Paso	77-59	.566
Dallas-Ft. Worth	63-73	.463
Amarillo	57-78	.422

1972

EASTERN DIVISION

Alexandria	84-56	.600
Memphis	75-64	.540
Arkansas	65-74	.468
Shreveport	64-76	.457

WESTERN DIVISION

El Paso *	78-62	.557
Amarillo	71-68	.511
Midland	68-71	.489
San Antonio	53-87	.379

1973

EASTERN DIVISION

Memphis *	77-61	.558
Shreveport	70-68	.507
Arkansas	69-71	.493
Alexandria	59-77	.434

WESTERN DIVISION

San Antonio	82-57	.590
El Paso	69-71	.493

Midland	64-74	.464
Amarillo	64-75	.469

1974

EASTERN DIVISION

Victoria *	79-57	.581
Arkansas	75-59	.560
Shreveport	59-79	.428
Alexandria	49-85	.366

WESTERN DIVISION

El Paso	76-61	.555
Amarillo	69-62	.527
San Antonio	68-64	.515
Midland	65-73	.471

1975

EASTERN DIVISION

Lafayette-Co	72-57	.558
Jackson	65-65	.500
Arkansas	63-72	.467
Alexandria	58-72	.446

WESTERN DIVISION

Midland-Co	81-53	.604
Shreveport	76-52	.594
El Paso	62-71	.466
San Antonio	50-85	.370

1976

EASTERN DIVISION

Shreveport	70-66	.515
Jackson	69-66	.511
Arkansas	59-76	.437
Lafayette	58-76	.433

WESTERN DIVISION

Amarillo *	81-54	.600
El Paso	77-56	.579
San Antonio	63-71	.470
Midland	62-74	.456

1977

EASTERN DIVISION

Tulsa	66-62	.588
Arkansas *	63-67	.485
Shreveport	62-68	.477
Jackson	62-68	.477

WESTERN DIVISION

El Paso	78-52	.600
Midland	70-60	.538
San Antonio	61-67	.477
Amarillo	56-74	.431

1978

EASTERN DIVISION

Arkansas	77-55	.583
Jackson	76-58	.567
Tulsa	57-78	.422
Shreveport	55-81	.404

WESTERN DIVISION

El Paso *	80-55	.593
San Antonio	79-57	.581
Midland	70-65	.519
Amarillo	44-89	.331

1979

EASTERN DIVISION

Arkansas *	76-57	.571
Shreveport	73-62	.541
Jackson	70-65	.519
Tulsa	58-75	.436

WESTERN DIVISION

Midland	76-59	.563
San Antonio	69-62	.527
El Paso	61-75	.449
Amarillo	54-82	.397

1980

EASTERN DIVISION

Arkansas *	81-55	.596
Tulsa	75-61	.551
Jackson	74-62	.544
Shreveport	49-87	.360

WESTERN DIVISION

Amarillo	77-59	.566
San Antonio	74-62	.544
Midland	64-72	.471
El Paso	50-86	.368

1981

EASTERN DIVISION

Tulsa	68-65	.511
Jackson *	68-66	.507
Shreveport	68-67	.504
Arkansas	52-80	.394

WESTERN DIVISION

San Antonio	76-57	.571
Amarillo	77-59	.566
El Paso	65-69	.485
Midland	62-73	.459

1982

EASTERN DIVISION

Tulsa *	70-66	.515
Jackson	68-65	.511
Arkansas	68-68	.500
Shreveport	62-73	.459

WESTERN DIVISION

El Paso	76-60	.559
Midland	67-66	.504
San Antonio	68-68	.500
Amarillo	61-74	.452

1983

EASTERN DIVISION

Shreveport	72-64	.529
Arkansas	69-67	.507
Jackson	69-67	.507
Tulsa	63-73	.463

WESTERN DIVISION

El Paso	74-62	.544
Beaumont *	68-68	.500
San Antonio	66-70	.485
Midland	63-73	.463

1984

EASTERN DIVISION

Jackson *	83-53	.610
Tulsa	62-73	.459
Arkansas	62-74	.456

Shreveport	59-77	.434

WESTERN DIVISION

Beaumont	89-47	.654
El Paso	72-63	.533
San Antonio	64-72	.471
Midland	52-84	.382

1985

EASTERN DIVISION

Jackson *	73-63	.537
Shreveport	72-64	.529
Arkansas	64-70	.478
Tulsa	60-76	.441

WESTERN DIVISION

El Paso	86-50	.632
Beaumont	69-67	.507
San Antonio	59-75	.440
Midland	59-77	.434

1986

EASTERN DIVISION

Shreveport	80-56	.588
Jackson	72-63	.533
Arkansas	67-67	.500
Tulsa	49-85	.366

WESTERN DIVISION

El Paso *	85-50	.630
San Antonio	64-71	.474
Midland	62-71	.466
Beaumont	60-76	.441

PLAYOFF RESULTS

1895 Fort Worth defeated Dallas 7 games to 6.

1896 Houston defeated Galveston 5 games to 2.

1903 Dallas defeated Paris-Waco 7 games to 3.

1904 Corsicana defeated Fort Worth 11 games to 8.

1919 Shreveport defeated Fort Worth 4 games to 2 with 1 tie.

1928 Houston defeated Wichita Falls 3 games to 1.

1929 Dallas defeated Wichita Falls 3 games to 1.

1930 Fort Worth defeated Wichita Falls 3 games to 2.

1932 Beaumont defeated Dallas 3 games to 0.

1933 Galveston defeated Dallas 3 games to 0. San Antonio defeated Houston 3 games to 0. **FINALS:** San Antonio defeated Galveston 4 games to 2.

1934 Galveston defeated Dallas 3 games to 1. San Antonio defeated Beaumont 3 games to 2. **FINALS:** Galveston defeated San Antonio 4 games to 2.

1935 Beaumont defeated Galveston 3 games to 2. Oklahoma City defeated Tulsa 3 games to 1. **FINALS:** Oklahoma City defeated Beaumont 4 games to 1.

1936 Dallas defeated Oklahoma City 3 games to 1. Tulsa defeated Houston 3 games to 1. **FINALS:** Tulsa defeated Dallas 4 games to 3.

1937 Oklahoma City defeated San Antonio 3 games to 2. Fort Worth defeated Tulsa 3 games to 2. **FINALS:** Fort Worth defeated Oklahoma City 4 games to 2.

1949 Fort Worth defeated Shreveport 4 games to 1. Tulsa defeated Oklahoma City 4 games to 2. **FINALS:** Tulsa defeated Fort Worth 4 games to 3.

1950 Tulsa defeated Fort Worth 5 games to 1. San Antonio defeated Beaumont 4 games to 0. **FINALS:** San Antonio defeated Tulsa 4 games to 2.

1951 Beaumont defeated Fort Worth in single game to determine fourth place. Houston defeated Beaumont 4 games to 2. San Antonio defeated Dallas 4 games to 3. **FINALS:** Houston defeated San Antonio 4 games to 0.

1952 Oklahoma City defeated Dallas 4 games to 2. Shreveport defeated Fort Worth 4 games to 0. **FINALS:** Shreveport defeated Oklahoma City 4 games to 1.

1953 Dallas defeated Oklahoma City 4 games to 3. Tulsa defeated Fort Worth 4 games to 2. **FINALS:** Dallas defeated Tulsa 4 games to 1.

1954 Fort Worth defeated Shreveport 4 games to 1. Houston defeated Oklahoma City 4 games to 1. **FINALS:** Houston defeated Fort Worth 4 games to 1.

1955 Houston defeated Dallas 4 games to 2. Shreveport defeated San Antonio 4 games to 2. **FINALS:** Shreveport defeated Houston 4 games to 3.

1956 Houston defeated Tulsa 4 games to 1. Dallas defeated Fort Worth 4 games to 0. **FINALS:** Houston defeated Dallas 4 games to 1.

1957 Dallas defeated Tulsa 4 games to 2. Houston defeated San Antonio 4 games to 3. **FINALS:** Houston defeated Dallas 4 games to 3.

1958 Austin defeated Fort Worth 4 games to 0. Corpus Christi defeated Houston 4 games to 1. **FINALS:** Corpus Christi defeated Austin 4 games to 3.

1959 San Antonio defeated Victoria 2 games to 0. Austin defeated Tulsa 2 games to 1. **FINALS:** Austin defeated San Antonio 3 games to 0.

1960 Victoria defeated Rio Grande Valley 3 games to 0. Tulsa defeated San Antonio 3 games to 1. **FINALS:** Tulsa defeated Victoria 3 games to 0.

1961 Austin defeated Victoria in single game to determine fourth place. Austin defeated Amarillo 3 games to 2. San Antonio defeated Tulsa 3 games to 1. **FINALS:** San Antonio defeated Austin 3 games to 0.

1962 Austin defeated El Paso 3 games to 2. Tulsa defeated Albuquerque 3 games to 0. **FINALS:** Tulsa defeated Austin 4 games to 1.

1963 San Antonio defeated El Paso 3 games to 2. Tulsa defeated Austin 3 games to 0. **FINALS:** Tulsa defeated San Antonio 3 games to 1.

1964 San Antonio defeated El Paso 3 games to 1. Tulsa defeated Albuquerque 3 games to 2. **FINALS:** San Antonio defeated Tulsa 3 games to 1.

1965 Tulsa defeated Fort Worth in single game to determine Eastern Division. **FINALS:** Albuquerque defeated Tulsa 3 games to 1.

1966 Austin defeated Arkansas 2 games to 1. Albuquerque defeated Amarillo 2 games to 1. **FINALS:** Austin defeated Albuquerque 1 game to 0 (series shortened by rain).

1967 No playoff.

1968 El Paso defeated Arkansas 3 games to 1.

1969 Memphis defeated Amarillo 3 games to 0.

1970 Albuquerque defeated Memphis 3 games to 1.

1971 Arkansas defeated Amarillo 2 games to 0. (Charlotte defeated Ashville 2 games to 1.) **DIXIE ASSOCIATION FINALS:** Charlotte defeated Arkansas 3 games to 0.

1972 El Paso defeated Alexandria 3 games to 0.

1973 Memphis defeated San Antonio 3 games to 2.

1974 Victoria defeated El Paso 3 games to 0.

1975 Midland and Lafayette each won two games, then were declared co-champions when rain prevented completion of playoffs.

1976 Amarillo defeated Shreveport 3 games to 2.

1977 **EAST:** Arkansas defeated Tulsa 2 games to 0. **FINALS:** Arkansas defeated El Paso 2 games to 0.

1978 **EAST:** Jackson defeated Arkansas 2 games to 1. **FINALS:** El Paso defeated Jackson 3 games to 0.

1979 **EAST:** Arkansas defeated Shreveport 2 games to 0. **WEST:** San Antonio defeated Midland 2 games to 1. **FINALS:** Arkansas defeated San Antonio 3 games to 0.

1980 **EAST:** Arkansas defeated Jackson 2 games to 0. **WEST:** San Antonio defeated Amarillo 2 games to 0. **FINALS:** Arkansas defeated San Antonio 3 games to 0.

1981 **EAST:** Jackson defeated Tulsa 2 games to 1. **WEST:** San Antonio defeated Amarillo 2 games to 1. **FINALS:** Jackson defeated San Antonio 2 games to 1.

1982 **EAST:** Tulsa defeated Jackson 2 games to 1. **WEST:** El Paso defeated Midland 2 games to 0. **FINALS:** Tulsa defeated El Paso 3 games to 0.

1983 **EAST:** Jackson defeated Arkansas 2 games to 0. **WEST:** Beaumont defeated El Paso 2 games to 1. **FINALS:** Beaumont defeated Jackson 3 games to 0.

1984 Jackson defeated Beaumont 4 games to 2.

1985 **EAST:** Jackson defeated Arkansas 2 games to 0. **FINALS:** Jackson defeated El Paso 4 games to 0.

1986 **EAST:** Jackson defeated Shreveport 2 games to 1. **FINALS:** El Paso defeated Jackson 4 games to 0.

DIXIE SERIES RESULTS

Texas League team listed first; winner in CAPS; record in parentheses.

1920 FORT WORTH v. Little Rock (4-2-1)

1921 FORT WORTH v. Memphis (4-2)

1922 Fort Worth v. MOBILE (2-4-1)

1923 FORT WORTH v. New Orleans (4-2-1)

1924 FORT WORTH v. Memphis (4-3-1)

1925 FORT WORTH v. Atlanta (4-2)

1926 DALLAS v. New Orleans (4-2-1)

1927 WICHITA FALLS v. New Orleans (4-0)

1928 HOUSTON v. Birmingham (4-2)

1929 Dallas v. BIRMINGHAM (2-4)

1930 FORT WORTH v. Memphis (4-1)

1931 Houston v. BIRMINGHAM (2-4)

1932 Beaumont v. CHATTANOOGA (1-4)

1933 San Antonio v. NEW ORLEANS (2-4)
1934 Galveston v. NEW ORLEANS (2-4)
1935 OKLAHOMA CITY v. Atlanta (4-2)
1936 TULSA v. Birmingham (4-0)
1937 FORT WORTH v. Little Rock (4-1)
1938 Beaumont v. ATLANTA (0-4-1)
1939 FORT WORTH v. Nashville (4-3)
1940 Houston v. NASHVILLE (1-4)
1941 Dallas v. NASHVILLE (0-4)
1942 Shreveport v. NASHVILLE (2-4)
1943–45 No series.
1946 DALLAS v. Atlanta (4-0)
1947 HOUSTON v. Mobile (4-2)
1948 Fort Worth v. BIRMINGHAM (1-4)
1949 Tulsa v. NASHVILLE (3-4)
1950 SAN ANTONIO v. Nashville (4-3)
1951 Houston v. BIRMINGHAM (2-4)
1952 Shreveport v. MEMPHIS (2-4)
1953 DALLAS v. Nashville (4-2)
1954 Houston v. ATLANTA (3-4)
1955 Shreveport v. MOBILE (0-4)
1956 HOUSTON v. Atlanta (4-2)
1957 HOUSTON v. Atlanta (4-2)
1958 Corpus Christi v. BIRMINGHAM (2-4)
1959–66 No series.
1967 Albuquerque v. BIRMINGHAM (2-4)

ALL-STAR GAMES

The first Texas League All-Star Game was played in 1936. One team was selected by popular vote of the fans from the four southern clubs in the league, and another from the four northern franchises. This format was followed through the 1941 season. When the All-Star Game was resumed in 1947, a new format was adopted: the team in first place on a given date would host the All-Star Game, playing against a squad of stars selected from the other seven teams by a vote of Texas League managers and sports writers. This format was used through 1949, and again from 1956 through 1958.

During the years of the Pan American Association — 1959–61 — Texas League All-Stars played the Mexican League All-Stars. In 1962 there were two games: another North vs. South contest; then, later in the season, a squad of Texas League All-Stars vs. the Houston Colt .45s, Texas' first major league team. The Texas Leaguers played Houston from 1962 through 1968, winning four of the seven games. In 1968 the Texas League aligned into four-team Eastern and Western divisions, and for two years the All-Star Game pitted East vs. West. During the Dixie Association season, 1971, Texas League All-Stars played the San Diego Padres.

From 1972 through 1974, and beginning again in 1976, Texas League All-Stars played the Texas Rangers. The 1982 game was played in Tulsa and pitted the All-Stars against the Class AAA Oklahoma City '89ers. Since 1983 the All-Star Game has returned to an East vs. West format.

Homer Peel is the only Texas Leaguer to have played and managed in the All-Star Game, while slugging outfielder Russ Burns is the only player named to six All-Star teams (1948–49 and 1951–54). Three players have appeared in five All-Star Games: Clyde McDowell, Fort Worth infielder (1937–41); J. B. Brillheart, Jr., Oklahoma City pitcher (1936–39 and 1941); and Harold Epps, Houston outfielder (1938–39, 1941 and 1947–48).

Year	City	Winner	Attendance
1936	Dallas	South, 4-2	9,050
1937	Houston	South, 3-1	7,705
1938	Oklahoma City	South, 2-0	7,510
1939	San Antonio	North, 7-2	8,998
1940	Fort Worth	North, 7-6	5,030
1941	Beaumont	South, 2-0	4,580
1947	Houston	All-Stars, 4-2	11,333
1948	Fort Worth	All-Stars, 4-2	12,636
1949	Fort Worth	Fort Worth, 2-1	8,442
1950	Fort Worth	South, 5-2	10,273
1951	Houston	North, 7-3	9,947
1952	Oklahoma City	South, 9-8	7,285
1953	Shreveport	North, 6-1	7,686
1954	Fort Worth	North, 9-8	6,177
1955	Beaumont	North, 6-2	3,626
1956	Dallas	Dallas, 7-1	9,966
1957	Dallas	All-Stars, 5-3	8,722
1958	Fort Worth	Fort Worth, 5-3	9,017
1959	Mexico City	Mexican League, 9-3	19,089
1960	San Antonio	Texas League, 7-2	8,061
1961	Mexico City	Mexican League, 8-3	13,850
	San Antonio	Mexican League, 13-3	3,850
1962	Tulsa	South, 2-1	3,814
	San Antonio	All-Stars, 8-1	5,168
1963	San Antonio	All-Stars, 7-3	8,832
1964	San Antonio	All-Stars, 7-3	8,881
1965	San Antonio	Houston Astros, 5-1	11,076
1966	Dallas-FW	Houston Astros, 7-6	10,434
1967	Dallas-FW	Houston Astros, 8-2	9,024
1968	Dallas-FW	All-Stars, 8-7	5,088
1969	Memphis	East, 2-1	5,579
1970	Albuquerque	West, 8-2	6,047
1971	Albuquerque	San Diego Padres, 4-3	2,664
1972	Alexandria	Texas Rangers, 4-3	2,930
1973	Little Rock	Texas Rangers, 9-6	2,816

1974	Shreveport	All-Stars, 10-5	4,487
1975	Lafayette	Lafayette, 5-2	2,317
1976	San Antonio	Texas Rangers, 18-4	6,134
1977	Little Rock	All-Stars, 5-1	6,675
1978	Little Rock	All-Stars, 7-6	6,879
1979	Little Rock	All-Stars, 11-3	5,689
1980	San Antonio	All-Stars, 5-1	2,416
1981	Tulsa	All-Stars, 9-5	4,202
1982	Tulsa	All-Stars, 10-4	4,821
1983	El Paso	West, 10-4	8,093
1984	Jackson	East, 8-7	4,828
1985	Shreveport	West, 6-4	4,341
1986	Shreveport	East, 4-3	4,596

PRESIDENTS OF THE TEXAS LEAGUE

1887–88	Fred W. Turner (Austin, TX; Dec. 15, 1887–May 15, 1888)
1889	Lewis Newburg (Waco, TX)
1890	Joseph Sensheimer (Galveston, TX)
1892	Si Packard (Houston, TX)
1895	J. C. McNealus (Dallas, TX; Oct. 27, 1894–May 25, 1895)
	C. P. Gregory (Sherman, TX; May 25–Sept. 2, 1895)
1896	John L. Ward (Fort Worth, TX; Oct. 1, 1895–Aug. 7, 1896)
1897	Louis Heuermann (San Antonio, TX; Aug. 8, 1896 through 1897)
1898	John L. Ward (Fort Worth, TX; Nov. 13, 1897–May 13, 1898)
1899	George Dermody (Galveston, TX)
1902	John L. Ward (Dec. 15, 1901 through 1902)
1903	Newton D. Lassiter (Fort Worth, TX)
1904	William A. Abey (Fort Worth, TX; Jan. 24–July 13, 1904)
	J. Doak Roberts (Corsicana, TX; July 14 through 1904)
1905	J. Doak Roberts (Temple, TX)
1906	J. Doak Roberts (Cleburne, TX)
1907–8	Dr. William R. Robbie (San Antonio, TX)
1909–13	Wilber P. Allen (Austin, TX)
1914–15	William R. Davidson (Waco, TX)
1916–20	J. Walter Morris (Fort Worth, TX)
1921–29	J. Doak Roberts (Dallas, TX)
1929	William B. Ruggles (Dallas, TX; interim for Roberts)
1930–53	J. Alvin Gardner (Dallas, TX)
1954	John L. Reeves (Fort Worth, TX)
1955–63	James H. Burris (Denver, CO)
1965	James H. Burris; Dick Butler (interim); and Hugh J. Finnerty (Tulsa, OK)
1966–68	Hugh J. Finnerty
1969	Hugh J. Finnerty; Dick Butler (interim); and Robert R. Bragan (Fort Worth, TX)
1970–75	Robert R. Bragan
1975–	Carl E. Sawatski (Little Rock, AR)

PRESIDENTS OF THE SOUTH TEXAS LEAGUE

1903	James C. Nolan (Galveston, TX)
	Max Stubenraugh (Houston, TX)
1904–5	Bliss P. Gorham (Houston, TX)
1906	Dr. William R. Robbie (San Antonio, TX)

BATTING CHAMPIONS

1889	Farmer Works, Galv.	.372
1895	Al McBride, Austin	.444
1896	Mike O'Connor, Den-SA	.401
1897	Bill Nance, Galv.	.395
1902	Allen Nickell, Dallas	.
1903	Harry Clark, Dallas	.326
1904	Trapper Longley, Corsi.	.372
1905	Scott Ragsdale, Waco	.292
1906	George Whiteman, Cleb.	.281
1907	Tris Speaker, Houston	.314
1908	Bob Edmondson, Houston	.391
1909	O. C. Downey, Ok. City	.346
1910	Hank Gowdy, Dallas	.312
1911	Bill Yohe, Ok. City	.329
1912	Frank Metz, San A.	.323
1913	Dennis Willie, Bmt.	.324
1914	Bob Clemens, Waco	.327
1915	Al Waters, Waco	.325
1916	Charles Bittle, Waco	.335
1917	Ralph Sharman, FW	.341
1918	Olen Nokes, Dallas	.333
1919	Al Nixon, Beaumont	.364
1920	Godfrey Josephson, WF	.345
1921	Clarence Kraft, FW	.352
1922	Homer Summa, WF	.362
1923	Ike Boone, San A.	.402
1924	Art Weis, WF	.377
1925	Danny Clark, San A.	.399
1926	Tom Jenkins, WF	.374
1927	Del Pratt, Waco	.386
1928	George Blackerby, Waco	.368
1929	Randolph Moore, Dal.	.369
1930	Ox Eckhardt, Bmt.	.379
1931	Ray Ratcliff, Spt.	.361

1932	Ervin Fox, Bmt.	.357
1933	Everett Purdy, San A.	.358
1934	Chester Morgan, San A.	.342
1935	Art Weis, FW	.331
1936	Les Mallon, Dallas	.344
1937	Homer Peel, FW	.370
1938	Harlon Pool, Dallas	.330
1939	Lou Novikoff, Tulsa	.368
1940	Gordy Donaldson, Tulsa	.319
1941	Grey Clarke, Dallas	.361
1942	Dick Wakefield, Bmt.	.345
1946	Dale Mitchell, OC	.337
1947	Al Rosen, Ok. City	.349
1948	Tom Tatum, Tulsa	.333
1949	Herb Conyers, OC	.355
1950	Francis Saucier, SA	.343
1951	Robert Nieman, OC	.3239
	Grant Dunlap, Spt.	.3235
1952	Grant Dunlap, Spt.	.333
1953	Joe Frazier, OC	.332
1954	Les Fleming, Dallas	.358
1955	Eddie Knoblauch, Dallas	.327
1956	Albie Pearson, OC	.371
1957	Jim Frey, Tulsa	.336
1958	Eric Roden, Corpus C.	.320
1959	Al Nagel, Amarillo	.344
1960	Charles Hiller, RGV	.334
1961	Phil Linz, Amarillo	.349
1962	Charles Dees, El P.	.348
1963	Dick Dietz, El Paso	.354
1964	Mel Corbo, Alb.	.339
1965	Dave Pavlesic, Tulsa	.344
1966	Tom Hutton, Alb.	.340
1967	Luis Alcaraz, Alb.	.328
1968	Bob Taylor, Amarillo	.321
1969	Larry Johnson, DFW	.337
1970	Mickey Rivers, El P.	.343
1971	Enos Cabell, DFW	.311
1972	Randy Elliott, Alex.	.335

1973	Morris Nettles, El P.	.332
1974	Jerry Remy, El P.	.338
1975	Butch Alberts, El P.	.342
1976	Fred Frazier, El P.	.363
1977	Tom Smith, El P.	.366
1978	Dan Goodwin, El P.	.360
1979	Jim Tracy, Midland	.355
1980	Daryl Sconiers, El P.	.370
1981	Steve Sax, San A.	.346
1982	Randy Ready, El P.	.375
1983	Earnest Riles, El P.	.349
1984	James Steels, Bmt.	.340
1985	Billy Joe Robideaux, El P.	.342
1986	Steve Stanicek, El P.	.343

BATTING CHAMPS — SOUTH TEXAS LEAGUE

1903	Ed Pleiss, Galv.	.360
1904	Ben Shelton, Galv.	.352
1905	Earl Gardner, SA	.306
1906	Sam LaRocque, Bmt.	.319

HOME RUN CHAMPIONS

1895	Charles Meyers, Galv.	15
1905	Ben Shelton, Temple	5
	Sam Stovall, Waco	5
1908	Pat Newnam, SA	18
1909	Dick Hoffman, Waco-Gal.	18
1910	Hank Gowdy, Dallas	11
	Harry Storch, Dallas	11
	George, SA	11
1911	Frank Metz, SA	22
1912	Frank Metz, SA	21
1913	Fred Wohleben, Waco	12
1914	Bob Edmondson, Bmt.	10
1915	Fred Wohleben, Waco	8
	Bob James, Waco	8
	Otto McIver, FW	8
	Harry Storch, Dallas	8
1916	Al Nixon, Bmt.	9
1917	Roy Leslie, SA	18
1918	John Mokan, Waco	9
1919	Roy Leslie, Hous.	16
	Jewel Ens, Dallas	16
1920	Dave Callahan, Galv.	12
1921	Henry Eibel, Spt.	35

1922	Clarence Kraft, FW	32
1923	Clarence Kraft, FW	32
1924	Clarence Kraft, FW	55
1925	Ed Konetchy, FW	41
1926	Hack Miller, Dallas	30
1927	Del Pratt, Waco	32
1928	Tom Jenkins, WF	27
1929	George Blackerby, Waco	30
1930	Larry Bettencourt, WF	43
1931	Joe Medwick, Houston	19
1932	Hank Greenberg, Bmt.	39
1933	Zeke Bonura, Dallas	24
1934	Paul Easterling, Tulsa	29
1935	Rudy York, Bmt.	32
1936	Jim Stroner, Dallas	27
1937	Cecil Dunn, Bmt.	33
1938	Stan Schino, Tulsa	24
1939	Nick Cullop, Hous.	23
1940	Carl Jorgensen, SA	23
1941	Murrell Jones, Spt.	24
1942	Mervyn Connors, FW	27
1946	Bob Moyer, Dallas	24
1947	Nick Gregory, Spt.	28
1948	Russell Burns, Tulsa	26
1949	Jerry Witte, Dallas	50
1950	Bob Lemon, Ok. City	39
1951	Jerry Witte, Houston	38
1952	Harry Heslet, SA	31
1953	Harry Heslet, Spt.	41
1954	Buzz Clarkson, Dallas	42
1955	Pidge Browne, Spt.	33
1956	Ken Guettler, Spt.	62
1957	Keith Little, Hous.	30
1958	Mike Lutz, Corpus C.	39
1959	Carl Warwick, Vict.	35
1960	Layton Ducote, SA	32
1961	Craig Sorenson, SA	27
1962	Jerald Robinson, El P.	36
1963	Arlo Engle, El P.	41
1964	Charles Harrison, SA	40
1965	Leo Posada, Amarillo	26
1966	Winston Llenas, El P.	25
	Larry Stubing, Alb.	25
1967	Nate Colbert, Amar.	28
1968	Jim Spencer, El P.	28
1969	Adrian Garrett, SA	24
1970	Adrian Garrett, SA	29
1971	Larry Fritz, Memp.	20
1972	Gorman Thomas, SA	26
1973	Hector Cruz, Ark.	30

1974	Jerry Tabb, Mid.	29
	Wayne Tyrone, Mid.	29
1975	Mitchell Page, Spt.	23
	Gary Alexander, Laf.	23
	Jack Clark, Laf.	23
1976	Willie Aikens, El P.	30
1977	Karl Pagel, Midland	28
1978	Bob Clark, El P.	31
1979	Mark Brouhard, 28	28
1980	Mike Bishop, El P.	33
1981	Greg Brock, SA	32
1982	Darryl Strawberry, Jack.	34
1983	Rob Deer, Spt.	35
1984	Ralph Bryant, SA	31
1985	Joe Meyer, El P.	37
1986	Kevin King, Mid.	30

RBI LEADERS

1920	Dan Clark, WF	99
1921	Henry Eibel, Spt.	145
1922	Clarence Kraft, FW	131
1923	Ike Boone, SA	135
1924	Clarence Kraft, FW	196
1925	Ed Konetchy, FW	166
1926	Hack Miller, Dallas	118
1927	Del Pratt, Waco	140
1928	Tom Jenkins, WF	122
1929	Fred Bennett, WF	145
1930	Larry Bettencourt, WF	145
1931	Joe Medwick, Houston	126
1932	Paul Easterling, Bmt.	134
1933	Zeke Bonura, Dallas	111
1934	Larry Bettencourt, SA	129
1935	Rudy York, Bmt.	117
1936	Murray Howell, Tulsa	127
1937	Homer Peel, FW	118
1938	Stan Schino, Tulsa	118
1939	Nick Cullop, Hous.	112
	John Stoneham, FW	112
1940	Vern Stephens, SA	97
1941	Willis Norman, Hous.	107
1942	Mervyn Connors, FW	101
1946	Bob Moyer, Dallas	102
1947	Al Rosen, Ok. City	141
1948	Russell Burns, Tulsa	113
1949	Russell Burns, Tulsa	153
1950	Bob Lemon, Ok. City	119
1951	James Dyck, San A.	146
1952	Russell Burns, OC	120

1953	Russell Burns, OC	120
1954	Frank Kellert, SA	146
1955	Jim Pisoni, San A.	111
1956	Ken Guettler, Spt.	143
1957	Spence Robbins, OC	95
1958	Mike Lutz, Corpus C.	111
1959	Al Nagel, Amarillo	123
1960	Harry Watts, Tulsa	99
1961	Dick Bernardino, Amar.	93
1962	Charles Peterson, El P.	130
1963	Arlo Engel, El P.	126
1964	Larry Stubing, El P.	120
1965	Leo Posada, El P.	107
1966	Tom Hutton, Alb.	81
1967	Joe Hague, Ark.	95
1968	Jim Spencer, El P.	96
1969	Carlos Trevino, El P.	92
1970	Chico Diaz, Memphis	102
1971	Gary Matthews, Amar.	86
1972	Randy Elliott, Alex.	85
1973	Hector Cruz, Ark.	105
1974	John Balaz, El P.	111
1975	Mitchell Page, Spt.	90
1976	Willie Aikens, El P.	117
1977	Steve Stroughter, El P.	116
1978	Bob Clark, El Paso	111
1979	Mark Brouhard, El P.	107
1980	Mike Bishop, El Paso	104
1981	Stan Davis, El Paso	109
1982	Bill Foley, El Paso	106
1983	Mark Gillaspie, Bmt.	122
1984	Mark Gillaspie, Bmt.	87
1985	Billy Joe Robidoux, El P.	132
1986	Jason Felice, Jackson	97

STOLEN BASE LEADERS

1895	Will Blakey, Galv.	116
1896	Henry Cote, Hous.	64
1897	Jake Gettman, FW	55
1903	Leon Ury, Dallas	46
1904	Leon Ury, Dallas	56
1905	George Andres, Dallas	44
1907	Harry Short, Austin	78
1908	Tony Thebo, San A.	90
1909	Tony Thebo, Waco	63
1910	George Jackson, Dal.	55
1911	Red Downey, Austin	48
1912	Oscar Dugey, Waco	54

1913	Oscar Dugey, Waco	69	1965	Walt Williams, Tulsa	36
1914	Gerald Davis, Hous.	65	1966	Jesse White, DFW	31
1915	Bob Stow, FW	70	1967	Nate Colbert, Amar.	26
1916	Bob Stow, FW	60	1968	Ralph Garr, Spt.	32
1917	Al Nixon, Spt.	37	1969	Stan Martin, DFW	30
1918	Bob Stow, FW	27	1970	Guy Rose, Alb.	37
1919	Al Nixon, Bmt.	49	1971	Bill North, SA	47
1920	Mel Silva, Spt.	39	1972	Matt Alexander, Mid.	38
1921	Fred Henry, SA	52	1973	Morris Nettles, El P.	41
1922	Homer Ezzell, Spt.	55	1974	Larry Herndon, Ark.	50
1923	Ernest Vache, Dallas	40	1975	Jimmy Sexton, Spt.	48
1924	Joe Rabbitt, Bmt.	52	1976	Keith Chauncey, SA	31
1925	Dan Clark, SA	29	1977	Ed Miller, Tulsa	80
1926	Ray Flaskamper, SA	30	1978	Greg Jemison, Tulsa	65
1927	Pepper Martin, Hous.	36	1979	Mike Wilson, SA	56
1928	Ray Flaskamper, SA	48	1980	Nick Capra, Tulsa	55
1929	Pepper Martin, Hous.	43	1981	Dan Gladden, Spt.	52
1930	Joel Hunt, Houston	55	1982	Henry Cotto, Mid.	52
1931	Joyner White, Bmt.	52	1983	Mike Felder, El P.	71
1932	Byrne James, Dallas	42	1984	Mike Felder, El P.	58
1933	Herman Clifton, Bmt.	49	1985	Stanley Jefferson, Jack.	39
1934	Hubert Shelly, Bmt.	42	1986	Lance Johnson, Ark.	49
1935	Lynn King, Houston	55			
1936	Lou Brower, Ok. City	38			

1937	Mark Christman, Bmt.	47

.400 HITTERS

1938	Pat Mullin, Bmt.	40	1895	.444	Al McBride, Austin
1939	Frank Metha, FW	66	1895	.405	William Kemmer, Spt.
1940	Walt Kazen, FW	30	1923	.402	Ike Boone, SA
1941	Thurman Tucker, OC	40	1896	.401	Mike O'Connor, Den.-
1942	Thurman Tucker, FW	34			SA
1946	Boris Woyt, FW	50			

PITCHERS
— MOST VICTORIES —

1947	Jack Cassini, Tulsa	52			
1948	Tom Tatum, Tulsa	37			
1949	Preston Ward, FW	29	1895	Al McFarland, FW	34
1950	Dee Fondy, FW	39	1896	John Roach, Hous.	29
1951	John Temple, Tulsa	30	1904	Charles Jackson, FW	26
1952	Billy Hunter, FW	24	1905	Walt Chrisman, FW	23
1953	Galeard Wade, FW	31	1906	Alex Dupree, FW	25
1954	James Neufeldt, OC	43		Rick Adams, Cleb.	25
1955	Sherman Dixon, Hous.	40	1907	Ivy Tevis, Hous.	24
1956	Bob Malkmus, Austin	21	1908	O. C. Peters, Dal.	24
1957	Jim Frey, Tulsa	21	1909	Harry Stewart, Hous.	23
	Martin Bullard, Austin	21	1910	Sanford Burk, FW	25
1958	Rod Kanehl, Dallas	28	1911	Rube Robinson, FW	28
1959	Jim Beauchamp, Tulsa	20	1912	Poll Perritt, FW	24
1960	Jim Beauchamp, Tulsa	29		George Foster, Hous.	24
1961	Jose Tartabull, Vict.	37	1913	Charles Rose, Hous.	24
1962	Joe Patterson, Tulsa	31	1914	Eddie Donalds, Waco	30
1963	Joe Patterson, Tulsa	54	1915	Emmett Munsell, SA	25
1964	Joe Patterson, Tulsa	67			

1916	Cliff Hill, Waco	23		1956	Bob Mabe, Hous.	21
1917	Snipe Conley, Dal.	27		1957	Tom Bowers, Dal.	20
1918	Harry Lee, FW	9		1958	Joe Kotrany, Dal.	19
1919	Joe Martina, Beau.	28		1959	Carroll Berenger, Vict.	19
1920	Joe Pate, FW	26		1960	Jack Curtis, SA	19
	Paul Wachtel, FW	26		1961	Paul Toth, Tulsa	18
1921	Joe Pate, FW	30		1962	Jose Santiago, Alb.	16
1922	Paul Wachtel, FW	26		1963	Camilio Estevis, Alb.	16
1923	Lil Stoner, FW	27		1964	Jim Ward, Alb.	17
1924	Joe Pate, FW	30		1965	Ken Nixon, Austin	19
1925	Paul Wachtel, FW	23		1966	Bill Larkin, Alb.	20
1926	Jim Walkup, FW	22		1967	John Duffie, Alb.	16
	Tiny Owens, SA	22		1968	Joe DiFabio, Ark.	13
1927	George Payne, WF	23			Rick Folkers, Memp.	13
1928	Jim Lindsay, Hous.	25			Carl Morton, Spt.	13
1929	George Payne, WF	28			Santiago Guzman, Ark.	13
1930	Bob McCabe, FW	20			Archie Reynolds, SA	13
	Dick Whitworth, FW	20			Phil Knuckles, Ark.	13
1931	Dizzy Dean, Hous.	26		1969	Bill Frost, Amar.	16
1932	George Murray, Dal.	24		1970	Jim Flynn, Alb.	19
1933	George Darrow, Galv.	22		1971	Wayne Garland, DFW	19
	Ed Greer, Houston	22		1972	Dave Freisleben, Alex.	17
1934	Ash Hillin, SA	24		1973	Rick Sawyer, SA	18
1935	Russ Evans, OC	24		1974	Dennis Eckersley, SA	14
	A. M. Butcher, Galv.	24			Isidro Monge, El P.	14
1936	Curt Fullerton, Dal.	20			Harold Rasmussen, Ark.	14
1937	Ash Hillin, OC	31		1975	Tim Jones, Spt.	16
1938	Max Thomas, OC	23		1976	Bob Nolan, El P.	15
	Ash Hillin, OC	23			John Caneira, El P.	15
	Emil Bildili, SA	23		1977	Mike Scott, Jack.	13
1939	Ed Greer, FW	22		1978	Jeff Reardon, Jack.	17
	Murray Dickson, Hous.	22		1979	Bob Tufts, Spt.	14
1940	Maury Newlin, SA	23		1980	Tim Leary, Jack.	15
1941	Fred Martin, Hous.	23			Brian Holton, SA	15
1942	Earl Caldwell, FW	21		1981	Dave Dravecky, Amar.	15
1946	Henry Oana	24			Mark Dempsey, Spt.	15
1947	Clarence Beers, Hous.	25		1982	Brad Mengwesser, Tul.	13
1948	Harry Perkowski, Tul.	22			Jon Perlman, Mid.	13
1949	Joe Landrum, FW	19			Doug Welenc, Mid.	13
1950	James Blackburn, Tul.	21		1983	Sid Fernandez, SA	13
	Wayne McLeland, Dal.	21			Joe Georger, Jack.	13
	Ernie Nevel, Beau.	21		1984	William Long, Bmt.	14
1951	Al Papai, Hous.	23			Tim Meeks, SA	14
1952	Dave Hoskins, Dal.	22			Calvin Schiraldi, Jack.	14
1953	Red Murff, Dal.	17		1985	Randy Bockus, Spt.	14
1954	Karl Spooner, FW	21		1986	George Ferran, Spt.	16
	John Andre, Spt.	21				
1955	Red Murff, Dal.	27				

PITCHERS   — WINNING PERCENTAGE —

1895	——— Woodruff, Dal.	11-0	1.000
1896	Dale Gear, FW	24-5	.828
1904	Walt Chrisman, FW	21-6	.778
1905	Rick Adams, Tem.	13-3	.812
1906	Alex Dupree, FW	25-7	.781
1907	Parson McGill, Aus.	15-4	.780
1908	Ed Griffin, FW	23-09	.719
1909	Harry Stewart, Hous.	23-8	.742
1910	John Eubank, Hous.	10-4	.714
1911	Rube Robinson, FW	28-7	.800
1912	George Foster, Hous.	24-7	.774
1913	Dode Criss, Hous.	16-4	.800
1914	Eddie Donalds, Waco	30-4	.882
1915	Ed Duffy, Spt.	11-2	.846
1916	Walt Dickson, Hous.	18-8	.692
1917	John Paul Jones, Spt.	15-7	.682
1918	Ed Matteson, Dal.	7-1	.775
1919	Dick Robertson, FW	12-1	.923
1920	Bill Whittaker, FW	24-6	.800
1921	Joe Pate, FW	30-9	.769
1922	Gus Johns, FW	21-5	.808
1923	Harry O'Neill, Spt.	10-4	.714
1924	Ralph Head, FW	15-3	.833
1925	Paul Wachtel, FW	23-7	.767
1926	Dick Schumann, Dal.	17-5	.773
1927	Fred Fussell, WF	21-8	.774
1928	Milt Steengrafe, WF	22-8	.733
1929	Earl Collard, Spt.	10-2	.833
1930	Dizzy Dean, Hous.	8-2	.800
1931	Whitlow Wyatt, Bmt.	11-3	.786
1932	James Minogue, Dal.	13-4	.765
1933	George Darrow, Galv.	22-7	.759
1934	Clarence Phillips, Bmt.	15-5	.750
1935	John Niggeling, OC	9-2	.818
1936	Jackie Reid, FW	16-3	.842
1937	C. E. Poffenberger, Bmt.	9-1	.900
	Ash Hillin, OC	31-10	.756
1938	Dizzy Trout, Bmt.	22-6	.786
1939	Jackie Reid, Spt.	9-3	.750
1940	Maurice Newlin, SA	23-8	.742
1941	Howie Pollet, Hous.	20-3	.780
1942	John Whitehead, SA	10-3	.769
1946	Jim Turner, Bmt.	11-3	.786
1947	Willard Ramsdell, FW	21-5	.808
1948	Everett Lively, Tul.	15-4	.789
1949	Omar Lown, FW	8-1	.889
1950	James Blackburn, Tul.	21-7	.750
1951	Octavio Rubert, Hous.	19-5	.792

1952	Thomas Reis, Tulsa	15-5	.714
1953	Howard Judson, Tul.	11-0	1.000
1954	Willard Schmidt, Hous.	18-5	.783
1955	Melvin Held, SA	24-7	.774
1956	Hisel Patrick, Dal.	13-4	.765
1957	Tom Hughes, Hous.	14-4	.778
1958	Harvey Cohen, SA	14-6	.700
1959	Carroll Beringer, Vict.	19-5	.729
1960	Ron Herbel, RGV	15-4	.789
1961	Harold Stowe, Amar.	14-1	.933
1962	Gordy Richardson, Tul.	13-6	.684
1963	Cliff Davis, SA	13-7	.650
1964	Chris Zachary, SA	16-6	.727
1965	Don Sutton, Alb.	15-6	.714
1966	George Gerberman, Amar.	12-2	.857
1967	Sal Campisi, Ark.	14-6	.700
1968	Carl Morton, Spt.	13-5	.722
1969	Robert Johnson, Mem.	13-4	.765
1970	James Flynn, Alb.	19-4	.826
1971	Wayne Garland, DFW	19-5	.792
1972	Dennis James, El P.	11-3	.786
1973	Dan Corder, Mid.	13-3	.813
1974	Dennis Eckersley, SA	14-3	.824
1975	Tim Jones, Spt.	16-6	.727
1976	Bob Noland, El P.	15-3	.833
1977	Ray Rainbolt, Tul.	10-3	.769
1978	Jeff Reardon, Jack.	17-4	.810
1979	Charles Phillips, El P.	10-2	.833
1980	Ted Davis, Tul.	10-3	.769
1981	Tom Niedenfuer, SA	13-3	.813
1982	Dan Burns, El P.	10-4	.714
1983	Robert Clark, Tul.	12-3	.800
1984	Calvin Schiraldi, Jack.	14-3	.824
1985	Juan Nieves, El P.	8-2	.800
1986	George Ferran, Spt.	16-1	.941

PITCHERS — MOST STRIKEOUTS —

1904	Jack Jarvis, FW	185	1917	Snipe Conley, Dal.	171
1906	Rick Adams, Cleb.	138	1918	Joe Martina, Hous.	105
1907	Bill Bailey, Aus.	234	1919	Bill Bailey, Bmt.	277
1909	Fred Winchell, SA	264	1920	Bill Bailey, Bmt.	216
1910	Harry Ables, SA	325	1921	John Hollingsworth, WF	218
1911	Harley Young, OC	245	1922	Rip Wheeler, WF	132
1912	Eugene Moore, Galv.	213	1923	Slim Love, Dallas	172
1913	C. H. Harben, Galv.	204	1924	Slim Love, Dallas	208
	Dave Davenport, SA	204	1925	Gus Johns, FW	211
1914	Eugene Moore, Galv.	240	1926	Slim Love, Dallas	216
1915	Cliff Markle, Waco	228	1927	William Shores, Waco	125
1916	Cliff Hill, Waco	251	1928	Bill Hallahan, Hous.	244

1929	Andy Messenger, WF	138
1930	Allyn Stout, Hous.	166
1931	Dizzy Dean, Hous.	303
1932	Henry Thormahlen, Galv.	186
1933	Elton Walkup, SA	146
1934	Vern Kennedy, OC	167
1935	Lee Grissom, FW	166
1936	Beryl Richmond, Galv.	172
1937	Ed Cole, Galv.	205
1938	Mort Cooper, Hous.	201
1939	Vallie Eaves, Spt.	165
1940	Bob Uhle, Dallas	205
1941	Howie Pollet, Hous.	151
1942	Ralph Hamner, Spt.	148
1946	John Van Cuyk, FW	207
1948	Cloyd Boyer, Hous.	188
1949	Dick Rozek, OC	145
1950	Joe Presko, Hous.	165
1951	Wilmer Mizell, Hous.	257
1952	John Gray, Bmt.	152
1953	Ryne Duren, SA	212
1954	Karl Spooner, FW	262
1955	Pete Burnside, Dal.	235
1956	Bob Mabe, Hous.	195
1957	Larry Sherry, FW	146
1958	Jim Tugerson, Dal.	195
1959	Charles Gorin, Aus.	173
1960	Denny Lemaster, Aus.	181
1961	Harry Fanok, Tul.	158
1962	Harvey Branch, SA	116
1963	Camilo Estevis, Alb.	196
1964	Jim Ward, Alb.	224
	Charles Spell, Alb.	224
1965	Larry Jaster, Tul.	219
1966	Fred Norman, DFW	198
1967	Ed Everitt, Alb.	200
1968	Paul Doyle, DFW	149
1969	Jim Strickland, Alb.	137
1970	Randy Cohen, DFW	151
1971	Tommy Moore, Mem.	160
1972	Frank Riccelli, Amar.	183
1973	Frank Tanana, El P.	197
1974	Dennis Eckersley, SA	163
1975	Frank Panik, El P.	126
1976	Bill Caudill, Ark.	140
1977	Juan Berenguer, Jack.	126
1978	Dick Sander, SA	159
1979	Scott Budner, Spt.	110
	Joe Carroll, Amar.	110

1980	Fernando Valenzuela, SA	162
1981	Alan Fowles, Spt.	152
1982	Jeff Bittiger, Jack.	190
1983	Sid Fernandez, SA	209
1984	John Young, Ark.	136
1985	Chris Bosio, El P.	155
1986	George Ferran, Spt.	147

PITCHERS — LOWEST EARNED RUN AVERAGE

1916	Walt Dickson, Hous.	1.06
1917	J. Paul Jones, Spt.	1.83
1918	Ed Matteson, Dal.	2.09
1919	Bryan Harris, Hous.	1.56
	John Verbout, Spt.	1.56
1920	Joe Pate, FW	1.71
1921	J. B. Hollingsworth, Spt.	2.13
1922	Gus Johns, FW	2.34
1923	Lil Stoner, FW	2.70
1924	Jack Knight, Hous.	2.34
1925	Russ Pence, Dal.	2.88
1926	Jim Walkup, FW	2.43
1927	Ken Penner, Hous.	2.52
1928	Bill Callahan, Hous.	2.25
1929	Vic Frazier, Dal.	2.61
1930	Ralph Judd, Hous.	2.61
1931	Dizzy Dean, Hous.	1.53
	Whitlow Wyatt, Beau.	1.53
1932	Lynwood Rowe, Beau.	2.34
1933	Mike Cvengros, Hous.	2.43
1934	Red Phillips, Beau.	2.16
1935	Earl Caldwell, SA	2.25
1936	Fred Marberry, Dal.	2.12
1937	Ash Hillin, OC	2.34
1938	Max Thomas, Tulsa	1.98
1939	Ed Greer, FW	2.29
1940	Sam Nahem, Hous.	1.65
	Howie Krist, Hous.	1.71
1941	Howie Pollet, Hous.	1.16
1942	John Whitehead, Hous.	1.20
1946	John Van Cuyk, FW	1.42
1947	Dwain Sloat, FW	1.99
1948	Elred Byerly, Tulsa	2.21
1949	Carl Erskine, FW	2.07
1950	John Rutherford, FW	2.21
1951	Tom Gorman, Beau.	1.94
1952	Joe Landrum, FW	1.94
1953	Floyd Woolridge, Hous.	2.46

1954	Bob Smith, Spt.	2.89
1955	Red Murff, Dallas	1.99
1956	Hisel Patrick, Dallas	2.03
1957	Murray Wall, Dallas	1.79
1958	Don Erickson, Tulsa	2.96
1959	Charles Gorin, Austin	2.96
1960	Gaylord Perry, RGV	2.83
1961	Larry Maxie, Austin	2.09
1962	Gordy Richardson, Tulsa	3.18
1963	Sterling Slaughter, Ama.	3.00
1964	Dick Burwell, FW	2.55
1965	Charles Hartenstein, DFW	2.18
1966	Pat House, Austin	2.13
1967	Sal Campisi, Ark.	2.26
1968	Joe DiFabio, Ark.	2.17
1969	Ramon Hernandez, Ark.	2.40
1970	George Manz, DFW	1.99
1971	Wayne Garland, DFW	1.70
1972	Dave Freisleben, Alex.	2.33
1973	Dan Corder, Midland	2.32

1974	Randy Willes, Ark.	2.56
1975	Mike Bruhert, Jack.	2.62
1976	Jay Dillard, Laf.	2.31
1977	Fred Honeycutt, Spt.	2.47
1978	Neil Allen, Jackson	2.09
1979	Greg Harris, Jackson	2.26
1980	Billy Joe Edelen, Ark.	2.62
1981	Tim Hamm, Amarillo	2.27
1982	Doug Sisk, Jackson	2.67
1983	Sid Fernandez, SA	2.82
1984	Ted Higuera, El P.	2.60
1985	Randy Bockus, Spt.	2.73
1986	George Ferran, Spt.	2.29

30-GAME WINNERS

1895	34-12	Al McFarland, FW
1937	31-10	Ash Hillin, OC
1914	30-4	Eddie Donalds, Waco
1924	30-8	Joe Pate, FW
1921	30-9	Joe Pate, FW
1895	30-16	George Bristow, Galv.

MOST VALUABLE PLAYERS

Beginning in 1931, Texas League sports writers voted each season for the league's Most Valuable Player. In 1933 and 1934, separate awards were made for the Most Valuable Player and the Most Valuable Pitcher, but was dropped in 1935 — only to be resumed in 1946. In the years where two players are listed, the second name represents the Most Valuable Pitcher. From 1955 through 1959 a Rookie-of-the-Year was also named; the third player listed below represents that seasons Rookie-of-the-Year. No MVP award was made in the years 1973 through 1976.

1931	Dizzy Dean, P, Houston
1932	Hank Greenberg, 1B, Bmt.
1933	Zeke Bonura, 1B, Dallas
	George Darrow, Galv.
1934	Charles English, IF, Galv.
	Ash Hillin, San Antonio
1935	Rudy York, 1B, Beaumont
1936	Les Nallon, IF, Dallas
1937	Ash Hillin, P, Ok. City
1938	Dizzy Trout, P, Beaumont
1939	Nick Cullop, OF, Houston
1940	Bob Muncrief, P, San A.
1941	Rip Russell, IF, Tulsa
1942	Dick Wakefield, OF, Bmt.

1946	Henry Schenz, IF, Tulsa
	Hank Oana, Dallas
1947	Al Rosen, IF, Ok. City
	Clarence Beers, Houston
1948	Irv Noren, OF, Fort Worth
	Harry Perkowski, Tulsa
1949	Herb Conyers, 1B, Ok. City
	Joe Landrum, Fort Worth
1950	Gil McDougald, IF, Bmt.
	Wayne McLeland, Dallas
1951	James Dyck, OF, San A.
	Bob Turley, San Antonio
1952	Billy Hunter, IF, Fort W.
	Harold Erickson, Dallas

1953	Joe Frazier, OF, Ok. City		Ken Nixon, Austin
	Don Fracchia, Beaumont	1966	Tom Hutton, 1B, Alb.
1954	Frank Kellert, 1B, San A.		Freddie Norman, DFW
	John Andre, Spt.	1967	Nate Colbert, IF, Amarillo
1955	Ray Murray, C, Dallas		John Duffie, Albuquerque
	Red Murff, Dallas	1968	Jim Spencer, 1B, El P.
	Pidge Browne, OF, Spt.		& Bill Sudakis, 1B, Alb.
1956	Ken Guettler, OF, Spt.		Santiago Guzman, Ark.
	Bert Thiel, Dallas	1969	Larry Johnson, 1B, DFW
	Ken Guettler, OF, Spt.		& Bobby Grich, IF, DFW
1957	Jim Frey, OF, Tulsa		Bill Frost, Amarillo
	Tommy Bowers, Dallas	1970	Mickey Rivers, OF, El P.
	Jim Coker, C, Tulsa		Jim Flynn, Albuquerque
1958	Mike Lutz, OF, Corpus C.	1971	Enos Cabell, 1B, DFW
	Joe Kotrany, Dallas		Wayne Garland, DFW
	Charles James, OF, Hous.	1972	Randy Elliott, OF, Alex.
1959	Carl Warwick, OF, Victoria	1977	Karl Pagel, OF, Midland
	Carroll Beringer, Victoria	1978	Bob Clark, OF, El Paso
	Al Nagel, OF, Amarillo	1979	Max Brouhard, OF, El P.
1960	Chuck Hiller, IF, Rio G V	1980	Tim Leary, P, Jackson
	Jack Curtis, San Antonio	1981	Steve Sax, IF, San A.
1961	Phil Linz, IF, Amarillo	1982	Darryl Strawberry, OF, Jack.
	Larry Maxie, Austin	1983	Mark Gillaspie, OF, Bmt.
1962	Charles Peterson, SS, El P.	1984	James Steels, OF, Bmt.
	Gordy Richardson, Tulsa		Calvin Schiraldi, Jack.
1963	Jim Beauchamp, OF, Tulsa	1985	Billy Joe Robidoux, 1B, El P.
	Camilo Estevis, Alb.		Juan Nieves, El Paso
1964	Joe Morgan, 2B, San A.	1986	Steve Stanicek, 1B, El Paso
	Chris Zachary, San A.		George Ferran, Shreveport
1965	Leo Posada, OF, Amarillo		

STAR OF STARS AWARD. In 1984 the Howe News Service, which compiles statistics for the Texas League and other minor circuits, began to name a "Star of Stars" in each league for overall statistical excellence. The Texas League Stars of Stars have been:

1984 Calvin Schiraldi, Jackson (14-3)
1985 Billy Joe Robidoux, El Paso (.342, 23 HR, 132 RBI)
1986 George Ferran, Shreveport (16-1)

MANAGERS OF THE YEAR

Beginning with the 1955 season, a Manager of the Year was chosen. The award was dropped in 1961, then renewed in 1964.

1955	Red Davis, Dallas	1959	Pete Reiser, Victoria
1956	Red Davis, Dallas	1960	Ray Murray, Rio G. V.
1957	Salty Parker, Dallas		
1958	Harry Walker, Houston		
1964	Grover Resinger, Tulsa	1966	Vern Rapp, Arkansas
1965	Whitey Lockman, DFW	1967	Buddy Hancken, Amarillo

1968	Chuck Tanner, El Paso		1977	Bob Rodgers, El Paso
1969	Joe Altobelli, DFW		1978	Jim Saul, Midland
	Johnny Antonelli, Memphis		1979	Andy Gilbert, Shreveport
1970	Del Crandall, Albuquerque		1980	Bob Wellman, Jackson
1971	Andy Gilbert, Amarillo		1981	Don LeJohn, San Antonio
1972	Duke Snider, Alexandria		1982	Tommy Burgess, Tulsa
1973	Tony Pacheco, San Antonio		1983	Nick Leyva, Arkansas
1974	Joe Frazier, Victoria		1984	Sam Perlozzo, Jackson
1975	Denny Sommers, Lafayette		1985	Terry Bevington, El Paso
1976	Bob Miller, Amarillo		1986	Wendell Kim, El Paso

TEXAS LEAGUE HALL OF FAMERS

(Hall of Famers Who Have Played or Managed in the Texas League)

Grover Cleveland Alexander (Dallas, 1930)
Dizzy Dean (Houston, 1930–31; Tulsa, 1940)
Hank Greenberg (Beaumont, 1931–32)
Chick Hafey (Houston, 1924)
Rogers Hornsby (Mgr. — Ok. City, 1940–41; FW, 1942;
    Beaumont, 1950)
Carl Hubbell (FW, 1927; Beaumont, 1928)
Ducky Medwick (Houston, 1932–32, 1948)
Branch Rickey (Dallas, 1904–5)
Brooks Robinson (San Antonio, 1956–57)
Frank Robinson (Tulsa, 1954)
Al Simmons (Shreveport, 1923)
George Sisler (Shreveport-Tyler, 1932)
Duke Snider (FW, 1946; Mgr. — Alb., 1967)
Tris Speaker (Cleburne, 1906; Houston, 1907)
Bill Terry (Shreveport, 1916–17)

LIFETIME RECORDS

BEST LIFETIME	RBIs	Paul Easterling	1,136
HITTING RECORDS	Stolen Bases	Pat Newman	422

Years	Homer Peel	14
	Arch Tanner	14
Games	Paul Easterling	1,777
Runs	Paul Easterling	1,134
Average	Homer Peel	.325
Hits	Paul Easterling	1,922
Doubles	Paul Easterling	378
Triples	Harold Epps	112
Home Runs	Paul Easterling	223

BEST LIFETIME
PITCHING RECORDS

Games	R. O. Whitworth	452
Victories	Paul Wachtel	231
Losses	Paul Wachtel	142
Strikeouts	Joe Martina	1,412
Years	Paul Wachtel	13
	Stuart Jacobus	13

SEASON RECORDS

BEST INDIVIDUAL SEASON BATTING RECORDS

Games	Randolph Moore (Dallas, 1929)	168
	Irvin Jeffries (Dallas, 1929)	168
Average	Al McBride (Austin, 1896)	.444
Runs	Jimmy Singles (Houston, 1896)	171
Hits	Randolph Moore (Dallas, 1929)	245
Singles	Randolph Moore (Dallas, 1929)	187
Doubles	Rhino Williams (Dallas, 1925)	70
Triples	Eddie Moore (FW, 1929)	30
Home Runs	Ken Guettler (Spt., 1956)	62
Grand Slams	Roy Ostergaard (Galv., 1923)	6
Extra Base	Clarence Kraft (FW, 1924)	
Hits	36 2Bs, 5 3Bs, 55HRs	96
Hitting Streak	Ike Boone (SA, 1923)	37
(Games)	Carlos Trevino (El Paso, 1969)	37
RBIs	Clarence Kraft (FW, 1924)	196
Stolen Bases	Will Blakey (Galv., 1895)	116
Walks	Ed Lake (Houston, 1939)	153
Strikeouts	Willie Crawford (Alb., 1966)	186
HBP	Ed Miller (Galv., 1916)	27

BEST INDIVIDUAL SEASON PITCHING RECORDS

Games	Chief Waters (FW, 1955)	77
Complete Games	Bob Couchman (Galv., 1920)	34
Victories	Al McFarland (FW, 1895)	34
Losses	Bill Doyle (Temple, 1907)	28
Winning	Ted Thiem (Tulsa, 1960, 12-0)	1.000
Percentage	Woodruff (Dallas, 1895, 12-0)	1.000
	Howard Judson (Tulsa, 1953, 11-0)	1.000
	Don Feerarese (SA, 1955, 9-0)	1.000
Lowest ERA	Hickory Dickson (Houston, 1916)	1.06
Most Innings	Bill Bailey and Joe Martina (bmt., 1919)	378
Consecutive Wins	Snipe Conley (Dallas, 1917)	19
Shutouts	Dizzy Dean (Houston, 1931)	11
Strikeouts	Harry Ables (SA, 1910)	325
Walks	Bill Bailey (Bmt., 1919)	185

CENTURY CLUB

Winners			**Losers**		
1924	Fort Worth	109-41	1914	Austin	31-114
1922	Fort Worth	109-46	1955	Beaumont	51-110
1920	Fort Worth	108-40	1925	Beaumont	42-108
1931	Houston	108-41	1940	Fort Worth	52-108
1921	Fort Worth	107-51	1956	Ok. City	48-106

1940	Houston	105-56	1928	Beaumont	50-106
1928	Houston	104-54	1932	Dallas	55-106
1925	Fort Worth	103-48	1942	Dallas	48-104
1941	Houston	103-50	1931	Galveston	57-104
1914	Houston	102-50	1920	Houston	50-101
1914	Waco	102-50	1920	Galveston	49-100
1957	Dallas	102-52	1924	Shreveport	54-100
1927	Wichita Falls	102-54			
1946	Fort Worth	101-53			
1937	Ok. City	101-58			
1932	Beaumont	100-51			
1949	Fort Worth	100-54			

Bibliography

Books

At the Texas Sports Hall of Fame in Arlington I was granted access to a collection of annual baseball guides. While two or three guides were available for a number of seasons, guides for about one-third of the years were missing. I photocopied the available Texas League records and other related items, and the library of the Baseball Hall of Fame in Copperstown graciously supplied photocopies from the missing guides. The guides I used were: *Spalding's Official Base Ball Record, The Reach Official Base Ball Guide, Spink's Official Baseball Guide,* and *The Sporting News Official Baseball Guide.* Other books containing pertinent information included:

Bailey, Jim. *Arkansas Travelers, 79 Years of Baseball.* Little Rock: Arkansas Travelers Baseball Club, Inc., [1980].

Goldstein, Richard. *Spartan Seasons — How Baseball Survived the Second World War.* New York: Macmillan Publishing Co., Inc., 1980.

Greene, A. C. *Texas Sketches.* Dallas: Taylor Publishing Company, 1985.

Hammond, Clara T., Comp. *Amarillo.* Amarillo: George Autry, Printer, 1971.

Harrison, W. Wentworth. *History of Greenville and Hunt County, Texas.* Waco: Texian Press, 1977.

Hornsby, Rogers, and Bill Surface. *My War With Baseball.* New York: Coward-McCann, Inc., 1962.

Kelley, Dayton, ed. *The Handbook of Waco and McLennan County, Texas.* Waco: Texian Press, 1972.

Lowenfish, Lee, and Tony Lupien. *The Imperfect Diamond.* New York: Stein and Day, Publishers, 1980.

MacFarlane, Paul, ed. *Daguerreotypes of Great Stars of Baseball.* St. Louis: The Sporting News Publishing Co., 1981.

MacLean, Norman, ed. *Who's Who in Baseball 1986.* New York: Who's Who in Baseball, Inc., 1986.

McComb, David G. *Houston, the Bayou City.* Austin: University of Texas Press, 1969.

Mitchell, Harley D. *Bicentennial Plus One, Harley Mitchell's Temple, Somewhat of a History of Sports.* Belton, Texas: Stillhouse Hollow Publishers, Inc., 1977.

Morris, Leopold. *Pictorial History of Victoria and Victoria County.* N.p., n.d.

Obojski, Robert. *Bush League, A History of Minor League Baseball.* New York: Macmillan Publishing Co., Inc., 1975

Parker, Al. *Baseball Giant Killers, The Spudders of the '20s.* Quanah, Texas: Nortex Press, 1976.

Reichler, Joseph L. *The Baseball Encyclopedia.* New York: Macmillan Publishing Co., Inc., 1979.

Reidenbaugh, Lowell. *Take Me Out to the Ball Park.* St. Louis: The Sporting News Publishing Co., 1983.

Rogosin, Donn. *Invisible Men, Life in Baseball's Negro Leagues.* New York: Atheneum, 1985.

Ruggles, William B. *The History of the Texas League of Professional Baseball Clubs, 1888–1951.* Published by the Texas League, 1951.

———. *Roster of the Texas League, 1888–1952.* Published by the Texas League, 1952.

———. *Texas League Official Record Book, 1888–1956.* Published by the Texas League, 1957.

———, J. P. Friend, Mike Halbrooks, and Ed Williams, comps. *Texas League Record Book, 1888–1982.* Published by the Texas League, 1983.

Ryan, Bob. *Wait Till I Make the Show, Baseball in the Minor Leagues.* Boston: Little, Brown and Company, 1974.

Society for American Baseball Research. *Minor League Baseball Stars.* Vol. I. Manhattan, Kansas: Ag Press, Inc., 1984.

Society for American Baseball Research. *Minor League Baseball Stars.* Vol. II. Manhattan, Kansas: Ag Press, Inc., 1985.

Somers, Dale A. *The Rise of Sports in New Orleans, 1850–1900.* Baton Rouge: Louisiana State University Press, 1972.

Texas Sports Hall of Fame, Its Members and Their Deeds. N.p., n.d.

Turkin, Hy, and S. C. Thompson. *The Official Encyclopedia of Baseball.* New York: A. S. Barnes and Company, 1956.

Tyler, George W. *History of Bell County.* Belton, Texas: Dayton Kelley, 1966.

Walker, John H., and Gwendolyn Wingate. *Beaumont, A Pictorial History.* Norfolk, Virginia: The Domingo Company, Publishers, 1983.

Articles

Aten, Earl V. "Speaker, Killifer & Co." *The Texas Magazine* (October 1912), 459–462.

Bablitch, John. "Jim Paul — El Paso's Top Rank Promoter of Minor League Baseball." *El Paso Magazine* (June 1984), 33–39.

"The Big Playoff." *Shreveport Magazine* (September 1954), 15, 31.

"Bucs Brighten the Ballpark." *Shreveport Magazine* (June 1975), 24.

Bullock, Jimmy. "When the Majors Trained Here." *Shreveport Magazine* (March and April, 1981), 26+ and 38+.

"Caps Take Early Lead in Texas League," *Shreveport Magazine* (June 1977), 28, 46.

Conwell, Bob. "The Parkers Have More Muscle." *Shreveport Magazine* (April 1951), 20–21+.

———. "The Texas League Pennant Chase." *Shreveport Magazine* (April 1950), 30.

Elgin, Jack. "Lone Star League." *Shreveport Magazine* (April 1953), 28, 48.

Farber, Jerome. "The Coming Baseball Season in Texas." *The Texas Magazine* (April 1911), 61–63.

Fiser, Jack. "Bossier's Boy in Blue." *Shreveport Magazine* (February 1963), 28, 44.

———. "Is Organized Baseball On Its Way Back?" *Shreveport Magazine* (February 1967), 22, 50.

———. "Return of the Sports (Braves?)" *Shreveport Magazine* (October 1967), 24, 45.

Harris, Otis. "Sports Open Season at Home April 16." *Shreveport Magazine* (April 1948), 20, 22.

"Home Ownership Back in the Ball Park." *Shreveport Magazine* (April 1974), 30, 51.

House, Bob. "City's Baseball History Colorful." Lake Charles *American Press*, Centennial Edition (1967).

Ingram, Bob. "The Dome — A Long Time Home." *Diablos Game Program, 1986,* 2–5.

Kepple, G. E. "Organized Baseball in Texas." *The Texas Magazine* (April 1910), 11–16.

Laird, John. "There's Nothing Minor About the Texas League." *Texas Sports* (April 1981), 60–62.

Lopez, Tommy. "Captains On Their Way." *Shreveport Magazine* (May 1971), 30, 44.

"Make Way for the Shreveport Captains." *Shreveport Magazine* (March 1971), 24.

Manasseh, Paul. "Baseball's Back in Town." *Shreveport Magazine* (April 1968), 32, 49–50, 52.

———. "Sports Prep to Defend Title." *Shreveport Magazine* (April 1956), 18–19.

———. "The Sports Will Be Hard To Beat." *Shreveport Magazine* (April 1954), 22, 38.

———. "Those Rampaging Sports." *Shreveport Magazine* (April 1949), 24, 58.

"The Men Behind the Sports." *Shreveport Magazine* (April 1952), 13–15, 42, 44–45.

Patoski, Joe Nick, and John Morthland. "Root, Root, Root for the Home Team." *Texas Monthly* (June 1986), 120–125.

Peebles, Dick. "Play Ball!" *San Antonio Express Magazine* (April 9, 1950), 12–13.

———. "Take Me Out to the Ball Game." *San Antonio Express Magazine* (April 10, 1949), 4–5.

Piercey, Joe. "Are the Minors Making a Comeback?" *Shreveport Magazine* (April 1960), 20–21, 35.

"Preview of the Sports." *Shreveport Magazine* (March 1948), 22–23.

Putnam, Pat. "Bananas in the Bushes." *Sports Illustrated* (September 12, 1977), 32–35.

Ruggles, William B. "Baseball in Texas." *Bunker's Monthly, The Magazine of Texas* (July 1928), 89–101.

Saulsberry, Charles. "Fifty Years of Baseball." *Oklahoma City Times* (long-running serial in 1940).

Shelton, Horace H., "Texans in the 'Big Show.'" *The Texas Magazine* (January 1911), 39–41.

"Southern Digs in for New Season of AA Ball." *Shreveport Magazine* (April 1961), 20–21.

Spander, Art. "Baseball No Longer Treats King Carl Royally." *The Sporting News* (March 24, 1986), 8.

"Sports Brace for Texas League Season." *Shreveport Magazine* (April 1957), 22, 40.

"The Sports Have It Again." *Shreveport Magazine* (April 1955), 26, 36.

"The Sports' New Stars." *Shreveport Magazine* (July 1955), 24–25.

"Stretch Drive." *Shreveport Magazine* (September 1952), 18.

"Texas League." *Shreveport Magazine* (April 1946), 16–17, 36.

"Texas League Champions." *Shreveport Magazine* (November 1952), 22.

"Third Base Coach for the Giants." *Shreveport Magazine* (April 1961), 29, 32.

Van Thyn, Nico. "History of Fair Grounds Field." *1986 Texas League All-Star Game Program* (July 9, 1986), 3–5.

Wallis, Michael. "The Bush Leagues Are Alive and Well." *Muse Air Monthly Magazine* (July 1985), 36 + .

Newspapers

The *Dallas Morning News* is on microfilm at Stephen F. Austin State University, and I used the files of that newspaper extensively. Where available I also sampled baseball history in the following newspapers:

Albuquerque Tribune (1966, 1969).

Alexandria Daily Town Talk (1972).

Austin American (1930, 1934).

Austin Statesman (1895, 1896, 1939, 1956).

Beaumont Enterprise (1926–41, 1945–56, 1958, 1976–77, 1986).

Corpus Christi Times (1976).

Dallas Morning News (1887–1958, 1965–71).

Dallas Sentinel (1934).

El Paso Herald-Post (1964, 1966, 1971, 1975, 1976, 1977).

Fort Worth Press (1925, 1950, 1957, 1959, 1968).

Fort Worth Star-Telegram (1949, 1950, 1970, 1980).

Galveston Daily News (1903, 1934, 19530.

Greenville Messenger (1906).

Houston Chronicle (1963, 1968, 1976).

Houston Post (1936, 1952, 1966, 1979).

Longview Daily News (1933).

Longview Morning Journal (1985).

Marshall News-Messenger (1932, 1933).

Midland Reporter-Telegram (1934–39).

Oklahoma City Times (1940).

Paris News (1931–34, 1936).

San Antonio Express (1892).

San Antonio Light (1963).

Sherman Democrat (1976, 1979).

Shreveport Times (1984–86).

Tulsa Tribune (1949, 1958, 1974, 1979).

Tulsa World (1965, 1967, 1969, 1971, 1976, 1977, 1983).

Waco Times-Herald (1967).

Local Baseball Files

The following libraries (all in Texas unless otherwise indicated) have files on local baseball teams or sports history. These files include newspaper clippings, old game programs, photographs, etc., and were a rich source of information.

Albuquerque (New Mexico) Public Library
Austin History Center, Austin Public Library
Beaumont Public Library
Corpus Christi Public Library
El Paso Public Library
Fort Worth Public Library
Rosenberg Library, Galveston
W. Walworth Harrison Public Library, Greenville
Houston Public Library
Nicholson Memorial Public Library, Longview
Midland Public Library
Metropolitan Library System, Oklahoma City (Oklahoma)
Aiken Regional Archives, Paris Junior College, Paris
San Antonio Public Library
Shreveport (Louisiana) Public Library
Temple Public Library
Tulsa (Oklahoma) Public Library
Waco Public Library

Miscellaneous

Blankenship, Maude Davis. "A History of Texarkana, My Texarkana." Unpublished master's thesis, East Texas State University, Commerce.
Brown, John C. "How the Longview Cannibals Got Their Name." Longview sports file, Nicholson Memorial Public Library, Longview.
Hart, Katherine. *Waterloo Scrapbook*. Files of the Austin History Center, Austin Public Library.
History of El Paso Baseball. Television script, provided by the El Paso Diablos.
"Jackson Mets . . . The Tradition Continues!" Release provided by the Jackson Mets Baseball Club.
Moegle, Bobby Jim. "A Survey of the Minor League Baseball Player." Unpublished master's thesis, University of Texas at Austin.
Rains, Marck C. "A Historical Survey — Organized Recreation in Victoria, Texas." Unpublished master's thesis, Baylor University, Waco.
Texas League Final Official Statistics, 1986. Howe News Bureau, Boston, Massachusetts.

Interviews

Antonelli, John. Jackson, Mississippi (6-12-86).
Bowlin, Art. Gary, Texas, by Tim Bush (10-15-86).
Butler, Dick. Shreveport, Louisiana (7-9-86).

Callow, John H. Jackson, Mississippi (6-12-86).

Dickson, Frank, Sr. Albuquerque, New Mexico (11-27-85 and 11-30-85).

Faulk, John "Lefty." Center, Texas, by Patresa Livingston (9-30-85).

Feder, Mike. Jackson, Mississippi (6-12-86), and Shreveport, Louisiana (7-9-86).

Finnerty, Hugh. Shreveport, Louisiana (7-9-86).

Ford, Steve. San Antonio, Texas (6-3-86).

Foster, Lana. Linden, Texas (7-8-86).

Gliatto, Mrs. Sol. Dallas, Texas (11-6-85).

Hanson, Vivian. Carthage, Texas (10-18-85).

Hughes, Dr. Bill. Texarkana, Texas (10-22-86).

Maloney, J. Con. Jackson, Mississippi (6-12-86).

McIntyre, Bill. Shreveport, Louisiana (5-12-86).

Moor, Ted, Jr. Shreveport, Louisiana (7-9-86).

Oden, Gene. Elysian Fields, Texas (5-12-86).

Parr, Rick. El Paso, Texas (7-22-86).

Peddlie, Inez. Dallas, Texas (12-20-86).

Peel, Homer. Shreveport, Louisiana (12-14-85 and 5-12-86).

Perlman, Jon. Carthage, Texas (1-24-86 and 11-5-86).

Perry, Matt. Midland, Texas (7-28-86).

Preseren, Joe. Tulsa, Oklahoma (6-24-86).

Sawatski, Carl. Little Rock, Arkansas (numerous conversations in 1985 and 1986).

Smith, Fred. Geneva, Texas, by Tonya Wilburn (9-30-85).

Underwood, "Rhino Red." Beaumont, Texas, by Guy Draper (5-16-86).

Valentic, Lou. Beaumont, Texas (6-1-86).

Valentine, Bill. Little Rock, Arkansas (6-11-86).

Vincent, Al. Beaumont, Texas (10-12-85).

Vitter, Joe. Carthage, Texas (12-1-85 and often thereafter).

Washington, Mrs. Vernon. Linden, Texas (11-9-85).

York, Mariana. Hubbard, Texas (12-20-86).

INDEX

Edelen, Benny Joe, 156, 274
Edens, J. E., 310
Edington, Stump, 55, 245
Edmondson, Bob, 28, 33, 36, 44, 259
 Roger, 42
Eduardo, Hector, 152
Edwards, "Frisco," 174
 "Monk," 173
Ehret, "Red," 3, 5
Ehrlich, Harry, 40
Eibel, "Hank," 52, 192, 303
Eisenfelder, C. W., 291
Elberfeld, Norman Arthur "Kid," 18,
 58
Eldred, R. C., 332
Elisha, Mrs. Sol, 215
Ellam, "Slippery," 175
Elliff, Harry, 11
Ellingsen, Bruce, 200
Elliott, Harry, 110, 306
 Randy, 144, 201, 202
El Paso, 132, 139, 145, 146, 147, 160,
 169, 176, 177, 178, 219, 221, 239,
 274, 279, 281, 307, 316
Elsey, Charles, 15
Elster, Kevin, 267
Engle, Arlo, 133, 240
English, Charles, 77, 253, 254
Ens, Jewel, 49
Epps, Harold, 349
 "Yo-Yo," 175
Erickson, Don, 124
 Hal "Moose," 112
 Harold, 109
 William, 8, 12
Erskine, Carl, 101, 102, 248
Espinosa, Arnulfo, 322
Estell, Tom, 60, 63, 331, 332
Eubanks, John, 39
Eueller, Walter, 331
Evans, Rube, 39
 Russ, 286
Everitt, Ed, 137
 Leon, 199
Ezell, Homer, 303

F

Fabian, Henry, 9, 11, 13
Fausett, Buck, 253, 254
Feder, Mike, 166, 265, 266, 267
Feller, Bob, 218, 314

Ferguson, Joe, 200
Fernandez, Sid, 161, 295
Ferran, George, 165
Ferrarese, Don, 116
Field, Dudley, 177
Fillingim, Dana, 60
Fillman, John, 41, 43
Finger, Tom, 105
Finnerty, Hugh, 134, 166, 167, 213
Fisher, Eddie, 225
Fitzgerald, Howard, 331, 332
 Lou, 296
 Mike, 157
Flaherty, Pat, 10
Flair, "Broadway," 174
Flannery, Tim, 206
Fleming, Les, 85, 113, 218, 233, 306
Flynn, James, 142, 200
 "Mikado," 5, 173
Folkers, Richard, 278
Fondy, Dee, 101
Ford, Steve, 166
Foreman, Gus, 55
Fort Worth, 2, 3, 4, 5, 6, 8, 9, 11, 12,
 14, 15, 16, 17, 18, 19, 23, 26, 27,
 28, 29, 30, 31, 32, 33, 39, 40, 41,
 47, 48, 49, 50, 52, 53, 54, 57, 58,
 59, 60, 64, 65, 67, 68, 69, 71, 80,
 82, 88, 99, 100, 101, 102, 125, 131,
 178, 179, 180, 181, 183, 190, 192,
 193, 194, 195, 204, 207, 209, 221,
 222, 223, 230, 231, 232, 234, 235,
 244, 249, 255, 256, 277, 315, 320,
 330
Foster, Rube, 42, 260
.400 Hitters, 354
Fowler, Art, 122
 Charles, 225
 Jesse, 262
Fox, Pete, 73
France, Carl "Bones," 291
Frantz, Joe, 187
 Walter, 187
Frazier, Fred, 242
 Joe, 287, 322
Freeman, Lavell, 167, 169, 242
Freisleben, Dave, 144, 201, 202
French, "Piggy," 173
 Sam, 3
Frey, Jim, 122, 314
Frierson, Buck, 102, 302